CAMBRIDGE SOUTH ASIAN STUDIES

BRITISH POLICY IN INDIA
1858–1905

CAMBRIDGE SOUTH ASIAN STUDIES

These monographs are published by the Syndics of Cambridge University Press in association with the Cambridge University Centre for South Asian Studies. The following books have been published in this series:

GOPAL, S., *British Policy in India, 1858–1905.*
PALMER, J. A. B., *The Mutiny Outbreak at Meerut in 1857.*

BRITISH POLICY IN INDIA

1858-1905

BY

S. GOPAL

CAMBRIDGE
AT THE UNIVERSITY PRESS
1965

PUBLISHED BY
THE SYNDICS OF THE CAMBRIDGE UNIVERSITY PRESS

Bentley House, 200 Euston Road, London, N.W. 1
American Branch: 32 East 57th Street, New York, N.Y. 10022
West African Office: P.O. Box 33, Ibadan, Nigeria

©

CAMBRIDGE UNIVERSITY PRESS

1965

Printed in Great Britain at the University Printing House, Cambridge
(Brooke Crutchley, University Printer)

LIBRARY OF CONGRESS CATALOGUE
CARD NUMBER: 65–19149

TO MY FATHER

TO MY FATHER

CONTENTS

MAPS

PREFACE

In 1858, after the suppression of the revolt in India, the British government decided to assume direct responsibility for the administration of the country. The rebels had failed to uproot British rule in India but they had succeeded in drawing attention to the anomaly of the East India Company governing an empire. The assumption of authority by the Crown marked, of course, no sharp cleavage in India's history. Many of the principles and methods which became prominent in the years after 1858 had been considered and formulated by the servants of the Company. Nor was there much replacement of personnel. But the fact that the British government and Parliament had accepted responsibility for India, for the proper administration of the country and for the betterment of her people, was in itself of significance.

It demanded, in the first place, that the two political parties in Britain should give thought to India and to the objectives of British rule; for the British government had now to make policy for India. It is true that, in the years after 1858, the emphasis was on administration. The machinery of government was organized, a corpus of statute was built and the civil service was strengthened. But these were no inanimate tasks. They were inspired by certain ideas; and in turn they set afoot certain forces. Education, encouraged mainly as an aspect of good administration, promoted the elements of political consciousness. After about fifty years, by the end of Lord Curzon's viceroyalty in 1905, it became clear that these new forces would dominate the scene. Thereafter it was the story of the growing strength of political ambitions and the gradual withdrawal of British authority.

This work is a study of the first phase of British rule in India under the Crown. It is primarily concerned, as the title makes clear, with British policy and not with Indian attitudes and reactions. It seeks to examine the ideas and aspirations of British parties and statesmen, their ways and methods of implementing them and the consequences, both anticipated and unintended, of these efforts.

I have not sought to deal with every development in India during these years. That would not only have been impractical; it is also, for the purpose of this book, unnecessary. I have attempted

Preface

to follow the main strands of British policy and to study their evolution during each of the periods into which these years can conveniently be divided.

I have relied mainly on the private papers of British and Indian statesmen and the official records of the governments of Britain and India. I have quoted extensively in order to reveal the free exchange of ideas and the friction of personalities that contributed to the formulation of policies.

This book has been a long time in the making. It was started in 1958, when the School of Oriental and African Studies in the University of London appointed me as a Rockefeller Research Associate. Thereafter, back in India and under what a writer in *The Economist* has termed 'the curse of the full in-tray', I could turn to it only in the intervals of my official routine. Fortunately, in 1963 the Faculty of Modern History at Cambridge invited me to spend a year at that University as Commonwealth Fellow; and Trinity College generously offered me its hospitality. This enabled me to complete the book. Parts of it formed the basis of my lectures at Cambridge.

When this book was in the press, the Committee of Management of the Centre of South Asian Studies at Cambridge University asked me whether I would be willing to have it published as the first of the new series of Cambridge South Asian Studies. I have gladly agreed to this.

I would like to thank Professor Butterfield, Dr Kitson Clark, Professor V. H. Galbraith, Professor Mansergh and Professor C. H. Philips, who have all given me encouragement in the years when this book was taking shape. The Earl of Harewood and Mr Michael Maclagan most kindly granted me access to the Canning papers. Dr C. C. Davies, Mr Christopher Hill and Mr J. Steven Watson have been good enough to read the typescript and to make many valuable suggestions.

S.G.

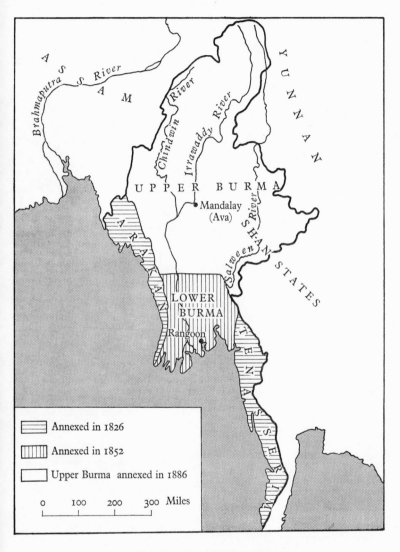

Annexed in 1826

Annexed in 1852

Upper Burma annexed in 1886

0   100   200   300 Miles

I   THE ANNEXATION OF BURMA

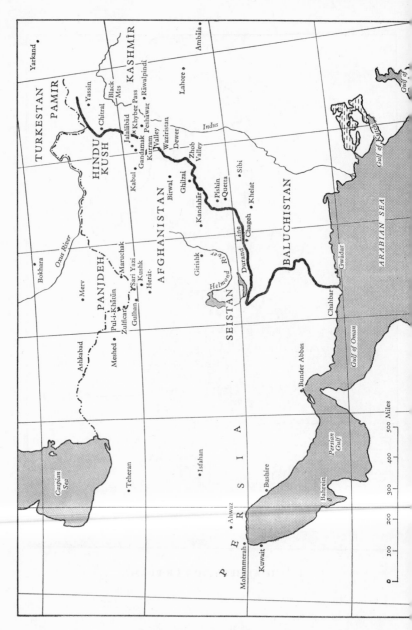

2   AFGHANISTAN AND CENTRAL ASIA

xii

CHAPTER I

THE AFTERMATH OF THE REVOLT
1858–69

I

Writing to his friend the Governor-General and Viceroy, Charles Canning, in India on 23 July 1859, Gladstone reported that the Cabinet had been informed the previous day 'that that mutiny which may also be called rebellion, civil war, or whatever else is most formidable, was now really at an end'.[1] It had in fact been much more than a mere mutiny. What had started as a rising of the Indian soldiers in the Bengal army gradually gathered support till it became the only large-scale revolt in India in the nineteenth century. The Indian *sepoy* (soldier) had some specific causes for discontent; but he was also in most cases only a peasant in uniform, and he could not but be affected by the general mood in the villages from which he came. Many of the soldiers of the Bengal army were Brahmins or Rajputs, and nearly a third of them had their homes in Oudh. They knew of the harsh and impatient manner in which the East India Company had set aside families which had been respected as royal for centuries. They were aware of the economic and social changes which were taking place in the country, of the land-holders who had been deprived and of the local industries which had been destroyed. They themselves had at times been marched in haste to stop such practices as the immolation of widows. So in 1857, when they mutinied, they incited as well as battened on sympathy from all the discontented. The army voiced grievances other than its own; and the movement spread beyond the army. The conservative and feudal elements in Bengal, Bihar, the then North-West Provinces and central India acted together, when the opportunity arose, in an effort to restore the past. Canning himself recognized the nature and seriousness of the rising. 'The struggle which we have had has been more like a national war than a local insurrection. In its magnitude, duration, scale of expenditure, and in some of its moral features it partakes largely of the former character.'[2]

The outbreak took most of the British in India completely by surprise. Statesmen in Britain, with less knowledge of detail, had shown more prescience. Canning in 1856, on the eve of his departure for India, had spoken of the possibility of such a rising.[3] Palmerston, despite his indifference to Indian affairs, was aware that the maintenance of the Indian empire might well become a military problem. 'No man can pretend to say that we may not have to defend India in India.'[4] But British officials, civil and military, had expected no violent uprising. 'None are more surprised at what has happened at Meerut than those who know the Sepoys best—and I have lost, *entirely*, all confidence in the Commanding Officers of Regiments, who with scarcely an exception swear to the fidelity of their men.'[5] Taken aback, these officials now moved to the other extreme; filled with alarm and fear, they demanded dire vengeance. But Canning stood firm and refused to sully justice with indiscriminate reprisals. With little support from Britain, where public opinion had been greatly stirred by the reports of the savagery of the rebels,[6] he did all he could to curb the racial feelings which had been aroused. Responsible opinion in Britain gradually came round to his side, and the man of whom Dalhousie had written years ago at Oxford that he would never 'make a figure'[7] stood in 1859 upon a pinnacle.[8] Canning's qualities were not spectacular, but they were suited to this crisis.

All sections of political opinion in England were agreed that, once the flames had been quenched, the East India Company should be set aside and the British government should assume direct responsibility for the administration of India. But there was no similar unanimity on the way in which this should be done. Palmerston introduced a bill for the management of Indian affairs in Britain by a president and council; but his ministry fell before the bill could be enacted. On behalf of the second Derby ministry Disraeli brought forward a bill providing for a president and a council elected by a complicated process. This scheme was so severely criticized that Disraeli replaced it by another measure which became the Act of 1858. India would be governed directly by and in the name of the Crown, acting through a Secretary of State. He would be aided by a council of fifteen members, of whom at least nine should have served in India for not less than ten years and have left India not more than ten years before their appointment to the council. This body would be presided over by the Secretary of State, who could if necessary overrule their decisions. Nor was he bound to keep them informed of all communications with the Government of India; it was for him to decide what would be kept secret.

In India the central administration continued to remain in the hands of the Governor-General in Council. Being now the representative of the Crown, the Governor-General was given the new title of Viceroy. This was intended to be a purely ceremonial title, for there was no definition of viceregal duties. But Canning, the first Viceroy of India, was pleased with his new designation and expected it to be of use,[9] probably in impressing the Princes and other conservative elements in Indian society. It certainly gave the head of the Indian government an exalted status and in the ninety years that followed it was as Viceroy—the empty title—rather than as Governor-General—the designation of responsibility—that he was best known.

The title of Viceroy was conferred not by the India Act of 1858 but by the Royal Proclamation which was issued on 1 November 1858. Canning was not consulted by the Derby Government in the drafting of this document, but the Queen, who 'is the strongest Canningite I ever saw',[10] ensured that it expressed most of his views. The Princes were assured that their rights, dignity and honour would be respected, and it was declared that Indians would be treated on a par with all other subjects of the Crown. There would be no religious discrimination, land rights would be protected, due regard would be paid to the ancient rights, usages and customs of India and the official service would be open to all. Unconditional pardon would be granted to all who laid down their arms by 1 January 1859, except those who had directly participated in the murder of British subjects or who had sheltered those guilty of such crimes or had acted as leaders or instigators of the revolt. It was only the failure to insist on the immediate return to the ways of peace, the suggestion that the revolt was legitimate for the rest of the year and the promise to protect all rights connected with land which seemed to Canning open to criticism.

II

The assumption of the government of India by the Crown was marked by no ceremonial *durbar*; but the Proclamation was read in all the Indian languages and copies were sent to all the Indian

3

Princes. The significance was not lost on the Indian people.[11] British civil servants also looked forward to the change; and it was only among the soldiers of the Company's armies that there was some resistance. Most men, having surmounted a revolt, would have regarded their work as done; but Canning wished at least to commence the task of seeking the objectives laid down in the Proclamation. The general amnesty had been his own suggestion. In September 1858 he had proposed to Stanley that when resistance was melting the rebels should be pursued with pardons. 'I do not believe that anything short of this forcible pardoning will impress into their minds the truth of our desire to pardon.'[12] He now instructed the withdrawal of all pending cases which did not involve the murder of British subjects, the harbouring of such criminals or the acting as leaders of the revolt. Sentences already passed would be effective but cases of confiscation should be favourably considered.[13] Canning's Government were of the view that while literally and legally, British subjects included Indians as well as Europeans, the Proclamation had intended that only murderers of Europeans should not be pardoned; and the local governments were directed to withdraw cases pending against alleged murderers of Indians to preclude the courts holding that the amnesty did not apply to them.[14] This interpretation was approved by the home government.[15]

It was in Oudh, more than in any other part of India which had been affected by the rising, that the military revolt had expanded into a popular rebellion involving all sections of society; and it was therefore here more than anywhere else that the government had thought it necessary to render the success of their arms complete. A large proportion, perhaps half, of those serving in the regiments which had mutinied in Oudh had been killed in the course of the fighting; and few of those who survived dared to come in and surrender. They hovered near the villages with the clandestine support of their friends, and the government thought it likely that a heavier retribution had overtaken them than those who had been killed or had died on the gallows.[16] Oudh, in fact, was thoroughly cowed. The Oudh government reported that all classes except perhaps the fanatical Muhammadan rabble of the towns admitted that they had been beaten after a trial of strength in which all the advantages had been for a long time on their side, and it was generally felt that this conquest had given the British government a

4

better right to govern Oudh than annexation had done.[17] Sir James Outram, the Chief Commissioner,[18] and John Lawrence[19] favoured a general amnesty for all rebels and mutineers, but Canning felt that so generous a step would be liable to misconstruction. It should be made clear that mutiny was 'not a game in which if they get safely through the first hot scurry they may reckon upon escaping scot free'. While hanging and shooting should be reserved for special cases, a large number of those captured should be sentenced to transportation.[20] The Chief Commissioner was informed that it was essential, considering the state of the province and the avowedly hostile temper of nearly the whole population, that criminal justice be administered with an iron hand. He was even authorized to declare that capital punishment would be awarded in all cases of personal violence even if death had not ensued.[21]

It was also decided to disarm the population and dismantle the forts. Outram thought that this could be done without difficulty.

The people of India respect power and they can well understand how a strong Government will suffer no armies or strongholds but its own. Popularity is not to be gained by a display of weakness, and if the people would have felt no temporary irritation against, neither would they have entertained any respect for, a Government that despite of the teachings of the late insurrection had left them the power again to attempt its overthrow with the slightest prospect of success. The Chief Commissioner has never met a native really attached to our Government who did not consider the disarming of the population one of the wisest acts of our policy.[22]

Outram directed that officials should go on tour directing villages to hand in their weapons; and if they failed to do so, vigorous searches should be conducted. If the number of arms recovered was less than that of the number of men in a village, it could only mean that the weapons had been buried; for every man was bound to possess at least one sword, spear or musket. Permission to carry arms should be granted rarely, and for some time to come licenses to make and sell arms and ammunition should not be given.[23]

As a result of the stern punishment of the guilty among the rank and file and the disarming of the whole province, by the end of 1858 Oudh was not merely subdued but tranquil.[24] Canning decided that as the whole population of Oudh, with a few exceptions, had taken part against the government, the latter should resume their proprietary right over the whole province and then decide what was to be done with it.[25] On 15 March 1858, after the fall of Lucknow, a proclamation was issued confiscating the proprietary right in the whole of Oudh with the exception of six specified estates; but the *talukdars*—the hereditary landowners—were assured that such of them as had not been accomplices in the cold-blooded murder of Europeans would have their lands restored to them. In addition, the Chief Commissioner was given the discretion to notify any talukdar that if he now came forward to support the government his lands would not be confiscated and even such lands as he had owned before Dalhousie's general measure of confiscation might be restored to him.[26]

The Oudh proclamation was generally condemned as too harsh, but in fact no greater lenience could have been shown; for under the discretionary powers vested in the Chief Commissioner, a large number of talukdars were not only pardoned but given back all the lands which they had owned. Some 22,658 out of the 23,543 villages in Oudh were restored to the talukdars in return for submission and loyalty in the form of collection and transmission of information.[27] Even active aid in pursuing the rebels was not demanded of them. The denunciation by John Bright of the proclamation and its public censure by Ellenborough were not unfair but irrelevant. Whatever the letter of the proclamation, Canning's Government had done very much more for the talukdars than even his critics had desired. His Liberal friends, who had sought to defend him by recounting the misdeeds of the talukdars, did not realize that he had sanctioned confiscation because that alone would enable the restoration of the talukdari system.[28] Apart from clearing the ground, it demonstrated British strength. 'This is native character. You must knock a native down before you pardon him. He will not accept your pardon till he is at your mercy.'[29] It was a puzzled Sir Charles Wood who, soon after taking over as Secretary of State, wrote to the Viceroy:

I cannot get over the confiscation in Oudh having enabled you to upset so completely all that we have been doing in settling the tenures in that country ever since we took it. It is so directly the contrary of what we supposed was the intention or could be the effect of the Proclamation that it takes one aback ... I am low about our Indian future as everything seems out of joint.[30]

But Canning was unrepentant. He visited Oudh and at a formal durbar granted the talukdars *sanads* or title-deeds of permanent ownership. He found the talukdars, who had expected to be mowed down by guns or at least permanently dispossessed, enthusiastically loyal, and he conferred on twenty-two of them authority in matters of land revenue on their own estates and the powers of magistrates.

Canning appealed to the British government 'not to consider humbug what has been done in Oude'.[31] The settlement of Oudh was part of his general scheme of strengthening an Indian aristocracy which would buttress British rule. 'It is a curse and blunder of that rule that this has never yet been done—and only very feebly and partially attempted.'[32] His clemency was more than a virtue; it was a shrewd act of policy. When details of the revolt were received in England, the first reaction was that no section of Indian society could be relied upon. All Indians appeared to share a detestation of the British rulers. 'In no instance is a friendly glance directed to the white man's carriage. Oh, that language of the eye! Who can doubt it? Who can misinterpret it?'[33] It was concluded, therefore, that British power in India would have to be based primarily on force. But to Canning this seemed neither desirable nor possible. He realized that as Englishmen would never be more than a small handful in India, they could not hope to govern the country effectively if they distrusted all Indians and proscribed whole classes. 'Saxon domination', unsupported by the collaboration of at least some section of the Indian public, would be unable even to retain the Indian empire. In Bengal and Bihar there was not a single European soldier more than at the beginning of the crisis. In Orissa the total number of Europeans was not more than a hundred. Peace and order were being maintained in these areas by the goodwill and loyalist efforts of the upper classes —the *rajas*, the *zemindars* and the Indian officials. Though it was, of course, in their interest to support the British, Canning believed that it would be worthwhile to strengthen this interest by trusting them and treating them well. The fact that the British had surmounted the revolt could be no source of complacency. The Sikhs had been loyal but they were not trusted by the Viceroy. There was a feeling among them that they had saved the British but that the latter would not recognize this; so if the Sikhs got another opportunity they would seize it.[34] It was true that the exclusion of Indians from the artillery minimized the dangers. An artillery manned exclusively by Europeans 'is to India what a Channel

Fleet is to England. As long as it is strong we are all but secure against any attempt at disturbance. It will keep all in check, Sikhs included.'[35] But the most probable and most serious danger was the harassment of British power in India in the context of a European war, when the despatch of troops from Britain would cease and perhaps even those already in India would be withdrawn. 'I believe there is but one way of meeting this danger, and that is to bring the influential classes—the native states first and afterwards our own chief subjects—into that condition and temper in which, when the moment comes, we may as completely as possible throw the reins on their necks and entrust to them the keeping of internal peace and order.'[36]

Towards the Princes Canning adopted a policy of punishing resistance and rewarding obedience. He held two durbars, in Agra and in Lahore, to which the loyal Princes were summoned, confirmed in rank and titles and in some cases given an additional decoration. He also considered restoring to the Nizam some of the territories acquired from him—'We should show convincingly that we can sometimes relax our grasp upon the good things that come within it'[37]—but finally nothing was done. However, Scindia (the ruler of Gwalior) was enabled to consolidate his principality by an exchange of lands with the British. On the other hand, states like Dhar and Kotah, whose rulers had not adopted a firm attitude of support to the British during the fighting, suffered loss of territory.

To conciliate the Princes further by ensuring continuity of title and possession—disturbed by Dalhousie's doctrine of lapse—Canning wished to grant them the right to adopt in the absence of a natural heir. 'There never was', he wrote to Wood, 'such a time for the stroke; and if we are to have troubles at home and troops are taken from here, we must lay out all the anchors we can.'[38] The sanction of adoptions would be a less spectacular measure than the lavish durbars and the bestowal of large rewards, but its effects would be far more general and its results would last for ever. It was the indispensable foundation of the policy of reliance on the great Indian influences, to which Canning wished to dedicate not only the remainder of his viceroyalty but the rest of his life. The British should lose no time in binding to themselves the chiefs and the landholders and impressing on them that the fall of British power would mean no gain to them. Only then would the empire in India be safe, in the face of either internal convulsions or external threats. Even fanaticism would give way to material interests.[39] Wood was not happy about firmly closing the door to annexations, especially of pleasant hill stations, but he approved of the principle of friendship with the Princes and, fortified by the approval of Stanley and the Queen, assented to Canning's proposal.[40]

An occasion soon arose for implementing this policy and testing the *bona fides* of the home government. The raja of Mysore was sixty, had no heir and did not wish to adopt one. He declared that he should be the last representative of his house and that the British government should inherit his possessions.[41] But the India Office entered into direct correspondence with the raja and, according to Canning,[42] jeopardized the arrangement and demonstrated that the Viceroy had no voice in, and not even a knowledge of, decisions taken in a matter under his direct supervision. For the raja was informed that Mysore affairs would hereafter be the responsibility of the government of Madras. Because of Canning's protest, this particular decision was revoked;[43] but the influence of the Government of India had been weakened and the raja began to reconsider his proposal to bequeath his kingdom. Canning, therefore, wrote a vigorously worded minute protesting against the manner in which the home government had ignored the Government of India. He explained to Wood that personally he would have much preferred to have been silent. 'But you are sapping the Governor-General's authority and dispelling the superstitious sort of reverence in which it is held. Half a dozen reversals of my decisions or disallowances of my acts would not operate so effectually towards that end as the complete ignoring of the Governor-General's office.'[44] Wood agreed that the autocracy of the Governor-General should be maintained and nothing derogatory to his authority should be done, though he could not understand in what way the viceregal authority had been shaken in this matter of Mysore.[45] He was now anxious to secure possession of Mysore as a bequest or with the consent of the raja, but realized that it could not be forcibly taken.[46] So he urged Canning, who had more influence than any other Englishman with the raja, to do all he could before his departure from India to prevent the raja adopting;[47] and he was greatly disappointed that Canning, instead of confirming the raja's half-promise to Lady Canning of a bequest, had been willing to permit the raja to adopt a successor.[48] Lord Elgin, who succeeded Canning in February 1862, was inclined to agree with Canning; but he was informed that the home government were keen that the state should revert to the Crown after the raja's death, with the exception of any one district which the raja might grant to any relative for whom he wished to provide.[49] The Viceroy was anxious to fall in line with the Cabinet and suggested somewhat uneasily that the raja could perhaps be bribed into abstaining from adoption.[50] But the India Council advised the Secretary of State to restore the administration to the raja and to trust to his avowed intention of making it over to the British on his death. Wood was not pleased with this but could think of nothing better. 'I am sadly puzzled between what seems to be our honest course, and my wish to secure Mysore.'[51] It was finally decided not to alter Canning's decision.[52]

John Lawrence, who came out as Viceroy on Elgin's death in December 1863, argued that if the administration of Mysore were to be retained in British hands, it was the government's clear duty and prerogative to refuse to recognize the right of adoption.[53] Cranborne (later Salisbury), Secretary of State in the Conservative Government, replied that he had no particular sympathy for these Princes 'who will certainly cut every English throat they can lay hands on whenever they can do it safely'; but the government should be scrupulously just to them and give them no reason for saying that Britain treated her promises lightly.[54] He decided that while the raja's treaty rights would terminate with his death, his adopted son, if he proved fit, might be given a portion of the kingdom under such conditions as the government might impose.[55] Lawrence welcomed this decision,[56] but Sir Stafford Northcote, who succeeded Cranborne, disclosed that his predecessor had announced his decision without consulting his council. Northcote himself wished to transfer the whole kingdom to the adopted heir on the attainment of his majority on such conditions as the government might like to impose.[57] Lawrence regretted the failure to apply Dalhousie's doctrine of lapse to Mysore but agreed to abide by Northcote's decision.[58] So Mysore was saved from absorption.

At the rung below that of the Princes, Canning sought to win the sympathy of the feudal gentry and even created such a class where none existed. In Oudh he had not merely dealt leniently with individual talukdars but had supported the talukdars as a class.

A similar encouragement of those who had traditionally exercised power by vesting them with magisterial authority was considered in the North-West Provinces,[59] even though in this area, judged by the demographic ratio formulated by Outram, disarming had been only a partial success. In Meerut, for instance, the collection was only one weapon to every four men, and in Benares one to every twenty-six. The government of the North-West Provinces, therefore, desired that the powers to disarm should be vested in them permanently; otherwise, once the powers lapsed, the manufacture and sale of arms would recommence and arms would soon be as plentiful as before.[60] But they were rebuked by the Government of India for their harsh and suspicious attitude towards the people and accused of using their powers with undue severity. The Government of India saw little necessity for continuing the powers to disarm, much less for rendering them permanent. The rebuke was meekly accepted,[61] although it had been estimated that of the total number of arms in the North-West Provinces only 3,576,317 had been collected and 1,487,641 had not been surrendered.[62]

Canning also instituted an inquiry in the North-West Provinces into the influence of land tenures in times of scarcity, for he believed that this might disclose strong reasons for rendering permanent a considerable extent of the settlement in the North-West Provinces without sacrificing a great share of the revenue, as had been done in Bengal in 1793.[63] For Canning was anxious to extend the permanent settlement to these areas. He was certain it would do for landholders what the right to adopt had done for the Princes in the way of binding them to the British government. 'It would be worth an army of European troops.'[64] But Wood warned the Government of India not to proclaim a permanent settlement without his approval, or to commit themselves to a general permanent settlement. His reason was that one had to be sure that the value of the land had been precisely ascertained and the land revenue carefully settled before it was declared to be permanent. Such a permanent settlement could easily be lowered if fixed too high, but it could never be raised if the assessment were too low.[65]

When Lawrence, like Canning, favoured a permanent settlement wherever this could be introduced without any large loss of revenue,[66] Wood advised him not to be in a hurry. There need be no change in the decision to introduce a permanent settlement, but care should be taken not to throw away any chance of an increase of revenue.[67] The Viceroy replied that the measure would result in the loss of little, if any, revenue but would do much to enlist the great mass of the people on the side of the government.[68]

By the end of 1864 the Secretary of State began to have misgivings about any form of permanent settlement, for none of such settlements, in the North-West Provinces, Bengal, Madras and Oudh, appeared to him to have borne the test of experience.[69] But Lawrence disagreed. He felt that the *ryotwari* settlements as introduced in Madras (which Lawrence considered as permanent in that they were not revised for a period of years) were preferable to all others and regarded Munro as perhaps the best administrator India ever saw. However, even Thomason's settlements in the North-West Provinces had proved beneficial; and Lawrence urged the home government to allow a permanent settlement to be implemented.[70] So the Government of India were authorized to effect a permanent settlement at the existing rate if that were equitable and if 80 per cent of the area were cultivated; but there should be no commitment to introduce in the future a permanent settlement at a rate that was fixed.[71]

Cranborne was not in favour of a permanent settlement. At the time of its introduction, it had been hoped to find some way of tapping the expected increase of agricultural wealth; but that had proved 'a philosopher's stone'.[72] Lawrence regretted this attitude for he believed that the political advantages of a permanent settlement were very great and the direct loss in revenue would be counterbalanced by the consolidation of British power and influence. But if a decision precluding permanent settlements were to be communicated, the sooner it was done the better.[73]

In the Punjab, which he visited, Canning was astonished by the contentment and cordiality of the people—testimony, though he did not recognize it, to the merits of the administration of Dalhousie and John Lawrence. There was not the silence and passiveness which Canning had found in Lucknow and elsewhere but a cheerful demonstration of loyalty. But Canning was pained to find that there were few Indians of 'influence, intelligence and good character'—by which he meant noblemen—remaining in the province. While pensioners, heads of decayed families and rich bankers were plentiful, there were few wealthy and influential landowners. It never struck Canning that this might be the explanation for the contentment of the Punjab, and he regretted what he termed 'a wide blank' between the government and the poorer landholders. 'If we are mad enough to think that a country can long be governed safely under so unnatural a system we shall deserve a second rebellion.' It was against all reason to attempt to govern a conquered country in which, under all changes of dynasty, feudalism had remained rooted, by obliterating the aristocracy or by maintaining it shorn of all authority. Canning thought there was a want in the Punjab of a class interested in the land, exercising influence on those below them and participating in the administration. So he rescinded the practice of scattering the lands of the *sirdars*, which had converted these landowners into a weak and idle aristocracy, and permitted them to consolidate their estates.[74] Canning also, during his last year in India, considered the possibility of introducing the law of primogeniture in the Punjab[75] and effecting a permanent settlement of the land revenue wherever it seemed suitable.

Wood was satisfied of the general soundness of Canning's policy. 'I wish you joy of your success in Oudh. I believe that a certain quantity of humbug is not only useful, but indispensable in dealing with Orientals; and I am afraid that it is not only with them that it succeeds beyond its deserts. However, you seem to have done quite rightly; and I trust that the good feelings will be as permanent as they appear to be satisfactory at present.'[76] Without an Indian gentry there would be a 'dead level of all the natives, who have so little to look to, except as clerks and subordinates, where they are not likely to acquire any masculine qualities'.[77] Wood agreed with Canning that it was very necessary to enlist on the British side and employ in its service those Indians who had from birth or position a natural influence in the country. The enforcement of British law had tended to alienate the landed proprietors and if Canning could secure their loyalty he would have commenced a new and most important era in the British administration of India. British rule would be stronger with 'the natural chiefs and leaders of the people' attached to it than if the people were left open to the persuasion and seduction of upstart leaders.[78] But Wood was not convinced that Canning had always implemented this policy in the correct manner. In Oudh the legitimacy of title of the talukdars had not been sufficiently examined; and Wood would have preferred the recruitment to official service of members of this class to the restoration of their private influence.[79] Nor was Wood satisfied that the rights of all those holding under the talukdars had been protected.

However, Canning himself was well pleased with the results of his efforts. 'The temper and success with which the native land-owners and chiefs have discharged their new duties is more perfect than I ever dared to hope.' The proof and knowledge that they were trusted and that it was intended that their authority should be treated with respect by British and Indians had made men of the talukdars and sirdars. In neither Oudh nor the Punjab did the Viceroy think that there had been the slightest trace of abuse of power, of undue favour or of malpractice. Of 609 criminal cases tried by the talukdars in the first year of their magisterial authority, the appellate British judges had modified the decisions in only thirty-four cases; and the talukdars had always erred on the side of leniency. Encouraged by this, Canning enlisted the assistance of the talukdars in the suppression of infanticide and authorized the constitution of a bench of Indian magistrates in Lucknow also. As regards the general effects of his policy, he was convinced that his measures had given rise to a wholesome temper in those areas which were crucial to the safety of India.[80]

Wood suggested to Elgin that even if he did not favour Canning's policy, he should modify and not upset what had been settled. Sudden transitions from one policy to another, even if the latter be right, gave an appearance of uncertainty which was never to the advantage of the government.[81] Elgin disliked Canning's policy; he felt that the sanads had given the talukdars a power over their estates that was repugnant to Indian custom and ideas of right.[82] But Wood wished to modify the details of Canning's action without appearing to do so, for it would be a great evil to shake the confidence of the chiefs in the permanence of the general arrangements. Canning's settlement had been approved by the home government with the full knowledge that it had sanctioned acts of usurpation and spoliation of the rights of the cultivating and non-proprietary class. Canning's policy had been to form an Indian gentry in the shape of the talukdars, and the Government of India could not, without great discredit, depart from it. This was especially necessary as Lawrence had the reputation of being opposed to Canning's views and eager to extend his levelling policy to Oudh.[83]

Lawrence replied that there was no need for alarm. He was doing all he could to smooth matters in Oudh short of giving up vital principles and was seeking to maintain Canning's policy in its essentials.[84] The relaxations which had been ordered would benefit many directly or indirectly; for though force and fraud had reigned successfully so long in Oudh that the rights of tens of thousands had been swept away, some still had a chance if there were fair play and unbiased judges.[85] Canning had ruled that while the superior right in the land should rest with the talukdars, 'all subordinate rights' should also be respected; and it could not be argued from this that Canning had wished to guard only one subordinate right under the talukdars.[86] Nor could the question be ignored, as the government of Oudh had undertaken the recording of all rights.

Wingfield,[87] the officer appointed to conduct the inquiry, reported that it had been found that no occupancy rights had existed at the time of annexation; and he and William Grey,[88] a member of Lawrence's council, took the view that any grant of rights to sub-proprietors would be a derogation of the rights conferred by Canning on the talukdars.[89] But Lawrence asserted that the government could not, consistent with their dignity and their duty, renounce their right to interfere for the protection of the subordinate interests in the land, in the event of any serious aggression on the part of the talukdars and the zemindars; and he insisted that the landholders should recognize all rights of subordinate holders which might be upheld by the courts on the basis of merits, usage or custom.[90] He was even willing to resign if the India Office declined to uphold his position.[91] The Viceroy was probably capable of such firmness because he received the support of Sir Henry Maine on this issue.[92] To no part of his administration, wrote Lawrence, would he look back in later years with greater pleasure than his success in this matter.[93]

III

As the first of the Viceroys and the head of an administration which would no longer be hampered by such distractions as trade, it was natural for Canning to devote attention to the methods of the Government of India of conducting business. Questions of policy and principle now arose daily, and there was a great increase of matters unruled by precedent in which decisions had to be taken. The existing practice was for all papers to be circulated to the Governor-General and members of his council, and decisions in every case to be taken by this collegiate body. The result was that the Governor-General in Council tended to become, in Canning's phrase, 'a gigantic Essay-Club'.[94] As a first step Canning laid down what seems obvious enough, that the secretaries to government should dispose of routine matters and members of council should each assume responsibility for a particular department of government. Only matters of importance demanding consultation should be referred to the Governor-General in Council.[95] This hastened the disposal of work to some extent, though the Governor-General himself benefited little by it because of the reluctance of his colleagues to take decisions without his knowledge on any matter of the least significance, while some members of council resented the taking of decisions without their knowledge.[96]

Clearly a more definitive solution was required. Despite the change introduced by Canning, the senior members of government continued to be inundated with paper. 'The Governor-General and the Governors are overwhelmed with BOXES; and the invaluable time of these highly paid functionaries is frittered away in attending to details which are entrusted at Home to Junior Clerks.'[97] Canning also reported that the work which pressed upon the members of the Viceroy's council, and chiefly upon the Viceroy, was enough to weigh down any human strength, and so the difficult and most important questions and those requiring continuous thought and application were just the matters which suffered and were delayed.[98] Sir Bartle Frere, member of council,[99] believed that this under-administration in important subjects had led to the failure to check the growing bitterness between the British and the Indians. There was a 'general hopeless repulsiveness towards India' among the Europeans, including the soldiers, and this discontent and distrust were beginning to spread among the Indians.[100]

Stanley and Wood were for dispensing with members of council altogether and authorizing the Viceroy to govern India with a team of secretaries.[101] Canning, too, was inclined to adopt the scheme of replacing councillors with secretaries occasionally assembling in council. A man who was primarily and essentially a head of a department and only secondarily and infrequently a councillor on matters outside his department would have more heart in his work

16

and would do it better. This would also enable the choice of men with special qualifications to administer particular departments.[102]

I could form a very pretty Cabinet of Secretaries; and if you leave me liberty to strengthen the subordinate staff in one or two of the Departments at a very trifling expense I will undertake to say that my successor will find to his hand a Government machinery that will do its work thoroughly and rapidly, without any need for his overtasking his own brain and fingers, and leaving him free to give his attention now and then to one subject for a few consecutive hours.[103]

But whatever the change effected by the home government in the form of executive government in India, Canning wished to remain in India long enough to initiate it. His experience would be helpful, while any change in the wake of his departure would be construed as a criticism of his methods of administration.[104]

Wood, however, began to have second thoughts about a 'Secretary Council'. Such a body would lack corporate capacity and would be too weak to assert control over the presidency governments in the absence on tour of the Viceroy. This encouraged the members of council to record minutes opposing any such change. They could see no justification for such a measure, while the objections seemed so numerous as to make any such step almost impossible. What the Governor-General required was not fewer but more responsible advisers without damage to his own authority to make the final decision. So what had informally been done, of vesting each councillor with the control of a department, seemed all that was necessary. Nothing should be done that would give the Governor-General any but the best talent, the greatest vigour and the ripest experience procurable for his council; but secretaries would still have many years of service ahead of them and would be inhibited in their advice by prospects of promotion. To expect the Governor-General, with the assistance of these nominees of his, to govern India would be a fatal mistake.[105] The Government of India therefore forwarded a proposal that Parliament enact a statute formalizing the procedure of vesting councillors with departmental responsibilities. This was necessary to preclude any member of council from disputing the division of work. So the Indian Councils Act of 1861 authorized the Governor-General to make rules and orders for the more convenient transaction of business in his council. This general authorization gave legal sanction to the departmental transaction of business.

Linked with this problem of administrative reform was the question of the legislative council. Dalhousie had created it in 1853 as a means of ascertaining official opinion in the presidencies; and a full expression of opinion had been secured. One consequence of replacing the Viceroy's executive council with a squad of secretaries would have been that the legislative council would have been deprived of many members and reduced almost to a nullity. But this in itself was not generally regarded as a disadvantage. Opinion in the India Office in London was unanimous that the experiment of 1853 had proved an expensive failure. The legislative council was distrusted and checked by the Governor-General in Council. The legislative council's relations with the governments of Bombay and Madras were also anomalous, for its members could not hope to have first-hand knowledge of every part of India. Stanley was of the view that the legislative council had for the most part done nothing and occasionally done mischief. Both he and Wood concluded that the governments of Madras and Bombay should be allowed to legislate for themselves and be generally relieved of too tight a control from Calcutta.[106] What Wood had in mind was a legislative council for each presidency with limited powers and with a few English and Indian non-official members nominated by the Governor.[107]

Canning also was disappointed with the legislative council and, departing from Dalhousie's practice, he attended it only on special occasions. He thought a great mistake had been made in dressing it up with all the forms and ceremonies of Parliament and opening it to the public. But it was too late to alter this and he could see no way of making the council permanently satisfactory. The admission of a few Indian and British non-officials might silence the critics for a while, but there would soon be new grounds for dissatisfaction. Madras and Bombay would complain that their representatives had been excluded, but this was bound to be unless these governments bore the expenses for their nominees to travel to Calcutta. Admission of non-official nominees 'would be in fact a sham, a mere sop to the discontented, and this would soon be discovered'. The other alternative, of replacing the central legislative council with these provincial councils, would tend to improvement in legislation but was unlikely to conciliate non-official opinion. And once a legislative council had been constituted, its abolition without any other body to take its place was unthinkable.[108]

Indian opinion, such as it was, would be outraged. Frere, one of the most experienced of British officials, observed that the number of Indians who read English newspapers and were accessible to all the influences which swayed public opinion in England was rapidly increasing, and the number of those indirectly open to the same influence was growing even more rapidly.

I know few things more striking than the change which has come over the Natives in this respect. Twenty years ago they were remarkable for their general indifference to all public questions which had no immediate local bearing. But this indifference has given place among the more intelligent classes to a feverish curiosity which has of late years frequently struck me as one of the most note-worthy changes in the general characteristics of Native society.

Non-official Englishmen would also resent any abolition of the legislative council. So Frere suggested improvement of the existing body by the appointment of non-official Englishmen and Indians. This alone could obviate the perilous experiment of continuing to legislate for millions of people with few means of knowing except by a rebellion whether the laws suited them or not. He was also in favour of the creation of local legislatures.[109]

Wood, providing one more instance of a change of mind on his part, thought that the proliferation of legislative assemblies would only add to the confusion and promote a conflict of powers. He therefore preferred the other alternative of increasing the membership of the central council by nominating Indians and non-official Englishmen; but a strong official element should remain to protect the interests of Indians against the independent British members.[110] Canning was not enamoured of this proposal but was anxious for immediate action. 'It is now or never. Two or three years hence it will be far more difficult, perhaps impossible, to go back from our present forms and mock-Parliamentary publicity and to bring the legislating body for India to its true bearings.'[111]

The question became more pressing with the two judges, who had been nominated as members of the legislative council, speaking in severely critical terms of the government. Canning suggested that provincial councils be set up for 'debating and spouting', while the central council met in secret.[112] Wood was inclined even to abolish the legislative council, whose members tended to act independently of or antagonistically to the government and regarded themselves as representative of non-official British opinion.[113] 'I will not constitute a House of Commons in India, which would be a farce, if not mischievous.'[114] But Canning was in his new phase of conciliating the British community and advised Wood not to take such drastic action.

It is the duty of the Government to stand against any degree of opposition and virulence when a principle is at stake—and it has done so on more than one occasion. But asperities are now being smoothed down, and I am not disposed to see them raised again upon questions of legislative forms—although I admit that the forms were of incalculable importance when they were so unwisely conceded. I would give a good deal to be rid of them: but I do not think that it is worth a chronic hostility on the part of our European community. That community is very small, very ignorant of and indifferent to India and very selfish; but it is compact and united, has the press on its side, and can make itself heard better than any class in India; and constant antagonism with it, especially if the legislature be the field, will in the end weaken the Government with its native subjects. Indeed it has done so already in Bengal.[115]

The Indian Councils Act of 1861 enabled the addition to the Governor-General's council for legislative purposes of six to twelve members. These were to be nominated by the government; but at least half the number were to be non-officials. On the other hand, the Act truncated the powers of the legislative council. It could deal only with legislative matters and was expressly forbidden to deal with any other subject. Measures relating to the public revenue or debt, religion, military and naval matters and foreign relations could not be introduced without the Governor-General's sanction, and his assent was required to every Act passed by the council. Powers of legislation, which had been taken away from the governments of Madras and Bombay in 1833, were restored to them, a legislative council for Bengal was sanctioned and the Governor-General was authorized to establish such councils in the North-West Provinces and the Punjab. All these councils were expanded for legislative purposes on lines similar to those of the central council. There was no distribution of subjects between the central and the provincial councils, but all acts of the provincial legislatures required the assent of the Governor-General in addition to that of the Governor. The Governor-General's sanction was also required for the introduction of legislation on certain specified subjects.

The Aftermath of the Revolt

The Councils Act of 1861, both in its provision for the creation of what is known as the 'portfolio system' of government and in its clauses laying down the methods of legislation, was fully according to Canning's suggestions. 'Wood has worked', wrote Canning to Granville,[116] 'the India Bills through the Commons like a brick'. The central legislative council in its new form met in Calcutta on the eve of Canning's departure and functioned to the Viceroy's satisfaction. The nominated Indian members, who, as was to be expected with Canning at the head of the government, were Princes and landholders, behaved sedately and with deference.

IV

Canning, sore and raw after the intense criticism to which his policy of clemency had been subjected by his fellow-countrymen in India, was anxious to placate them in other respects. He decided to sanction the sale of waste lands on terms such as would attract British capital. This would also help to counter the agitation that was developing in Britain for increased cotton cultivation in India in view of the likelihood of diminished cotton supplies from the United States. Canning expected the Manchester interests to participate in such cultivation by purchasing these waste lands, but in fact the cotton manufacturers looked to the Government of India to promote cotton cultivation and ship the supplies to Britain.[117] Canning also wished to concede the demand of the Europeans for permission to redeem the land tax. By allowing such redemption up to a certain percentage of the revenue of each district and making sure that only the rights of the government and not those of any under-tenant were affected, the Viceroy thought that the experiment could be tried without risk.[118]

The Government of India published two resolutions on the sale of waste lands and the redemption of the land tax without reference to the home government. Wood generally approved of the schemes but objected to certain details and resented the failure to consult him.[119] While the home government agreed that waste lands should be sold, it seemed to them unduly generous for the State to forego all advantage from it and wrong to fail to protect tenant rights; and as only those landowners who had been assessed at a low rate would redeem, the State would never have the opportunity of raising the assessment. A permanent settlement was not likely to lead to such an improvement in the condition of the people that

21

the consumption of taxable articles would make up for the loss of revenue;[120] yet the home government were inclined to prefer such a settlement after a careful revision of the assessment.[121] As for redemption, if it were meant to provide an example of British improvement it was too much; but if it were intended to improve the general condition of the cultivators it was too little. More limited terms for the sale of waste lands, redemption in special cases and a permanent settlement seemed the best.[122]

It was realized that cancellation of the resolutions was bound to have a harmful effect on opinion in India. They were the grand measures of Canning's last years, intended to propitiate non-official British opinion in India and in Britain; and their revocation would lead to criticism from not only those who had been deprived of advantage but also the believers in the theory that India should be governed in India and not from London. It would certainly not help to establish the influence of the new Viceroy if he were seen to await instructions from the home government on a matter which had been decided by his predecessor and finally to carry out countermanding orders. In fact the newspapers owned by Englishmen denounced Elgin as a 'weak fool'.[123] Even so, the home government drafted a despatch censuring Canning's conduct in assuming such independence of action; but just then Canning died, and the draft was cancelled.[124] However, the Bombay government were authorized to declare a settlement permanent wherever the assessment was fair.[125]

Another delicate problem of administration concerning the non-official British community was created by the clashes between the British planters seeking to enforce the cultivation of indigo and the *raiyats* who resisted it. In 1860 there was a strong and nearly unanimous reluctance on the part of the raiyats in several districts of Bengal, especially Nuddea, Jessore and Malda, to sow indigo, even though some of them had received advances for this purpose; and the determination of the planters to avoid heavy losses by either themselves sowing or enforcing cultivation seemed likely to lead to serious affrays. The government were in an awkward position. They themselves were monopolists of opium, the cultivation of which they enforced on terms disadvantageous to the raiyats and on lands which were sought by the entrepreneurs of indigo;[126] but they realized too that as between the planters and the raiyats they owed a duty to their Indian subjects. The planters reported to the government that 'a general rebellion throughout Lower Bengal is *inevitable*, unless strict and decided measures are without delay taken by Government to put it down. It is entirely out of the planter's power to quell without the aid of Government. Unless matters improve within a fortnight not a man's life will be safe, leaving alone the destruction of property that must be the result.'[127] The planters, in other words, associated themselves with the government as fellow-exploiters of the land and the cultivators; and what they meant by their exaggerated references to a general rebellion was that their own position was becoming untenable. So they requested the government to issue a notification which would disabuse the raiyats of the idea that the government intended to interfere with the cultivation of indigo and to provide by law for the summary trial and punishment of breaches of contract in the districts.[128]

The belief was certainly current that the government were opposed to the cultivation of indigo;[129] so the government authorized the issue of a half-hearted notification which would help the planters without outraging the government's conscience. The raiyats were told that they were not obliged to take advances and to enter into contracts for the cultivation of indigo, and in this matter the law was equally fair to all parties. But if they did opt for the cultivation of indigo, they were required to fulfil their contracts, and would be liable to the lawful consequences of misconduct and failure to act up to their engagements. In a letter forwarding this notification, the Bengal government informed their officials that the sole object was to remove the false impression which appeared to exist regarding the government's views on indigo. It was not intended that the police should enforce these civil contracts; for that purpose the planters should have recourse to the courts.[130] However, as a few affrays had already occurred, and in view of the general excitement which prevailed, troops were sent down to these districts, the powers of the magistrates to compel fulfilment of contracts were increased by a temporary enactment, and it was decided to set up a special commission of inquiry.[131] Trevelyan[132] in Madras, always inclined to look at Calcutta with jaundiced eyes, commented that the raiyats of Bengal, proverbially the meekest and most easily governed of men, had been goaded into a state of smothered insurrection and were kept from open resistance only by a coercion act and the military police.[133] This was, of course, a gross exaggeration; but the Bengal authorities themselves recognized, with embarrassment, that they had sided with the planters.

Despite this, the resistance of the raiyats continued. In Nuddea district nearly 400 of them preferred imprisonment for alleged breaches of contract to the sowing of indigo, and in Thana district a riotous crowd, armed with sticks, repulsed a police detachment which sought to assist the planters.[134] The Secretary of State expressed his alarm and displeasure. To Wood the system of indigo cultivation in India seemed forced labour and he thought it would have to end. It could not be enforced by law or penal statutes, and the measures taken by government could only be justified as temporary ones. If the planters wished to secure indigo, they should deal equitably with the raiyats and pay a fair price. This might mean bankruptcy for some of them, but it could not be avoided.[135] With official reprimand added to their own lurking sense of guilt, the Bengal government instructed their officers that the great object should be to avoid the appearance as well as the reality of supporting misconduct on either side. Only then could magistrates hope to be accepted as just and neutral, and their advice and persuasion were likely to do real good and the people would not doubt that the government meant to act justly and fairly to all. Planters and raiyats should be reasoned with and advised in a kindly, considerate and temperate spirit so long as no offence had been committed. But once there had been an offence, the sole duty of the magistrate was to enforce the law equally against planter and raiyat. As long as planters conducted themselves lawfully they would be protected to the utmost and every assistance that could properly be given would be available to them. But they should be warned that if they resorted to oppression, the consequences would be upon their own heads. And nothing would be more unpardonable in an official than inducing the cultivators to do anything that would in the least degree prejudice their position in the future.[136]

It was now the turn of the planters to criticize the Bengal government. They said they were convinced of the desire of the Government of India to encourage them; but Sir J. P. Grant,[137] the Lieutenant-Governor of Bengal, and his officials were accused of having given rise to the impression that they were opposed to the cultivation of indigo. Indeed, Grant had stated in a letter published by official authority: 'I am myself of opinion that the indigo cultivators have and long have had great and increasing ground of just complaint against the whole system of indigo cultivation.' By informing the raiyats that the enactment compelling them to fulfil their engagements applied only to the current season and not to the coming years, the Bengal government were said to be driving the planters to ruin. Grant was also accused of interfering improperly and most indiscreetly with the sentences passed by magistrates and creating a general impression that decisions in favour of planters would incur the disapproval of the Bengal government. As a result, according to the planters, the people of Lower Bengal were losing all respect for officials and the minds of the people in the indigo districts were being kept in a state of greater excitement and uncertainty than before the statute of compulsion.[138]

There was, in fact, as Grant himself acknowledged in private, a measure of truth in this complaint. For Grant agreed with Wood that the system of indigo cultivation was an unjust one fit for destruction, did what he could to subvert it and was pleased with his success. 'On the whole', he reported to the Secretary of State, 'I think I am not too sanguine in believing that a very rotten and dangerous edifice has fallen to the ground and that by the care taken the fall has been as little destructive as possible.'[139] In his official minute he was more reserved but no less firm. He pointed out that there was no general unrest in the indigo districts and that the ill-will between the planters and the raiyats had only occasionally taken a violent form. He regretted any losses suffered by the planters. 'But as a national interest, the owners and cultivators of the soil must be ranked second to none in an agricultural country like India. Both interests should be treated, not only with justice but with consideration. Any less impartial view would err as much in point of sound economical policy as in point of fair dealing.' Grant said he was not hostile to indigo planting, and the quotation from his letter proved nothing. Conducted justly and by the free will and to the mutual benefit of all concerned, indigo cultivation could be a source of national wealth; but conducted otherwise it was an evil of great magnitude to be urgently corrected. 'I have objected to the police forcing unlawfully, or assisting or protecting others in forcing unlawfully, any unwilling person to cultivate any sort of crop whatsoever; and I have insisted that the police shall not support one man in unlawfully sowing another man's land by force, on any plea whatsoever.' If the planters had paid the raiyats a price which would have made it worthwhile for them to sow indigo, they would have got every year as much indigo as they wanted. In a sudden emergency the government had sponsored a special law for six months, but they had also provided for an inquiry and redress of all grievances; and this is what he had made known to the raiyats. 'I should have taken shame to myself if I had so acted as to gratify either party, at the expense of the just rights of the other.'[140]

Canning described Grant's minute as an excellent paper and a very clear exposition of a thoroughly right policy;[141] and the planters were informed that the Government of India were satisfied that the Bengal government had administered the law to all classes in a strictly impartial manner.[142] Their only criticism, expressed confidentially, was that it should have been made clear to the raiyats who had already entered into contracts for subsequent years that they should fulfil their engagements.[143] Wood too was satisfied. He thought that the indigo system as practised had probably received its death-blow, and he directed Grant to administer justice impartially and to protect the raiyats without giving the planters any opportunity for attributing their losses to the conduct of officials.[144] Nothing should be said or done to suggest that the government were opposed to indigo cultivation, and violence should be prevented. The planters were losing money heavily and required all the soothing they could get. Wood's new mood of moderation seems to have been the result of angry feelings in the India Council, of whose members many had invested in indigo firms.[145] But Grant's minute was not worded to calm ruffled tempers. The planters objected to what they believed to be its tone of prejudice and claimed to see little prospect of British capital being again invested in Lower Bengal. They protested also against what they deemed to be the Lieutenant-Governor's interference in judicial process.[146] Grant reiterated in reply that throughout the time of trouble he had had but two principles in mind: equal justice to both parties and every effort to make the inevitable disintegration of an unsound system as little of a calamity as possible.

It would be vain, even if it could be justifiable, after the publication of the Government records relating to the dispute between ryots and planters and of the evidence taken by the Indigo Commission, to attempt to conceal the fact that while in Bihar, the North-West Provinces and

Madras, nothing objectionable in the manner in which this trade is conducted is apparent, there have been grievous abuses in the indigo system in operation in Bengal.

So, while he was not hostile to indigo planting or to the planters, he regarded the removal of these abuses as a paramount duty both to the raiyat and to the honour of the British government. Coercive cultivation had now come to an end and it would be a wiser and more helpful course for the planters to try some reformed system.[147]

In fact, as Grant pointed out to the Secretary of State, the destruction of the old indigo system was no achievement of his. The raiyats had taken the matter into their own hands and had the law and the right wholly on their side. The raiyats knew their rights and felt that they were worth fighting for. To compel them to sow indigo at a heavy loss when they could sow other crops at a profit was now beyond human power. 'I think we have escaped a great tumult in which the destruction of every sort of property would have been infinite, more narrowly than I thought at the time. Such a rising would not have been a nice after-piece to the mutiny.' As it was, the raiyats in the indigo districts were in a state of 'fervent loyalty'.[148] Canning and his government again upheld Grant[149] and the Viceroy received Wood's congratulations for what was in every way his Lieutenant-Governor's achievement.[150] As the support in London for the planters extended from the India Council to Parliament, Granville, who had been greatly concerned, was shown Grant's minute; he said of it that he had never read an abler paper, and was convinced by it of the correctness of the policy of the Government of India.[151] Stanley, on behalf of the Conservatives, was not so easily converted. He felt that Grant's language to the planters 'has been to say the least unlucky'. But the Conservatives, though in opposition, were still too conscious of the shock of 1857 to criticize the Government of India and allowed Parliament to return to what Stanley described as 'its normal state of forgetting the existence of India'.[152]

Canning, with the wind blowing in his favour, now took a more direct interest in indigo affairs. In an official despatch to the Secretary of State in December 1860, he agreed with Grant that the administration of the law had not been impartial and the raiyats had not been adequately defended against the planters and their agents. If the Indigo Enforcement Act of April 1860 had not been temporary, it would have been unjust to the raiyats. On the other hand, the raiyats had been cautioned against pressing just grievances with violence or excitement and against repudiating contracts. However, the system had broken down from its own unsoundness, and Canning observed that he could 'not look upon the emancipation of Lower Bengal from such a system and the changes which will follow that emancipation as other than a great national good'.[153] Three months later he again wrote privately with vehemence on the subject. He told Wood that out of six hundred contracts over forty had been proved to be forgeries, and that it could be fairly presumed that another two hundred had also been forged. 'It makes one's blood creep to think of what may have been done under cover of this gigantic system of fraud, bearing in mind the cases of blind men, lepers, bed-ridden men and children' who in some districts were found imprisoned on pretence of violating contracts. 'Really it is worse than slavery, for it is deceit in place of force and it involves honourable men unknowingly.' Many senior officials also had been conniving at it because they had invested privately in indigo concerns; and this fact, being generally known, had been utilized by the planters to compel acquiescence in malpractices and to extort hard terms.[154] But soon, under pressure of local British opinion, Canning allowed his ardour to cool and, to Wood's astonishment,[155] introduced a bill to punish as a criminal offence any fraudulent breach of contract to grow or deliver agricultural produce. It is difficult to recognize in the Canning of these years the man who had withstood the howls for vengeance in 1858; and one can only conclude that the long agony had dented his powers. His lame excuse was that the indigo problem was not settling down, that the raiyats, with a foundation of right, had in some places put themselves in the wrong and that the cases were threatening to become very complicated in point of law.[156] But the bill was withdrawn.

The same note of pliancy and appeasement is to be seen in Canning's handling of the *Nil Darpan* affair. *Nil Darpan*, or Indigo Mirror, was a play in Bengali lampooning the planters and describing the harsh conditions under which indigo was sown. Grant ordered that the play be translated for his perusal, for he thought it likely that the play depicted popular feeling on the subject. Semi-isolation from all classes of Indian society and lack of information as to their views seemed to Grant to be the reason why the revolt of 1857 had come as an unexpected eruption, and he wished to avoid a similar ignorance in the indigo crisis.[157] The play was translated and thereafter circulated, without Grant's permission, to a large number of officials by Seton-Karr, secretary to the Bengal government.[158] The planters heard of this and objected.[159] Though the circulation had not been sanctioned, there was no reason to regret it, for *Nil Darpan* was not libellous or likely to excite any class of persons to sedition or breaches of the peace. So Grant stood his ground. He apologized for the fact that copies of the play had been posted with an official frank, but did not retract the translation itself.[160] The planters then brought an action for libel against the translator and the distributor. Meantime the Viceroy also, in his anxiety to please the planters, intervened. He informed the Secretary of State that it had been an 'unpardonable act of inconsiderateness' on Seton-Karr's part to identify his office with 'a party squib on so sore a subject'.[161] Seton-Karr was asked to explain. He acknowledged his inadvertence in circulating the play officially without the knowledge of Grant, and offered to resign from the legislative council. Grant did not think it necessary to accept the resignation;[162] but, in the wake of a judgment by the High Court, which even the Viceroy recognized as displaying 'indecent partizanship',[163] sentencing the translator to imprisonment with fine, the Governor-General in Council issued a resolution on the subject. It was declared that even if the passages impugned were completely vindicated it would go but a small way to lessen the regret of the Government of India at the whole proceeding. Grant was rebuked and told that he should have disavowed and disapproved Seton-Karr's proceedings as soon as they had been brought to his attention. Seton-Karr was censured for an unwarrantable assumption and indiscreet exercise of an authority which did not belong to him and for neglect of his duty to inform the Government of India. Despite his apology, his resignation of membership of the legislative council was accepted and, in addition, he was not allowed to continue as a secretary to the Bengal government.[164] It was no wonder that the planters expressed their appreciation of the Viceroy's action.[165] The home government felt that Canning had been too severe, especially as no one agreed with the judgment of the Calcutta High Court; but, in deference to Canning's wishes, they did not disturb the decision.[166]

This was not the end of the indigo question. The problems of its cultivation and of land tenures, rents and tenant rights in general were rendered acute by certain observations made by the Chief Justice, Sir Barnes Peacock.[167] 'I think', commented Wood, 'Peacock ought to be whipped for the *inconsiderate folly* of what he has done. No man is justified, especially a Chief Justice, in throwing out *doubts* on the legality of titles to land or property. Our Chancellor says he ought to be recalled.'[168] The sooner Peacock resigned, the better.[169] Elgin felt that the uncertain state of the rent law and tenant rights was a great evil and he was willing to consider remedial legislation.[170] But Wood was not inclined to override the decisions of the courts by a legal enactment until it became necessary.[171] It was impossible to expect the proper rent in each case to be fixed by a court of law, but if a reasonable decision were reached in one or two cases some sort of compromise could be reached in most cases, and the question might in practice be settled.[172] But the decision of Peacock seemed likely to cause a revolution in land tenures in India by extinguishing the rights of subholders, confirmed by the Tenancy Act of 1859, which had recognized a right of occupancy on the basis of continuous holding for twelve years and had limited the landlord's rights to enhance rents or to evict his tenants. Wood was of the view that tenancy rights in Bengal required modification, particularly in view of the decision of the Calcutta High Court, and that the Act of 1859 should be amended to lengthen the period for acquiring occupancy rights from twelve to twenty or twenty-five years.[173] But this was not in accordance with Lawrence's thinking; and he was more concerned about a possible conflict with the planters, who wished to have the power of enhancing rents in order to enforce the cultivation of indigo.[174] Lawrence braced himself for the 'tough fight. . . .But I fear the ryots will never see fair play; there are too many, too strong interests against them.'[175] The planters, the great body of zemindars and most of the lawyers led by the Chief Justice formed a formidable combination, and the civilians were rather afraid of meddling with the rent question.[176]

Raising the rent was regarded by the landholders as their right. 'An increase of rent is in all countries a source of discontent to the tenant; but Indian officials are probably the only Government servants in the world who do not recognize that this claim by the landlord of his share of the increased value of his own land is as natural and as blameless as the official's own claim to an increased salary for increased efficiency and for length of service.'[177] It was the established practice to offer the raiyat the option of either executing an agreement to cultivate indigo or receiving a notice for enhancement of rent under the Act of 1859. It was difficult to say which of these two alternatives was more obnoxious or the cause of greater discontent; but most raiyats considered indigo contracts for limited periods preferable to permanent enhancement. This, supplemented on many occasions by the employment of force, led to a large number of raiyats contracting to cultivate indigo at rates which were clearly unremunerative.[178] Such cultivation was therefore undertaken with a sense of injustice; and as the planters had no scruples about tampering with the terms and conditions of the contracts to the detriment of the raiyats, sporadic disturbances became the rule. The landholders urged the government to support them and to explain to the raiyats that indigo cultivation was to their advantage as it took the place of the fallow in the system of crop rotation.[179] But it was by no means certain that indigo had the effect of a fallow crop on the soil; and usually the agents of the planters chose the best land available without reference to any system of crop rotation. So the Bengal government refused to interfere.

The Bengal Ryot is not slow to learn what is and what is not profitable to him, and if on such a question he will not follow the advice of the Planter who may be supposed to have some knowledge of Agriculture, he will not willingly follow the advice of a Government Officer who pretends to no such knowledge. Advice unwillingly followed is but another name for compulsion.[180]

When the matter came up for consideration to the Government of India, the home department felt that any effort to fix the rent in perpetuity, thereby removing the threat of periodic enhancements, would be wholly opposed to the intentions of the permanent settlement.[181] But the Viceroy thought it would be most desirable if the proprietors of land could be induced to reach a compromise with the hereditary raiyats, whereby the rent would be greatly enhanced and fixed in perpetuity. Alternatively, Lawrence suggested legislation fixing rent in hereditary tenures of land fairly and in a simple manner. Otherwise it would be better that indigo was not cultivated; for it was the bounden duty of the Government of India to take measures to prevent the recurrence of agrarian violence on such a wide scale as in 1860.[182]

Lawrence, however, received little support from his council. Maine believed that the officials of Bengal were biased against the planters. He thought the state of affairs disclosed by the report of the Indigo Commission had passed away and the remedy for such evils as still existed lay not in depriving the planters of their methods of coercion but in establishing a regular system of civil courts.

I would frankly [wrote Maine to Lawrence][183] ask Your Excellency whether you have ever seen anything in the Bengalis of the present moment which indicates an oppressed race. I would rather say that their principal characteristic is 'cheek'. It comes from their at last understanding that the Government, both Home and Indian, has their interest at heart; and that their rights and privileges on paper are really given to be used.

A measure to ensure by civil justice the prompt performance of fair contracts should be a condition precedent to any rent reform. Instead of impounding the bullocks of a raiyat when he proposed to violate his contract, an order of a civil court should be served on him. A silent revolution would then speedily be effected, the character of the contracts would be completely altered and Europeans would be weaned from burdening themselves with proprietary interests in land. Legislation would be difficult and delicate, while the abandonment of indigo cultivation could not be considered. 'Now, we should surely look facts in the face. Is it not a fact that, the total collapse of the great indigo interest would be not simply a severe wound to the prosperity of India but almost a fatal moral blow to the credit of the Indian Government?'[184] Trevelyan contended that it was neither proper nor possible for courts to fix rents. This belonged to the private arrangements and not to the public polity of society. But a commission should be appointed to investigate and adjudicate landed tenures in Bengal.[185] Both Maine and Trevelyan were agreed that there should be, not fixity of rent as Lawrence had suggested, but permanency of tenure, 'a permanent sub-settlement' as Maine described it.

Wood feared that as the planters now had the decision of the High Court in their favour, they would probably provoke violence and then call upon the government to put it down, thus driving them into collision with a large section of the population. He therefore asked Maine to examine the extent of the government's obligation to protect the rights of the cultivator;[186] but Maine was believed to have no heart for the subject as his leanings were all on the side of the zemindars and the planters and he was not the man to face unpopularity.[187] Wood's own view was that some period, perhaps longer than twelve years, should be fixed which would serve as prima facie proof of hereditary occupancy and the rent should only be raised in proportion to the rise in value of the produce or the potential of the land, assuming that the rent had originally been fixed on a fair and equitable basis.[188] The government should not be placed in the position of being the apparent oppressor of the raiyats; and it would be impossible to maintain the legal position, whatever it be, against the feelings of a large majority which believed the law to be inequitable and unjust.[189] Wood also asked Maine to support mitigation of 'the fraudulent and disgraceful system of indigo contracts', which Canning had sanctioned in an effort to conciliate the non-official British community, by restricting the enforcement of specific performance to registered contracts; for then the registrar could satisfy himself that the raiyat had acted as a free agent.[190]

Lawrence felt sure that while the abuses described by the Indigo Commission might have become less frequent they had not disappeared, and that small cause courts could provide no adequate remedies.[191] But his determination to improve matters had begun to weaken and he did not urge the reluctant Maine to take up the rent question for he himself could not see his way to a successful solution. No great improvement could be effected by any modification of the Act of 1859. Maine was very anxious to secure a collective opinion from the High Court on the Act; but the judges shrank from giving one. 'The simple fact is that public opinion is on the planters side, and all the English press is in their favour.'[192] Unless the government defined in each case what the raiyat should pay, there was little they could do. Registration of contracts would afford the raiyat no effectual security.[193] The result was that nothing was done; and Wood feared, on giving up office in February 1866, that under his successors the selfish policy of the planter might gain ground. 'I am firmly convinced that our permanent hold of India would be fearfully loosened if the cultivating population felt that their *customary* rights were in danger.'[194]

Ripon, who succeeded Wood, was not in favour of fresh rent legislation unless it were absolutely necessary.[195] So Lawrence

33

abandoned all efforts to alleviate the situation. He did not enact a law of specific performance regarding agricultural contracts as that might become a means of fraud and oppression. The raiyat was not a free agent and did not enter into contracts of his free will. A statute providing for specific performance would therefore 'only serve to rivet his chains which I would gladly help to knock off'. But the members of his council, as Lawrence knew, while they did not really approve of the system of indigo cultivation, had no wish to incur the odium of the influential class.[196] For other reasons also Sir John Strachey advised Lawrence not to initiate any revision of the Act of 1859. 'I dread the consequences of mooting such a question with a new Governor-General who is pretty sure to be a Tory with strong sympathies in favour of land-lords and none in favour of tenants.'[197]

Conditions in the indigo plantations in Bihar were probably worse than in Bengal. Lawrence reported that there the raiyat was no better than a serf and cultivation was being carried on under a system of pressure and terror. Serious discontent was therefore bound to develop sooner or later.[198] The planters staved off a *iacquerie* by consenting to raise prices; but Lawrence believed that no final settlement of the indigo problem in Bihar was possible until there had been an outbreak such as had occurred in Bengal in 1860.[199]

v

The problem of the relations between the European planters and the Indian labourers working on their estates was not merely an economic one; it automatically spilled over into the more serious question of the relations between the two races. Wood heartily disliked this clash of the private interests of Englishmen and Indians.[200] Maine was inclined to side with his fellow-countrymen. It was the European party which should win in the end, and the great task of the Government of India was but to guide them and to compel them to be just to the weaker race.[201] As it was, however, there seemed to Maine to be no need for intervention; for the Bengalis felt themselves amply protected against the Europeans and were ready to stand up against them at the smallest chance. Maine believed that the success of their stand against the planters had turned their heads, and the protest of the British Indian Association against the speech of the Lieutenant-Governor in the legislative council was 'positively the most impertinent document I ever read in my life'.[202]

But Wood was not so easily deceived and distrusted the planters and the British community as a whole.

I don't think I was ever more shocked in my life than by a story I heard the other day that in the case of a gross outrage perpetrated by some officers on a foreigner residing in Calcutta the advocate explained that they took him for a native. While I would do every justice to the English settler, we should, I think, abdicate our most sacred duty if we did not take good care to prevent oppression. We must approach the consideration of these cases with the consciousness that there will be a disposition on the part of one side to use the powers for their own purposes.[203]

The question of the relations between the British and the Indians raised in turn the wider issue of the future of British rule in India. Wood did not believe in its permanence. How it would end no one could foresee; but it was difficult to suppose that, when urban Indians were educated and the hardier races were ill-treated by Englishmen of low character and position and resented it, British rule could be maintained.

Of course there will be a struggle; and blood and treasure to an enormous amount will be spent in rain [*sic* vain?]. This is, I am afraid, the most probable end of our Indian rule, but good conduct, wise measures, and sound policy towards the natives may avert it for many years, if it can do no better. Whatever may be the result, our course ought to be the same; to improve the native, reconcile him if we can to our rule, and fit him for ruling himself. I don't believe that his fitness to rule well will make him a worse subject, till his time arrives.[204]

But as regards the army, Wood was more cautious. He rejected the absurd idea of the Government of India of raising a force of Christian converts in India.[205] But he favoured the mixing of castes in the regiments and advised Canning and Elgin to raise the regiments as much as possible from different parts of India. There should never again be an Indian army very much the same in its feelings and prejudices and connexions. Rather, if one regiment mutinied, the next one should be so alien as to be ready to fire on the first.[206]

Rose[207] says that the inhabitants of India will not neglect any good opportunity of throwing off our yoke. We have maintained our power by playing off one part against the other, and we must continue to do so. . . .Do what you can therefore to prevent all having a common feeling. You cannot create a military body apart from the people alto-gether, for the soldiers are constantly going home, and renewing their relations with their families and connexions—but I think you may pre-vent any common feeling amongst the different component parts of the army and that I am anxious to do.[208]

Each province should be manned with its own troops, with the Sikhs and the Bengal regiments kept in readiness to deal with each other if necessary. The natural antagonism of Indian races was a considerable element of British strength; so 'a dissociating spirit' should be kept up. 'If all India was to unite against us how long could we maintain ourselves?'[209]

Such advice, born clearly of fears of a second revolt, was wel-comed in India. Elphinstone,[210] Governor of Bombay, thought the Brahmins would never be well disposed towards the British,[211] and Frere, his successor, was convinced that the Muhammadans and the Brahmins would for many generations remain apart from the British, unwilling to be conciliated and extremely difficult to incorporate. These two powerful and compact classes would never be without leaders and their attempts to do mischief would always secure sympathy even from those who were well off and by no means discontented.[212] The Commander-in-Chief felt no anxiety regarding Indian troops;[213] but there were alarmist rumours in circulation. In June 1862 a panic was caused by the report that the assassination of all Europeans was being planned; and even British officials became savage. The life of an Indian, according to the Viceroy, was estimated by most Europeans as no higher than that of a dog. 'Our greatest source of embarrassment in this country is the extreme difficulty of administering equal justice between natives and Europeans.'[214] But Elgin insisted on a firm and impartial enforcement of the law; and the home government supported him in this, for Wood had no deep regard for the Euro-pean settlers in India. In fact, on the issue of bringing Europeans to trial before Indians, which tended to become the most sensitive aspect of race relations, Wood was not opposed in principle. He believed that the deficiency of Indian judges was not in learning or acuteness but in moral courage and those qualities which enable a man to act alone. So he declared that he would not hesitate to appoint an Indian to the High Court where he would sit along with other judges, but would not feel confident in appointing an Indian as sole judge in a *mofussil* (country) district.[215] Though

Indians might generally not be a fine or superior race, it was impossible to believe that there were not good men among them.

But what is to become of us if we are to treat all Indians as unworthy of trust or employment except in the lowest places? How are we ever to improve them? I fully agree that they can be admitted to high places only sparingly, but I should be sorry to have to administer the affairs of India if I did not think and believe that there were the elements of improvement amongst them.[216]

But apart from the argument of moral duty, Wood saw a great political advantage in employing Indians as much as possible in official service. Active and stirring spirits among the Indian population should be associated with British rule in order to make them its supporters.[217] He therefore resisted Maine's suggestion for replacing Indian officials in the subordinate judicial service with English barristers. Reduction of the number of Indians in the army and the civil services had been a matter of necessity; but removal of Indians from the judiciary would give rise to the impression that the British were seeking to rule India without the assistance of Indians.[218]

Lawrence too was conscious of the potential danger of bad feeling between the races as a result of clash of interests. 'These things are never out of my mind night nor day; but how to reconcile people to what is wise and politic and good for both, there is the rub!'[219] Indeed the Viceroy, in his anxiety to be impartial between the races, forwarded officially an application from a raja of Bengal for a Queen's Commission in the army. The Secretary of State rejected it, though with considerable embarrassment, on the grounds that British soldiers would never obey an Indian officer and a Brahmin would be out of place in a British officers' mess.[220] Though he directed Lawrence to consider other ways of employing 'the better class of Indians' in the army,[221] he could not free his thinking of memories of 1857. These fears were strengthened by Lawrence's report that there was 'a good deal of *quiet* dissatisfaction' among Indian soldiers.[222] So the Bombay government were censured for issuing Enfield rifles to an Indian regiment.[223] The Madras government were advised not to display any official interest in the propagation of Christianity.[224] The law member was directed to make sure that English criminals were punished promptly and severely without being produced before Indian judges or juries; for while Europeans should not be alienated by subordinating them to the subject race, Indians should see and feel assured that Europeans enjoyed no immunity.[225]

This desire to provide equal justice even if by different procedures found expression in the Grand Jury Bill; but there was loud opposition from the European community. Lawrence, whose experience in the Punjab had not equipped him to face such a reaction, was inclined to give way; and Maine, though he saw the folly of such a retreat, was incapable of strengthening the Viceroy.[226] Wood urged the Government of India to hold firm, for surrender to such senseless agitation would be ignominious to the last degree and most injurious to the government and the public good.[227] 'If the opinions of the Home Government, of the Indian Government, of the Law Commission, of the Chief Justice of Madras and of all improving lawyers generally are to be overborne by clamour in Calcutta, matters are come to a pretty pass indeed.'[228] Were the Government of India to allow themselves to be bullied on this occasion, they would ever be at the mercy of the agitators of Calcutta.[229]

In 1868 Lawrence reported that all was quiet in India. There was, according to his assessment, much natural docility and respect for power and authority in the Indian people. In Bengal, the educated middle classes had political aspirations but were aware of their weakness. The great danger arose from the large extent of country to be administered and the number and strength of the predatory races scattered over upper and central India.[230] Rumours had been reaching London that a fresh rising would shortly occur in India, and Cranborne suggested the exclusion of Hindus and Moslems from the army. 'Can you find no races that have neither caste nor Koran to defend nor deposed rulers to avenge?' Withdrawal of many British troops from India was not improbable, and they might be replaced by soldiers recruited in Burma, Ceylon or Borneo.[231] But the Viceroy regarded the rumours as groundless. There were many disturbing causes at work in India and the result was much latent discontent; but no serious matters causing irritation existed. The two great issues on which a very strong feeling did exist was the general want of employment and the treatment of Indians by Englishmen. It was the widening gulf between the two races which Lawrence regarded as the great danger to British rule.[232] As for recruitment of non-Indian soldiers for the Indian army, the Viceroy thought that only Africans could be considered, and their employment would be unpopular in India. So he preferred recruitment within India on a provincial basis and segregation of troops.[233]

Cranborne's successor, Northcote, was so alarmed by the possibility of a revolt that he advised a weakening of the central government, the adaptation of the administration to the wants and prejudices of each district and the exercise of caution and forbearance in the introduction of modern ideas.

It seems natural to say, a Christian nation, a nation possessing what it believes to be the highest form of civilization, ought to apply itself to Christianize and civilize those who have been committed to its charge. But it would require an iron will to carry it into effect. You would need a Strafford with his policy of Thorough. To accomplish a benevolent purpose you would have to do many things which are extremely disagreeable to the object of your benevolence: you would have to improve a good many of them off the face of the earth; your means would often come to be very unworthy of your ends. A Government such as that of England never will pursue such a policy with any vigour at all. I look therefore to the opposite policy. . . .[234]

This did not, however, frighten Lawrence into abandoning what was perhaps his only positive effort as Viceroy—the attempt to better the lot of the raiyats. He thought India was as quiet and the people as well disposed as they had ever been since 1857 or were ever likely to be; and the government had ample means of maintaining the public security.[235] He attached no importance to the reports circulating in Britain of widespread Fenian plots in India, of contacts with revolutionary organizations in Europe and of a conspiracy fomented by Silenites with headquarters in the United States and subsidized by some Princes. The Viceroy was convinced that Fenians could gain no influence with Indians; they might have sympathizers in British regiments but even there the proportion of Irishmen was much smaller than in former days.[236] All that Lawrence thought necessary, particularly after an anonymous letter had led to the fear of another military rising in Meerut in June 1867,[237] was to caution against arming Indian troops with Schneider rifles and to insist on the stationing in India of a sufficient number of British troops to keep in check the Indian sepoys whom he described as strangers and mercenaries and belonging for the most part to warlike tribes and hardy races.[238] Otherwise he thought it sufficient to give attention to the improvement of the condition of the tillers of the soil and the promotion of better relations between the races. If there were any parallel with Ireland at all, it lay in the extreme poverty of the peasants. The main cause of discontent in Ireland arose from agrarian circumstances. 'No people can be contented and loyal, who have not the means of decent subsistence. Ireland on a small scale is a type of India. Agriculture is the chief employment of the people and hence the poverty of the masses.'[239]

Lawrence recognized that relations between the two races were also deteriorating and that the conduct of the British in India oscillated between extreme insolence and acute apprehension;[240] but he did not consider any remedial action. Northcote wished to make it easier for Indians to join the covenanted civil service, and for this purpose was willing to consider recruitment in India or grant of scholarships to a few Indians every year to complete their education in Britain.[241] But the Government of India were unwilling to make any change in the rules for admission of Indians to the civil service. 'We conquered India mainly by force of arms and in like manner we must hold it.'[242] All that Lawrence and his council were prepared to do was to let Indians hold more posts;[243] and Northcote, despite his earlier attitude, was satisfied with this.[244]

VI

In foreign policy, the first decision Canning had to take was on the proposal of John Lawrence that Peshawar be abandoned to the Amir, Dost Mohamed, as a measure of economy and a pledge of good behaviour by the Afghans.[245] The Viceroy was wholly opposed to such a cession. It would diminish British prestige—no insignificant consideration at that time—and the security of India, while the immediate saving was overrated. British influence over the tribes inhabiting this area was greater than ever before, and it was incomprehensible why Lawrence wished to convert them into subjects and soldiers of the Amir, who would at all times be far more amenable to the influence of Britain's enemies. Nor could any such transfer be justified as consideration for services rendered or friendliness shown by the Amir. He had done nothing except remain aloof during the disturbances of 1857 in return for a monthly bribe of ten thousand pounds. The whole scheme was described by Canning as 'madness' and the most effective recipe for keeping the whole frontier and some of the internal provinces of India 'in hot water'. Rather than implement such a scheme, Canning was prepared to resign. 'If the measure is to be adopted (which I cannot believe) and if this reason or excuse is to be alleged for it, I hope that it will fall to some other Governor-General than me to set his hand to the paper which conveys the grant.'[246]

However, if Canning was averse to relinquishing territory, he showed no desire to acquire it. Raiding operations by the Maharaja of Sikkim opened out the prospect of annexing at least part of that hill kingdom, and Wood suggested that the government 'could, without taking *a great deal*, acquire a more defensible line. I would take what makes Darjeeling safe for the future, and no more.'[247] But Canning was emphatic in rejecting the practice of turning the aggressions of a semi-barbarous people into an excuse for appropriating their territory. While an addition to the hill country around Darjeeling would be very pleasant, that was not a sufficient ground for action, especially after the recent professions of anti-annexation.[248] Wood hastily withdrew his suggestion.[249]

Elgin was strongly of the view that there should be the least possible interference in Afghan affairs; but when British self-interest necessitated it, the government should speak with determination and follow it up if necessary with a blow.[250]

I am wholly opposed to that prurient intermeddling policy which finds so much favour with certain classes of Indian officials. It is constantly thrusting us into equivocal situations in which our acts and our professions of respect for the independence of other nations are in contradiction—and in which our proceedings become tainted with the double reproach of inconsistency and selfishness. Nothing in my opinion can be more fatal to our prestige and legitimate influence. My modest ambition for England is that she should in this Eastern world establish the reputation of being all just and all powerful.

The British should cease to attempt to play a great part in small intrigues and interfere only where they could put forward an unimpeachable plea of right or duty; and when they announced a decision it should be understood by the neighbours as the decree of fate.[251] Such a policy of general abstention would be not only dignified but prudent as well, for there was uneasiness and excitement in the minds of Moslems in India, who were awaiting the prophesied advent of the twelfth Imam in 1863 and watching the development of events in Afghanistan.[252]

Wood, while he agreed that no interest should be shown in internal conditions in Afghanistan, was at first for a positive policy of making Afghanistan a bulwark of India. The Amir should be assured of British friendship and goodwill. He should also be advised against marching on Herat; but if the rulers of Herat and Persia attacked him he should be assisted with money and arms.[253] The next year, influenced by John Lawrence who was a member of his council, the Secretary of State retracted his suggestion. Dost Mohamed was so old that no arrangement with him seemed likely to be permanent; and any advice given to him, if rejected would weaken British prestige and if accepted would give the Amir a claim against the British government.[254]

However, the Viceroy was obliged in October 1863 to sanction an expedition to crush the embryo conspiracy among the Sitana tribesmen on the frontier with Afghanistan; and Wood warned him against any move which might create the impression that the British were intending to interfere in Afghan affairs.[255] Elgin's death at this stage virtually determined the choice of his successor. For one main reason for Lawrence's appointment as Viceroy was his knowledge of the frontier areas and the belief that he would bring the Sitana expedition to a rapid and successful conclusion. Pushing large bodies of disciplined troops, who were only formidable in masses, into the hills where they could not function effectively, seemed to Wood to be folly. 'For Heaven's sake avoid this if you can. India was going on so well prospering in every corner, the finances in a comfortable state, the revenues improving, public works pushed on to some greater extent than formerly, and then all at once without adequate cause we are plunged into an expedition in which we have lost men, money and audit.' A defensive frontier policy seemed to Wood to be the best. The plains should be held, but no attempt should be made to advance into the hills. The Liberal Government were also for a policy of non-intervention and refusal to seek any permanent influence in Afghanistan. The Government of India should not meddle in Afghanistan in ordinary times for whenever the assistance of the Afghans was required it could always be made worth their while to give it.[256] These were views wholly in accordance with those of Lawrence. The man who had in the crisis of 1857 recommended the abandonment of Peshawar was not likely in more tranquil times to engage in aggrandizement on the frontier; but the virtual war on which the Commander-in-Chief, Rose, had embarked with the consent of Sir William Denison,[257] the weak individual officiating as Governor-General, had been brought to an end before Lawrence reached India.

After the death of the Amir, Dost Mohamed, in 1863, there were wars of succession in Afghanistan which lasted till almost the end of Lawrence's term, and the frontier with India was virtually forgotten. On his part the Viceroy was happy to watch events in Afghanistan as a spectator. 'I do not believe we shall have any difficulties or complications with the Afghans if we only leave them alone. The greater the enmity between the two parties in Kabul, the less likely are they to meddle with us.'[258] Both parties would be glad to have British assistance in arms and money but neither party, when the difficulty was over, could be relied upon a moment longer than it was in their interest to be on the British side.[259]

Like their Liberal predecessors, the Conservative Government of 1866 also approved of Lawrence's policy of neutrality; for the Conservative party had not yet awakened to the imperial argument. Cranborne wrote to Lawrence that the Viceroy's observant attitude towards the contending parties was the only one in accordance with British interests. 'Indian resources are wanted for other work besides extension of territory just now.'[260]

In fact Cranborne was more interested in Upper Burma than in Afghanistan. No European Power should be allowed to interpose itself between British Burma and China, and British influence should be paramount in Upper Burma. This could be effected by diplomacy; but Cranborne added that when the hour struck for absorbing Burma he would hear of it without regret.[261] This frightened Lawrence. He thought that annexation was bound to come but there was no need to anticipate events; twenty years of peace wisely employed would do great things for India.[262] But the conquest of Upper Burma was still far below the horizon. The immediate problem was Afghanistan and Central Asia, and in this respect the policy of Lawrence had the support of both parties in Britain.

Shere Ali, whom the Government of India had formally recognized as Amir, sent an envoy to Peshawar with requests for a new treaty of friendship, 6000 muskets and the recognition of his son as heir apparent. He was told in reply that as the old treaty signed with Dost Mohamed was still in force there was no need for a fresh one; the request for arms was also refused but the son was recognized as the heir. When Shere Ali's brother and rival, Azim Khan, sought asylum in India, he was granted it only on the condition that he would not intrigue against the Amir. When another brother of Shere Ali, Amin Khan, sent a mission to India, it was informed that the treaty relations of the Government of India were with the Amir and no countenance would be given to proceedings which sought to establish the independence of any of the Amir's relations.

At first Shere Ali was triumphant and captured Kandahar; but the death of his son and heir lowered his spirits, and his enemies gained ground and occupied Kabul. The Government of India made it clear that so long as the Amir retained any material hold on Afghanistan, their recognition of him would continue unimpaired and that they would not interfere in the affairs of Afghanistan.[263] However, Shere Ali suffered further reverses and on 22 May 1866 the Government of India authorized their agent in Kabul to congratulate another brother of Shere Ali, Afzul Khan, who had installed himself at the capital. But the Viceroy wrote to him:

that it would be inconsistent with the fame and reputation of the British Government to break off its alliance with Ameer Shere Ali Khan, who has given to it no offence, so long as he retains his authority and power over a large portion of Afghanistan. That Ameer still rules in Candahar and in Herat. My friend! The relations of this Government are with the actual Rulers of Afghanistan. If Your Highness is able to consolidate Your Highness' power in Cabul, and is sincerely desirous of being a friend and ally of the British Government, I shall be ready to accept Your Highness as such. But I cannot break the existing engagements with Ameer Shere Ali Khan, and I must continue to treat him as the Ruler of that portion of Afghanistan over which he retains control.[264]

Afzul Khan was given all honorific titles short of that of Amir.

In January 1867, with Shere Ali suffering another defeat, this position had to be abandoned; and Lawrence wrote to Afzul Khan recognizing him as Amir of Kabul and Kandahar and Shere Ali as the ruler of Herat. In return for British goodwill, Afzul Khan was expected to adhere to the treaties signed by Dost Mohamed.[265] But Lawrence still saw no necessity for, or advantage in, closer relations with the Afghan rulers. 'A day may come when it is wise to do so, but that day has not yet arrived.'[266] But if Shere Ali, in his distress, sought support from Russia or Persia he should be told plainly that Britain would aid his enemies. This could hardly be expected to deter Shere Ali, but 'it is a card we are bound to play'.[267] Northcote, who had succeeded Cranborne as Secretary of State, was in full agreement.[268]

On 7 October 1867, Afzul Khan died and was succeeded by his brother Azim Khan. Though he did not formally notify the Government of India of his accession, Lawrence sent him a letter of good wishes. But Azim Khan's reign did not last long, and by September 1868 Shere Ali was back in Kabul. Even though Lawrence's government had throughout insisted on keeping alive their *de facto* recognition of whatever authority had remained with Shere Ali, the latter had not been satisfied.

From the very commencement of the union and friendship of the two Governments until now, notwithstanding the confusion and troubles that have befallen the Cabul Government, I have so carefully kept in view the integrity of our former friendship, that I have neither publicly nor privately, neither by sign nor hint, held any, even the smallest, communication with any other Government far and near, except with the great British Government. Notwithstanding all this, during all this season of anarchy, neither by way of assistance nor by way of friendship and condolence or sympathy, have I received any attention. Now that God Almighty, apart from or beyond the aid, secret or public, of another, has of his own mercy restored to me the country of my inheritance,

Shere Ali was anxious to strengthen his position by proceeding to India for talks with the Viceroy.[269] Lawrence agreed to this, for he too was keen on meeting the Amir. The Viceroy expected that at the interview Shere Ali would promise and seek much. 'An Afghan. . . has a large maw; and it is next to impossible to content him.' No offensive and defensive alliance should be signed but he should be given a grant from year to year, strictly dependent on the general satisfaction of the Government of India with his good conduct and adherence to engagements. All that should be expected of him was that he kept his subjects on the Indian frontier in good order and maintained true relations of amity with the Government of India.[270] In fact, Shere Ali was not able to leave Afghanistan in the winter of 1868; but, with the approval of the home government,[271] Shere Ali was presented with a sum of twelve lakhs of rupees and 6000 muskets. Lawrence, on the eve of his departure from India, assured Shere Ali that 'as long as you continue, by your actions, to evince a real desire for the alliance of the British Government, you have nothing to apprehend in the way of a change of policy, or of our interference in the internal affairs and administration of your kingdom'.[272]

Beyond Afghanistan, Lawrence favoured an understanding with Russia. There could never be any Russian menace to India from the north-eastern areas of Central Asia. If ever India were invaded by a Russian army, it could only be via Herat. So it would be to British advantage to involve Russia in Yarkand and Bokhara. This would absorb her energies, deplete her resources, lessen the danger of her inciting the border tribes and promote anti-Russian sentiment among the Muhammadans of India. But Lawrence did not really fear a Russian advance or feel convinced that it would prove injurious to British interests; at any rate, the further they advanced the greater would be their difficulties, while British interference would not retard them but only waste British effort and money.[273] Wood took a more pessimistic view, for he feared that Russian presence in the neighbourhood might have a disquieting effect on the Afghans and the tribesmen by leading them to believe that there was a powerful force to protect them if necessary against the British. He therefore preferred to give no encouragement to Russia in Central Asia or to take any interest in that region; British interests would be sufficiently safeguarded if they remained on good terms with the Afghans. Sir Henry Rawlinson's[274] scheme to occupy Herat and Kandahar as a counter-move to a Russian advance in Central Asia seemed to him the most unwise step possible, for it would extend the British further from their base and excite the opposition of those on whose resistance to any Russian invasion the British had to rely in the first instance. It was better to stay out of Afghanistan and keep on good terms with the people, for then their alliance could be bought whenever required.[275] Wood's successor, Ripon, agreed that Britain should stay out of Afghanistan and Central Asia; the truest wisdom consisted in a strict abstinence from all meddling.[276]

The replacement of the Liberals by the Conservatives in the

summer of 1866 and the advent of Cranborne as Secretary of State led Lawrence to reaffirm his views, for he seems to have feared a change of policy.[277] He said that it would be 'absolutely suicidal' to send troops into Afghanistan to forestall any Russian advance.

Dear Lord Cranborne, believe me, our dangers and perils lie *in India* and not from beyond the Border. All our money, all our resources are wanted in India. We are educating the people in wholesale fashion, and the difficulty will be how to employ the leading spirits, the men who will have knowledge, spirit and aspiration, and who will chafe for want of an outlet for their energies.[278]

But there was no need for concern; Cranborne approved of Lawrence's policy. 'I cannot bring myself to look on the alarms of Russian advance even seriously. When there is so much room for her to the eastward of Bokhara, it would be sheer wantonness on her part to provoke a powerful antagonist by turning to the south.'[279] As Britain was strong enough to give Russia a warm reception if she did advance, it would be impolitic and premature to take immediate action.[280] 'I would as soon sit down upon a beehive than occupy Quetta.'[281] Northcote, who succeeded Cranborne in 1867, was even warmer in his support of the Viceroy's policy.[282]

With such approval from both parties, the Government of India formally suggested, in September 1867, an understanding and preferably an engagement with Russia defining a border up to which the two sides could extend their influence. As there was considerable agitation for a more forward policy, Lawrence recorded a long minute on the subject. The further Russia extended her power the weaker would be her influence; nor would her presence in the neighbourhood lead to insurrection within India. The wise course for the Government of India would be not to send their troops beyond the border or their officers into Central Asia but to give the people of India the best possible administration by conciliating all classes and consolidating resources.[283] Any Russian advance on India in that generation was 'a perfect delusion'.[284] The home government agreed with this, and did not think it necessary to do anything more with regard to the Russian advance than to await an opportunity for reaching an understanding with Russia.[285]

As, in the summer of 1868, Sir Henry Rawlinson restated the

arguments for military and diplomatic initiative across the border[286] and was supported by some officers in India, the Government of India reiterated their views.

Should a foreign power, such as Russia, ever seriously think of invading India from without, or, what is more probable, of stirring up the elements of disaffection or anarchy within it, our true policy, our strongest security, would then, we conceive, be found to lie in previous abstinence from entanglements at either Cabul, Candahar, or any similar outpost; in full reliance on a compact, highly-equipped, and disciplined army stationed within our own territories, or on our own border; in the contentment, if not in the attachment, of the masses; in the sense of security of title and possession with which our whole policy is gradually imbuing the minds of the principal Chiefs and the Native aristocracy; in the construction of material works within British India, which enhance the comfort of the people, while they add to our political and military strength; in husbanding our finances and consolidating and multiplying our resources; in quiet preparation for all contingencies, which no Indian statesman should disregard; and in a trust in the rectitude and honesty of our intentions, coupled with the avoidance of all sources of complaint which either invite foreign aggression, or stir up restless spirits to domestic revolt.[287]

VII

The administration of the Crown in India found itself compelled to levy new taxes. Canning, on his own responsibility, raised the customs duties on a larger number of imported goods from $3\frac{1}{2}$ and 5 per cent to 10 per cent. The Derby Government agreed to support him because the measures were necessary, but they resented the failure of the Government of India to anticipate the requirement and to act with less haste and greater consultation.[288] They decided to send out to India an expert in finance who could serve as finance member in the Viceroy's council. Seeking the best talent available—'a man of the Chancellor of the Exchequer class'—Stanley offered the post to Edward Cardwell and to Robert Lowe and, when they both declined, appointed James Wilson.[289] Canning welcomed the appointment half-heartedly,[290] for he doubtless realized the criticism inherent in it. However, he found Wilson easy to work with, and the Government of India for the first time gave serious consideration to the long-term problems of Indian finance. Trevelyan in Madras believed that all that was needed was reduced expenditure and efficient administration; but Wilson considered that mere paring was not enough. India should become self-sufficient in financial matters; and for this it seemed essential to Wilson that over a period of years income and expenditure should be at least equalized. While expenditure should be controlled, revenue should be judiciously increased. This appealed to the new Secretary of State, Wood, who believed that unless more taxes were levied and expenditure, especially military expenditure, was reduced, there would be bankruptcy and consequent loss of India.[291]

In his first budget Wilson imposed a license tax on trades and a low income tax for five years. This opened up new sources of revenue which could, if necessary, be further exploited in years to come. It also, according to Wilson, laid down firm principles of taxation which could be understood and would be accepted by the people of India. 'Vacillation and hesitation will ruin anything in this country. They like to be *ruled* if you only are just and equal in your dealings. At the present moment they are not in the mood to resist anything.'[292] Canning, as usual concerned about the impact of such measures on the landholders, directed Wilson to raise the level of the income tax from Rs 100 to Rs 200, and inserted a clause that in the case of landholders income should be reckoned at half the assessment. 'Come what may we must run no risk of putting the mass of the more intelligent and influential zemindars against our measures. We must keep them on our side, so that if the towns should give us trouble we may be at ease in the country at large.'[293] Wood feared that the collection of income tax might cause discontent in the army,[294] and thought it possible that Wilson had 'been run away with' by his English notions, by the British community in Calcutta and by the support of the British press in India.[295] Elphinstone in Bombay thought the scheme of taxation was too sweeping.[296]

But Wilson's most violent critic was Trevelyan of Madras. Canning had welcomed the appointment of Trevelyan as Governor of Madras although Granville had warned him that Trevelyan's head seemed to have been completely turned.[297] Trevelyan had had experience of India and had studied the problems of the country in great detail. But from the start there was friction between him and the Viceroy.[298] Trevelyan believed—with considerable justification—that he knew India better than the rulers at Calcutta did, and he resented the uniformity and supervision which were sought to be imposed. The efforts of the legislative council to enact laws for all India were particularly galling to him.[299] Matters came to a head with Wilson's budget in February 1860. Trevelyan thought that by levying an income tax the Government of India had created for themselves a crisis more serious than that of 1857. 'There is only one way of dealing with a Mutiny, which is to *put it down*, but now we have to choose between two opposite lines of policy pregnant with the most portentous results.'[300] Wood, an intimate friend of Trevelyan, warned him that his criticism appeared to be unjustified; it ill became the government of Madras, who had been unable to reduce their expenditure, to shirk taxation. Wood added that, whatever the merits of the case, it could never be right for a Governor to set himself so openly against the central government.[301] 'I hope not to see Lord Canning marching to put down the insurrection of Madras, headed by its Governor; but you are running hard upon raising the standard of revolt. Do, for heaven's sake, be prudent. I am very anxious to give you every support in my power; but your last outbreak on this matter is indefensible.'[302] But it was already too late for prudence. Trevelyan's dislike of the Government of India, which he considered to be under the undue influence of Bengal, was accentuated by his personal distrust of Wilson. To save India from what he felt would be the most serious calamities, much worse than the Afghan war, he published his minutes of criticism.[303]

Canning, as acknowledged by Trevelyan himself, expressed his displeasure '*like a gentleman*'[304]; but this was clearly inadequate, and the Cabinet, acting on Canning's demand, unanimously decided to recall Trevelyan.[305] Anything less would have shaken the prestige of the Government of India and confidence in their budget. 'The man has lost his head, and is as dangerous as a mad dog— more so, for his mischief reaches (by means of the unwarrantable publication of his Minutes) all over India.'[306] Wood's comment was that Trevelyan had done more to create difficulty in Indian administration than Nana Sahib or Tantia Topi.[307]

There was no doubt, however—apart from Trevelyan's explosive animosity—that the income tax was generally disliked and Wilson was misled when he declared that it was popular. Canning himself said that he hated it but thought it was unavoidable. India as a whole acquiesced in rather than welcomed it and, except in Bombay, it was collected without resort to force.[308] Wood was relieved because not only had law and order remained generally inviolate but the tax also lightened British expenditure in India. 'If any disturbance arises and further expenditure is necessary, India will be hardly worth, in a money sense, preserving at the price. You must not suppose I am giving it up; but this country will grumble sorely at being taxed for the purpose of maintaining the Indian Empire.'[309]

At this stage Wilson suddenly died and Indian financial policy was again in flux. The manufacturing interests of Britain took advantage of his death to protest against the 10 per cent duties on their goods.[310] As Wilson's successor Northcote was considered but finally Samuel Laing, Financial Secretary to the Treasury, who had Gladstone's warm support, was selected.[311] Laing[312] was a cleverer but less weighty man than Wilson. Wood urged him and the Viceroy not to concern themselves with further increase of revenue but to scrutinize and reduce expenditure. 'If I could only see an equilibrium of income and expenditure, I should consider your course and my own well expended, but I should not like you to come away or to go away myself till this is accomplished. You have done so much that I should wish this last laurel added to your wreath.'[313] But Laing could not resist the attractions of tax policy. He thought Wilson's schemes too theoretical and complicated for Indian conditions.[314] 'The income tax is the most horrid hash conceivable. It is not possible, admitting the principle, to apply it worse, and I can only say that India must be a deal more patient than England if it does not worry and tease it to fever heat.'[315] He wished to replace it with a poll tax and it required strong pressure from the Viceroy to restrain him.[316] It seemed to Canning that the appointment of men of the highest class as finance members was risky, as they were eager to make quick reputations; it would be wiser to select mediocre men from the Indian service and to send out accountants from Britain.[317]

Laing, however, had his way to the extent of dispensing with the license tax. The Viceroy agreed that it would be worthwhile to avoid the harassment of millions of Indians if they could be prevented from drawing false conclusions from such tenderness.[318] Wood expressed his disgust with Laing's proceedings and wrote that he was almost ashamed for having sent Laing to India at all.[319] But Laing believed that the decision to dispense with the license tax was a wise one; nothing but necessity could make it politic to impose a new tax directly affecting about five million taxpayers for the sake of about six hundred thousand pounds. He hoped too to be able to reduce the import duties.[320] Wood objected to the correctness and wisdom of Laing's statement that if European troops had not been posted in India in excessive numbers import duties would have been reduced earlier; but Laing refused to retract. 'It is a matter of history that from the time of the first Chinese and Afghan wars, Indian finance has been more or less sacrificed to English policy, and three of the most powerful Departments in England, the Treasury, the War Office and the Horse Guards, are, from their position, under a constant inducement to continue the practice.'[321] However, because of the pressure from British manufacturing interests, Wood suggested a reduction of the duties on manufactured goods to 5 per cent if possible,[322] although, despite the 10 per cent duty, exports to India were increasing. He favoured diverse taxation, on the ground that the greater the number of items of taxation the more lightly they would be felt and the more evenly they would bear on the people.[323]

Elgin agreed with Laing that the repeal of the license tax had been a popular measure and in many ways a commendable one. He thought that the income tax also should be repealed along with the import duties. The cost of the collection was great, the levy was attended by deceptions and extortion and the amount realized was inconsiderable. Indeed, according to the Viceroy, 'the misrepresentations and villainies which have their pretext and origin in this tax are the main cause of those troubles on our North-Eastern Frontier which are obliging us to resort to measures of severity against wretched savages who are harmless enough, but the ready victims of those whose interest it is to rob and deceive them'.[324] But he wished to consider other means of taxing directly the monied, as distinct from the landed, classes. There was a great need of elastic sources of revenue which could be depended upon in times of crisis, but customs duties were not very productive and were particularly objectionable because of their bearing on the relations between Britain and India, excise duties were as odious in India as elsewhere, there was a limit to the burden which even salt could bear, the revenue from opium was precarious and the effect of recent resolutions regarding the sale of land and the redemption of the tax on that portion of the land revenue which was in the nature of rent was uncertain.[325]

In May 1862 Laing reported happily that he did not see a cloud[326] and, to Wood's great relief,[327] departed. Elgin felt that men like Wilson and Laing, 'members of the middle class speculative business hierarchy, a sort of Brahmins in the sect', had had a purpose to fulfil at a time of commercial and financial revolution in England, when there was a new interest in enterprise in India; but the new order was now well established and with the return of financial ease only a pedestrian character was required as Laing's successor.[328] Wood, however, sent Trevelyan back to India as finance member, again pressed Elgin to consider a license tax and a tax on cotton-spinning factories in India to counter the 5 per cent duty on British cotton piece-goods,[329] and directed Trevelyan to promote the increase of cotton production in India. The prospects in Lancashire were anything but cheering, and the Government of India should not leave themselves open to the charge of dawdling and trifling with so vital a matter.[330]

This meant the construction of roads and railways; but Trevelyan wished to restrict public works. Elgin and Frere, who was Governor of Bombay which was the centre of cotton production, urged Trevelyan to change his mind. Once the main railway lines were completed and India remained at peace, economy could be effected to counter the capital outlay on railways by reducing the army by one-third, because increased mobility would make a smaller force as effective as the larger one had been. The construction of such public works would also raise the wages of labour and promote a class of skilled labourers, thus imparting a kind of education which would do more for the elevation of the masses than any other form which the British could provide.[331] 'Nothing', wrote the Viceroy to the Queen, 'that has been done by the British in India has affected the native mind so powerfully, and produced so favourable an impression as these railway undertakings.'[332] Wood too insisted on the development of these means of communication.

Imagine the outbreak in the House of Commons if it should appear you have delayed instead of accelerating construction of these roads. For Heaven's sake do not commit so suicidal an act. I fairly warn you I shall have no alternative but to express my strong disapprobation of any monetary stint in public works and to throw you over. . . . Unless there is something which I do not understand you seem to have gone out of your senses at Calcutta on this public works question. Just when money considerations were beginning to have less weight, and when every other was in favour of accelerating them, you pull in!!! I write strongly for I confess that I never have been so surprised in my life as at this proposed course.[333]

However, both Elgin and Trevelyan were agreed that the income tax should not be renewed after the five years for which it had been imposed.[334] '*Our power of future taxation,* EVERYTHING *I may say, depends upon this reputation for good faith.*'[335] But in order to reach the classes paying the income tax, Trevelyan suggested that a part of it be converted into a local charge. He also suggested that the import duties be reduced from 10 per cent to the standard 5 per cent. But the Viceroy felt that this would not be attended by an increase of trade and consumption, while Wood thought that the import duties and the tax on salt were the only ways of securing revenue from the mass of the population. So, while the income tax was reduced, the project to reduce the import duties was abandoned.[336]

With the development of cotton manufacture in Bombay, Wood began to consider an excise or a license duty on Indian cotton goods as a form of protection to the British industry.[337] Wood, and Frere in Bombay, were both agreed that the role of India was to produce a plentiful supply of raw cotton and that it would be most unwise for any British government to do anything to foster or promote the use of machinery to produce that which Britain could produce and export well and cheaply. But though the Government of India had never acted with such a purpose, the low cost of carriage and the abundant supply of skilled labour made the manufacture of cotton in India a worthwhile endeavour.[338]

In December 1863 Trevelyan prevailed on his colleagues to agree to a reduction of the duties levied at 20 per cent to 10 per cent and those at 10 per cent to $7\frac{1}{2}$ per cent. Wood was not in favour of such a policy of reduction in taxation[339] and gave his reluctant consent; and when the corresponding effort to effect economy in expenditure produced little result, he authorized the Viceroy to devise 'a new and not unpopular' tax.[340] He had not favoured the reduction in the income tax carried out in 1863, but was now strongly for replacing it by a local tax for local purposes. He also recommended the restoration of the license tax.[341]

Lawrence was greatly concerned about the state of the finances and, despite the pledge given to discontinue the income tax after five years, was in favour of retaining it; and both Wood and Trevelyan finally agreed.[342] Indeed, as there seemed little scope for development of fresh sources of revenue, Wood was against a commitment to the repeal at any time of the income tax.[343] But in the executive council Trevelyan, mercurial as ever, joined the opponents of the income tax and it was decided to repeal the tax and levy export duties instead. The majority would not even permit Lawrence to refer the issue to the Secretary of State, on the ground that this would be virtually an abrogation of duty. The Viceroy regarded export duties, levied without a proper inquiry, as harmful and the withdrawal of the income tax as 'an enormous evil deliberately incurring debt', but was incapable of standing his ground. All he was able to do was to prevent a tax on salt which would have transferred the burden from the rich Europeans to the poor Indians.[344] So Wood intervened and refused to approve of the export duties. He thought they could have been justified as an additional measure of taxation but not as a substitute for the income tax. Taxation of rich Indians could not be replaced by duties payable by English planters and merchants.[345] 'Heaven help us from such selfish and short-sighted statesmanship.'[346] But revival of the income tax had now become much more difficult. The quandary drove the Viceroy to a conclusion which did him no credit. 'One thing is clear to me, that it is worse than useless in deciding what should be done in financial matters without first getting your consent.'[347] Lawrence could neither restrict expenditure nor revoke the increase of what seemed to him to be the wrong kind of taxation. 'One way or the other, the influence of the G.G. is now a days weaker than ever it was, and will daily become more so . . . I am as fully impressed as ever with the impolicy of increased taxation, but the matter is practically not in my hands, the views of the day are the other way, and I have not the authority to resist. At every turn one is met by opposition.'[348]

Wood then suggested, in place of the income tax, an estate duty or a duty on gold and silver ornaments.[349] But these appeared to be impractical and both Wood and Massey, the new finance member,[350] favoured greater local rather than central taxation.[351] Lawrence believed that discontent would follow the imposition of any direct tax while any increase in indirect taxation was almost impracticable. So the wisest course for the government would be to abstain from fresh taxation, husband old sources of revenue and practise as much economy as was consistent with efficiency.[352] But Cranborne wished to secure more revenue from the rich, and Massey declared that additional revenue of one million rupees was required. Lawrence therefore suggested an income tax collected from the rich non-officials and a license tax levied on the lower classes.[353] Cranborne agreed to a license tax but preferred local taxation to an income tax. 'As you are a despotism the only result of attempting increased taxation you have to fear is popular discontent, and that can only shake your power if it is concentrated upon you from all parts of India at once. If instead it is split up into a number of small local grievances and directed at different times against subordinate local officers, it can never constitute a serious political danger.'[354] To levy a license tax alone was to lay the whole burden on the poorer classes; and when Cranborne was succeeded by Northcote, the Viceroy appealed to him to sanction an income tax and not a license tax. It would be a surrender to non-official British pressure to exempt them from taxes and to tax only the poorer class of Indians.[355]

Northcote agreed with Lawrence and favoured an income tax, if a succession tax were not feasible, and a remission of export duties.[356] With this support the Viceroy was able to persuade his council to recommend the imposition of an income tax of 2 or 3 per cent and the repeal of the license tax.[357] But his colleagues soon retracted and the budget of 1868 only provided for a revised license tax which could be amplified later, if need be, into an income tax. Lawrence's parting advice to the finance member was to effect this as soon as possible.[358]

VIII

Canning's powers were at their finest during the years of revolt. He showed firmness, courage and humanity. British authority was asserted without compromise and yet without surrender to vindictiveness. But the single-minded statesmanship which Canning had attained in the time of high crisis was never to be his again in the years which followed after. Canning had shaped himself by character and seemingly to his own exhaustion to a leadership that was not by nature his bent. The fair and unenvious mind, the dedication of purpose, the stubborn application to the task—

these qualities were always his. But the indifference to hostility and the precision and punctiliousness of intellect weakened. Canning, during his years as Viceroy, was anxious to win the favour of the British community in India, and he gained their applause by supporting their interests and resisting the home government on their behalf. His wavering policy on indigo, his attitude in the *Nil Darpan* case and his encouragement of the sales of waste lands and redemption of the land tax admit of no other explanation. Indeed, he informed his successor that the desire to establish more amicable relations with the European community had influenced him considerably in the years after 1858.[359] The same desire doubtless induced him to do little that was positive to improve relations between the British and the Indians, which by all accounts were at this time at their worst, although he realized the importance of this question. 'The word "niggers" is now in daily use by every newspaper's correspondents. It will be a bad day for us when that word becomes naturalized in India.'[360]

Canning contended that his efforts to create an Indian aristocracy of wealth and influence would have the ancillary effect of lessening the bitterness of race relations; for when the British saw the government doing all they could to place Indians in the position of gentlemen they would be less disposed to call all Indians 'niggers' and to treat those Indians with whom they came into contact as inferior animals.[361] But this was to expect too much. Far from his policy—which he described as not a conciliatory but a just policy,[362] but which in fact was almost a fawning one—having a beneficial effect on the Europeans, it did not even, in the long run, hold together Indian opinion in support of British rule. Canning initiated a strand of British policy which remained alive for the rest of the century, and often became prominent; but it was a policy which had no potential. The future lay with the classes other than the feudal one, and particularly with the educated middle classes, who were eager to take advantage of the universities set up in Canning's time, in the very year of the outbreak of the revolt. It was perhaps unfair to expect Canning to see so far ahead. But he cannot escape responsibility for encouraging the opposite bias and seeking to buttress British authority with the loyalty of men who belonged to the past and who had sought to harness the rising of 1857 in the cause of that past. There was a measure of truth in Bright's criticism: 'Since the revolt I cannot see that *one single thing* has been done to show that we have learned anything.'[363]

If the policy of Canning was flawed, the performance also was ragged. It should be added in mitigation that, like Dalhousie before him, he toiled with his health deteriorating and, in the last months, under the shock of bereavement. The death of his wife in Calcutta in November 1861 was a blow from which Canning never recovered. He would have done well to have departed from India at the end of the normal term of five years. This was the advice which his friend Granville gave him, in words of dramatic irony: 'How many of your friends are already gone, who can say what havock another year may make among the remaining.'[364] As it was, Canning deluded himself into thinking that he could serve India better than any newcomer and stayed on, with the encouragement of Wood, till February 1862, while his efforts became increasingly untidy as well as lacking in vision. Many matters of importance frequently did not receive his attention at all, and on other matters the home government were not kept fully informed and decisions were often taken and announced without the prior approval of the Secretary of State and the Cabinet. It is true that Wood was pert and waspish and inclined to interfere in the details of administration. The Viceroy complained to Frere that Wood 'is one of the most insensitive public men I ever came across as well as one of the most provocative'.[365] To Wood himself Canning once wrote in despair: 'You are hard to please, my dear Sir Charles.'[366] But Wood had as much reason to complain of the Viceroy's frequent assumptions of final authority and his rough-hewn actions.

So the second phase of Canning's work in India was in every sense a period of anti-climax. But it would be unfair to judge him by this. His monument was built in the crisis of 1857, and his epitaph is in the paragraphs of the Proclamation assuring justice and equality before the law to all British subjects, whatever their colour. 'I will not', he wrote in a famous sentence, 'govern in anger.'[367] The magnitude of his achievement can only be comprehended if one bears in mind the atmosphere in India[368] and the state of opinion in Britain. Gladstone, meeting Canning on his return to England, wrote that he had been greatly delighted with Canning; he was in every way expanded and matured in mind, and after all he had done his modesty was incomparable.[369] When, soon after, Canning died, Gladstone recorded, 'Few men have had such an opportunity as he had in India—of witnessing and striving for the things dearest to God, for justice, mercy and truth; fewer still have so used it.'[370] And over thirty years later, Gladstone, looking back on the long stretch of British rule in India in his time, spoke of Canning as the greatest Viceroy he had known.[371] It was the achievements in the years of disaster and tension, and not the pettifogging and clumsiness of the viceroyalty, which Gladstone justifiably had in mind.

Canning's successor was Elgin, the man who had, in the crisis of 1857, agreed to divert the troops under his command from China to India. He came with considerable prestige and was 'like the card which the conjurer forces you to take. He is inevitable.'[372] But those who knew him had no high regard for him. Granville described him as very vain and a bore with no promise whatever,[373] and Canning expected him to sail with the wind.[374] The same view was stated more scathingly by a kinsman. 'My namesake is very knowing and very shrewd and possessed of a perfect knowledge of the side upon which his bread is buttered! So much so that if he ever gets into a sinking ship every blessed thing will go overboard including crew, passengers and even perhaps little Elgins to boot!'[375]

Elgin had a very limited conception of his role as Viceroy. He was succeeding, he is reported to have said, a great man and a great war with a humble task to be humbly discharged.[376] 'We must, for a time at least, walk in paths traced out by others, filling up here a little hole, removing there a bit of dirt—confining our- selves in short to a sort of scavenger work—all of it very humble, and some rather nasty.'[377] He felt, too, that in time of peace the Viceroy had few powers. With the provincial governments ad- ministering large territories and the home government pronouncing final judgments, the Governor-General in Council appeared to have little authority or responsibility. 'If I were to tell you what I *now* think of the relative amount of influence which I exercised over the march of affairs in Canada, where I governed on strictly constitutional principles and with a free Parliament, as compared with that which the Governor General wields in India when at peace, you would accuse me of paradox.'[378] Yet Elgin was earnest and sought to do the best he could. Such powers as he regarded himself as possessing were exercised either by himself or by his officers acting under his direct control. After a year in office, he decided, despite his poor health, to visit the extremities of his dominions, and it was in the course of this endeavour that he met his death in December 1863. To the last his sense of duty never failed him and when his doctors informed him that he was about to die, he sent a message not to his family but to the Governor of Madras requesting him to be ready to assume the office of Viceroy.

Elgin's viceroyalty lasted only eighteen months and has therefore to be judged in torso. Diffident by temperament, Elgin was still feeling his way when the end came. The general impression of him in India was expressed by Col. Bruce, a serving officer, who wrote on hearing of the Viceroy's death, 'This is very sad of course but I cannot say on public grounds that I can bring myself to think it a calamity.'[379] All that he had achieved was an abatement of the differences between the home government and the Government of India, caused by the fact that Canning in his last years had announced policies and decisions of significance without consulting the Secretary of State. But Elgin had hardly begun to initiate policies of his own. The claims[380] that he established sound relations between the white and the brown races and initiated the harmonization of relations between the different parts of the administration cannot be sustained. Elgin's whole time in India was spent under the shadow of Canning.

The vacancy created by Elgin's death was filled unimaginatively. John Lawrence had a distinguished reputation as an Indian civil servant, but to send him out as Viceroy was to lift him to a level to which he was unequal. Experience is one of the minor ingredients of leadership and cannot, however massive, make up for the lack of the basic talents. Lawrence had a slow intellect which was suited to the detailed problems of district and provincial administration and could be harnessed to carrying out the orders of others. It was, however, unfair to the man to expect him to formulate policies and assume final responsibility. Wood himself had earlier remarked that Lawrence was 'excellent in practice; but I have not the same confidence in the long-sightedness of his views'.[381]

Moreover, Lawrence's powers, such as they were, were not at this time at their height; he was by 1864 an aged man and returned to India as Viceroy with his vitality much diminished. Indeed, he spoke of himself as a cracked pot which would never be quite sound again.[382] To his subordinates the new Viceroy was an unglamorous figure with the remains of greatness, 'a rough, coarse man; in appearance more like a "navvy" than a gentleman'.[383]

Lawrence commanded no superiority of mind or influence over officials in India. Frere at Bombay set himself, according to the Viceroy,[384] to make his government independent of the Government of India and Lawrence interfered as little as possible with Bombay affairs. In his own council, Lawrence relied, with the encouragement of Wood,[385] on those members who had no previous experience of India, and they liked it. Trevelyan wrote to Wood that 'Lawrence HAS *turned out* a first rate Governor-General'[386] and Maine commended his unprecedented practice of keeping the council fully informed. 'I really believe that all India outside Bengal proper would be as safe in his single hands as in those of any one human being.'[387] In fact, Lawrence proved to be one of the weakest of Viceroys. He confessed that it was very difficult for him to get a thing done in any department if the member in charge of that department resisted action;[388] and even in matters which fell within his general responsibility he often found himself helpless. He wished, for example, to sanction import of food grains into the famine-stricken province of Orissa but was prevented by his council from doing so.[389] His ineffectiveness drove him to condemn the machinery of conciliar government. An element of despotism seemed to him valuable in giving unity, force and consistency to the administration of India; and faced with the obduracy of Sir Henry Durand,[390] he suggested that the Viceroy should be permitted to select his members of council. He complained that, as it was, the Government of India was becoming weaker every year and the Viceroy's authority and influence were, in proportion to his responsibilities, less than those of a Lieutenant-Governor.[391] Indeed, he had to appeal to the Secretary of State to give Durand 'a hint of his duty' and to direct him to accept the guidance of Lawrence;[392] but even after Durand, to Lawrence's great relief, temporarily left the Government of India, the Viceroy complained that the council was in a thwarting mood.[393] Northcote submitted a memorandum to the Cabinet proposing that the Viceroy be authorized to select the members of his council;[394] but the method of selection remained, not surprisingly, unaltered.

The Viceroy fainéant in India appeared to the Secretaries of State in London as a senior foreman awaiting orders. Lawrence had been too long a civil servant to be able to resist the directives of the home government. According to him, a Governor-General should not only obey instructions but even conform to a great extent with the wishes of the Secretary of State; it was a mere waste of time and labour to reiterate his own views.[395] This led Wood, who had earlier been convinced that Lawrence was unsuited to the post,[396] to take advantage of his amenability. 'I infinitely prefer your remaining in India working at half power, as one would say of a steam-engine, than to replace you by anybody else.' It was the good fortune of Lawrence that none of the successors of Wood sought to assert the same authority and initiative. Ripon and Cranborne were not in the India Office for long and had as yet no pronounced views on Indian affairs; and Northcote was temperamentally attuned to Lawrence.[397]

So the five years of Lawrence's viceroyalty saw little impact on the Indian scene. It was a period of tired authority with little perspective or hint of the future. Lawrence was overawed, with the memories of the revolt still fresh, at the prospect of a small minority of foreigners ruling an immense poverty-stricken population; and he believed that the objectives of British rule should be limited to the collection of the minimum revenue necessary for good government and the greatest possible expenditure on the development of resources.[398] That beyond these might lie other long-term objectives of greater significance he could not see. But even his immediate purposes Lawrence was unable to promote to any marked degree. The financial policy of his term was in the main the work of others, with Lawrence a powerless critic. His past achievement in India had, of course, lain in administration; and, as was to be anticipated, he sought as Viceroy to apply the experience of the Punjab to the rest of the country. Indeed, he tended to look on the whole of India as Punjab writ large, and to treat the governors of the various provinces as if they had been deputy commissioners. Repair of the executive machinery, which had been badly damaged by the turmoil of the revolt, and the strengthening of the paternalist influence in the governance of India were Lawrence's prime efforts in administrative matters. In the construction of public works and the improvement of sanitation, substantial advances were made. But even in the narrow sphere of the mechanics of government, Lawrence's achievements were disappointing. The steps taken to deal with the famine in Orissa, which was the major administrative problem that confronted the Viceroy, were tardy and inadequate. He was at his best in matters of land revenue, where he had the advantage of the right approach. Wood unfairly accused him, before he became Viceroy, of being 'very anti-native' and imbued to excess with the missionary spirit.[399] In fact he was eager to better the lot of the ordinary cultivators, whose marginal existence was often jeopardized by revenue settlements and indigo contracts. His most outstanding achievements were the strengthening of tenant rights in Oudh and in the Punjab.[400] 'It seems to me', wrote his brother to John Lawrence over ten years before the latter became Viceroy, 'that you look on almost all questions affecting *jaghirdars* and *mafeedars* in a perfectly different light from all others; in fact, that you consider them as nuisances and as enemies. If anything like this be your feeling, how can you expect to do them justice, as between man and man?'[401] The answer, of course, was that the higher ranks of rural society were well able to look after themselves and it was from them that others required protection. To the extent that Henry Lawrence's comment was justified (and it had a pertinence throughout John Lawrence's Indian career) it was an unintended tribute.

CHAPTER 2

THE CONSERVATIVE ADVENTURE, 1869–80

I

For a dozen years from 1869, the Conservatives were able to impose their ideas on India. Their opportunity came in 1868, when, for the first time, they were required to select a Viceroy. Disraeli's choice was Mayo, a young Irish nobleman. This was one of those many instances when Disraeli relied on his intuition rather than on any careful assessment of merit and achievement; and on this occasion Disraeli's instinct did not play him false. Energetic, buoyant, and self-assured, Mayo was suited for India, which at that time demanded a strong hand. While, as is clear from his correspondence, Mayo was not a highly educated man, he had a sturdy and unhesitating mind which grappled firmly with the problems of administration. As Kimberley discerned,[1] Mayo was 'a somewhat dull, heavy man' by no means endowed with first-rate powers; but he had sound sense and independent character, qualities more important than brilliant talents in an Indian Viceroy. Soon after his appointment had been announced, the Disraeli Ministry fell; and the Liberal Government, in the glad morning of success, seriously considered the cancellation of Mayo's appointment. Gladstone believed that a Viceroy should not be appointed by a government in its last agony,[2] and it was expected that Mayo would be recalled, even though he had sailed, and Argyll sent in his stead.[3] However, there was no such drastic assertion of party spirit. Argyll contented himself with the Secretaryship of State and assured Mayo of his support.[4] With Gladstone's approval he even offered the finance membership to Stafford Northcote, the Conservative expert on Indian problems.[5] Mayo, on his part, helped to insulate India from party politics in Britain both by appealing to his Conservative friends to support the government and by allowing his policies to develop from the Indian situation. He came with no preconceived ideas but took his decisions on the basis of the facts; and he was the master of his policies.[6] In no other sphere did the first Gladstone Ministry have so little impact as on India. The viceroyalty was very much Mayo's own. When, just over three years after his arrival, Mayo was murdered, the tragedy was more than a personal one. It removed a man who had placed his impress on events and developments.

Mayo's successor was, of course, chosen from the Liberal party. But Northbrook had more in common with Palmerston than with Cobden or Gladstone. An imperialist with little respect for local or popular sentiments, Northbrook came out to India, not to apply the Liberal principles of increasing trade and training Indians for self-government but to maintain the empire. Little, if any, heed was paid to Gladstone's hopes for India: 'My own desires are chiefly these, that nothing may bring about a sudden, violent, or discreditable severance, that we may labour steadily to promote the political training of our Native fellow-subjects, and that when we go, if we are ever to go, we may leave a good name and a clean bill of account behind us.'[7] The principle of Walpole, *Quieta non movere*, inspired Northbrook in India. The replacement of a Conservative by this Liberal Viceroy only meant inactivity in administration and not a change of policy or of direction. Northbrook should, therefore, on grounds of approach and attitude, have been acceptable to the Conservatives when they returned to power in 1874. In fact both Northbrook and the new Secretary of State, Salisbury, sought to work in harmony. Indian affairs, wrote Northbrook,[8] were quite apart from English politics; and Salisbury observed that a 'break of gauge' in Indian governments was much to be deprecated.[9] But differences both of temperament and of policy soon developed.

Salisbury, with previous experience of the India Office, had well-formed views on Indian affairs and, contrary to general belief, he was not indolent. Like Mayo, he believed that the duty of Britain in India was to promote prosperity. British rule would never be popular. 'One thing at least is clear—that no one believes in our good intentions. We are often told to secure ourselves by their affections, not by force. Our great-grand children may be privileged to do it, but not we.'[10] But lack of *rapport* with the people should not discourage the government from working for their welfare. 'Speaking generally, I am desirous to push forward the argument from the interests of the people more than has hither-to been done. As I have said, I consider it to be our true rule and measure of action, and our observance of it is the one justification for our presence in India.'[11]

Holding such views, Salisbury was naturally irritated by what seemed to him to be Northbrook's lifeless outlook and tendency to leave the initiative to local authorities. But the Viceroy's personality was not as grey and self-effacing as his policy; and the hustling methods of the Secretary of State often rasped on his rigid mind. He and his supporters gradually came to the conclusion that Salisbury's intention was to conduct the government of India largely by private correspondence with the Viceroy and to reduce the latter to the level of an ambassador at a foreign court.[12] So points of friction arose, and by the time the Viceroy left India in 1876, a year before his time, he and the Secretary of State were far apart. Indeed, Salisbury had cause to complain that the Viceroy had acted on his own in a matter of importance in defiance of the declared views of the British government.

As Northbrook's successor, Disraeli approved of the selection of the son of his old friend Bulwer Lytton. The appointment was welcomed by the Conservatives, for Lytton, as Derby described him, was 'able, popular, Conservative and literary'.[13] In 1875 Salisbury had offered him the Governorship of Madras on the grounds that Lytton was young, clever, had great hereditary claims on the party and had served efficiently in all posts to which he had hitherto been appointed.[14] Lytton had then declined, and in December 1875 Salisbury suggested his name for the higher post of the viceroyalty. 'Lytton—with an occasional bilious fit—will be better than any other candidate you have at your disposal.'[15]

It is not, therefore, fair to Disraeli to suggest, as is generally done, that he had once more, as in the case of Mayo, relied on intuition in sending out Lytton. The choice was in fact that of Salisbury. A poet and a romantic, Lytton sought as Viceroy to implement in earnest the new Conservatism of Disraeli. His was not the policy of preservation and construction which had inspired Mayo, or the passivity of Northbrook, but a grandiose effort of expansion and glitter. The result was disaster.

II

When Mayo arrived in 1869, the civil war in Afghanistan seemed over and the retiring Viceroy advised him to meet the Amir, Shere Ali.[16] Mayo agreed that such an interview, if prudently conducted, would be productive of great good. As it had been widely reported that Shere Ali was completely under the control of Russia and

66

Persia, the effect of any meeting would also be considerable throughout Central Asia. Shere Ali, on his part, made no secret of his desire to meet the Viceroy.[17] Mayo, therefore, acted quickly. He favoured a meeting at Ambala in the Punjab towards the end of March. The government would then be in transit from Delhi to Simla, and would not give the impression of deviating much from normal arrangements to enable the Viceroy to meet the Amir. If the venue were Ambala rather than Peshawar, it would imply that the interview had been sought more by the Amir than by Mayo. But the Viceroy was willing to go elsewhere too, if necessary, for this purpose. 'I myself attach the greatest possible importance to the interview and I should be sorry to think that anything should now happen to prevent it from taking place.' Shere Ali should be assured that nothing would be left undone to receive him with the highest honour and make his journey as agreeable as possible.[18] The only expression of opinion from the home government—no decision was sought or received from them—was a mild warning to maintain Lawrence's policy of reserve and abstention from interference in Central Asian politics.[19]

The Amir expressed his preference for Peshawar but agreed to Ambala and arrived there on 27 March. Mayo was clear in his mind as to what he should settle with his guest. The creation of a strong and independent government in Afghanistan, complete abstinence from direct interference in the internal affairs of that country, the development and protection of trade with Central Asia, a well-policed frontier and access to accurate information about events in Central Asia—these were the main objectives of Mayo's policy. The safe course lay between the two extremes of interference and inaction, in a policy of watchfulness and friendly intercourse. The advance of Russia could be checked mainly by pushing British commerce northwards. There should be a definite arrangement whereby the British would, without interfering in the internal affairs of Afghanistan or posting troops and residents there, assist the Amir in forming a strong and permanent government in return for increased facilities for trade and active measures for maintaining order in all those portions of the Indian frontier over which the Amir had any influence. Mayo was opposed to treaties and subsidies of a permanent character but was willing to pay Shere Ali well for any services performed.[20]

In all matters of ceremonial Mayo treated Shere Ali as an equal.

'I now begin', Shere Ali said at Lahore, 'to feel myself a king.'[21] But this courtesy was blended with firmness on matters of substance. Shere Ali sought a promise that the British would never recognize anyone but himself as Amir, a fixed subsidy and a treaty of mutual assistance. Mayo, on his own responsibility, resisted all these demands and would give no more than an assurance of 'cordial countenance and some additional support as it may be advisable'. Even Mayo's advisers urged him to sanction immediately a large addition to the Amir's subsidy, but the Viceroy refused. All that Shere Ali secured were a siege battery, 6000 muskets and a letter of friendship and general support, in which a sentence discouraging the Amir's enemies was inserted at his request.[22]

Although, as already intimated to you, the British Government does not desire to interfere in the internal affairs of Afghanistan, yet, considering that the bonds of friendship between that Government and Your Highness have lately been more closely drawn than heretofore, it will view with severe displeasure any attempts on the part of your rivals to disturb your position as ruler of Cabul and re-kindle civil war, and it will further endeavour from time to time, by such means as circumstances may require, to strengthen the Government of Your Highness, to enable you to exercise with equity and with justice your rightful rule, and to transmit to your descendants all the dignities and honours of which you are the lawful possessor.[23]

Neither side mentioned Russia or Central Asia. The Amir appeared to be unaware of the Russian shadow, while Mayo did not raise the subject as he wished to show that the British had no fear of Russia.[24]

The Viceroy was satisfied with the results. He believed that if the policy of moral support and *ad hoc* assistance, which had been clearly explained to the Amir, were rigidly adhered to, Britain might hope both to obtain a faithful ally for the first time since 1841 and to extend to Afghanistan a civilizing influence, thus providing her with the possibility of a strong and merciful government.

So far [Mayo wrote to his patron][25] your Governor General has had good luck. I hope it may last. I believe that if I am allowed to carry out my policy I shall be able to form round our frontier from the Mekran coast to the confines of Northern Turkestan and China a cordon of friendly and independent states whose interest it will be to keep well

68

with the great English Raj. This policy is a great one. It has been lost sight of for years. I hope too to complete it as I have begun it before I see you again.

Shere Ali also seemed to be satisfied with the Ambala Conference and declared that the letter was worth a crore of rupees to him.[26] Only the home government were concerned that the Amir might expect an annual payment—the withdrawal of which would become a grievance—and armed British intervention on his side in any civil war. The statement in the letter that the British would 'view with severe displeasure' all rebellions against the Amir seemed to imply that such displeasure would take the form of fighting for the Amir against his enemies; and the use of the term 'rightful rule' might be construed as an acknowledgement of Shere Ali's *de jure* sovereignty. Argyll suggested, therefore, that the oral provisos given by the Viceroy to Shere Ali, making clear that no intervention was intended, should be put in writing as soon as possible. How little the Secretary of State knew the Viceroy was shown by a further caution to Mayo to beware of his very able advisers who favoured a more active policy and were likely to lead him into compromises which might later be causes of embarrassment.[27] For no Viceroy was more the maker of his own policy. Mayo brushed aside Argyll's fears and deprecated the idea of correspondence with the Amir as that would lead to further demands.[28] As Sir Henry Durand, the military member of council, observed, to state to the Amir under what conditions aid would not be granted implied a promise of aid when such conditions did not arise.[29] The argument satisfied Gladstone.[30]

The effects of the conference at Ambala appeared to the Viceroy to exceed his hopes. The Amir believed that British policy had been altered in his favour and responded with friendship. In 1871 the rebellion of the Amir's son, Yakub, and his seizure of Herat imperilled the whole achievement; and Sir Henry Rawlinson suggested that the Government of India should send troops to support Shere Ali. But Mayo was more prudent. Any such action would have resulted either in a military defeat or in maintaining a hated ruler in Afghanistan and alienating Yakub, who would be prominent in Afghan politics in the future. Mayo, therefore, with the home government's approval, preferred to watch and wait and, when he heard that Yakub had written to his father seeking to be forgiven, promptly wrote to the Amir advising him to seek a settlement.[31] Shere Ali was at first reluctant to do so and, having reoccupied Herat, planned vengeance; but Mayo's letter cooled his spirit and father and son were reconciled. The Viceroy rightly concluded from this that, despite the civil war, the influence obtained by him at Ambala was still very strong.[32] This advice given and accepted at a crucial stage certainly ensured Mayo personally of a commanding position in Afghan affairs.

Ambala and subsequent developments had an impact even beyond Afghanistan. Throughout Asia British influence was considerably strengthened as every enemy of Britain felt weaker. The belief was spreading that the Government of India was the paramount power in Asia. Mayo thought too that it was beginning to be understood that British policy was one of peace and non-intervention; and once it was realized that Britain was the only non-aggressive power in Asia, she would stand on a pinnacle of strength she had never reached before.[33] For this reason, Mayo spurned suggestions for an advance to Quetta. Britain's strongest argument with Russia would be her own example.[34] 'I am sick of the nonsense talked about Russia.' If Russian troops tried to advance beyond the Oxus and were so demented as to attack India, they would be driven back in one summer campaign.[35] A few British agents and a few hundred thousand pounds could incite in a short time a *jehad* (holy war) against Russia throughout Central Asia. An envoy of Yakub Beg, the ruler of Yarkand, told the Viceroy that if he gave the signal such a war would be proclaimed from the Caspian Sea to the frontiers of China; and Mayo believed this to be true. 'I could make', he wrote on 14 December 1870 to the British Ambassador in Russia, 'of Central Asia a hot plate for our friend the Bear to dance on.' But instead of secret intrigues against Russia, a cordial and honourable understanding on the basis of specified spheres of influence rather than a neutral buffer zone[36] should be sought. Mayo had warned the Amir against interference in the territories north of the Oxus; and Russia should be similarly warned against subverting British influence in the states bordering the frontiers of India. Were this done, the Central Asian question might cease to exist; for more faith could be placed in Russia's political wisdom, foresight and knowledge of her own interests than in her assurances.[37]

The clarity and common sense of Mayo's frontier policy ensured quick and complete success. He wrote to Derby that some day people might admit that without firing a shot or moving a soldier he had made British influence paramount in regions which had been for years the 'hard nut' of Anglo-Indian politics.[38] He had gained peace and security by departing from 'masterly inactivity' but avoiding direct intervention.

The policy which we believe the Government ought to exercise with regard to frontier nations is, to endeavour to show to the rulers of these States, and to the world, that in respect to them our policy of annexation has passed away; that it is the desire of the British Government to assist them in becoming strong and independent; that their safety against foreign aggression lies mainly in an alliance with Great Britain; and that by just and good administration it is within their power to command the willing allegiance of their own subjects and the respect of neighbouring States.[39]

As the Viceroy explained to his military member, 'In countries where events march so fast, it is pedantry to lay down fixed rules of policy. We desire peace and non-interference; but at the same time we wish to maintain over our neighbours that moral influence which is inseparable from the true interests of the strongest Power in Asia.' A policy of isolation had been tried and had failed. Mayo firmly believed that in Asia a bold front was the first element of success and that such a front could be well maintained without aggression, oppression or injustice. 'I am confident we are in the right groove. . . . Risk is never absent from existence in the East.'[40]

Events showed that whatever risk had been taken by Mayo had been more than justified. By the time his term in India came suddenly to an end, he had achieved peace with dominance. Afghanistan was quiet and the Amir was a friend. Encouraged by reports that Russian policy was not expansionist,[41] the Viceroy, acting almost as the head of an independent government, sent his own emissary, Sir Douglas Forsyth,[42] to St Petersburg in 1869; and Forsyth's detailed exposition of Mayo's policy elicited from the Tsar himself a statement that his government had no intention of extending his empire. A party of troops from Bokhara, which had crossed the Oxus, was promptly withdrawn. So the Viceroy was satisfied with the position of Central Asian affairs and declared that the Russians had given him no cause for complaint.[43] The Russian government also declared that they would not intervene in Afghan affairs and requested the Government of India to define the frontiers of Afghanistan.[44]

Relations with other states on the borders of Afghanistan also improved. The ruler of Yarkand sent an envoy to Calcutta for support and advice, and it was decided to send a British mission to Yarkand in return. Trade with Central Asia developed and a treaty was signed with the Maharaja of Kashmir providing transit facilities through his State for this purpose. A boundary dispute between Afghanistan and Persia seemed likely to cause embarrassment as support for either party would cause the other to turn to Russia; but this was avoided by Persia's offer to submit the case to arbitration.

No man, wrote Northbrook many years later, had had sounder views on frontier policy than Mayo;[45] and throughout his own viceroyalty he strove to continue that policy. He was convinced that the less the Government of India had to do with Afghanistan and Central Asia, the better. Indeed, Northbrook was inclined to believe that even Mayo had striven too hard to please the Amir, who was drifting into trouble and was always in need of money.[46] Argyll, by no means a protagonist of a 'forward policy', hinted that the Viceroy might be running the risk of being too indifferent to Afghan affairs. The stationing of a British agent at Herat, for example, would be useful if it could be done without exciting suspicion.[47]

Northbrook agreed with Mayo that Russia and Russian expansion in Central Asia need not be feared either militarily or politically. The more Russia extended her possessions, the more open she became, as she herself knew, to injury from Britain; and the nearer Russia came to India, the less her intervention was likely to be looked forward to 'as a blessing by the Indian Mussalmans who are our most dangerous class'.[48] Yet an agreement with Russia would be worthwhile because the smothering of rumours of Anglo-Russian differences would be of some advantage and give a sense of confidence and security to Shere Ali.[49] Encouraged by Russia's request for the British definition of the boundaries of Afghanistan, Northbrook suggested that Russia might be warned that she should not interfere in Persia or Afghanistan without clear provocation.[50] But the Cabinet was against reopening negotiations with Russia.[51]

The refusal of the Gladstone Government to seek an understanding with Russia led Northbrook to fear a drift into war. For Russia would not be aware that it might become at some stage inconsistent with British honour and Indian interests to allow the further progress of Russia in the direction of Afghanistan.[52] The Disraeli Ministry which came into office in 1874 also, however, saw little hope in any fresh diplomatic overtures to Russia.[53] Northbrook replied that he did not worry about the result of a war with Russia; but no one who considered what it would involve could contemplate it without repugnance, for the British would be forced to use as allies the whole fanatical Moslem population of Central Asia, retard the 'civilizing mission' of Russia in these countries and excite a religious enthusiasm which would probably react against British rule in India itself.[54]

If Northbrook in vain urged the Disraeli Government to diplomatic activity in St Petersburg, the roles were reversed with regard to Afghanistan. Salisbury, like Argyll before him, wished the Viceroy to strengthen British influence in that country.

Have you entirely satisfied yourself of the truth of the orthodox doctrine that our interest is to have a strong and independent Afghanistan ? My impression is that, if ever you get it, it will turn against you. I have many misgivings as to the wisdom of making the friendliness of the Amir the pivot of our policy. If with our help he subdues rebels, and accumulates warlike stores, and fills his treasury, and drills his people, perhaps some day he may fancy, without our help, adding to all these blessings the loot of Hindustan. And there will be no lack of advisers at his side, with plenty of reasons in their purses for enforcing and recommending such a policy.[55]

Salisbury was in favour of maintaining secret agents—even if necessary Englishmen in disguise—at Kabul and Herat.[56] As Northbrook was willing to do no more than appoint a British Consul at Meshed in Persia,[57] Salisbury, who felt increasingly that the British had thought too highly of, and relied too heavily on, the Amir, advised the Viceroy to study the details of any military movement which the British might be called upon to undertake to Quetta or Herat.[58]

The divergence between the views of the home and the Indian governments on Russia and Afghanistan began rapidly to widen. While Northbrook desired an understanding with Russia and was confident that the Amir had no dealings with her adverse to British interests,[59] Salisbury trusted neither. 'The great question we have to settle is—what shall we do when Russia goes to Merv ? for thither she will inevitably go. If we sit still, you will have great trouble in India, and the Amir will tender his faithful allegiance to the Czar in a panic.'[60] Tighter control of the Amir seemed to Salisbury essential. Lawrence had had no judgment or breadth of view and had been influenced too greatly, in developing his policy of non-intervention, by his recollections of the Afghan war. 'He is like a man who has seen a ghost in early life; he cannot get 1842 out of his mind.'[61] It had been an error to allow the Amir to refuse to receive a British agent, and the first opportunity should be taken to correct this. As Salisbury saw the scene, the British were in the humiliating position of giving the Amir arms and money and being called upon to guarantee his position against Russia and receiving nothing from him in return.[62] This description of Anglo-Afghan relations was, to an extent, borne out by expert observers nearer the scene of events. The Lieutenant-Governor of the Punjab reported that there had recently been a change in Shere Ali's attitude towards the Government of India. The Amir was now convinced that he was indispensable to the British.[63]

Towards the end of 1874 Salisbury, with Disraeli's support, again urged the Viceroy to secure the posting of Englishmen as British representatives, if not at Kabul, at Herat or Kandahar and preferably at both.[64] Disraeli and Salisbury were now no longer thinking of only the security of India. It was the beginning of the new Conservative imperialism, motivated by a determination to make Britain a great power in Asia. But Northbrook remained of the view that there was no need to revise the policy of Lawrence and of Mayo. The idea of Russia making a serious attack on India seemed to him militarily next to impossible, and he presumed that the home government did not contemplate an advance into Afghanistan against the Afghans for the purpose of protecting them against Russian aggression. An advance into Afghanistan could only be contemplated with the co-operation of the Afghans and at their invitation. As for obtaining more information from Kabul, Northbrook still thought that this could be best done through Persia; but he was willing to press for a British agent at Herat when circumstances rendered it appropriate. There was no advantage in forcing one upon the Amir against his will.[65]

The correspondence continued but the lack of communication was clear. Northbrook argued in terms of the old policy and objectives without understanding that in Britain there was a new spirit and context. Salisbury agreed that a Russian advance upon

India was a chimera but said that there might well be an attempt to throw the Afghans upon India. The idea of Afghanistan as neutral territory was fundamentally impossible; it would be within either the British orbit or that of Russia. British policy should therefore be to check and divert Russia.

It is evident that this Russian avalanche is moving on by its own weight, not in consequence of any impulse it receives from St Petersburgh. If so, it is likely to go on, whatever diplomacy may do. Surely our policy is to divert it into some channel where it will not meet us. If it keeps north of the Hindu Kush, it may submerge one dynasty of Mussulman robbers after another, without disturbing our repose. It will at last break itself harmlessly over the vast multitudes of China. If any frontier ever gave safety, we may surely contemplate with equanimity what goes on north of the Himalayas.[66]

But for this it was essential to have a representative in Afghanistan. The lack of such an envoy had resulted in the development on India's frontier of a thick covert behind which any amount of hostile intrigue and conspiracy might be masked. Unless the principle of the British right of representation in Afghanistan, as in the territory of every other friendly country, was speedily established, Russian influence might well gain ground and greatly endanger the British position. The goodwill of Shere Ali alone was no security, and a very small advance in money and arms would probably tempt the Afghans to try once more the looting of India. 'Afghanistan is undoubtedly *our* difficulty. We cannot conquer it— we cannot leave it alone. We can only give to it our utmost vigilance.' Salisbury made it clear to Northbrook that he should attempt to establish a mission in Afghanistan during the coming months. With a fair start and sufficient information, the British should be able to keep their moral hold on the Afghans.[67]

The Viceroy, who had earlier agreed in principle to a British agent in Herat, now replied that it was the unanimous opinion of the Government of India that the Amir would view any demand for British representation with intense dislike.[68] But Salisbury, fortified by the counsel of the two members of his council who belonged to the 'forward' party, Frere and Rawlinson,[69] demanded speedy action. He contended that the British government had virtually guaranteed to Russia the Amir's peaceful conduct without being in a position even to know if he committed an act of aggression. It was in Russia's interest to make herself mistress of

Afghanistan not by force of arms but by 'influence', and the British would not know what she was doing till it had been done. Russia would then be able, wrote Salisbury, quoting the Russian phrase, 'to besiege Constantinople from the heights above Peshawar'. It might, therefore, be better, if a British agent could not be posted in Afghanistan, to withdraw altogether 'from that *quasi*-friendship and protection of which the advantages are all on his [the Amir's] side and the dangers are all on ours'. A refusal to agree to a British agent signified either disloyalty or feebleness. But rather than adopt this extreme step of withdrawal from Afghanistan, which was to Salisbury the logical conclusion of Lawrence's policy, Salisbury suggested that Sir Lewis Pelly be sent on a special mission to Kabul to secure the Amir's assent to British representation in his country.[70] The Government of India should not be seduced into solving a difficult question by the attractive alternative of doing nothing. 'We cannot leave the keys of the gate in the hands of a warder of more than doubtful integrity, who insists, as an indispensable condition of his service, that his movements shall not be observed.'[71]

Such pressure aroused the element of stubbornness in Northbrook, and he insisted on deferring action on his earlier commitment to seek the posting of a British agent in Herat. A careful scrutiny of the discussions at Ambala in 1869 did not show that Shere Ali had ever accepted such a proposal, and his objection to any such scheme could be consistent with loyalty to the British government.

Unless, therefore, it is the desire of the Government at home to change the policy with regard to Affghanistan [*sic*] and to show less desire to keep on cordial terms than has hitherto been thought advisable, we cannot recommend a formal announcement to the Amir that we desire the establishment of a British Agent at Herat. The time, just as the Ameer has kept under a civil war, and while there cannot but still remain elements of disturbance, is by no means favourable to such a representation.[72]

Northbrook did not think there was any reason to believe that Shere Ali was in the least inclined to rely on Russia. All that the Viceroy did, therefore, was to make informal arrangements for obtaining more news from Kabul.[73] To Salisbury's insistence that it was 'absolutely necessary' to have some one who could watch and report on developments in western Afghanistan, Northbrook replied that it was his firm opinion that to force the Amir against his will was likely to have an opposite effect to that desired, and subject Britain and India to the risk of another unnecessary and costly war in Afghanistan before many years were over.[74]

The differences had become unbridgeable and could only have been overcome by either the Secretary of State or the Viceroy giving way. On 12 September 1875 Northbrook requested the home government to relieve him of his post. The grounds were said by him to be personal.[75] Without disbelieving Northbrook, one can assume that he also took into account the lack of agreement with the home government on various basic issues of policy, including Afghanistan. The resignation was accepted promptly, though with stylized courtesy, and the pretence that Northbrook was resigning in order to look after his children was maintained.[76]

Disraeli and Salisbury now prepared the ground for the implementation of their policy by Northbrook's successor. A despatch was sent by the Cabinet requesting the Viceroy to make the effort to obtain the Amir's consent to the posting of a European agent in Afghanistan.[77] Salisbury thought this could best be done by granting limited recognition to Abdulla Jan, Shere Ali's favourite son, and sending a mission of congratulation. Otherwise Russia might become mistress of Afghanistan and then either invade India or cause it to be invaded or excite a revolt in India or tie down a considerable English force in upper India. 'The Prime Minister is, I think, chiefly anxious for some measure bringing Afghanistan more within our influence, and securing us against the danger of Russia pre-occupying the ground.'[78] Northbrook protested that any such recognition of Abdulla Jan and a congratulatory mission would result in deeper British commitments and greater demands on the part of Shere Ali; and he warned the home government that the policy of greater intervention which their communications seemed to envisage would be a serious error.[79] The foreign secretary of the Government of India, Sir Charles Aitchison,[80] described the new policy as proceeding 'from the infatuation of ignorance'.[81]

The Disraeli Government, however, were set on their course. Salisbury did not believe that the Amir would be antagonized by the British proposals; but if he were, this in itself, according to Salisbury, would have justified the reconsideration of policy. Nor was there reason to fear that the presence of a British agent in

Kabul would draw the British into a renewed attempt to occupy Afghanistan. The avoidance of this could be left to British self-restraint. 'We cannot shape our policy by an ascetic rule, and shun temptation on the side where we believe our moral nature is weak.' However, Salisbury did not believe that the British had shown any great aptitude for unprofitable conquests.[82] Northbrook, who had written again criticizing the new policy,[83] was asked to defer action on the Cabinet's despatch[84] and Lytton, chosen as Northbrook's successor, was fully briefed. 'It may be', Salisbury wrote to the retiring Viceroy,[85] 'that I have not the gift of explaining in writing what I really wish, and that Lord Lytton, to whom I have naturally talked much on the matter, will on that account be in a better position to seize our exact meaning and design.'

The secret instructions[86] which the new Viceroy carried with him had been drafted by himself and signed by Salisbury after securing Disraeli's approval.[87] In place of what they regarded as Northbrook's short-sighted and timid policy influenced by Gladstone, the Conservative Government were determined to establish British political ascendancy in Afghanistan and, if necessary, divert Russian interests elsewhere.[88] The Prime Minister's farewell words to the Viceroy were reported to have been, 'There is now fortunately a reaction in favour of pluck, and in boldly carrying out this policy you may confidently reckon on the cordial support of Salisbury and myself.'[89] The principles of the new policy having been laid down, their implementation was left largely in the Viceroy's hands.

Lytton approached what he knew was a difficult task with confidence. 'We inherit a huge capital of blunders which has been accumulating at compound interest. I hope that by the end of the year I may have something to show in the shape of a definite frontier policy, but the whole situation is now in such a state of drift and flux, that one has to spin one's way, painfully and invisibly—like a spider—out of one's own inside, with not a point left on which to hang the lightest web.'[90] His first move was a communication to the Amir, not inviting him to receive a British mission but informing him that a mission would be sent and inquiring where he would like to receive it.[91] The Viceroy told the home government that if the Amir declined to receive the mission, another effort would be made; but if that effort too failed, then a policy of coercion would be tried. 'I believe it will not be difficult to put the screw on Shere Ali.'[92]

78

The Amir declined to receive the mission.[93] No one was surprised and Lytton declared that he was not disappointed. 'It brings us at least a long step forward on the road to firm ground, and out of the quicksand in which we have been floundering for so long.'[94] He was confident that success was only a matter of time as the British position was a strong one and that of the Amir weak.[95] Disraeli agreed with the Viceroy and hoped that his own posture of firmness in Europe would advance and assist Lytton's course in Asia.[96] A mild reply was sent to the Amir,[97] but Lytton thought it was enough to frighten and convince Shere Ali that the Government of India were in earnest. He, therefore, anticipated little difficulty in securing a permanent hold over Afghanistan by a treaty which the Amir could not violate without risking his throne and which Russia would be obliged to respect. 'But if he resists all our bribes and threats, we can with the greatest ease clip his claws by strengthening our position in Khelat, and allowing Cashmere to absorb Yassin and Chitral. This can be done in a few months without moving a soldier.'[98] Relations could no longer be left ambiguous. 'One hand washes another, and it is now time for the Amir to shew us some of his soap.' The Amir had to choose on which of his two powerful neighbours he would rely; and if he did not promptly prove himself a loyal friend of the British, he would be treated as an enemy. 'A tool in the hands of Russia I will never allow him to become. Such a tool it would be my duty to break before it could be used.'[99] To Lytton there was 'no longer such a thing as a Khelat question, or an Afghan question; these are only departments of the great Russian question, and should be treated accordingly'.[100]

Shere Ali, however, delayed his answer, and for the first time the Viceroy's confidence was shaken. He feared that the Amir's commitments to Russia might have gone much further than he had supposed. The Liberals had wasted four years. 'Gladstone has played the game of Russia in England to perfection and the Czar ought to give him a pension.'[101] Lytton believed, too, that Rawlinson's book on Central Asia—which earlier he had hailed as by far the most statesmanlike review of the whole question yet written, the most suggestive and the most far-reaching[102]—had had the worst possible influence on the Amir's confidence in British good faith.[103] All that the Amir, who was believed to be in constant touch with Russian agents in Kabul,[104] suggested when he finally replied was that Lytton should confer with the Amir's agent in India and ascertain from him the Amir's views and difficulties; and the Viceroy was constrained to agree to this.[105] But he blamed Russia for Afghan intransigence and spoke airily of going to war with her.

The prospect of a war with Russia immensely excites, but, so far as India is concerned, does not at all alarm me. If it is to be—better now than later. We are twice as strong as Russia in this part of the world, and have much better bases both for attack and defence. . . .If war *is* declared, I would propose that the Government of India should at once take the offensive in Central Asia, where Russia is really very weak, and where I believe that, without any great expenditure of force, we could easily raise the Khanates against her, and put a sea of fire between us. I think it would be a mistake to await attack from her.[106]

The best policy would be to let Russia reach Merv and then attack her. 'So far as India is concerned, no event could be so fortunate as a war with Russia next spring.'[107]

At first Disraeli and Salisbury had confidently left the execution of policy wholly to the Viceroy. They had even encouraged him to ignore his council.[108] Lytton was, of course, elated. 'I eagerly welcome', he wrote to Salisbury,[109] 'your concurrence in my deeply-settled conviction that the foreign policy of India must be exclusively in my own hands, supported by yours.' He rejoiced that the Viceroy could fairly say in matters of foreign policy, 'L'état, c'est moi.'[110] But the omnipotent Viceroy, within a few months of his assumption of office, gave much concern even to the home government. Salisbury did not share Lytton's enthusiasm for a war with Russia. He did not expect a Russian attack on India; it was only Russian diplomatic activity which seemed to him to demand attention.[111] Lytton, while assuring Salisbury 'that it is not my views but *your* views that I hold myself bound to carry out with the utmost efficiency in my power',[112] protested at the indifference of the Cabinet to the Russian advance in Central Asia. This he described as a policy 'dictated by the heart of a hen to the head of a pin. . . .I have lost confidence in my own capacity to understand what it (your Indian policy) now is, and am haunted by a horrible fear that, for want of a common signal code, we may be acting at cross purposes.'[113]

There was also a lack of understanding between the Viceroy and the India Office on policy towards Turkey. Lytton reported that if Britain were suspected by Indian Moslems of connivance with Russia in the spoliation of Turkey, their loyalty would speedily dissolve; 'we should not only have to reckon on a real *jehad* all round our frontier, but in every Anglo-Indian home there would be a traitor, a foe and possibly an assassin. Such a danger might possibly be more difficult to deal with than the mutiny, which cost us such an effort to suppress.'[114] The Viceroy was supported by Sir Henry Layard, the Ambassador at Constantinople;[115] but Salisbury, who had returned from a conference at Constantinople with contempt for Turkish administration, expressed surprise that British policy in Europe should be determined by people conquered in the East.[116] Sir Louis Mallet,[117] Permanent Under-Secretary at the India Office, was of the same opinion. 'It seems to me a policy turned upside down. How can it be supposed that our hold on India depends on the love of our Mahomedan subjects? or that they will regard us for years to come with anything but inextinguishable aversion. And yet to conciliate these irreconcilable enemies, you are prepared to exasperate a great nation eminently needing your friendship and guidance.'[118]

These differences were soon reflected in events. The negotiations with the Amir's envoy proved fruitless.[119] Lytton had earlier discounted the importance of the Amir. Shere Ali's hostility was 'great, indubitable and probably now unchangeable', but if he ever ventured to attack, he could be crushed like a fly. So the Government of India need do no more than strengthen their own frontier and weaken and embarrass the Amir by all the indirect means available.[120] But now, in the summer of 1877, he, on his own, ordered immediate military preparations for the temporary occupation of western Afghanistan and canvassed support in Britain against the Secretary of State. If Salisbury, who seemed to be considering an Anglo-Russian alliance against Germany, directed him officially to co-operate with Russia, he would resign at once. If a Russian occupation of Merv could not be prevented, it should at least find British political power firmly established along the western frontier of Afghanistan from Kandahar to Herat. Otherwise Peshawar would have to be abandoned. The Viceroy could, without moving a soldier or firing a shot, ensure the deposition of Shere Ali within a fortnight; but he was being directed instead to tolerate humiliation lest he compromise Britain's relations with Russia. If such a policy were ever adopted, 'I would not

6   81

give a year's purchase for our tenure of India'. Already the excitement of not only the Muhammadans but also the Hindus was rapidly rising. This was for all practical purposes a purely Indian question, which could only be settled by Indian diplomacy, troops, money, energy and skill. The Government of India were more competent to define and appreciate the true character and magnitude of the danger than a Cabinet far removed from the daily and hourly evidence of its existence and chiefly occupied in the consideration of other matters. But in fact the Government of India could not act without the sanction of the Cabinet. 'The result is that nobody is dealing with the situation; except, indeed, our inevitable rival, and virtual enemy, Russia, who *is* dealing with it unchecked, unopposed and most energetically!' Throughout Central Asia the Russian Governor of Turkestan was regarded as a far more powerful personage than the Viceroy of India, because he could do his utmost with the assured support of a grateful government acting in accordance with a well-considered rational policy, while it was 'well known that the Viceroy of India is dependent, in the most trivial details of his external policy, on the never-assured sanction, and always undefined opinion, of a generally weak and often divided Cabinet', which was in turn dependent for its existence on the uncertain support of a popular assembly and an uninstructed but powerful public. But whether the British Parliament and public liked it or not, both Kandahar and Herat should be brought under British control as soon as possible. 'Failing purchase, we shall have to take them by force.' To let Russia take Herat would be a proclamation of weakness; the Government of India would then have either to invade Afghanistan immediately for permanent occupation and the speedy reconquest of Herat or to fall back behind the Indus, a movement which would involve the loss of the whole empire.[121]

The home government were not convinced. The political ascendancy in Afghanistan which they had sent Lytton out to secure did not mean military campaigning in that country or a war with Russia. The pluck which Disraeli had commended was being construed by the Viceroy as foolhardiness. Salisbury regarded 'a Candahar' the next year as much more mischievous than a policy of inactivity because it ran the risk of plunging Britain into a useless war for which she was by no means prepared. The Viceroy seemed to Salisbury to be out of touch with the opinion prevailing in Britain on the issue of war or peace. The complete breakdown of Russia as a military power had made British opinion disinclined to believe in any danger to India, and, whether right or wrong, the feeling of Parliament and the British government should govern. He appealed to Lytton to exercise great circumspection to prevent the 'muskets going off of themselves', and to resist 'military seducers, if they are besetting your virtue'. It was neither war nor inactivity but a 'middle holding ground' which the home government sought—the strengthening of British influence in Afghanistan through diplomatic action.[122] The suggestion of Lytton, that elements of resistance to Russia among the tribes in the vicinity of Merv should be encouraged, was sharply rejected.[123] 'The period when Russia was an object of apprehension seems centuries ago.'[124] Never more than a phantom, it had faded, according to Salisbury, during the past two months to 'the shadow of a shade'.[125] Lytton resented what he regarded as a betrayal at a time when the Indian frontier was the scene of raids and outrages which he believed Shere Ali had been inspiring;[126] but he promised to abide loyally by the decisions of the British government.[127] He even took credit for preventing officials in the Punjab from dragging the Government of India into a vast frontier campaign.[128]

However, when Cranbrook[129] succeeded Salisbury at the India Office in the spring of 1878, Lytton made a fresh attempt to gain support for his views. He argued that though the occupation of Quetta had rendered the Government of India less dependent than before on the Amir's goodwill, he could not be ignored. Shere Ali might dislike and mistrust Russia, but he felt a bitter personal animosity towards the British. His ruling passion was greed of territory, and the territory he most coveted was British. He overrated his own military strength and underrated that of the British, and unless he could soon justify to his subjects the strain he had put on them by finding foreign employment for the army he would be faced with threats of rebellion and assassination. Steps that would enable the British to punish promptly any Afghan act of aggression and to occupy Herat if the Russians entered Merv should, therefore, be taken at once. All that was required was a forward post in the Kurram valley which, along with Quetta, would serve to hold Afghanistan in a vice. Lytton, who had been for many years a diplomatist and had promised, when he first came out to India, to weave a web of subtle diplomacy, had by now

6-2

lost faith in that art. 'Diplomacy is a weapon with which we cannot fight Russia on equal terms. And she knows it. . . .It seems to me, therefore, that we should be unwise to neglect any opportunity which circumstances may offer us of settling scores with her by means of that weapon, in the use of which we are strongest, and she weakest. This weapon is the sword.'[130] Failure to act in Afghanistan might have harmful effects in India also, where the ex-king of Oudh and his partisans were on the alert and all the disaffected and dangerous social elements were active.[131]

Cranbrook, like Salisbury, was inclined to discount fears of a Russian advance, and informed the Viceroy that no more than watchfulness was needed.[132] He authorized in addition, on 3 August, a reiteration of the demand that the Amir should receive a diplomatic mission in Kabul.[133] Cranbrook intended such a mission to convince the Amir of the advantages of an alliance with Britain and, at most, to apply pressure on him.

Our object is to secure Afghanistan whoever may be its ruler and that by the ties of a common interest. Make it clear that we are far from wishing to annex and that our agencies would be for the advantages of the Afghans as well as ourselves. Some responsibilities must be incurred to achieve such ends but let us undertake none which we will not or cannot completely fulfil. Say nothing which any Government in India will not feel bound to do and so say it as to bind the future.[134]

But the Viceroy's ideas were very different. He proposed to establish British influence in Afghanistan by rousing the Amir's fears rather than by raising his hopes; and if, as Lytton expected, the Amir failed to come to terms, the Viceroy intended that British forces should occupy the Kurram valley and, temporarily, Kandahar. 'I believe that the Ameer could not live a week at Kabul in *known* hostility to us and with our hands so close to his throat.' As, with the settlement at Berlin and peace in Europe, the Amir could not expect active assistance from Russia, his kingdom might disintegrate, with northern Afghanistan being administered by the Russian protégé, Abdur Rahman, and southern and western Afghanistan falling under British influence. Even if the Amir complied with British demands, Lytton had no doubt that the presence of a permanent British agent at Herat would eventually lead to the absorption of the whole area between Kabul and Herat by the British.[135]

On the earlier occasion when the Viceroy had differed with the Secretary of State, it was Lytton who had had to give way; but Cranbrook was no Salisbury. He was extremely idle, with little knowledge or interest in Indian affairs and altogether, as Sir John Strachey wrote after meeting him, 'a poor sort of a creature'.[136] So the Viceroy could now take the bit between his teeth. Unaware that the British government had already protested at St Petersburg against the despatch of a Russian mission to Kabul,[137] he considered Shere Ali's ostentatious reception of it as a public slight to Britain and instructed the British mission which was setting out to Kabul to demand the withdrawal of the Russian mission as a preliminary to negotiations.[138] Cranbrook rather uncomprehendingly nodded assent. 'It is not easy to forecast what will be right in the event of the refusal to receive your mission as that may be based upon many different grounds but "inactivity" will not be a safe retreat. You have so far stepped in that to go over some way or other will be a necessity.'[139] But Salisbury was more alert. He complained that Cranbrook's views on Afghanistan were inclined to be bellicose[140]—in fact they were virtually non-existent—and Salisbury and the Prime Minister instructed Cranbrook to curb the Viceroy.[141] Lytton was directed to await a reply from St Petersburg and informed that the demand for the withdrawal of the Russian mission, being an affront which a great power could not endure and a matter vital to European peace, should not be made without the full sanction of the Cabinet or at least of the Prime Minister and the Foreign Secretary.[142] Lytton pretended to fear assumption of responsibility.

But scalded cats mistrust cold water; and I cannot help remembering that, although, for more than twelve months, Lord Salisbury, in his private letters and telegrams, unreservedly approved, and encouraged, every detail of my policy and action in regard to frontier affairs, yet, when these were publicly challenged, or officially opposed, at the first sound of the enemy's trumpet, he threw me over the parapet without a moment's hesitation; and the language he then publicly held to others was absolutely irreconcilable with that which he had been privately holding to myself.[143]

But in fact preparations had gone so far ahead and there seemed so much confused indecision in London that Lytton, in defiance of orders, ordered, on 20 September, the British mission to advance; and the next day he directed it to enter Afghanistan.[144]

The British mission was refused permission to enter Afghanistan by the Afghan troops on the border, and Chamberlain,[145] the leader of the mission, urged that the safety of British rule in India depended now on British ability and determination to crush Shere Ali and prevent at any cost the final establishment of Russian ascendancy in Afghanistan.[146] Lytton thought that the annexation of a country 'which contains nothing but stones and scoundrels' would be a huge political mistake, but that military operations had become absolutely necessary.[147] This led him to rejoice at developments; 'to secure public and official support of ulterior measures it was absolutely necessary that affront offered to Mission should be conspicuous. This has now been effected without loss of life, and I consider the service rendered and the result secured quite inestimable.'[148] Disraeli, Salisbury and the Cabinet as a whole resented the Viceroy's disobedience of explicit instructions but recognized that military measures had become inevitable.[149] On 1 October Cranbrook approved of all the measures proposed by Lytton—the massing of troops on the frontier, the issue of a proclamation calling on the Afghan people to rise against the Amir and the immediate despatch of a force to assist the Khyberees if they should be attacked.[150] A few days later, the home government reprimanded Lytton and urged moderation even at this stage. But the Viceroy made it clear that he would continue to act on what he believed to be the instructions of Disraeli and Cranbrook rather than on those of the Cabinet. The later telegram

contains nothing which can guide, assist, or support me—very much which seems deliberately calculated to discourage, confuse and embarrass me, in the execution of a task from which it still leaves me unrelieved. For it neither recognises, nor mitigates, my responsibilities. Every word of it breathes mistrust, suspicion, timidity, and a fretful desire to find fault on the most frivolous pretext. Yet no single word of it affords me the faintest clue to a leading idea, a governing principle, or an intelligent object and purpose on the part of Her Majesty's Government, to which I may conform the action, or whereby I may direct the efforts of the Government of India.[151]

The disposition of some members of the British government to rely on the Amir was regarded by the Viceroy as the greatest and most serious danger, for in his opinion the friendship of Afghanistan depended entirely on the early and complete downfall of Shere Ali. 'We really have the game in our hands; our antagonist is by no means a first-rate player; and, if only our partners will kindly help us to play the game according to the obvious rules of it, without trumping our best cards, and then revoking, we cannot fail to win it, and, with it, a stake of the highest value.' Unless prompt action were taken, the Amir would strengthen his position; and the apparent want of courage, power and policy on the part of Britain would seriously undermine both external prestige and internal security. To accept apologies would be to run a risk of losing India.[152]

The Prime Minister's attitude was now lukewarm, while Salisbury, perhaps the most important member of the Cabinet, feared that Cranbrook was disposed to trust the Viceroy too much and that the latter was misleading the home government. Lytton required vigilant supervision to prevent him exaggerating both the action and the splash and thereby landing the government in vast expense and possibly in a vast disaster.[153] But Lytton was not wrong in believing that he had the goodwill of the Secretary of State in his challenge to the Cabinet.[154] Cranbrook, with a disregard of Cabinet decisions even more unpardonable than Lytton's, told the Viceroy that he saw no honourable escape from military measures, apologized for the obstreperousness of his colleagues, agreed that the Cabinet's instructions were objectionable and held out hopes of modifying them. 'I cannot help feeling, much as I deplore it, that the knot can only be cut and that in spite of European and Parliamentary obstacles we shall be compelled to cut it— if so the sooner the better.'[155] It was not the Viceroy's policy but his haste that seemed to Cranbrook to be open to criticism.[156]

Lytton could, therefore, assume powers of decision without much fear of being repudiated. On 19 October he informed the government that British troops would cross the frontier, and the Cabinet, at Cranbrook's instance, approved of war.[157] On 21 November, no reply having been received from the Amir to the British ultimatum, the invasion of Afghanistan began. Lytton assumed an air of sorrowful self-righteousness. 'I assert, without fear of competent contradiction, that at no time has the Government of India ever done as much as it has done during the last two and a half years to conciliate Shere Ali, justify his confidence, and secure his friendship.'[158] Cranbrook gave his unqualified approval and blessing. 'Your great work is begun—God give you a good deliverance.'[159] Even Salisbury was now reported to be a wholehearted supporter of Lytton's policy.[160]

However, though the advancing troops met with no resistance,[161] the Cabinet became uneasy and anxious for a settlement.[162] The Viceroy still favoured a fragmentation of Afghanistan, but as the home government showed a great repugnance to any extension of territory, Lytton sought only to replace Shere Ali by his son Yakub and to reach an agreement with the latter.[163] This could obviously not be achieved rapidly; and meanwhile opposition mounted in Britain to the whole campaign and the secrecy in which decisions were being taken and war had been precipitated. The work of following Lytton, as Argyll observed,[164] was the work of a detective. To criticize the British government on these grounds was unfair, for they themselves had often had no previous knowledge of Lytton's actions; but it was a good weapon with which to belabour the government.[165] In face of this agitation, the Disraeli Government considered whether they should announce their intention not to annex any territory. Finally it was decided to make no such announcement and Cranbrook sanctioned the principle of annexation almost by implication. 'I hope whatever portion of Afghanistan or its annexes comes under our control that we shall not too hastily introduce Indian government but leave much to existing law and custom.'[166] Later, Cranbrook advised Lytton to leave out the word 'annexation' if control of territory could be obtained.[167] Salisbury was inclined to transfer Herat, or at least parts of Seistan, to Persia, but the matter was not discussed by the Cabinet, while Lytton expressed himself strongly against it.[168] His own policy of seeking to install Yakub as Amir had been approved.[169] This was facilitated by the death of Shere Ali soon after, and Yakub came to Gandamak as a suppliant for peace.

By the treaty of Gandamak signed on 26 May 1879, Yakub agreed to conduct his foreign relations in accordance with British advice and wishes. In return Britain would support him against foreign aggression with money, arms or troops, to be employed in whatever manner the British government might judge best. There would be a British Resident at Kabul, and British agents would be posted on the Afghan frontiers whenever considered necessary. To facilitate communications and commerce between the two countries, the British were authorized to construct a telegraph line from Kurram to Kabul. The districts of Kurram, Pishin and Sibi would remain 'under the protection and administrative control' of the British government. They would also retain control of the Khyber and Mishmi Passes and of all relations with the independent tribes in the vicinity. An annual subsidy of six lakhs of rupees would be paid to the Amir.

Lytton was congratulated warmly on his achievement by his masters. 'My dearest Lytton', wrote the Prime Minister, 'you did your work admirably on our "scientific frontier".'[170] Cranbrook remarked that the government were satisfied with the treaty, the public had made no protest, and the Lawrence school was silent.[171] He even proposed for Lytton's consideration the garrisoning of Herat by British troops with the Amir's permission.[172] Salisbury too expressed his satisfaction. 'If only the Queen was served in Africa as she is in Asia!' Salisbury's only suggestion was that the Viceroy might also give some attention to Persia.[173] Lytton himself believed that he had secured all his objectives and, in addition, Yakub's goodwill. 'The Ameer is behaving angelically, and shewing, by every means in his power, that he is really grateful for our treatment of him, and loyally bent on the observance of his obligations towards us.'[174] As for the sharp criticism in Britain, Lytton commented disdainfully that Argyll seemed to have set himself on fire with his own hair and the toothless growl of Lawrence was amusing.[175] He was encouraged in this attitude of contempt by his friends among the Opposition. The Afghan settlement, wrote John Morley, was contrasted in public opinion with the odious mess in South Africa; and Wilfrid Blunt assured the Viceroy that he had 'only to sit still now and win. You will come home to the sound of dulcimers and all kinds of music.'[176]

The elation was short lived. In July Sir Louis Cavagnari[177] arrived at Kabul as the British Resident and received a cordial welcome from Yakub. But it is said that Cavagnari himself believed he was going to his death—a fear that was shared by most observers with knowledge of Afghanistan.[178] Even Cranbrook in London had vague premonitions:

I quite see what is the danger to European residents and he (Cavagnari) ought to be careful of himself for the sake of his country. Fanatics indifferent to life are masters of the situation where there is the least carelessness and one deadly blow may bring results out of all proportion to the intent of the assassin. Everything according to your telegrams is going so smoothly that one becomes sanguine but [one] must not forget Afghan nature, Russian intrigue. . . .[179]

The Viceroy assured him that there was no real cause at all for anxiety,[180] and was taken completely by surprise when, on 3 September, Cavagnari and his small escort were murdered by some riotous Afghan soldiers.

This was a sudden, unpremeditated act for which Yakub was not responsible, and the tragic accident could not by itself be regarded as a violation or abrogation of the treaty. Yet it was felt in both London and Simla that the blow to British prestige required to be avenged. Even the Liberals were of this view. Ripon thought it made annexation a matter of necessity, while Halifax was not sure that annexation might not be the best and cheapest course.[181] Lytton reported that he was anxious but not discouraged. 'We have fresh difficulties to face, but they are *only* difficulties, not impossibilities; and the recess gives us time to deal with them more energetically than might otherwise have been possible.'[182] Once more British armies were ordered to advance. The home government had no clear ideas as to what their policy should be in the changed circumstances. Cranbrook thought that disintegration of the country after a long period of British occupation was almost inevitable;[183] but the Cabinet was unwilling to accept Lytton's proposal, made on hearing of Yakub's abdication the day the British army entered Kabul, for immediate annexation of Kandahar and the neighbouring districts.[184] It preferred to transfer Herat to Persia and hand over Kandahar to a ruler loyal to Britain. Annexation was regarded as of less consequence than practical supremacy; and to make such supremacy easier a railway to Kandahar was sanctioned.[185]

The Viceroy now agreed that this was the correct policy, and reported as extremely satisfactory the unanimous conclusion of all the military authorities and advisers on the scene that the 'scientific frontier' secured by the treaty of Gandamak was the best possible. 'Not one of them wishes to recede from it an inch. Not one of them wishes to advance an inch beyond it.'[186] Negotiations over Herat were begun with Persia and amenable rulers sought for the remaining parts of Afghanistan. The Shah, advised by the Russian government that if he accepted Herat on the terms offered he would be nothing more than a vassal of England,[187] declined. The province of Kandahar was declared an independent state under British protection, with a local chieftain as its ruler.[188] Both Disraeli and Lytton were strongly opposed to Yakub's restoration to Kabul;[189] and Cranbrook suggested that Abdur Rahman, son of the late Amir Afzul, who had just returned to Afghanistan after a long exile in Russia, might be considered.[190] This was a counsel of despair, for it was generally recognized that Abdur Rahman had been sent to Afghanistan by the Russian government to act as a fresh element of disturbance. But the Viceroy accepted Cranbrook's advice and offered to hand over unconditionally Kabul and the rest of Afghan territory, excepting Kandahar, to Abdur Rahman. Assistance would also be given him to establish his position and to meet his immediate wants.[191] Abdur Rahman had not replied by the time the Disraeli Government fell after a resounding defeat in elections in which Afghanistan had been a major issue; and Lytton departed, knowing that he left behind him the debris of a policy.

III

From the start, Mayo was confronted with internal conditions which were far from normal. Scarcity of food developed in the North-West Provinces and other areas; and before it deepened into famine, Mayo sanctioned a programme of public works to relieve unemployment and the provision of advances for the sinking of wells. Determined to save life at any cost, he even examined the possibility of importing corn from abroad.[192] Providentially, the danger of a widespread famine soon passed away. Had it materialized, it might well have been one of the worst calamities that had till then befallen India and might have aggravated the prevailing tension.

Other problems, which were man-made, could not be so easily escaped. The finances of India demanded reorganization. For some years expenditure had exceeded revenue, and the Viceroy was determined to secure an equilibrium by both reducing expenditure and increasing revenue. The decision was a sound administrative measure, even though it was reached by faulty economic reasoning.

We hold India by a thread. At any moment a serious danger might arise. We owe now 180 millions, more than 85% of which is held in England. Add 100 millions to this and an Indian disaster would entail consequences equal to the extinction of half the National Debt. The loss of India or a portion of it would be nothing as compared to the ruin which would occur at home. . . . I do declare that with such a revenue

91

as ours, borrowing in time of peace and so increasing a formidable political danger which already stares us in the face, is little short of a crime.[193]

All the departments were informed that they should not spend more than had been received by the government. 'I don't care', Mayo used to say, 'if I stop every public work and suspend every improvement in India, but I *will* have the public expenditure brought within the public income.'[194]

In fact, however, Mayo's policy did not necessitate a retrenchment of essential public works. Mayo reported to Argyll that there was not a place he went to where public funds were not urgently required for sanitation, education, hospitals, roads, bridges and navigation. 'We are trying to do in half a century in India a work that in other countries has occupied the life of a nation.'[195] The Viceroy did not stint money for these requirements; indeed, he expanded the scope of administrative activity in order to build a modern India. He wished the country to be self-sufficient as far as possible, and prospected for coal and iron. As private enterprise had failed to locate good iron ore in India, he thought the government should lead the way and take advantage of probable railway construction by the State to utilize the vast quantities of iron ore. The services of an oil expert from the United States were sought for prospecting petroleum.[196] What Mayo set his face against was dissipation of public funds. 'I am no screw but I cannot bear waste—and *that* is going on fearfully in every concern of the Empire.'[197] By 1872 Mayo had reduced expenditure from £52 million to £47.3 million.

Complementary to this economy was the development of sources of revenue. If the salt duty were revised, Mayo insisted that it should be done thoroughly; any minor change would only endanger the revenue. Even if the salt duty were raised, the people of India would still be taxed less than any other people in the civilized world. The internal customs could also be abolished, the cost of carriage reduced and the salt duty equalized throughout India. An income tax would prove another major source of revenue, and Mayo's Government decided to rely on it. But as the law member, Sir Henry Maine, was opposed to the introduction of a wholly new mode of assessment for this purpose, it was proposed to adopt the system of license tax-collection.[198] In the budget of 1869 an income tax was introduced. 'You have now got', Mayo wrote to Argyll,[199] 'what Gladstone used to call the great financial weapon hanging on your wall, to be only taken down and used in an emergency.' In times of peace Mayo hoped to keep the income tax at one per cent. It was received in India without protest. Only the zemindars of Bengal were inclined to complain, as they knew that Mayo was strongly opposed to exempting them from taxation; but the Viceroy and the Secretary of State agreed that the zemindars were not to be pitied, as no class in India profited more by the rising prosperity of the country and gave so little in return.[200]

Even with such increased taxation, there was, and could be, no great increase in revenue. India, wrote the Viceroy, was a much poorer country than was generally supposed. Taxing the rich brought in very little, while the poor, though lightly taxed, could afford to pay little more.[201] But the financial situation was becoming desperate.[202] So Mayo, in concert with his finance member, Sir Richard Temple,[203] conceived of another device: to place on local resources a larger proportion of the charges for local requirements. As it was, the local governments spent heedlessly, in the knowledge that the funds would be secured from the Government of India. 'I wish our Indian officials would lay aside a little of their provincialism and give up the idea that the whole duty of man is to get as much as possible out of the Imperial Exchequer.'[204]

Mayo had also a political object in transferring this responsibility for local expenditure to the local authorities. He deplored that, after a rule of one hundred years, there were no signs of any serious British attempt to train Indians in public administration.

I hope gradually to commence the establishment of native municipal institutions. We must gradually associate with ourselves in the Government of this country more of the native element. We have neglected this too much. Were we to quit India tomorrow we should leave whole Provinces in which would not be found a man capable of administrating [sic] the affairs of a small district. It can only be a work of time; and, as in other countries, to the growth of municipal institutions has generally been traced the development of the powers of self-government, so in India do I believe that we shall find the best assistance from natives in our administration, not by competitive examination or the sudden elevation of ill educated and incapable men, but by quietly entrusting as many as we can with local responsibility, and instructing them in the management of their own district affairs.[205]

But this would not, of course, mean any devolution of political authority. For Mayo was convinced that once the central government were weakened, diluted or 'deputed', from that day the decay of British rule would commence and the British might begin to prepare for ultimate departure.[206]

The home government were at first of the view that it was premature to decentralize finance, but later they agreed that local expenditure should be met out of local funds.[207] There was some resistance both from the departments of the Government of India and from the provincial governments; but Mayo refused to be discouraged by this jealousy and what he termed 'huffiness'.

In the struggle between the Bureaux most people seem to forget that there is such a thing as an Empire and a People of India, that national bankruptcy is national ruin, and that we hold the purse strings not in the interest one day of the Madras army, at another of the education of Bengalee Baboos, and on a third to build palaces in Bombay, but that our sole object is to work for the good of all.[208]

The scheme of financial devolution was implemented successfully. But Mayo cautioned the local governments to effect economy in expenditure and to tax the districts no more than was necessary.[209] There should be no sudden increase in the burdens of the people,[210] for India was still in an irritable mood. As a measure of security, Indian soldiers were not supplied with breech-loaders; but a policy of deliberately withholding from the sepoy the best available arms seemed calculated to promote, and almost justify, disaffection.[211] Argyll was of the view that any possible threat arising from the provision of the latest type of arms could be avoided by maintaining the system of provincial armies, each with its own *esprit de corps*.[212] But the Viceroy preferred to rely on the strength of the British Army in India. 'One thing I implore you not to consent to, and that is the removal of a single British bayonet or sabre in India.'[213] This precaution seemed especially necessary when, in the middle of the financial year, by what Mayo termed 'almost a monetary coup d'état',[214] he was obliged, because of a continuing deficit, to raise the income tax from one to 2·5 per cent, and to increase the salt duty in Madras and Bombay. The principal newspapers were not unfriendly and the visit to India of the Queen's son, the Duke of Edinburgh, in the winter of 1869 appeared to strengthen loyalty and the recognition of the power and

94

dignity of British rule. But there were murmurs in the Madras army;[215] and the budget of 1870, which further enhanced the income tax to $3\frac{1}{8}$ per cent, was severely criticized by both Indian and British-owned newspapers. There was no doubt of the unpopularity by this time of the income tax. Mayo was prepared for this. Had the government, he observed, instead of taxing 'the screaming few', doubled the salt duty or in any other way laid the burden on the silent masses, there would have been no criticism.[216] But the articulate opposition did not make his task easier and he was alarmed to hear that the Indian revenues might dwindle further by a sudden stoppage of opium exports to China. 'We have committed many follies for the sake of "an idea" but I hope we shall not perpetuate such an act of idiotcy [*sic*] as this.'[217]

The danger lay in that, unlike in the revolt of 1857, when the leadership had been wholly reactionary, the landed interest might now be joined by the new moneyed classes, who resented the increasing taxation, in giving a lead to any violent opposition. That the possibility of another revolt could not be excluded was becoming clear. Mayo's belief that his foreign policy of peace and friendship would have a healthy effect within India also[218] seemed to be illusory. On 1 July 1870 the Viceroy warned the Commander-in-Chief: 'There is I believe a slight Mussalman rustle in the country but I have heard nothing tangible.'[219] Such Moslem discontent was, according to the Viceroy, periodical and would perhaps always recur from time to time, especially as there was a large and constant stream of sedition from Mecca; but there was cause now for greater watchfulness.[220] Though Sir William Muir[221] reported that there was no unusual or serious activity among the Muhammadans in the North-West Provinces, he was instructed to direct district officers to discourage quietly any meetings to discuss such subjects as the income tax.[222]

It was also possible that the opposition to the income tax was not entirely selfish and that the rate was excessive and the methods of collection probably often oppressive. Not having considered the difficulties in practice of collecting a high levy of income tax, the instances of corruption and of certain assessees seeking to transfer the incidence to others came as a shock to Mayo; and he sought refuge in a generalization: 'The corrupt habit is engrained into every native's mind.'[223] The governments of Bengal and of the North-West Provinces advised the Viceroy to reduce the rate of income tax; but Strachey, while recognizing that a great mistake had been made, urged the Viceroy to stand firm.[224] With such varied counsel and acute pressures, even Mayo began to flinch. The task, he wrote to Argyll,[225] of successfully governing the Indian empire was daily becoming more difficult.

Meantime, in contradiction of Muir's assurances, the uneasiness among the Moslems became clear. It appeared to be the consequence, not of taxation, but of a far-flung Wahabi conspiracy. As far back as 1820, a Moslem preacher, Syed Ahmed, of Rae Bareilly in the North-West Provinces, had wandered over northern India, demanding that Islam be cleansed of all idolatrous and superstitious innovations. As this corresponded closely with the Wahabi teachings in Arabia of the eighteenth century, it came to be known as the Indian Wahabi movement. War was declared by the Wahabis on the Sikhs in 1826, only to end in the rout of the Wahabis and the death of Syed Ahmed; but rumours spread that he would reappear and lead his followers in a jehad against all infidels, including the British. Thereafter the movement, in both its religious and political aspects, never died out. The British authorities were not concerned with the doctrines preached; but they could not ignore the political repercussions and the rebellious actions. Patna became one of the centres of the movement, and in 1852 Dalhousie noted that treasonable correspondence was being carried on between Patna and the north-west frontier. As it was taught by the *Moulvis* that, according to the Koran, a jehad could not be carried on against an infidel government by Moslems who lived as subjects of that government, the Wahabis sought to gather on the other side of the Indian frontier. They did not join the rebel forces in 1857 for fear of retaliation on their families in India; but their gathered strength was regarded by the government as dangerous enough to justify in 1862 a military expedition. This, however, was not the end of the Wahabi menace. There was fighting in Multa Sittana on the north-west frontier in 1863, and supplies of men and money continued to be sent regularly from Patna. Emissaries toured all parts of the country, especially Bengal, urging Moslems to join the jehad or, as the official documents of the time term it, 'crescentade'. Thousands volunteered and were taken to Patna, where they were feted and sent in small bands via Ambala across the frontier. Moslems were also required to provide funds liberally. It was held a sacred duty to put aside a percentage of the daily earnings for this purpose; and those who were too poor to give money provided handfuls of grain. What was required to eradicate the movement was extermination of the nests of conspiracy within India rather than of the hostile bands hovering on the frontier.[226]

In 1864 the leaders of the Wahabi cells in Ambala and Patna were arrested and sentenced to long terms of imprisonment; but this did not retard the movement. It had ramified throughout the north, while letters were sent to rajas in the Deccan, in the name of the Mogul, reminding them of promises said to have been made during the revolt of 1857 and requesting them to send money to Emperor Ferozeshah and to meet him on the Oxus. There was no evidence that political Wahabism had gained ground in Madras or Bombay; but Bengal and Bihar remained fertile recruiting areas. A military expedition had again to be despatched in 1868 to deal with the Wahabi marauders on the frontier. Mayo was convinced that large sums of money were still being despatched from Patna to the frontier, and he directed the Punjab government to ascertain how this money was being transmitted and to break up the Wahabi settlements. Once more many Wahabi agents were arrested, and the Calcutta High Court rejected their habeas corpus petitions.[227]

Mayo believed that this judgment and the conviction of the leaders would deter the conspirators considerably.[228] But within a week he was led by disturbances in Allahabad to change his mind and to conclude that there was 'a somewhat unusual bubble' in the Indian mind. The Princes generally believed that Britain had not taken sides in the Franco-Prussian war because she was not strong enough; and the Wahabi movement and the discontent caused by taxation were feeding on each other. The Governor of Bombay reported widespread discontent even in his presidency. The Viceroy declared that it might be better to reduce the army by half than to run the risk of the chronic disaffection which was produced by the prevalent feeling that the government were determined to increase the tax burden every year.[229]

This was a Mayo shaken in nerve; but he soon recovered his poise. He had decided to reduce the income tax as much as possible, but deemed it absurd to say that the tax was likely to provoke resistance in any district. Though there was much talk of discontent, not a single fact indicative of the prevalence of discontent among any particular class of the population had been reported.[230] The influence of the press was far less than was generally supposed, and its criticism of the income tax seemed to draw inspiration from a few non-official Europeans in Calcutta.

> They are a class who do not care a farthing for the country. They come here to get as much money out of the blacks as they can, and desire to go home as soon as possible. They object to pay a farthing towards the welfare and good government of the country which is to them a source of wealth, and their general tendency is to abuse and resist any government who tries to do its duty. I have no sympathy with this class and they know it.[231]

British military strength in India was also quietly and gradually increasing, being double what it was in 1857, and therefore no rising need be feared.[232]

The policy of the Government of India now was to arrest and prosecute only the offenders among the Wahabis, thus establishing that conspiracy and treason could not be carried on with impunity; and it was believed that this was approved by the bulk of the Moslem community.[233] When it was found that many men had been arrested on insufficient evidence, for 'being' Wahabis and, in one case, for 'looking like a Wahabi', the Punjab government were directed to release all except those who were believed to be dangerous characters or against whom there was evidence to justify criminal charges.[234] As for the Hindus, Mayo considered that they had always been accustomed to be ruled by foreigners. 'There is no real patriotism in India.' But all, Moslems and Hindus, were like suspicious children, whose confidence the British government in India had never yet obtained. So increase of expenditure and of taxation—'squeezing more out of the niggers'—should be avoided as the only real danger.[235] Though expenditure remained high and what Mayo described as a 'gigantic waste of public money'[236] continued, in the budget of 1871 the income tax was reduced by two-thirds, and all the agitation against it disappeared.[237]

Resentment of high taxation, however, as the Viceroy well knew, did not comprehend the whole area of Indian disaffection. It was not the attitude of sections of the Moslem population alone which gave the government cause for concern. The Wahabi movement in Islam had its counterpart in the Kuka sect among the

Sikhs of the Punjab. Started in 1847 by a Sikh in Rawalpindi, it called on all true believers to abandon temples and mosques, disregard distinctions of caste and lead lives of abstinence. Nominally it was open to men of all religions to become Kukas, and at least two Moslems were known to have joined. But most Hindus and Moslems disliked the sect, which was recruited mostly from the Sikhs. This was especially so after 1863, when Guru Ram Singh became the leader of the Kukas. He preached that Guru Govind Singh was the only *guru* (teacher), and his disciples frequently demolished tombs and idols. The Kuka sect developed a well-knit organization, and the whole Sikh community was divided into districts under lieutenants directly subordinate to Guru Ram Singh. More important, the movement gradually drifted from iconoclasm to a zeal for the cleansing of the Sikh faith and then to a yearning for the revival of Sikh political supremacy.[238] Agents were sent to Nepal and Kashmir, and the Maharaja of Kashmir sanctioned the formation of a Kuka regiment in his militia.[239]

On 14 June 1871 a Kuka band raided a slaughter-house in Amritsar, killing four; and the next day a similar attack was made at Raikote. The culprits were caught and executed after confession. It became clear that the offences had been carefully planned. But what alarmed the authorities most was the knowledge that this campaign against cow-killing would secure the sympathy of the vast Hindu population, which had little, if any, interest in religious austerity or Sikh ambitions. However, it was hoped that with the example of the executions, the Kuka movement in its rebellious aspect would die out.[240] The Maharaja of Kashmir disbanded the Kuka regiment; and Mayo warned the Punjab government against prosecuting Ram Singh.[241]

In fact Mayo confidently reported to the Queen in August 1871 that tranquillity generally prevailed in India.[242] The Kuka movement had been scotched and the Wahabi movement seemed to have collapsed. An order of the Madras government, which raised once more the bogey of the 'greased cartridges' by distinguishing between lubricated and non-lubricated ammunition for 'caste reasons', was quietly rescinded.[243] The early advent of the rains in 1871 was reported to have caused horoscopic uneasiness in the Indian mind and there were prophecies of disaster; but these Mayo could naturally laugh away. 'I hope', he commented to Argyll,[244] 'the horrors of Paris may satisfy the Goddess of Evil for this year.'

To Mayo's dismay, however, the calm was again shattered on 20 September 1871, when the officiating Chief Justice of the Calcutta High Court was stabbed to death by a Pathan. Despite the best efforts of the governments of Bengal and India, nothing was discovered to suggest that the crime was the result of a conspiracy and not an act of personal frenzy.[245] But as the Chief Justice had been reputed to be hostile to the Wahabis and it was known that he would try the appeals from Patna, the general conclusion was that the murder had been organized by the Wahabis.[246] This was, therefore, in the eyes of the public, the first political murder in India since 1857, and it revived an atmosphere of panic. Sir William Hunter, regarded as an expert on Indian affairs, announced that the Moslems of India formed a source of chronic danger to the British power as they were 'seditious masses in the heart of our Empire'. He added that they had good grounds for their deep sense of wrong.[247] The Government of India considered proscription of the book but soon abandoned the idea.[248]

There was now in many provinces a general air of tension. Communal disturbances occurred in Bareilly and Pilibhit and there was a riot in Bareilly jail. The Commissioner of Rohilkhand reported considerable religious excitement and the Chief Commissioner of the Central Provinces wrote of an undefinable uneasiness prevalent everywhere.[249] But Mayo, whose optimism was irrepressible, declared that there was not the least ground for apprehension. All that was required was quiet, though active, watchfulness. Even the assassination of the Chief Justice was beginning to be forgotten. Kukaism was at a discount and a great terror had fallen on Ram Singh and his disciples. There was no reason to anticipate the recurrence of either Wahabi or Kuka disturbances.[250]

Once again, Mayo was proved wrong. On 15 January 1872 a band of two hundred Kukas attacked Malodh Fort killing two men; and the next day five hundred Kukas attacked Malerkotla, a state ruled by a Moslem prince, killing seven. The troops of the Sikh Maharajas of Patiala, Nabha and Jind promptly took the field and dispersed the Kukas.[251] But the officials of the Punjab lost their nerve. The men who had informed the Viceroy two months before that the Kuka sect had been broken now telegraphed that there was 'an incorrigible conspiracy';[252] and Ram Singh and his principal lieutenants were arrested and deported from the province. The Deputy Commissioner, who arrived on the scene after the Kukas had been quelled, summarily had forty-nine men blown away from guns; and the Commissioner set aside his earlier qualms and followed up his subordinate's action by executing sixteen more Kukas in the same manner.[253] The Viceroy promptly ordered the Lieutenant-Governor to forbid such summary executions for which there was no precedent even during the revolt of 1857. The Viceroy's council was unanimous that such actions, which weakened authority and brought the government into disgrace, could not be passed over, and the Deputy Commissioner was suspended till a full inquiry had taken place.[254] The Lieutenant-Governor, without condoning the blowing from guns, pleaded mitigating circumstances.[255] But the last act of Mayo's government was to observe that nothing short of immediate and urgent necessity could justify such actions. The Deputy Commissioner appeared to have believed that his conduct might prevent a general insurrection; but such a general apprehension of a rising was insufficient justification. Nor did the Government of India believe that there was sound reason for fearing a widespread revolt.[256]

It was in this atmosphere of crisis and fear of another Kuka outbreak[257] that news came that the Viceroy himself had been murdered on 8 February 1872 in the Andaman Islands by a Moslem. The conclusion was immediately drawn that this too was the result of a conspiracy, on this occasion of the Wahabis and Moslems. The senior officials who were present conducted an immediate investigation and reported that the assassin was not related to the murderer of the Chief Justice and that no political significance need be attached to the murder.[258] But the general opinion, both in Britain and in India, was, as *The Spectator* had written just before, 'that we have found the most dangerous foes who ever faced us; that our dominion hangs even now, today, by a hair; that at any moment in any year a Mussulman Cromwell may take the field, and the Empire be temporarily overwhelmed in universal massacre'.[259]

The first reaction of the Government of India to Mayo's death was one of almost hysterical anger. Fitzjames Stephen,[260] the law member, informed his wife that he and Strachey had decided that if the High Court acquitted Mayo's assassin, they would hang him on their own.[261] But gradually the sense of shock wore out and the Government of India returned to the path of sanity marked by Mayo himself. The Deputy Commissioner at Maler-kotla was removed from service and the Commissioner transferred to another province.[262]

To administer justice with mercy is the fixed and settled policy of the Government of India, but it is absolutely essential to this great object that justice should be administered according to known rules; with due deliberation and with discrimination between degrees of guilt. . . . His Excellency in Council cannot consent to be forced by the crime of a few fanatics into the sanction of acts repugnant to the whole spirit of British rule.[263]

Thus the atmosphere had become much calmer by the time of Northbrook's arrival, and being freer than his colleagues from the emotion roused by the murder of Mayo, he viewed the scene with a greater measure of detachment. Northbrook concluded that there was no evidence of any serious Moslem conspiracy. Bombay, Madras and the Punjab were tranquil, and such unrest as there was in Bengal could be attributed to a great extent to the abrasive methods of Sir George Campbell, the Lieutenant-Governor.[264] But the increase of local taxation had much disturbed the minds of the people; and perhaps too many changes, good in themselves but beyond public understanding, had been made recently. So 'a little rest, and, if possible, reduction of taxation, seems to me to be the right policy at the present time—a policy for which the change in the Governor-Generalship will give a fair excuse, and so will not appear to be an alteration from what has gone before'.[265] He would endeavour to keep things quiet and make no changes that were not absolutely required.

Northbrook, therefore, administered India with a light hand. A careful watch was kept on the classes likely to be disaffected and on any possibility of a combination among the Moslem soldiers in the army.[266] Campbell of Bengal was advised not to prosecute any newspapers for sedition but to exercise official influence and to divert the attention of educated men to professions and trades;[267] and the Viceroy was greatly irritated that, counter to his directive, Campbell continued to 'over-legislate' for Bengal. Campbell ordered a census, levied a road cess and sought to develop local self-government. To the Governor of Madras the Viceroy suggested that it would be wise to employ a certain number of Moslems and to induce them to send their children to English schools.[268] Northbrook also considered that taxes in general—and not merely local cesses—were too high and that nothing would tend more to quiet the Indian mind than the repeal of the income tax, which was unpopular and unsuited to India. 'I am fairly convinced that the only people who really like it, why I can't say, are Temple and Strachey, that is the real truth of it *between ourselves.*'[269] The petty amount derived from it was not worth the loss of confidence of the people; and the argument that only by an income tax could the zemindars and commercial interests be made to bear their fair share of the public burden was true only in theory, for in practice there was considerable evasion.[270] On the question of repeal, the Cabinet was divided; Kimberley and Gladstone were of the same view as Northbrook, but Argyll, the Secretary of State, favoured retention of the tax at a low rate.[271] Taking advantage of this division of opinion, Northbrook decided to administer India what he regarded as a general sedative and repealed the tax in March 1873.[272]

A similar relaxation of official interest and authority was sought to be effected in the sphere of land revenue. Northbrook stated in the legislative council that the Government of India did not approve of Campbell's desire to impose heavy rents, as the agricultural population formed the mainstay of British rule in India and should be kept in a state of contentment.[273] Argyll went even further. He favoured, in conjunction with general and varied taxation, not merely a lightening of the revenue assessments but a permanent settlement for all India.[274] To further this objective he sent a despatch which nominally dealt with irrigation works but in fact advocated the recognition of private proprietorship in land.[275] Northbrook agreed in principle but, knowing that it would arouse strong opposition in his council, awaited the arrival of Sir William Muir, an official with great knowledge of land problems in the North-West Provinces, before taking action.[276]

Further consideration of these long-term problems was prevented by the development of severe famine conditions in parts of Bengal and Bihar in the winter of 1873. This crisis Northbrook handled firmly, with sole regard to saving life and without counting the cost. Lavish effort to combat famine also seemed to Northbrook politically wise 'because no firmer hold can be taken of this vast country by us aliens than by establishing the conviction in the minds of the people that they are saved in times of danger by the exertions of a vigorous executive'.[277] Famine relief was the only aspect of Northbrook's internal administration which enhanced his reputation.

In February 1874 Salisbury became Secretary of State in the Conservative Government. His interest lay mainly in foreign affairs as they concerned India. He sought detailed information on Indian problems but the Viceroy had little cause at the start to complain of undue intervention. Salisbury disapproved of the North-West Provinces Rent Bill which incorporated Argyll's dislike of occupancy rights for tenants and support of the landowners; but he did not withhold his assent.[278] Indeed, often the Viceroy's timidity and Salisbury's instinctive conservatism led them to the same conclusions. They agreed that there should be no move to restore the Berars to the Nizam of Hyderabad. Northbrook described that State as 'the most powerful Mohamedan power in India', and Salisbury replied, 'He [Salar Jung, the minister of Hyderabad] can hardly imagine that we should look on a Mohamedan and a Native State in the same light. The Nizam is a real danger, and I would never willingly strengthen them [*sic*].'[279] Salisbury did not trust the Moslems and believed that the demand for the Berars was itself a result of the recrudescence, spontaneous or organized, of Moslem fanaticism throughout Asia.[280]

Again, the Viceroy discontinued the practice of permitting discussion of the budget in the legislative council and Salisbury approved, as these discussions had seemed to him

an unmeaning mimicry of the forms of popular institutions where the reality is impossible. What is called public opinion in India is frequently the opinion of a clique, and presents none of the guarantees for sound judgment possessed by a public opinion which represents the combined views of a large mass of different interests and classes. I have the smallest possible belief in 'Councils' possessing any other than consultative functions.[281]

Salisbury was even suspicious of the Viceroy's executive council and feared that it might one day appeal to Indian opinion against the British government 'and then we should have before long an Independence cry fostered by white leaders'.[282] Salisbury preferred to regard the Governor-General rather than the Governor-General in Council as the highest authority in Indian administration; and this, in Lytton's time, led to calamitous results.

It is possible, however, that if Salisbury had taken a more active interest in the details of Northbrook's administration, the clumsy handling of the case of the Gaekwar of Baroda might have been avoided. Malhar Rao, who had become Gaekwar or ruler of Baroda in 1870, was regarded by the Residents who served at his court as a man of feeble intellect and savage habits; but he was aware of his rights and shrewd enough to engage the services of the most distinguished Indian of that generation, Dadabhai Naoroji, to argue his case. He avoided attendance at Northbrook's durbar at Bombay in November 1872 for fear of insulting treatment and secured a confirmation of his rights of precedence from the British government against the wishes of the Bombay and Indian governments.[283] But the rapid deterioration in the administration of the State enabled the new Resident, Col. Phayre,[284] and the Bombay government to recover lost ground. Phayre sent detailed reports of oppression and corruption, and the Governor of Bombay sought Northbrook's permission to intervene. When the Gaekwar, hearing of this, fell at Phayre's feet and sought pardon, the Bombay government deemed this a good opportunity to demand of him the suspension of his ministers and the acceptance of an inquiry by a British commission.[285] Northbrook agreed to the appointment of such a commission and preferred to await its report before demanding the removal of the ministers.[286] He became aware, too, that while Phayre's charges were, in the main, valid, his manner was not conciliatory;[287] and the Bombay government had encouraged and not restrained him.[288] The commission, from which Phayre was excluded, reported early in 1874, substantially upholding his charges. Salisbury favoured action to bring the Gaekwar to heel even while his honorific claims were recognized. 'Native Princes must submit, in the inevitable course of things, to constant retrenchments of power at our hands, and therefore, I should be inclined to be the more cautious not to diminish the ceremonial observances to which they have been accustomed. They care most about the show; we care most about the power. For some time at least we may hope to travel along peaceably with them upon those lines.'[289]

With such a general sanction from the Secretary of State and constant pressure from the Bombay government,[290] Northbrook assented to action against the Gaekwar. Indeed, he was frightened by reports that the Hyderabad government, discomfited by the decision on the Berars, were in communication with the Gaekwar. 'I am not a bit of an alarmist; but if there is a danger, it seems to me to be likely to come from the great Mahomedan State, and there is every facility, in the annual stream of pilgrims as described to me, for the circulation of rumours all over India, or worse.'[291] So though Northbrook was informed that there were other States into whose affairs inquiries would reveal even worse maladministration,[292] he gave the Gaekwar a serious warning and threatened, if that proved ineffective, to depose him.[293] But he doubted if deposition would be practical and, realizing that control of the Baroda case was slipping from his hands, he appealed to the India Council for assistance. 'I should be positively *afraid*, in the condition of "susceptibility" of the Bombay Government, to hint at the advantage it would be to put Baroda under the Government of India; but if you were to do it at home, I would accept the responsibility.'[294] Friction between the Central and Bombay governments was an Indian tradition of long standing; but no other Viceroy fared so badly in the contest or sought succour from the India Council.

The Governor of Bombay realized, in his turn, that it was not he but Phayre who was in command of the situation and that Phayre had allowed his dislike of the Gaekwar and of Naoroji, now the Gaekwar's minister, to distort his judgment. The Resident was summoned and told that unless he were prepared to co-operate with Naoroji, he would himself be replaced. Phayre protested at 'a true Christian like himself' and 'a traitor' such as Naoroji being placed on the same footing, but agreed to conform to instructions.[295] In fact, he continued to place obstacles in Naoroji's path and to encourage local resistance to his reforms. The Bombay government tolerated this insubordination[296] and rejected Northbrook's suggestion that Phayre should retire quietly. The Viceroy now realized that he had been given very little information by the Bombay government and he recalled Phayre at Naoroji's instance.[297]

The elated Gaekwar, in the belief that Naoroji's services were no longer required, secured his resignation; but soon a fresh crisis developed. Phayre had alleged that there had been an attempt to poison him on the eve of his departure. There was at first no evidence to suggest that the Gaekwar had been in any way involved;[298] and Sir Lewis Pelly, Phayre's successor, was favourably impressed by the Gaekwar.[299] But thereafter confessions implicating the Gaekwar were received. The Viceroy proposed a temporary assumption of the administration by the Government of India and the appointment of a commission of inquiry. If Malhar Rao were found guilty, he should be deposed and another ruler installed in his stead.[300] 'I need hardly tell you that I am entirely against a policy of annexation. I quoted the Queen's Proclamation almost *ad nauseam* when I was first appointed, but in no way as a matter of form, and any idea of a change of policy is quite incorrect.'[301] Salisbury agreed, even though the India Council was unanimously in favour of annexation. While the punishment should be sufficiently penal to deter other Princes from poisoning their Residents, 'we must avoid the charge that our love of justice has been sharpened in this instance by a love of territory'.[302] Annexation should be reserved for cases of open rebellion. But the Secretary of State was willing to consider the fragmentation of Baroda by recognizing feudatories as rajas.[303]

Northbrook was unwilling to do even this. He desired to hand over the State in its entirety to a relative of the Gaekwar without any particular stipulations as to internal government.[304] But this generous decision was so vitiated in implementation as to lose all its grace. Three Indians, of whom two were Princes, were appointed to serve on the commission, whose sessions were public. Throughout the country there was subdued excitement and expressions of sympathy for the Gaekwar. For this the Viceroy blamed the educated class; 'there is growing up a mass of people with a smattering of English education, just enough to make them conceited, and ape the English habit of grumbling at and criticizing everything done by the Government. It would have the worst effect to flatter this class by making them suppose their merits are equal to any posts. The way the public opinion of this people has been shown in the case of the Gaekwar is not satisfactory.'[305] But the general sympathy for the Gaekwar had deeper roots. He had become a symbol, however unworthy, of patriotic sentiment. Even the people of Baroda, who had suffered so much at his hands, rallied to his side; and they were supported not only by Mahratta opinion outside the State but also by the Gujeratis.[306]

The Indian commissioners, in accord with the sentiments of their countrymen, dissented from their British colleagues and refused to find the Gaekwar guilty. Sir Erskine Perry, a member of the India Council, commented bitterly 'that to trust a Maratha Brahmin in such a case would be like relying on a Jesuit in a matter where the Pope was concerned'.[307] It is true the Indian commissioners were greatly moved by the sight of the Gaekwar, degraded and dishonoured, being brought into court day after day.[308] But theirs was not a purely emotional verdict. So eminent a lawyer as Sir Henry Maine observed that the evidence could hardly sustain a conviction.[309]

The division of opinion in the commission thrust the final decision on the government, and the fact that this division was on racial lines made the decision an embarrassing one. The press in London was almost unanimous in warning the Government of India not to punish the Gaekwar in defiance of the dissenting report of the Indian commissioners. Salisbury and the Cabinet were inclined to compromise. Deposition, wrote Salisbury, would nullify the effect of appointing distinguished Indians to the commission and, though possibly right in policy, it would be very hard to defend in argument. The Liberals were of the same view, while the Queen, as was to be expected, was strongly against deposition. But for once the India Council had its way and prevailed on the home government to support the Government of India in whatever decision they might wish to take;[310] and Northbrook announced his decision to depose the Gaekwar not because the Government of India regarded him as guilty but 'having regard to all the circumstances relating to the affairs of Baroda from the accession of Malhar Rao; his notorious misconduct, his gross misgovernment of the State and his evident incapacity to carry into effect necessary reforms'.

So Northbrook took what was probably the right step in entirely the wrong way. Malhar Rao was utterly unfit to rule and there was sufficient evidence to justify his replacement. Even so large-hearted a patriot as Naoroji had found it impossible to remain in his service. Moreover, when deposing Malhar Rao, Northbrook refused either to annex the State or to partition it or even to strengthen British control over the administration. But the Viceroy had allowed Phayre, with the support of the Bombay government, to dominate the State and provide what some objective observers regarded as good reason for the deterioration of the administration. Thereafter the Viceroy had set up a commission to investigate a particular charge and selected with great care the

Indians who would serve on it; but when the commission could not arrive at an agreed decision on the facts, he had set aside its report and had acted on general grounds. The only purposes which the commission had served were to strengthen the probably wrong presumption in the public mind of Malhar Rao's innocence and to convince opinion both in Britain and in India that the government were acting on an earlier political decision after failing to secure a judicial verdict to their satisfaction. Northbrook contended that the commission was not intended to be a judicial tribunal.[311] It is true that the Government of India had from the outset asserted that the inquiry was of a political and not of a purely legal origin, and in framing the heads of charge they had carefully avoided legal terms and used popular expressions.[312] But the inquiry had assumed the forms of a judicial trial and it was universally believed that judgment had been delivered on the basis of evidence. So the argument of the Government of India carried no conviction. There was more agreement with Salisbury when he concluded, with disarming honesty, that the inquiry only showed that if ever an Indian prince were to be tried again, the tribunal should be composed of English lawyers only and the defendant should not have the benefit of Old Bailey Counsel.[313]

There was one issue, however, on which Northbrook found that he could not take Salisbury's support for granted; and that was the question of tariffs. To Salisbury this was a matter in which British interests were heavily involved, and he was not prepared to allow the Viceroy to deal with it as if it were a purely Indian issue. The Viceroy, though a nominal adherent of the theory of free trade, was keen on promoting industrial production in India. 'I am very happy also on the progress of Indian manufactures ultimately. Whisper it not in Manchester.'[314] He was, therefore, alarmed when in October 1874, Mallet, the Permanent Under-Secretary at the India Office, requested him to consider a gradual reduction of the tariffs imposed on British cotton goods and the development in their place of other sources of revenue.[315] Northbrook denied that the 5 per cent duty on cotton manufactures was protective, for the Indian cotton industry had hardly been born; but he offered to levy an excise duty on cotton manufactures in India to redress the balance.[316] Salisbury, however, under pressure from Manchester interests, directed the Viceroy to examine the possibility of not merely reducing but abolishing the cotton duties.[317]

Northbrook decided, as a compromise, to reduce import duties on various articles other than cotton goods and to impose an *ad valorem* duty of 5 per cent on raw cotton. The annual loss, as a result of these measures, was estimated at £80,000.[318] Salisbury replied that this enactment, which had taken him by surprise, was at variance with policy as stated in his public speeches and in his despatch of 15 July 1875,[319] and might have to be disallowed.[320]

The Viceroy sought to assure Salisbury that the measure was a small and safe one which had had to be enacted immediately without reference to the Secretary of State. The Government of India had not been aware that they might be violating the declared policy of the British government, as the despatch had not been received in time.[321] The duties imposed on cotton manufactures were not protective, for the cotton goods imported into India consisted mainly of the higher qualities, which could not be manufactured from the cotton grown in India.[322] So the demand by Lancashire interests for the total abolition of cotton duties in India was unreasonable and should be resisted. 'The duty of the Government of India is to govern India for the best interests of the people of India, and not for the interests of the Manchester manufacturers.'[323]

Salisbury, who had always felt that the Viceroy was not keeping him fully informed,[324] resented Northbrook's failure on this occasion to consult him before taking action.[325] He informed Northbrook that he could not assent to a new duty on raw cotton and the maintenance of the duty of 5 per cent on manufactured cotton goods. Besides the commitments to the British public, there was also the risk that the abolition of these duties at a later stage, when Indian opinion was politically awakened, might lead to friction between Britain and India.[326] He suggested that Mallet, who was one of Northbrook's oldest friends, should go to India for personal discussions to smooth matters out.[327] Northbrook, in the belief that Mallet was coming out with an open mind and with full powers, agreed.[328]

Mallet, however, was in complete agreement with Salisbury. He was a staunch member of the Cobden Club and believed in a rigid adherence to free trade. Abolition of the cotton duties was to him—as to Gladstone—not an inglorious concession to Manchester but impeccable doctrine, an encouragement to the investment of British capital in India and a strengthening of the purchasing power of the Indian people by lowering the prices of goods.[329] His terms of reference were limited to ascertaining the manner in which Salisbury's decision could be implemented with the least disturbance.[330] On the other hand, the Viceroy had no doubt that his own views were correct. 'I formed them deliberately upon the best information that I could obtain as regards the effect of the duties themselves, and upon the general knowledge which I have obtained since I have been in India of the condition of the finances and the feelings of the people: and you will, I am sure, feel that opinions upon so important a subject cannot be lightly set aside.'[331]

Mallet's mission, therefore, had no chance of success; and his long journey only served to gain time. The hope that Mallet would remove Northbrook's suspicion that Disraeli was resolved to drive him out of office in order to appoint a Conservative[332] also proved unfounded. Salisbury, with Northbrook's resignation already in his hands, had no need to be accommodating, and his tone became increasingly masterful. 'The ultimate policy to be pursued is fixed, not only by our decision, but by a public opinion here which will survive Ministries. But the mode and time and the conditions under which it can be done compatibly with the interests of the Treasury must necessarily be matter for discussion.'[333] An official despatch was also sent, firmly recording these views and calling upon the Government of India to enact amending legislation immediately.[334] Mallet, to soften the blow to an old friend, recommended as a compromise the withdrawal of the despatch, the abolition of the duty on raw cotton and the reduction of the duty on cotton goods to 3½ per cent.[335] The Viceroy agreed to this,[336] but Salisbury insisted that the duties should be repealed and not reduced. He also asserted that the withdrawal of the despatch disapproving of the action of the Government of India would make the position of the Ministry untenable.[337]

It was with such censure and humiliation that Northbrook departed, prophesying discontent in India, supporting his council as loyally as they had supported him in this matter and complaining of the unpleasant tone of Salisbury's official communications.[338] 'The Natives used to believe the Viceroy to be a very great man, and it is good policy that they should continue to believe it; and such language is a complete puzzle to them.'[339] In both Britain and India it was known that the home government had overridden the Government of India in British interests.[340] Instructions were given to Northbrook's successor to abolish the tariffs as soon as possible,[341] and Lytton made no secret of his anxiety to act in accordance with this directive.[342] Though advised by Mallet not to act piecemeal and to await a time when he could deal with the matter as a whole, he planned to repeal immediately the duty on long staple cotton.[343] That the members of council in India were in a mood of sullen antagonism and arrayed against him like 'all the elephants of Porus' worried neither him nor the Secretary of State.[344] Muir was replaced as finance member by John Strachey. At this stage Salisbury had second thoughts and told Lytton that hurried action might give an impression of heedlessness.[345] The Viceroy, with all his thoughts dominated by the Afghan question, willingly agreed to postpone consideration of the tariffs till the end of the year.[346] But thereafter failure of the monsoons and the indispensability of the revenue which was derived from the cotton duties obliged the government to delay repeal for a further period. 'All I can say is', wrote Lytton apologetically, 'make only fair allowance for difficulties not of our own creating, and give us only fair time to overcome them; and I think we shall be able to satisfy you that we are neither hydrocephalus idiots, nor invertebrate abortions.'[347]

On 11 July 1877 the House of Commons passed, without a division, a resolution that the Indian duties on cotton manufactures were protective and contrary to sound commercial policy and should be repealed without delay as soon as the financial condition of India permitted. However, Salisbury agreed that, faced with the prospect of a general famine, it would be wrong to reduce the tariffs, particularly if direct taxation would have to be increased to replace the revenue surrendered.[348] As it was, the expenditure on famine relief obliged the government to seek fresh sources of revenue. Lytton regretted Northbrook's repeal of the income tax and would have liked to restore it, but he knew that the home government were opposed to any such step[349] while the outcry throughout India would be 'strong enough to swamp our whole administration'.[350] He was, however, obliged to levy a famine cess in 1878. This was followed, at the suggestion of the home government,[351] by the repeal of the duty on coarse cotton goods. As Lancashire interests were not satisfied with this, Cranbrook suggested more comprehensive action.[352] Lytton was willing to undertake it if assured of support from the home government, for it might be necessary for him to overrule his own council.[353] On receiving this assurance he sanctioned in March 1879 a further reduction of import duties on cotton manufactures. But total repeal he was unable to achieve. 'It has long been my dream to leave India one great free port; and some day I have no doubt this will be done though not perhaps in my time.'[354]

If the dry subject of tariffs was a matter of significance to Salisbury, it was the new title of the Queen which warmed the imagination of the Prime Minister. The visit of the Prince of Wales during the last months of Northbrook's regime was followed by legislation declaring the Queen to be Empress of India. This was Disraeli's scheme, which he had had in mind since 1858[355] and now formulated with the enthusiastic approval of the Queen, for providing his concept of imperialism with a symbol. Even Salisbury had not been aware of the suggestion. 'I know nothing about the "Empress of India"—what *does* the Queen mean?'[356] Salisbury thought that the Queen should be satisfied with the fact that she was already referred to as Empress in a few formal documents in India.[357] When the Royal Titles Bill was severely criticized by the Liberals in Parliament, Salisbury regretted the move even more.[358] Mallet considered it 'one of the most gratuitous of blunders' which had damaged the government more than they suspected or admitted.[359] But the Viceroy, who had a stronger sense of theatre than his masters at the India Office, reported to the Prime Minister—without any evidence—that the Queen's new title seemed immensely popular with Indians. He proposed that it be announced in a grand durbar and the occasion utilized to strengthen the loyalty of the Princes by appointing the chief of them to the legislative council.[360]

Your Majesty's Indian Government has not hitherto, in my opinion, sufficiently appealed to the Asiatic sentiment and traditions of the Native Indian aristocracy. That aristocracy exercises a powerful influence over the rest of the native population. To rally it openly round the throne of Your Majesty, and identify its sympathies and interests with British rule, will be to strengthen very materially the power, and increase the éclat of your Majesty's Indian Empire. I think we have hitherto relied too much for popular gratitude on the great improvement we have undoubtedly effected in the position of the ryot by means of costly canals and irrigation works, which have embarrassed our finances and are as yet so little appreciated by the Hindu rustic that they do not pay the expense of making them. If we have with us the Princes, we shall have with us the people.[361]

The Viceroy developed in detail his concept of an imperial throne supported by an Indian nobility. Disraeli's scheme for binding India to Britain with sentimental loyalty was converted by Lytton into a feudal pattern. He wished to make twelve of the leading Indian Princes members of an Indian Privy Council.[362] He also planned to register the titles of all Princes and thus create an Indian peerage, to raise their ceremonial rank and to give them military commands with specific duties and services to be performed. 'Why not make Cashmere, for instance, a Warden of the Marches? The moral effect of employing him and his forces for the permanent defence of the frontier would be considerable.' The existing system seemed to Lytton 'one of half confidence, which always tends to provoke half loyalty'. The Princes were allowed to maintain large military establishments but not to make use of them; they were allowed to retain vast revenues and great powers from which the Government of India derived no direct benefit. 'The whole social structure of this Empire is essentially feudal and eminently fitted for the application of the salutary military principles of the feudal system.'[363]

Salisbury agreed that the nobility was, of all the classes in India, the one over which the British could hope to establish a useful influence. The masses were for the most part asleep, and to expect political support from the Indian people as a consequence and recognition of good government was an optimistic dream.

Good government avoids one of the causes of hate; but it does not inspire love. The literary class—a deadly legacy from Metcalf(e) and Macaulay—are politically alive enough: but under the most favourable circumstances they never give any political strength to a state, whatever other benefits they confer; they seldom go further in the affirmative direction than to tolerate the existing order of things.

In India an educated class had been unwisely warmed into life before its time, and was by nature *frondeur*. It could not provide anything other than an opposition in peace time and rebels in time of trouble.

There remains the aristocracy and—I quite agree with you—it is worth making an effort to secure their loyalty. If they are with us, we can hardly be upset; and they run so bad a chance under any possible substitute that their self-interest must be strongly on our side. The point is to get their sentiment with us too; and that with English arrogance working against you will be no easy matter. But it is worth trying.[364]

However, it was not to guard against any middle class or popular opposition in the future that Salisbury planned to secure the support of the Indian aristocracy. With inexplicable short-sightedness he applied to India the precedents of other parts of the empire where British settlers formed the majority of the population; and he believed that in India too the British non-official community would constitute the great danger to British rule.

If England is to remain supreme, she must be able to appeal to the coloured against the white, as well as to the white against the coloured. It is therefore not merely as a matter of sentiment and of justice, but as a matter of safety, that we ought to try and lay the foundations of some feeling on the part of the coloured races towards the Crown other than the recollection of defeat and the sensation of subjection.[365]

The British empire in India, if it were to endure, should stand not on one leg but on two; it should be provided with an oriental as well as a European footing.[366] Salisbury warned the Viceroy against delegating authority over the internal government of British India to an Indian Privy Council as it would stimulate elected representatives of the 'white' community to claim similar powers. 'The only enemies, I believe, who will ever seriously threaten England's power in India are her own sons.'[367]

It was, therefore, with the approval of the home government[368] that Lytton convened on 1 January 1877 an Imperial Assembly. Stress was laid on the Queen as the first among the Indian Princes. The purpose was both to enthrone her as an oriental potentate and to exalt the role of Indian noblemen. At a gorgeous pageant the Princes, with special banners before them, paid homage to the representative of the Empress. The spectacle was considered by both the home and the Indian governments to have been an unqualified success,[369] but in fact it was of little political consequence. The Viceroy could not create a Privy Council, for the India Council contended that it was *ultra vires* and was willing only to sanction the award to the leading Princes of the title of Councillor of the Empress.[370] Salisbury, scheduled to leave London for Constantinople, had no power to overrule the India Council from abroad;

and the Cabinet had no desire to precipitate an angry controversy in the House of Commons.[371] Lytton, while disappointed, accepted the compromise.[372] These new Councillors of the Empress had no influence whatever on developments in India. The statement of Lord Roberts many years later, that Lytton's durbar was the turning-point in Indian history, for 'that one day and that great meeting had more effect in welding the people of India to England than anything that has ever happened before or since'[373] is conclusive evidence only of that soldier's lack of political acumen.

More successful in strengthening the administration and securing for it Indian support were Lytton's less grandiose efforts. His famine policy was recognized to be effective. He visited the famine-stricken districts of the Madras presidency in 1877 and introduced a measure of order into the provincial government's wildly prodigal policy of famine relief. 'It is a struggle with exasperated lunatics which must be conducted without breaking any of the furniture.'[374] What appealed to Indian opinion even more was his declared determination not to compromise on the fundamental issue of relations between British and Indians. In 1876 Fuller, an English barrister at Agra, struck his groom who died of the injuries. The Joint Magistrate fined Fuller thirty rupees, and the High Court of Allahabad held that the sentence, though perhaps lighter than the High Court would have been disposed to inflict, was not specially open to objection. Lytton decided to take official notice of the case. 'If I could help it, the case should not be allowed to drop, until it dropped upon the head of Mr Fuller. For I am persuaded that, if it drops otherwise, some portion of the good character of our administration will drop with it.'[375] With the full approval of his council,[376] he published his letter to the government of the North-West Provinces, deploring Fuller's conduct, suspending the magistrate and criticizing both the provincial government and the High Court.[377] Lytton himself attached no great importance to this matter—it was, he wrote to Delane of *The Times*, 'a twopenny halfpenny case';[378] but what had been to him a minor matter of administrative propriety aroused the anger of the Anglo-Indian press and community, and in consequence won him the sympathy of Indians.

Further testimony of his impartial outlook was provided by his efforts to increase the avenues of official employment for Indians. Lytton found that little action had been taken under the Act of

1870 empowering the Government of India to appoint Indians to any post in the civil service even if they had not been admitted by competition. 'It seems to me a disgrace to our Government that an Act of Parliament, solemnly promising natives admission to Government service, should have practically remained a dead letter for six years.'[379] Salisbury's warning that there was nothing of which British officials were so jealous as an admission of Indians to 'a share of the cake'[380] did not deter Lytton from dealing with the problem. His own idea was to divide all official posts into two categories. To the first, Indians could never aspire; to the second the government would promote by all means at their disposal the free introduction of the best Indian candidates.[381] Salisbury, however, preferred gradual and tentative measures to any rigid decision and shifted the emphasis from a division of posts to an increased proportion of Indian recruits.[382] This at once vivified Lytton's prejudice against educated Indians and desire to secure the goodwill of the upper classes. 'As for the Babus, I thought it necessary to tell them plainly that the encouragement of natives does not mean the supremacy of Baboodom.'[383] With this attitude Salisbury wholeheartedly agreed. 'I can imagine no more terrible picture for India than that of being governed by competition-baboos.' The provision of a new method of recruiting Indians to the public service would furnish a more respectable excuse for denying them entry through competition.[384]

In accordance with this shared prejudice, the Viceroy proposed the establishment of a new service which would be confined to Indians selected from families of social standing. This would ensure the loyalty not only of the entrants but of all the members of their families and provide the government with the support of their influence.[385] After consulting the local governments,[386] he formally proposed that the covenanted civil service, which was recruited by examination, should be closed to Indians and a 'native branch' of the civil service created for the employment by selection of those with inherited qualifications, early habits of authority and a commanding influence over large numbers of their fellow-countrymen.[387] Cranbrook, who had by now succeeded Salisbury, replied that legislation to 'separate the black and white sheep into two distinct flocks' was not feasible and might savour of discrimination.[388] Lytton then declared that he was not in favour of legislation excluding Indians from competing for admission to the covenanted civil service and agreed to frame rules creating a 'native' civil service, thereby avoiding recourse to Parliament.[389] In May 1879 it was decided that a proportion not exceeding one-sixth of the total number of recruits to the civil service in any year would be 'natives' selected in India by local governments.[390] But the statutory civil service, despised by the covenanted civil servants and not attractive to able Indians, proved, as expected, a failure.[391]

Lytton's impartial attitude as between Indians and Europeans was, therefore, to a considerable extent vitiated by his obsession with the feudal elements of Indian society[392] and his consistent underrating of all other groups. It clouded his admirable conduct in such matters as the Fuller case and resulted in such generous impulses as the desire to extend the employment of Indians leading to nothing. Indeed, Lytton went further and embarked on self-defeating attempts to curb the activities of the educated classes. For some years the Government of India had been concerned at what they regarded as exaggerated criticism and wild allegations in the newspapers published in Indian languages, but had not thought it necessary to do more than occasionally warn the editors concerned. Lytton regarded this as weak tolerance and decided, with the support of Salisbury and Sir Ashley Eden,[393] the Lieutenant-Governor of Bengal whom the Viceroy considered the ablest administrator in India,[394] to impose statutory control over the vernacular press. The objection of the law member that the exemption of newspapers in the English language would render it 'class legislation of the most striking and invidious description, at variance with the whole tenour of our policy',[395] was set aside on the ground that the newspapers in English had a limited circulation and had no desire to subvert the government.[396] In March 1878 the Vernacular Press Act, which would 'enable us to behead the hydra at one sudden stroke',[397] was passed, with the approval of the Secretary of State, at a single sitting of the legislative council after suspension of the standing orders. Lytton himself described the procedure as 'a sort of coup d'état to pass a very stringent gagging Bill'.[398] Magistrates of districts and commissioners of police in presidency towns were authorized, with the previous sanction of the local governments, to demand bonds from printers and publishers and either a deposit of such sum as the local government might think fit or the submission of proofs for inspection. If the government found any matter they regarded as objectionable, they would publish a notice of contravention in the *Gazette*. If this warning were disregarded, the deposit, the machinery and copies of the paper could be confiscated. All proceedings under the Act were final and conclusive, subject only to appeal within three months to the Governor-General in Council. As the Secretary of State disliked the clause regarding submission of proofs,[399] this was repealed in September 1878. A Press Commissioner was appointed, whose real function was to manage the press; but as Lytton acknowledged, this proved a failure.[400]

Even as amended, the Vernacular Press Act was a flagrant violation of democratic principle and constitutional practice. It indicated Lytton's autocratic cast of mind and imperfect sympathy with the principles of British rule in India. The Viceroy believed that the fact that only one paper had ceased publication[401] and one editor had had to be warned under the provisions of the Act[402] was confirmation that the Act had served as a successful deterrent. 'What curs these Bengalis are! They seem to glory in proclaiming their own cowardice.'[403] But this was to exult at cowing an imaginary enemy. It was not among the readers of the vernacular journals in Bengal that the danger of seditious action lay.

In the Western Deccan the raiyats experienced great hardship. This had been clearly stated by a commission of inquiry,[404] and the India Office urged the Viceroy to act promptly upon its report. 'To leave the state of things revealed by the Commissioners without any attempt at remedy, would be a lasting disgrace to British administration in India.'[405] The Government of India proposed legislation to facilitate loans to the cultivators and provide additional judicial remedies;[406] and the Act of 1879 authorized the courts to scrutinize contracts in cases of debt and permit only reasonable rates of interest.[407] But agrarian legislation to deal with rural distress was in itself inadequate. Sir Richard Temple, the Governor of Bombay, reported the presence also of political discontent leading 'almost to organized sedition', with its centre in Poona.[408] Lytton agreed that there was active agitation.

Conspiracy of some kind, and in some form, is always smouldering in the Bombay Presidency; and this makes it a very difficult Presidency to manage. At the present moment, I am afraid that a good deal of dangerous ferment is simmering there. The dacoits, which [*sic*] have lately been increasing in magnitude and audacity, are not, I fear, mainly agrarian. We have proof that the Brahminical literati of Poona and Bombay are directly connected with them.[409]

If this proof could be established in court, Temple was instructed to act.[410] Even had the Bombay government been able to do so— which they were not—this was obviously to tinker with a major problem.[411]

IV

The Conservative impact on India during these eleven years was the result of the endeavours of Mayo, Northbrook, Salisbury and Lytton. Mayo, though he served under a Liberal Government, implemented fully his understanding of the new Conservatism. He believed that the British were in India by right but that it was their duty to provide efficient administration. Northbrook, nominally a Liberal, believed in keeping India static. This in itself should have irritated the Liberals of Gladstone's way of thinking and pleased the Conservatives who returned to office half-way through Northbrook's term. But Northbrook's immobility of mind and thought exasperated even Salisbury; and for the first time in the nineteenth century a Secretary of State settled the contours of Indian policy and administration despite the protests of the Viceroy. Salisbury then sent out Lytton in the hope that the Conservative Government would at last have a Viceroy fully in accordance with their views. But Lytton proved too enthusiastic and rash. His was almost a parody of the new Conservatism. Perhaps he took Disraeli's imaginative fancies too seriously. But by the time Lytton resigned, India had witnessed the full spectrum of the imperialist policy of British Conservatism.

Office often makes the man. Power and responsibility may serve as catalysts of the best in him. Mayo always felt that India was his destined ground of service and success. 'At last', he is reported to have said when the Indian appointment was offered to him;[412] and the young and relatively unknown Irish squire shouldered for three years 'as heavy a responsibility as falls to the lot of man'[413] with a capacity and courage which surprised all but a few men of percipience.

Mayo came to India when imperialism was becoming a part of the Conservative creed and he shared the enthusiasm for it. As he wrote, 'we are determined as long as the sun shines in heaven to hold India. Our national character, our commerce, demand it;

and we have, one way or another, two hundred and fifty millions of English capital fixed in the country.'[414] He considered too that racial consciousness was the basis of the empire. 'Teach your subordinates', he directed the Lieutenant-Governor of the Punjab,[415] 'that we are all British gentlemen engaged in the magnificent work of governing an inferior race.' He was shrewd enough to realize that new forces were emerging in India and changes 'which happily we cannot stop if we would are going on around us'.[416] His policy was flexible and he reckoned with the need to promote education and to associate Indians with the administration. He desired opportunities for education to be provided by the government for the masses rather than for the middle classes who could afford to pay for their education. The first duty of the government was to instruct the poor; and Mayo rejected the filtration theory 'that like the cow's tail education will grow downwards'. Nor was he deterred by the fact that the educated Indian was becoming discontented.[417] Believing that this discontent was caused by unemployment, he expressed his willingness to declare Indians eligible for all posts in the legal and judicial branches of government and most posts in the police service.[418] But a self-governing India was to Mayo not even a remote possibility. It was perhaps this lack of political sensibility which led him, time and again, to assume that all was well in India.

Mayo's objective was to provide India with efficient administration. 'The days of conquest are past; the age of improvement has begun.'[419] His passionate and tireless energy was enlisted in the service of the Indian people. 'But I feel sure you will agree with me that the line of duty is very plain and that we ought never to depart from it. . . we have no right to be here at all unless we use *all* our power for the good of the blacks.'[420] The maintenance of peace, the removal of disaffection and the promotion of prosperity would be the best ways of strengthening the imperial connexion. The purpose was limited but the work was noble; and it coincided with India's need. A firm basis of administration had to be laid before the horizons could be pushed back to encompass political development; and this Mayo sought to do. To the end he was hampered by local resistance. 'I have subdued', he remarked in the last letter he ever wrote,[421] 'many demons, but obstruction and delay are the many headed monsters which bear on the present occasion.' Even so, the achievement was marked. Mayo was in the line of the great administrators, of Warren Hastings, Dalhousie and Curzon, and had he lived his full span in India, he might well have ranked among the greatest of them.

Mayo's task might have proved insuperable but for his easy command of men. Though his council was composed of some of the ablest Englishmen who ever came out to India, he never found himself in a minority. Minute-writing or, as Mayo described it, 'paper shots at one's colleagues', ceased to a great extent. 'We are all', the Viceroy reported,[422] 'exceedingly good friends in Council.' There could be no more conclusive proof of his outstanding powers and personality than the fact that he gained the esteem and affection of two such self-sustaining individualists as John Strachey and Fitzjames Stephen. Strachey wrote that he had felt for Mayo a deeper personal regard than for almost any man in the world. 'He seemed formed by Nature to be a great Indian Governor. His noble bearing, his magnificent liberality, the dignity and courtesy of his demeanour, the unfailing kindness and unselfishness of his frank and genial nature, made everyone proud of him, and made everyone love him.'[423] Stephen's assessment was 'that of the many public men whom it has been my fortune to meet in various capacities at home and in India, I never met one to whom I felt disposed to give such heartfelt affection and honour'.[424]

Though nominally Liberal, Strachey and Stephen gave unqualified support to Mayo's objectives of a strong executive, a paternal administration, the maintenance of the rule of law and no pretence of promoting self-government. If the Viceroy's opinions were the result of his intelligent Conservatism, Strachey and Stephen were influenced by conditions in India. British power in India was based on force and justice. The British owed their position to conquest and their task was to introduce the fundamentals of European civilization. For reasons of economy and convenience, educated Indians had to be employed; but this could never lead to any form of representative government. Some day in the remote future Indians might wrest power, but if the British 'never let go of the thin rope of power' and were firm and resolute, there was no reason why the existing position should not continue indefinitely. And Mayo's methods seemed to them the best way of assuring this.[425] 'There [in India]', wrote Stephen on his return to Britain, 'you see real government. Here you see disorganized anarchy which is quickly throwing off the mask.'[426] No

Viceroy could have hoped for more brilliant lieutenants or more effective propagandists; and that he had successfully harnessed their talents was a measure of Mayo's own quality.

Mayo enjoyed his work with a youthful zest. 'The work here', he wrote to Disraeli a few months after assuming office,[427] 'is tremendous. Everything comes to the Viceroy, and the bigness of the questions would surprise you. I do not think I have made a mistake yet. At least if I have, it has not been found out.' Later in the year he remarked, 'I enjoy the life, the enormous interests and the great power, but the work is tremendous and the anxiety at times very great'.[428] This enthusiasm drove him to work hard—twelve hours a day and every day. In India, he observed, everything rested on the shoulders of the Viceroy.[429] Mayo's was the effective voice in all the significant decisions of the Government of India; and he revised, and often rewrote, every despatch and communication to the home and provincial governments. He took charge, not only of the foreign department but also of the public works department, because of its importance at that time. A separate department of agriculture was created to cope with this basic sector of the Indian economy, and Mayo proposed to take charge of this department if a member of council were appointed to deal solely with public works.[430] In addition, Mayo interested himself in the details of administration in every part of India, invited even junior provincial officers to be his guests and acquaint him with their work, and undertook long tours to secure first-hand knowledge of men and matters in his domain. As a result, Mayo had seen more of India in three years than most British civil servants in a lifetime and knew more about India's problems than any other Viceroy of his century. He encouraged representations to the central government, instructed the home department to inquire into every allegation of injustice and reserved the right to communicate directly with any official in India.[431] If England, wrote Mayo,[432] wanted to lose India, the best way she could set about it was to create a federal constitution. It was this avid attention to all problems of administration which led to the occasion of his death.

Northbrook lacked Mayo's vigour and drive and was always a withdrawn and indeterminate figure.[433] That he was not unpopular with the educated Indians[434] was probably because they were grateful for being left alone. His assessment of the Indian situation, that the country needed a rest, was confirmed, surprisingly enough, by both the civil servant with the greatest knowledge of Indian opinion and by the head of the intelligence department. Allan Hume, then still a senior official of the Government of India, complained in 1872 that British opinion had insisted on a show of progress in all directions, far more rapid than was justified by any real improvement in the condition of the people. The British were legislating and governing by virtue of their bayonets and artillery and in systematic disregard of popular feeling; and the result was general discontent. The fate of the empire was trembling in the balance and a single stone under a single wheel would probably upset the coach. 'We hurry on from change to change, seeking to force in a lifetime growth that to be healthy must be the product of ages. We will not rest content with doing a little and doing it well; securing for each little step the foundation of popular assent; we are building a palace on the sand, and great will be the fall thereof.' So he advised Northbrook to avoid innovations and to determine tax policy not by European theories but by the wishes and prejudices of the Indian tax-payer.[435]

The same opinion was expressed, though in more sober language, by the official whose duty it was to secure information regarding the public mood. He was certain that most Hindus, who had formerly been contented because they had been left alone, now distrusted and disliked the British. There were so many changes of every description in progress that they did not know what was being done and was likely to be done—but for all of which they would have to pay. 'In a word, if what everyone tells me is to be believed, the Natives look on themselves as being hustled (if I may use the expression) into a state of premature civilisation and wish to be allowed to settle down.' Indians hated change and complained that since 1857 the whole country had been turned upside down by new laws, new taxes and new institutions.[436]

There is no doubt, too, that Northbrook's policy of quietude helped to lower tension. Rumours about the circulation of *chapatis* proved, on inquiry, to be baseless.[437] There was no evidence of any general uneasiness among the Moslem population or of any fresh Wahabi stirrings that required notice. The rioting by Moslems in Bombay in 1874 was an isolated instance. The Kuka movement declined and the assemblies and seditious speeches which were reported in 1875[438] were the last splutter of the flame.

The agrarian uneasiness, which was noticed in 1873 and 1875 in the districts of eastern Bengal, did not lead to disturbances.[439] But the drag of apprehensive caution weakened the regular administration of these years. However justified the refusal to consider new measures, there was no excuse for letting the ordinary machinery of government run down. Northbrook was frightened into inertia. His understanding of his task was recorded in a letter which was later published over a pseudonym in *The Pall Mall Gazette.*

But what is the Government of India? A few Englishmen engaged in, perhaps, the most difficult Government in the world, who can be actuated by no other motives than to do what is right, and whose task is to maintain the honour and the safety of the British Possessions, whose every act is watched with jealousy by able men, natives of India, with feelings and interests adverse to British rule, either from a real desire to overthrow it, or from an unthinking wish to show their independence and use their English education to argue freely in all cases against the actions of their rulers.[440]

This diffidence and sense of encirclement led to a fussiness which complicated, and often spoiled, even matters of the most minor routine, while on important issues, such as the Baroda case, it carried the Viceroy out of his depth. Hume's description of Northbrook—'the best, kindest, officially most disagreeable, hard-working, conscientious, little-minded, feeble being that I have met in any high position'—was, in the main, fair.[441]

The contrast between Northbrook and his successor was striking. Lytton was volatile, a man of warmth and wit, with an impish streak in his behaviour. Impulsive, indiscreet and tactless, he could also inspire almost passionate devotion among men like John Morley and Wilfrid Blunt, who had very different political views. Even Delane, the editor of *The Times*, unbent so far as to promise Lytton, on the eve of his departure for India, that if in the course 'of your great proconsulship any occasion should arise in which your policy should require defence it will give me sincere pleasure to obtain for you that suspension of judgement which generally is alone necessary'.[442]

Lytton's power to charm was born of his quicksilver mind. He was perhaps the only intellectual ever to become Viceroy of India. Grant Duff thought he had more ability than any man who had held the Governor-Generalship since Warren Hastings.[443] Northbrook, by no means prejudiced in his favour, recognized soon after meeting him in India that he was clever and able.[444] Nor was he idle. His interest in women, reputation for heavy drinking and committing of what in those days was the grave offence of smoking in council strengthened the general opinion that he was an indolent young man wanting in seriousness; but amusement played only a minor part in Lytton's Indian life. 'I am scribbling morning, noon and night, without intermission, and yet barely able to keep pace with my work.'[445]

Few Viceroys determined their own policies so fully as Lytton did. John Strachey, the ablest member of Lytton's council, always gave the Viceroy vigorous and unqualified support. Some of the other members occasionally disagreed and recorded minutes of dissent, but Lytton could afford to ignore them. From London also there was little rein on the Viceroy. Salisbury supported him in both internal and foreign affairs; and by the time Salisbury began to be alarmed by Lytton's impetuosity, he had been succeeded by Cranbrook, an almost weightless personality in Indian affairs. Cranbrook was firm only in overruling the India Council whenever its members ventured to criticize the Viceroy's actions. So Lytton had at no time cause to worry about either 'the six second-rate men'[446] in his council or 'the coalesced stupidities'[447] of the advisers of the Secretary of State. So accustomed did he become to having his own way that, lacking any experience of Parliament, he resented even the little interest which was taken by its members in Indian matters.

I have always regarded the Secretary of State as the buffer, without which the despotism of India would be in constant collision with the democracy of England, and I shall always be on the lookout for your danger-signals. At the same time I venture to think that one of the many unrecognized advantages which we derive from the possession of India is a field of administration which furnishes us with the practical confutation of a great many liberal fallacies; and I feel sure that any attempt to administer this country, with undue deference to the exigencies of the Party and Parliamentary Government at home, would be fatal to our permanent possession of India.[448]

The viceroyalty, therefore, was an untrammelled opportunity to a man of Lytton's ability and ambition. But he failed for lack of understanding and vision. His flashy clevernessnever broke through the surface. He had given no serious thought to Indian problems and had no well-considered views as to Britain's role in

India. Britain was an imperial power; and, as far as Lytton was concerned, there was nothing more to be said. In his view, the Government of India should remain a despotism conducted in the interests of the British people and particularly, whenever possible, in the interests of the Conservative party. 'He is the first Viceroy', wrote a British civil servant in India, 'who has throughout his administration worked as the servant of a Party at home only, regardless of the views of his Council, and he has done all that was possible to render the office an unstable one dependent on the success or failure of the Ministry.'[449] When the Conservatives were defeated in the elections in 1880, Lytton resigned as a matter of course; and even among the British community in India none except a few personal friends sincerely regretted his departure.

Of real achievement Lytton could show little. He had sound impulses on such matters as the official attitude to the subject race and the employment of Indians in the civil service. His famine administration was efficient; and the gross error in the financial estimates in the last year of the viceroyalty was not a substantive one. Yet on the whole Lytton's domestic policy was irrelevant. He believed in symbol and ceremony, exalted the feudal princes and sought to terrorize the middle classes of Bengal when in fact the areas of political sensitivity were Bombay and the Western Deccan.

Yet, had this been all, Lytton's term in India might have escaped condemnation. It was his adventurism in foreign policy which turned the viceroyalty to ashes. He was eager in 1879 to annex a major portion of Upper Burma. 'But I know not whether I shall greatly shock you by the confidential avowal that few things would better please me than a really good pretext and opportunity for annexing a large slice of Upper Burma.'[450] However, he restrained his ardour, especially as his enthusiasm was not shared by the home government and he was being criticized at that time for his forward policy in Afghanistan.[451] There he acted as a runaway horse. The Afghan policy of the Disraeli Government was to secure information and a measure of ascendancy, but no more. 'I should deprecate', wrote Salisbury, on the eve of Lytton's departure, to the Prime Minister, 'as strongly as anyone a policy at all resembling Auckland's. But I hope Lytton will have flexibility enough to see that you may get information and tender advice on matters of foreign policy without committing yourself to any measure inconsistent with the independence of the country.'[452] Salisbury would have agreed with Gladstone's conclusion that there seemed to be one thing even worse than making the Afghans enemies and that was to make them subjects.[453] But Lytton deemed this too modest a policy. Once he was in India his 'gaudy and theatrical ambition'[454] took control and the Government of India adopted a bullying attitude. This seemed to be justified by the treaty of Gandamak; but soon British troops were marching into Afghanistan not in furtherance of any policy but solely on a mission of retribution. Lytton's policy could have been vindicated only by success; but this, to the surprise of few, was denied him. He had fought with a sword but no shield; and he paid the price.

CHAPTER 3

THE LIBERAL EXPERIMENT— RIPON AND DUFFERIN

I

When, after the elections of 1880, Gladstone returned to office, the appointment to the Indian viceroyalty received his special attention. He urged Kimberley to accept what seemed to him to be a post more important than all except perhaps two of the offices for which he had to recommend in Britain. 'To mere ambition I do not desire to appeal, but I feel that at no period of its existence has the office offered brighter promise of reward in the highest forms of which it is susceptible.'[1] The Prime Minister believed that it was an unprecedented opportunity for erasing the blots of the Lytton regime and introducing the principles for which Gladstone and the Liberal party stood. Kimberley, however, declined, whereupon the Prime Minister sought to persuade Goschen; and it was only when the latter also refused that the post was offered to Ripon.[2] Compelled to consider Ripon because of the unavailability of others whom he thought more suitable, Gladstone finally selected Ripon more with a view to fulfilling party commitments and avoiding Ripon's claims to membership of the Cabinet than because of his aptitude or ability. But Gladstone never later regretted his decision. Ripon had not the vibrant and compulsive influence of his leader, but he shared the latter's hopes and ideals and did his utmost to implement them in India. The immediate achievements were minor, but the impact on the minds of Indians was far-reaching. Because of Ripon, the influence of Gladstonian Liberalism became a permanent element in the political scene of British India.

Whatever the intrinsic merits of Ripon's policies, everyone in Britain, Liberal or Conservative, was agreed that his ways of promoting them had created high tension in India. It was an axiom of British policy at that time that the people should be kept in almost a stupor of contentment, for memories of the revolt of 1857 were still live enough to serve as a reminder of the thin surface of the stability of British rule. Ripon's administration had caused the volcano to rumble, and what seemed to be required thereafter was a period of tranquillization, when the placidity of Indian public life could be restored. For such a task, after Spencer had shown a lack of interest,[3] the choice was unanimous. No man seemed better suited than Dufferin to convert the high and commanding office of the Indian viceroyalty into a sedative. In him indolence had been developed into a virtue, and tact raised to the level of a policy.

The viceroyalty of India had for long been the goal of Dufferin's ambition. In 1863 Argyll wrote to him that 'only Lawrence's name stood in competition with yours for the Indian appointment'.[4] He had wished his name to be considered in 1872,[5] and was disappointed that his claims had been overlooked in 1880. 'My ambition', he wrote to Gladstone,[6] 'has always pointed East.' But Dufferin had no sense of duty or of mission. He was attracted not by the unrivalled scope for public service but by the grandeur and good living which attended the office. He had not given Indian problems serious thought and had no policies or programmes of his own. To him India provided only the highest office under the Crown, by occupying which he would attain the summit of his stylish, professional career. If Liberalism survived at all, it would be because it was to Dufferin's advantage.

II

The Afghan war had formed one of the main issues of the 1880 elections, and Ripon had, along with Gladstone and Argyll, been among Lytton's most vehement critics. 'We have now a real battle against a very wicked and base policy and must quit ourselves like men.'[7] Of the massacre of Kabul he observed, 'How swift the retribution has been—truly the Lord God omnipotent reigneth. . . . Who is the statesman now, Lawrence or Lytton.'[8] But by 1880 Lytton was a beaten man who was anxious to extricate himself from the Afghan morass as soon as possible;[9] and while some of his commitments were embarrassing, the Liberal Government were, on the whole, prepared to continue his efforts. Ripon was keen that all British troops should be withdrawn from Afghanistan by the end of the year and every effort made to establish as Amir the man likely to prove the best and most acceptable ruler. From this point of view, Abdur Rahman appeared to be the best candidate. The Amir, once established, should be assisted with arms and money but not with troops. British Residents need not be forced on the Amir, but a non-European agent might be stationed at Kabul. British troops should withdraw on the first favourable opportunity from Kandahar, unless this were contrary to the pledges given to the new ruler, all of which should be maintained. Persia should not be allowed to acquire Herat and the new Amir should be left free to take it. The British should withdraw from the Khyber and Kurram districts, though at one or two points the old frontier might be improved. But Ripon favoured the retention of Sibi and Pishin districts and the completion of a railway to Pishin.[10]

The negotiations with Persia were easily terminated. Granville, the Foreign Secretary, informed the Persian Minister at London that the treaty of 1857 precluding Persian intervention in Afghanistan was still in force and he was not inclined to resume the discussions initiated by Salisbury.[11] But otherwise the situation was difficult to disentangle. Lytton's policy of a series of petty chieftainships seemed to Ripon to be anarchy under another name;[12] but the 'late Government have made our bed, and we must lie on it'.[13] So often has Ripon been depicted as a reckless innovator that it is necessary to emphasize how firm was his respect for continuity in Indian policy and administration. That was the factor which determined his attitude in the first, and perhaps the most delicate, problem with which he was confronted in India. Ignoring the suggestions of Sir Lepel Griffin and Sir Donald Stewart, his political and military advisers in Afghanistan, that negotiations with Abdur Rahman be broken off and Yakub restored,[14] and taking no advantage of the Cabinet's decision liberating him from any obligation to find a sovereign for Afghanistan,[15] Ripon continued to deal with Lytton's nominee. Abdur Rahman was informed that he could establish his authority over all Afghanistan except Kandahar, Pishin and Sibi, and there would be no interference in his internal administration. As regards external relations, he should abide by British advice and have no political relations with any other foreign power; and in return the British would aid him if attacked.[16]

'It is felt on all hands', wrote Griffin, 'that the crisis has now come.'[17] Abdur Rahman had raised levies in different parts of the country, and Stewart's troops were ready for action. But the Government of India informed Griffin that a rupture with Abdur Rahman was most undesirable and no communications unfavourable to him should be sent to any other person even if negotiations with him failed.[18] Soon after, Abdur Rahman's reply accepting the offer was received. Though it was ambiguous in tone, the Viceroy considered it adequate enough to justify the continuance of negotiations. But in deference to the home government, who were anxious for an early withdrawal from Kabul, Stewart was authorized, if military circumstances required it, to terminate negotiations with Abdur Rahman and call upon his opponents to form a *de facto* government to which Kabul could be transferred.[19]

Stewart too wished to return to India as soon as possible. 'The people are sick of us and I am sure we are sick of them, and as we have publicly avowed our determination to withdraw this autumn, I am wholly unable to understand how anyone can advocate our clinging to Cabul a day longer than is necessary for our own purposes.'[20] He stopped work on constructions, reduced his staff, sent back some of his troops and made arrangements for total withdrawal.[21] But Ripon continued to seek a settlement with Abdur Rahman. On being informed that the latter had publicly expressed his desire for public recognition,[22] the Viceroy directed that Abdur Rahman be recognized, but not proclaimed or appointed, as Amir.[23] The distinction was intended to emphasize that the Government of India were not committed in any way to his future fortunes. So on 22 June Abdur Rahman was recognized as Amir of Kabul, and the British prepared to leave Afghanistan.

The Viceroy's self-congratulatory mood was, however, soon ended. Yakub's brother, Ayub, outmanoeuvred a British force in the vicinity of Herat and inflicted a crushing defeat. Such troops as escaped sought refuge in Kandahar. 'That 4600 effective troops including 1243 English should be cooped up by 10,000 Afghans of whom some 3000 are quite undisciplined can only be accounted for in the last way one would wish to account for it.'[24] To retrieve the situation and relieve Kandahar, General Roberts[25] was sent with a strong force from Kabul and negotiations with Abdur Rahman were expedited. The Amir, whom Griffin described as 'a singularly intelligent, pleasant and courteous man',[26] had no illusions about British policy. 'I am only a beast of burden; you are anxious to transfer to me the burden you no longer care to carry, and leave.'[27] Though disappointed in his efforts to secure a treaty and more money, Abdur Rahman assisted the British expedition. Roberts set out for Kandahar, and simultaneously the British withdrew from Kabul. Ripon believed that otherwise the tribes would have risen and the Afghan war would have been reopened; and this the state of the Indian army rendered it impossible to consider.[28] Stewart had reported that supplies were meagre, the number of troops was very few, sickness was prevalent, and the transport was rapidly wearing out.[29]

On 3 September Roberts routed Ayub's army. An influential school of thought now urged the annexation of Kandahar, as the troops of its Wali (ruler) set up by Lytton had joined Ayub and the Wali himself had abdicated; but the Viceroy and the home government were opposed to annexation.[30] Gladstone indeed was anxious that British troops should be withdrawn immediately from Kandahar. He was even prepared to consider, if need be, the restoration of the town to the defeated Ayub.[31] This was not thought practicable by the Government of India. But, despite the protests of a majority in council and Stewart's disclosures that the people of Kandahar were greatly opposed to the new Amir of Kabul and that he had informally assured them that they would never be placed under Abdur Rahman's authority,[32] Kandahar was transferred to Abdur Rahman in April 1881. The Khyber and Kurram districts were also evacuated; but the Viceroy desired to retain Pishin and Sibi. Though such clinging to a shred of the policy of the 'scientific frontier' seemed to the home government an unjustifiable compromise, they allowed Ripon to have his way.

The Viceroy wished to reinforce this Afghan settlement with an understanding with Russia. The British Ambassador at St Petersburg, Lord Dufferin, had stated even while the Conservatives were in office that it would be possible, if the British government desired it, to reinforce the defences of India with the 'collateral security' of some form of arrangement with Russia.[33] Salisbury had ordered that action on this information should be left to the new government;[34] and the response of the Liberals was warm. An agreement with Russia seemed far more important and valuable than any convention with Persia or friendship with Afghanistan could ever be; and once Lytton's dream of shattering the authority of Russia in Central Asia had been abandoned, there was no reason why the two powers should not be on the best of terms.

The professions of good faith of the Russian government were contradicted by the actions of the Russian generals. In the first year of Ripon's viceroyalty Russian armies pushed south to Ashkabad, hardly two hundred miles from Merv. The Russian Ambassador explained to Granville that this campaign had been unavoidable in the interests of law and order but the Russian government had no intention of getting entangled in further military operations in Central Asia and were anxious to end the prevailing antagonism between Britain and Russia.[35] Dufferin confirmed that this was the sincere intention of the Russian authorities from the Tsar downwards.[36] But the situation was really in the control of the local commanders, and their ambitions were stimulated by the Russian press. 'The Russian nation instinctively believes that the East belongs to it and its sons are ready to maintain their right by sacrificing their lives.'[37]

The British government, therefore, felt it necessary, despite official Russian assurances, to make a public declaration on 1 August 1881 that they would not tolerate any foreign interference in Afghanistan. Ripon and Hartington favoured a treaty with Russia on this basis. This was certainly more logical than the unilateral engagement with Abdur Rahman to assist him if he complied with British advice but with no obligation on his part either to seek or to follow such advice. Granville, however, did not regard such a treaty as worthwhile. He believed that whenever the English were on bad terms with the Russians, the latter, treaty or no treaty, would intrigue with the Afghans; and if the English wanted to fight, there would be plenty of excuses even without a treaty.[38] So Granville and the Foreign Office, when authorized by the Cabinet to make informal overtures to Russia, acted half-heartedly. Meantime Hartington, perhaps under the influence of his advisers Burne[39] and Rawlinson, had changed his views. Tsarist imperialism now seemed to him a carefully organized effort to menace British authority in India and he wished to challenge it vigorously. He proposed that Persia be strengthened and, when that scheme failed, suggested a close alliance with Abdur Rahman. Ripon thought that this would be to court disaster. The pivots of Liberal policy were non-interference in Afghanistan, the refusal to post British officers beyond the frontier and the consideration of Russian influence in Afghanistan as a matter to be taken up with the Russian government rather than with the Amir; and there seemed to the Viceroy no adequate reason for abandoning them.

The result of these differences of opinion was that no firm decision on policy was taken and there was a surrender to drift and fatalism.

But it does appear to me the most perplexing and almost hopeless question which it is possible to conceive. That we shall have trouble with the Russians in Afghanistan, I have very little doubt; and that it will be very unpleasant when it comes, appears to be equally certain. But I doubt whether there is any policy (Russian Treaty included) which would materially help to prevent the arrival of this trouble sooner or later.[40]

In December 1882, as part of a general shuffle, Hartington was succeeded at the India Office by Kimberley. Ever since his service at the British Embassy in St Petersburg in 1856, Kimberley had been interested in the problem of the Russian menace to India; in fact he admitted that this was the only topic connected with India of which he had any detailed knowledge.[41] He, like Granville and Hartington, had no faith in direct negotiations with Russia; and the home government directed the Viceroy, against his will, to promote closer relations with the Amir and to increase the subsidy paid to him. That this in itself was no barrier to Russian advance became clear in February 1884 when Merv was occupied. The British failure to formulate and act on a Central Asian policy had now borne fruit. There was only an ill-defined frontier separating the Russian empire from Afghanistan, and the Cabinet began negotiations with Russia, not for a treaty, of which Russia was now in no need, but for joint demarcation of the boundary. To this the Russian government agreed, for they too seemed interested in having defined limits for their territory.

Dufferin, who succeeded Ripon as Viceroy in December 1884, had the advantage of experience at St Petersburg, and was quickly seized of the Central Asian problem. The Secretary of State was of the view that Russia desired to be friendly and that a temporary understanding, even if not a final agreement, might be possible, although it was clear that Russia had designs upon Herat which she was certain to pursue at a convenient opportunity. So there was no immediate necessity for an interview with the Amir.[42] Dufferin agreed that any settlement with Russia, however disadvantageous, was preferable to none at all; for even during a little time thus secured, Herat could be fortified, Britain's position in Europe strengthened, the Egyptian imbroglio ended and preparations on the north-west frontier improved. India could do nothing to prevent Russia taking Herat; such a seizure could only be prevented by fear of the consequences. Indeed, if Russia occupied the town, British forces would either have to occupy all the passes in Afghanistan or retire behind the Indus. However, in addition to negotiations with Russia, an early interview with the Amir seemed desirable to Dufferin. He wrote that even Ripon had advised such a step.[43]

The initiative was taken by Russia. She proposed that the two governments should define the zone to be surveyed by boundary commissioners. Britain agreed and suggested that, to facilitate the commission's work, the Russians should withdraw from Pul-i-Khatun and the Afghans from Sari Yazi. Rejecting this proposal, Russia demanded instead that the Amir should withdraw from Panjdeh, which he had occupied in June 1884. According to Russia, both Pul-i-Khatun and Panjdeh lay outside Afghanistan.[44] Both the home and the Indian governments were convinced that these frontier claims were only a prelude to further aggression. The British military attaché at St Petersburg reported that Russia intended to attack Herat in the spring or as soon as British troops were tied down in the Sudan.[45] Kimberley warned the Russian Ambassador informally that Russian policy might lead to war. He also asked Dufferin to consider the feasibility of sending British troops into Herat. He said the Cabinet had decided that the Russian attitude of soft assurances and stealthy advances should be tolerated no longer, for public opinion in Britain favoured a firm policy and if at this crisis the Amir were deserted, the effect on Britain's position in India would be disastrous.[46] Granville instructed the British Ambassador to inform the Russian government that Britain was committed to regard as a hostile act any aggression upon the Amir's territory of which Herat was a salient point.[47] Dufferin agreed with this firm attitude and asked for more troops.[48]

Before the Government of India could assume this posture of defiance, Russian troops expelled the Afghans from Panjdeh on 30 March 1885 and forcibly occupied it. The news reached Rawalpindi, where the Amir had come, on the Viceroy's invitation, for an interview. Abdur Rahman spoke of wiping out the stain and said his people would compel him to do so even if he did not himself desire it. He, therefore, requested the Government of India to continue negotiations with Russia until he secured a chance of retaliation. When Dufferin remarked that the Russians were likely in that case to advance on Herat, he replied that it would be well defended. But for this purpose he would not seek British military assistance. He said his people were ignorant and suspicious and the presence of British troops in Afghanistan would be misunderstood. He would not permit even a few Muhamma- dan engineers in British service to go to Herat to strengthen its fortifications. He agreed only to British troops moving up to Kandahar in case Herat fell.

This seemed to Dufferin adequate. Kimberley said in the Cabinet that Russia should be told that an advance on Herat would be regarded as a *casus belli*, and that if Russia invaded undisputed Afghan territory Britain should support the Amir with troops.[49] But the Viceroy believed that Kandahar, and not Herat, was the outpost of British defences, and British commitments should not extend up to the frontiers of Afghanistan with Russia. That Russia was determined to take Herat, Dufferin had no doubt. He told the Amir that, as he was unwilling to rely on British military support, he should reach an agreement with Russia. 'In fact, in order to save a fatal blow at your heart, it would be better to cut off a bit of your little finger, especially as you say that it aches a good deal.' The Amir studied maps and agreed to accept any border that did not come further south than Zulficar and left Gulhan and Maru- chak in Afghanistan. To the loss of Panjdeh he was obviously, despite his bluster, indifferent, and Dufferin, greatly relieved, hinted to the home government that it could be quietly surrendered. 'It is out of the question that all England and India should be thrown into a flurry of excitement and a deluge of expense every time that a wretched Cossack chooses to shake his spear on the top of a sandhill over against Panjdeh.'[50] Thereupon the British govern- ment agreed to submit the issue to arbitration by the king of Denmark, and it was eventually decided to give up Panjdeh for Zulficar.

Though Lord Randolph Churchill, who in June 1885 took over from Kimberley as Secretary of State in the first Salisbury Govern- ment, regarded the arbitration as 'a highly ridiculous episode' and hoped to oust, with Bismarck's co-operation, Russia from Panjdeh,[51] Salisbury made no change in policy. Indeed, the Conservative Government placed their trust in Dufferin; and the Viceroy, who had been impressed with the Amir's shrewdness and moderation, wished to rely on him.[52] The Amir was given the one million rupees for which he had asked and 25,000 breech-loaders and heavy artillery for the defence of Herat. This support of the Amir had important consequences, for Britain was again nearly involved in war. A dispute regarding the extent of Zulficar led almost to the outbreak of hostilities with Russia.[53] A settlement of this issue was reached, but Salisbury publicly declared that the independence of Afghanistan was vital to the British position in India.

Dufferin thereafter maintained cordial relations with the Amir and also strengthened the frontier defences, and in this he received the support of both the Conservative and the Liberal Governments.[54] These efforts to promote friendship with Abdur Rahman seemed to Dufferin to yield results; 'every year', he wrote to Cross,[55] the Secretary of State in the Conservative Government of 1886, 'is improving our relations with the Afghan people, and if the battle of Armageddon be sufficiently delayed, we may really have coaxed and persuaded them out of all their ancient prejudices and hostilities'. What gave the Viceroy concern was the Amir's brutality, which almost destroyed whatever popular support he enjoyed;[56] and Dufferin was reluctant to side openly with the Amir in domestic affairs.[57] He wrote to the Amir offering to mediate between him and his enemies; but the home government disapproved of this. British officials were warned not to give the tribes the slightest encouragement to overthrow the Amir's rule.[58] For bloodthirsty as Abdur Rahman was, any successor might be worse.

With Russia, frontier negotiations made slow progress, and an agreement was finally reached on 22 July 1887.[59] Dufferin thought that though Britain had had, as usual, the worst of the bargain,[60] a definitive settlement was worthwhile if Russia could be convinced that any violation of this defined boundary would mean war. 'Russia should be kept where she is almost at any cost, for, mischievous as is even now her distant neighbourhood, she would become an intolerable nuisance when actually seated within our very skirts.' If she moved forward and occupied Herat, Britain would be compelled to advance to Kandahar; and while the Government of India took this into account and made preparations such as the storage of rails which would enable the occupation of Kandahar within three weeks, Dufferin was unwilling to assume such a step to be inevitable and to build railways for this purpose. The control of territory right up to the Hindu Kush mountains would, apart from everything else, involve a heavy outlay of money and a considerable increase of taxation.[61] Salisbury approved of this policy. The agreement with Russia should not induce the Government of India to relax the defence of the frontier; but the construction of a railway pointing straight at Kandahar might set alight the very inflammable chauvinism of the Moscow press.[62]

Dufferin, perhaps because of the presence of his private secretary, Mackenzie Wallace,[63] at his elbow, displayed in his conduct of Afghan and Central Asian affairs a wisdom which was absent in other spheres of his activity. The Amir was dealt with carefully. War was avoided over Panjdeh—a delicate achievement, for had Abdur Rahman insisted on recovering it, Britain was committed to his support. Moreover, the Amir was persuaded to accept the frontier demanded by Russia, even though this meant his abandonment of certain territorial claims. On the other hand, though convinced of the Amir's loyalty to Britain, Dufferin was unhappy at his treatment of his subjects, and the assistance given to him never went beyond the grant of money. The Viceroy had no wish to see Afghan tribesmen shot down by British bullets. At the same time, the refugees who flocked into Quetta were treated with consideration. To provide for the contingency of Abdur Rahman's overthrow or death, the Government of India took into custody all the possible claimants.

As for Russia, the agreement of 1887 was accepted as a final settlement. No provocation was given to Russia by thrusting British military influence into Afghanistan. But railway communications on India's own frontier were completed and the defences generally strengthened. Almost, as it were, as proof of this strength, Dufferin, in his last year in India, despatched a military expedition to the Black Mountain district on the north-western border to subdue the tribes which had murdered two British officers. This was intended as much to impress Russia and the Amir as to maintain peace on the north-west frontier.

III

The same moderation was not to be found in Dufferin's policy on the eastern frontier. The existence of a truncated independent kingdom in the northern part of Burma had always seemed to British expansionist and commercial interests to form a gap in the Indian empire. Mayo had sternly warned the officials in British

Burma not to interfere in the affairs of Upper Burma, as the annexation of this or any of the adjacent states was not an event which
the Viceroy contemplated or desired.[64] Northbrook, realizing that
this kingdom was at the mercy of British troops, took care to avoid
flimsy temptations for intervention although official opinion in
India demanded it and the home government would have accepted
it. Lytton had cast covetous eyes on Burma; but Ripon had refused to go to war. 'I have no belief in a policy of war to extend
trade.'[65] Remonstrances at the restrictions placed on British
commerce were sent to Mandalay, but the Burmese Court was
encouraged to send an envoy to discuss the matter. King Thibaw
responded to the suggestion and sent a mission to Simla. Though
the terms demanded by the mission were severe, Ripon believed
that negotiations would be worthwhile; for while the Burmese
expected great generosity from a Liberal Government, once they
were disillusioned they would probably accept whatever terms
were offered.[66] The Viceroy's efforts proved fruitless; but he had
succeeded in avoiding war and annexation.

On arrival, Dufferin found that Sir Charles Bernard,[67] the Chief
Commissioner of Burma, had changed his mind and was for intervention in Upper Burma. The moment seemed opportune; France
and China were preoccupied elsewhere, Thibaw was incapable of
firm resistance and his people would be indifferent. But the
Viceroy, 'with only one foot in the stirrup', had no desire to undertake a military adventure and directed Bernard to inform the
merchants of Rangoon that the Government of India had no intention of annexing Upper Burma.[68] The attitude of the home government was more qualified. While Kimberley agreed that Bernard's
proposal for a military expedition should not be acted upon at
once, he favoured annexation if that were required to exclude the
French, whose policy seemed to him to be governed by an aggressive and unquiet spirit. The Cabinet committee on foreign
affairs was for intervention not only to exclude the French but
even if there were a revolution in Burma; but it preferred the
establishment of a protectorate to annexation, as the latter might
alarm the Indian Princes.[69]

In the Viceroy's council there was a strong feeling that even a
protectorate should be postponed as long as possible and that mis-
rule and slackness of trade were not in themselves sufficient reasons for action. 'Let the Upper Burmese stew in their own juice,

but not boil over.' A Monroe doctrine should be applied to Burma and no European power should be allowed to secure financial or mercantile ascendancy there; but for this purpose pressure should be exercised in Paris rather than in Mandalay.[70] The home government were informed that the time for coercive measures in Burma was most inopportune and that the Government of India were opposed on principle to an annexationist policy.[71] Churchill also, surprisingly less bellicose than his Liberal predecessor, told Salisbury that the proper course would be to demand explanations from France and not from Burma.[72] But the Conservative Cabinet finally decided to leave the decision to the Viceroy, so that in the election campaign which seemed imminent they could attribute responsibility for any action to Dufferin.[73]

Despite the hesitancy of the home government, the opinion in his council and the advice of the two men in India with experience of Burma, Crosthwaite and Aitchison,[74] Dufferin now, in contrast to his earlier attitude, decided to force the issue. 'I am naturally an enemy of annexation, war and everything that can result in the loss of human life, but the violence of the Mandalay authorities compelled us to remonstrate, and they have returned a very unsatisfactory answer to a very friendly and moderate communication. This being the case, we must bring them to reason; and as when once one has to move, half measures too often lead to very bad results; with the consent of the Secretary of State, I have taken the bull by the horns, and have despatched an ultimatum which, if not replied to in a proper manner, will be supported by the despatch of ten thousand men up the Irrawaddy.'[75] Early in November General Prendergast[76] was directed to move into Upper Burma and conduct a sharp, certain and decisive campaign. While Thibaw and his family should be treated with every courtesy and consideration the primary objectives were a successful advance to Mandalay, the submission of the country and the safety of British troops. Prendergast carried out instructions and a kingdom larger in size than Britain was conquered with the loss of little over twenty men.

Once the Viceroy had, on his own responsibility, established British ascendancy in Upper Burma, the Salisbury Government became enthusiastic.[77] Of Dufferin's predecessors in India, Lytton sent his congratulations on Dufferin's doing what he himself should have done—an espousal of his cause which should have alarmed Dufferin—and urged him to annex; but both Ripon and Northbrook advised against annexation.[78] Dufferin told his Liberal friends, with disregard of truth, that his mind was as yet 'a perfect blank' upon the subject;[79] for he wrote the next day to Churchill that annexation might possibly prove the best policy.[80] Indeed, many weeks earlier, soon after the campaign, Dufferin had acknowledged that his instincts pointed to annexation and 'making a clean sweep of Upper Burmah'. Subordinate states were only possible if they were enclaves in British territory.[81] But before events could be pushed past the point of revocability, the Liberals returned to power. Dufferin had now to persuade. He wrote to Kimberley, again Secretary of State, that the border of the empire was not a good location for a protected state and there was no candidate whom the British could trust or the Burmese were specially anxious to adopt. He, therefore, 'perfectly unprejudiced by any Jingo sentimentality', pleaded for annexation. 'I look upon the necessity of having to take this country as a great nuisance, and I am well aware that, though ultimately its acquisition may prove advantageous to us, for some time to come it will breed nothing but trouble and annoyance.'[82]

Kimberley, as was to be expected of a man who had suggested annexation even in 1885, was more of Dufferin's new way of thinking than either Ripon or Northbrook. It was, in his opinion, indispensable to cancel the treaties between Burma and foreign powers; and this could be done only by annexation. The lawyers who had been consulted declared that after these treaties had been erased Burma could again be set up as a princely state; but Kimberley thought that such juggling was not likely to deceive anybody. Nor was any prince available who, if set up, could maintain himself. So, considering all the circumstances, Kimberley thought there was no alternative to Dufferin's proposal.[83] 'The annexation of Upper Burmah was a necessity, and when that is said, all is said.'[84] Northbrook felt that a mistake was being made,[85] Ripon acquiesced reluctantly[86] and Gladstone was uneasy;[87] but the majority in the government and Parliament warmly supported Dufferin, and Upper Burma was annexed 'with great reluctance'.[88]

This, however, was not the end of the Burma problem. Dufferin soon found that administering the area was even more difficult than acquiring it. He complained that the very reasons which had enabled occupation without opposition gave rise to the greatest difficulty. For the Burmese were like children; there was no co-hesion amongst them and it was as difficult to coerce them into a consistent whole as it was to solidify a handful of sand.[89] Bernard did not possess the administrative vigour to cope with such a problem and the correspondent of *The Times*, who had a personal dislike of Dufferin, magnified the shortcomings in his despatches. The indolent optimism of the Viceroy was severely shaken.

I cannot help sometimes smiling at the anomaly of a Viceroy of India in the midst of his many cares and anxieties being compelled to spend so much time as it has already cost me to refute and disprove the fabri-cations disseminated by a rowdy and discredited Barrister,[90] especially after his untruthfulness has already been so fully exemplified. But I suppose I must command my patience, as this is one of the characteris-tics incident to the new aspects of modern Parliamentary Government.[91]

He wrote a long minute justifying his conduct of the administra-tion of Burma and sent copies to prominent figures in Britain, including both the Prime Minister and the Leader of the Opposi-tion.[92] Salisbury at least was satisfied. 'I think you completely establish your case that the Indian Government has done its work well, and that no blame can attach to it for the apparent delay in the restoration of complete tranquillity. . . . When the operation is looked at as a whole from the distance of the future, it will be held to be a very remarkable achievement.'[93] But such minutes and encomia could not conceal the fact that disorder and discontent prevailed in Burma; and Allan Hume, the retired civil servant who had gained the confidence of the educated Indians and had helped them to organize for political purposes, suggested to the harassed Viceroy that the British withdraw from Burma.[94] The Viceroy sought to argue that marauders and robbers and not patriots or guerrilla fighters were responsible for the troubles; but it is doubtful if even he himself was fully convinced of this. 'Of course I do not mean to say that the Burmese like having their country taken from them; but, as far as I can ascertain, the great mass of the people will cheerfully acquiesce in our rule, if only they see that we can give them protection from their tormentors, justice and decent government.'[95] Anxious to rid himself of this problem—and to let the world forget it—as soon as possible, Dufferin ordered the army to act with humanity but without undue leniency or excessive expenditure.[96]

The world being what it is, it soon did forget the harsher aspects of Dufferin's Burma policy, and by 1888 one of his friends could write that everybody in Britain was agreed that annexation had not only been an inevitable necessity but was proving very satisfactory and promising.[97] Salisbury encouraged the Viceroy to choose for his marquisate a title connected with Burma. 'No such splendid acquisition has been made certainly since Dalhousie's time; possibly since Wellesley's.'[98] So Ava, where the Burmese court met in its final phase, found its place into Debrett; and in return Dufferin left as his last command to the Chief Commissioner, Crosthwaite, instructions that some place in Upper Burma should be called after him.[99] A hill station, therefore, was given the name of Dufferin. To the Viceroy the acquisition of Upper Burma was the peak of his Indian career, worthy of immortalization. In fact, it cast a dark shadow on an otherwise colourless viceroyalty.

IV

It was, however, internal rather than foreign affairs which offered full scope for any positive Liberal achievement, for any effort to establish that India was being governed as a trust in the interests of her people and not solely as a means of advancing British interests. If the Conservative adventure was mainly in foreign affairs with India serving as a base kept in order, a Liberal experiment would have to be centred within India.

Ripon's first impact on domestic affairs was vigorous and effective. In spite of half-heartedness in London and Simla and vigorous opposition from the Bengal government, he introduced factory legislation into India. The Act itself was a halting measure with which the Viceroy was not satisfied. 'I shall always regret that I yielded to Sir A. Eden's strong wish that the minimum age for the employment of a child should be reduced from 8 to 7. I was quite wrong, and I wish to have my opinion on that point on record.'[100] Even so, this Act opened a new phase in the industrial history of India.

The Viceroy next, acting on what was virtually a specific mandate from Gladstone, repealed Lytton's Vernacular Press Act. 'A free press,' Ripon told the editors who presented him with an address of thanks,[101] 'wisely conducted, must always be of great assistance to the Government, and, in my opinion, the limited extent to which representative institutions exist in this country

The Liberal Experiment

makes the provision of an unfettered press especially important.'
This removal of restrictions on the press was a step which the
Government of India never had cause to regret for the rest of the
century, even in periods of high tension.[102] Ripon also planned to
amend the rigorous Arms Act of 1878, which had made it difficult
for Indians to possess firearms; but his bill failed to receive,
despite the support of Gladstone, the approval of the India Office.

Apart from the Factory Act, however, these early domestic
reforms of Ripon were all part of the 'great undoing process which
the late Government bequeathed to us'.[103] It is the later, construc-
tive efforts, which form the core of Ripon's Liberal policy and vest
his term with significance. Eager to strengthen local self-government, he drafted, with the assistance of Evelyn Baring,[104] the
finance member, resolutions inviting the provincial authorities to
consider ways and means of increasing both the association of non-
officials with the activities of government and the powers of the
local bodies. As the agencies of 'deprovincialization', the Government of India favoured municipalities and district committees, with
ancillary subdivisional committees. The provincial expenditure
which could be transferred to local control with the greatest advantage appeared under the heads of health, education and public
works, but other items could also be considered. On the other
hand, municipal bodies should be relieved of charges for police
administration as they exercised no control over it and could hardly
be expected to take any interest in it. Transfer of items of responsibility should not involve additions to the existing financial
burdens of the local authorities; adequate receipts should also be
made over. These should be of such a character as to afford a
reasonable prospect of increase if administered carefully and with
local sympathy and knowledge.

Such great attention to detail on the part of Ripon's government only served to smother the spirit of his policy; and most
provincial governments considered his reform of local self-
government a matter of administrative reorganization rather than
a scheme to make official authority more responsive and the non-
official element more responsible. In Bombay, for example, the
system of local government was acknowledged to have fallen into
complete desuetude. The municipalities outside the presidency
towns were a 'set of dummies', and the district and *taluk* (sub-
division) committees were 'dead and buried'.[105] Yet the Bombay

government were satisfied that no further powers could be transferred and were prepared to do no more than extend the elective system to ten city municipalities.[106] So in May 1882 Ripon and Baring issued another resolution stating clearly the principles which had inspired them. The development of local self-government should be essentially an effort to promote self-confidence among the educated classes of India and to train them for participation in government. In all local bodies, therefore, non-officials should constitute at least two-thirds of the total number and should preferably be elected. These bodies should then, under the supervision of the government, exercise considerable initiative of action with regard to matters transferred to them; and if any of these bodies were ever found to be consistently remiss in the performance of its duties, it could be superseded with the permission of the central government.

These ideals, while unexceptionable, were also unpalatable to most British officials, who set to work, with the staunch support of the retired seniors of the India Council, to defeat Ripon's policy in practice. When in the Central Provinces the Viceroy sought to introduce a very limited measure of local self-government in the rural areas, a despatch was received from London stressing the need for official control of local bodies and criticizing the general application of the principle of election. In the North-West Provinces the brilliant but cynical Lieutenant-Governor, Sir Alfred Lyall,[107] was not enthusiastic. 'I think the general idea, if moderately developed, is good enough, but it is all experimental.'[108] However, Lyall implemented Ripon's policy loyally, at least in the municipalities. Aitchison of the Punjab framed legislation in accordance with the views of the Government of India; but the bills formulated by the Bengal government fell, even after revision, far short of expectations, and Kimberley, no ardent advocate of local self-government, rejected the draft statute pertaining to the districts. The government of Bombay initiated a public controversy with the Government of India on the merits of Ripon's policy, and implemented that policy in a very weak form. The Viceroy had more faith in Madras, whose Governor was a Liberal. 'If Bombay is to blow its Tory penny whistle, why should not Madras sound its Liberal trumpet?'[109] This was to exaggerate Grant Duff's command of his executive; whatever his personal beliefs, the decisions lay with his officials, and it required Ripon's intervention to secure legislation which at least enabled, if it did not stipulate, elected non-official chairmen of local bodies.

It is, in fact, surprising not that Ripon achieved so little advance in local self-government but that, despite the massive official inertia, he yet managed to attain so much. He himself attached the greatest importance to his efforts in this sphere. To instruct Indians in public administration and political responsibility was to him not merely expedient but in the highest traditions of imperial trustee-ship. 'Among the political objects attainable in India I see at present none higher.'[110] If Indians could not with safety be edu-cated and allowed a share in the management of their own local affairs, then the days of British rule were numbered and its justi-fication had ceased.[111]

'I hope', wrote Ripon of his local self-government policy, 'that I am planting a tree which will afford food and shelter to many generations of men.'[112] It proved to be a tree which never took firm root. Local self-government never gained major significance in the political history of modern India. The most seminal occur-rence of Ripon's viceroyalty was not the extension of local self-government but a development which was well nigh unplanned.

Most Englishmen, official and non-official, in India were still, in Ripon's words, of 'the type who regards India and her inhabi-tants as made for his advantage and for that alone, who never looks upon himself in any other light than that of conqueror, and upon the natives otherwise than as "subject races"'.[113] They resented the creation of an educated Indian class and the encouragement given to it to develop a political consciousness. Any suggestion that this class would inherit the future was anathema to them. But this, of course, was the heart of Gladstone's Indian policy. 'We have undertaken a most arduous but a most noble duty. We are pledged to India, I may say to mankind, for its performance; and we have no choice but to apply ourselves to the accomplish-ment of the work, the redemption of the pledge, with every faculty we possess.'[114] It was, too, in this spirit that Ripon carried out his duties. 'I get more Radical every day and am rejoiced to say that the effect of despotic power has so far been to strengthen and deepen my liberal convictions.'[115] Gladstone expressed his satis-faction; but the uneasiness of the British community deepened to apprehension.

There were many minor points of friction between the viceregal executive and the various elements of Anglo-Indian society in the early years of Ripon's term. Apart from the very different ideas as to the ultimate purpose of British rule in India and the feeling of the British community that Ripon's acts were throughout inspired by a desire to humiliate it, the Viceroy's personality irritated his fellow-countrymen. Indeed, Baring believed that it was not so much what he did as what he said that excited so much adverse criticism.[116] In converse proportion, Indians began to look to him almost for leadership.

The new factor in India is Lord Ripon's popularity—a very astonishing phenomenon to one accustomed to go round the provinces year after year, and to find the people unconscious of any governing personality more remote than the District Officer. I have observed, in the great cities which the Commission has visited, if the municipal orator is at a loss in his address he merely begins some irrelevant sentence with the words 'Lord Ripon', and the people cheer so loud and so long that he has ample time to recover himself.[117]

Thus the Viceroy had already become a controversial figure when a fresh, and more serious, crisis developed in 1883. In the preceding year, an Indian member of the civil service had protested that if Indians were in theory eligible for all posts in the administration, it was improper and unreasonable, under an Act of 1872, passed soon after Mayo's death, to deny them jurisdiction over Europeans in the country districts even for trivial offences. The law member commented that the case had been stated very fairly.[118] The Viceroy was sympathetic[119] and the executive council unanimously decided to give the matter careful consideration.[120] Thereafter the matter was referred to the local governments; and while there were differences of opinion among them as to the way in which the anomaly should be redressed, there was only one warning—and that from Madras—of possible opposition from the British community to any change. Not a single official in northern India, where the outcry was to be the loudest, had any premonition of it. As Baring wrote many years later, the main lesson of the events of 1883 was the proof that it was possible at times for the whole body of Indian civilians, taken collectively, to be unsafe guides in matters of state policy.[121]

Beguiled by these reports, the Government of India considered the matter as one almost of routine. Baring admitted that he merely glanced at the papers and initialled them without giving the subject much attention.[122] Even the civilian members of council sounded no alarm.[123] Proposals to amend the Act of 1872 were forwarded to the home government, who agreed that the time had come to remove racial discrimination among judges. Only Sir Henry Maine, then a member of the India Council, thought it possible that there might be resistance in India; but his reservation was inadvertently never communicated to the Viceroy. So in February 1883 the new law member, Sir Courtenay Ilbert, introduced a bill abolishing the principle of jurisdiction on the basis of race.

To the surprise of the government, the reaction was immediate and spontaneous. The correspondent of *The Times* reported from Calcutta on the 4th, two days after the bill had been published, that the government 'has suddenly sprung a mine on the European community' and that there could be no doubt that the bill would be intensely unpopular with them.[124] The general dislike of Ripon and the home government which he represented crystallized round this particular issue; and the opposition was quickly organized.

The Viceroy recognized and regretted his mistake. He had acted after consulting those with much greater experience of India, and the excitement clearly had roots reaching far deeper than this particular measure; but the Ilbert Bill (as it soon became known) was 'an error in tactics, which has exposed my flank to the enemy, who has made the utmost use of the advantage thus offered him'.[125] However, retreat was impossible. Ripon declared that the bill was a right and a reasonable measure which could do no harm.[126] Indians had shown themselves capable of judicial work, there would be few cases in practice when they would be required to exercise criminal jurisdiction over European British subjects, and the government could not openly justify a distinction which, as Macaulay had observed in 1836,[127] proclaimed to the Indian people that there were two sorts of justice—a coarse one which was thought good enough for them and another of superior quality which the British kept for themselves. But the British non-official community was impervious to argument, and it was encouraged in its blind fury by British officials. Rivers Thompson, who had succeeded Eden as Lieutenant-Governor of Bengal, opposed the bill in the legislative council as unnecessary and inopportune;[128] and he had the support of all the British civil servants in Bengal and of the Chief Justice and the ten British judges of the Calcutta High Court. The Chief Commissioner of Assam also advocated withdrawal of the bill as it did not seem to him important or urgent enough to justify permanently alienating the British community. In Madras, the Governor in Council thought withdrawal of the bill in deference to opposition would be a grave political error; but he suggested that jurisdiction of this nature should be granted only to those Indians who had been admitted to the civil service by competition. The governments of the other provinces also suggested amendments of the bill and the grant of judicial powers over Englishmen to a few very senior Indian judges. The Chief Justice of Madras approved of the principle, but the Chief Justices of Bombay and Allahabad expressed their unqualified condemnation.[129]

The Viceroy and the home government, while they deplored the pusillanimity of these officials who had surrendered to the pressure of the society in which they lived,[130] realized that it gave the problem a new complexion. The British community had openly organized themselves for almost mutinous opposition. The educated Indians too, though less vociferous than the British, began to show signs of irritation; and the editor of *The Englishman*, the leading British-owned newspaper of Calcutta, believed that 'we are on the eve of a crisis which will try the power of the British Government in a way in which it has not been tried since the Mutiny of 1857'.[131] To persist with the bill as it stood would, of course, have been the right thing to do; but it is doubtful if anyone in authority in Britain or India, barring Gladstone, had the necessary courage and determination. Certainly Ripon was not the man for this crisis. He believed in his master's principles but lacked his moral stamina and intellectual strength. The Government of India, setting aside considerations of prestige, offered to reduce the scope of the bill and grant criminal jurisdiction over European British subjects only to Indian district magistrates and sessions judges, with the right vested in the High Courts to transfer any case if they regarded the judge before whom it was posted as unfit to try it.[132] To have modified the bill any further, wrote the Viceroy,[133] would have reduced it to a sham.

Gladstone was not pleased with Ripon's anxiety to compromise.

In principle [he wrote to the Viceroy][134] I have been and am strongly with you, and as to tactics my own judgment has never gone beyond keeping the question open. After reading what you very candidly say,

I feel that an error may have been committed, but I am by no means sure that it has been committed. . . . There is a question to be answered: where, in a country like India, lies the ultimate power, and if it lies for the present on one side but for the future on the other, a problem has to be solved as to preparation for that future, and it may become right and needful to chasten the saucy pride so apt to grow in the English mind towards foreigners, and especially towards foreigners whose position has been subordinate.

When a Conservative Member of Parliament described Ripon as 'a crotcheteer, a sentimentalist and a pseudo-humanitarian', Gladstone retorted that so were all the members of the Liberal Government and party. They believed that Ripon was a wise and just man, and no part of his long public career had been more honourable or more beneficial than the years in India.[135] But Gladstone and the Cabinet were unwilling to go beyond general assurances of confidence and to take a specific decision on the particular issue of the Ilbert Bill. It was for Ripon, with his knowledge of the situation in India, to determine the steps to be taken; the home government would not relieve the Viceroy of his responsibility but would accept whatever modifications he suggested, however damaging to the principle of which they approved. When Ripon telegraphed that a discussion in the House of Commons on the bill would be very desirable, he was informed that the state of parliamentary business quite forbade it and that delay in passing the bill should be avoided.[136]

So the Viceroy could neither evade nor postpone a decision. The proposed changes in the bill did not satisfy European opinion in Bengal and its resistance continued to be as dogged as ever. When the Viceroy returned to Calcutta for the winter, the 'Mammon of unrighteousness whose temple has been set up on the banks of the Hughli'[137] was subjected to petty impertinences. The atmosphere overwhelmed all his colleagues in the executive council except Ilbert,[138] and they advised Ripon to weaken the bill further. They argued that the question of jurisdictional privileges took the place with Europeans of religious fanaticism and that a wise government should put an end as quickly as possible to any contest concerning these privileges. Otherwise agitation would become increasingly violent, no jury in Calcutta would convict a European and 'Calcutta would soon be a place where the Viceroy could not safely reside'. European policemen were not stationed in the districts and any effort by the Indian police to subdue the English in those areas would cause a 'white' revolt, civil war and chaos. To these dangers a defeat, however serious, for the Government of India was preferable.[139] Ripon was persuaded to approve of negotiations with the leaders of the European opposition. He authorized Sir Auckland Colvin,[140] Baring's successor as finance member, to conduct these negotiations; and after many schemes had been considered and rejected, Colvin finally evolved a formula whereby mixed juries, consisting of Europeans to the extent of at least half the number, would be associated with trials of European British subjects before district magistrates and sessions judges. It was in this almost unrecognizable form that the Ilbert Bill was finally enacted. The British community in India had gained a resounding victory and the Liberalism for which Gladstone stood had received a severe buffeting. It was primarily a failure of the Viceroy.

> The mistaken attempts to correct mistakes
> By methods which prove to be equally mistaken.

Dufferin's first task in India on his arrival in December 1884 was to restore the equilibrium of Indian society, so badly jolted by Ripon. In Calcutta Ripon had been distrusted by the civil servants and cursed by the non-official British community, while Indians had hailed him as a deliverer; and the Governors of Bombay and Madras reported that conditions were little better in their presidencies.[141] Dufferin's own inclination to smooth things over and be popular with all was supported by Grant Duff, who urged 'a soothing, cautious, nay even dull policy',[142] and by the Secretary of State. 'I need not say', wrote Kimberley,[143] 'how entirely I agree with you that it is most important to put an end to the division of whites and blacks into two hostile camps. Besides the annoyance it causes, the prolongation of such discussions might have serious political results.' Kimberley was right in that, while the vast majority of the Indian population was unconcerned with these developments, the Government of India could not afford to be confronted for any length of time with a resentful British community and smouldering Indian opinion. So the new Viceroy offered what he termed peace to his fellow-countrymen in India and informed his council that there would be little activity for some time once the pending tenancy bill had been disposed of;[144]

but he also took care to pay a tribute to his predecessor and to stress that continuity was the chief characteristic of British rule in India.[145]

This was intended, of course, to win over Indian opinion. If Dufferin can be said to have had a policy at all, it was at a personal level; he was eager to be popular with Indians, even more popular, if possible, than Ripon, without losing the favour of the British. Unlike Ripon, he soon developed a dislike for the educated Indians whom he saw around him.

I have already discovered that the Bengalee Baboo is a most irritating and troublesome gentleman, and I entirely agree with you in thinking that we must not show ourselves at all afraid of him. He has a great deal of Celtic perverseness, vivacity and cunning, and seems to be now employed in setting up the machinery for a repeal agitation, something on the lines of O'Connell's Patriotic Associations.[146]

But he believed he could outmatch them.

To placate Indian opinion further, Dufferin proposed the formation of two Indian regiments with Indian officers. While Northbrook supported the suggestion, Kimberley was more inclined to give Indians only appointments in the higher ranks of the army and not to raise Indian regiments, though it was unlikely that British officers and soldiers would consent to serve under Indians.[147] But the demand in India was for an Indian volunteer corps. Gibbs, the retiring home member, thought such a body would do no harm and might even do good if recruitment were limited to the gentry.[148] A contrary opinion was held by Lyall of the North-West Provinces. He believed that volunteering was a peculiarly English institution which was no more suited to the political conditions of India than to the atmosphere of Austria or Russia. Any extensive recruiting of Indian volunteers would alarm the British community and further complicate any future occasion of Hindu-Moslem discord. He, therefore, advised the Government of India to avoid a decision as long as possible.[149]

The Viceroy, reluctant to reject outright an offer that seemed to be born of loyalist sentiment at the time of the Panjdeh crisis but also unwilling to create what might acquire the proportions of a large Indian citizen army,[150] played for time by consulting Hume, with whom Ripon had advised him to cultivate friendly relations.[151] The fact that under the law volunteer companies could not be formed without the sanction of the Secretary of State and might even require an Act of Parliament enabled him to avoid an immediate decision. Hume met the Viceroy and thereafter issued a circular assuring his Indian friends that there was no apathy on the part of the government and the country could not do better than trust in the Viceroy and be patient. 'Be the issue what it may, I think I am justified in saying that Lord Dufferin thoroughly appreciated the loyal spirit in which our people have tendered their services as volunteers, and that we shall find in him a consistent and earnest, and at the same time, a wise and prudent friend.'[152] Dufferin secured this testimonial despite his rejection of Hume's suggestion that the Governor of Bombay should preside over the Indian National Congress which was to hold its first session that winter.[153]

The demand for Indian volunteers was soon almost forgotten, no doubt to Dufferin's great relief, for all the Residents except the one in Mysore and all the local governments except the Punjab, Bombay and Burma were opposed to any concession in this respect.[154] In the council, only Ilbert and Colvin were strongly in favour of it.[155] But it had served to win the Viceroy the friendship of Hume who told Dufferin that the government's failure even to express sympathy for the demand had hurt the Indian community. 'They are grumbling away about this matter, of course unreasonably, but children will be children, and our grown up *men* are few and far between.'[156] The Viceroy's almost deferential attitude to Hume, even while he paid little serious attention to Hume's proposals, acquired for him an undeserved reputation of being a true successor of Ripon; 'you are already *suspect* . . . of entertaining pro-native ideas'.[157]

Dufferin had, of course, no intention of following in Ripon's footsteps and, as he termed it, 'Midlothianizing' India.[158] 'It is our duty carefully to watch the signs of the times, and cautiously and conscientiously to liberalize the administration of India, but I am sure it would be a mistake if we identified ourselves personally either with the reforming or the reactionary enthusiasts.'[159] He believed that Ripon had had an exaggerated opinion of the educated Bengali. Dufferin for his part preferred to pay more attention to the landed interests and other conservative sections of society. With the instincts of a landlord, he was full of misgivings about the Bengal Tenancy Bill drafted by Ripon's Government in order to alleviate the conditions of the tenants. Dufferin thought it had been conceived in great ignorance of the facts and impressed with an unnecessarily violent and one-sided character by its two Irish draftsmen, MacDonnell and O'Kinealy.[160] Even MacDonnell admitted that two separate bills were required for Bengal and for Bihar, as conditions in the two areas were wholly different; in Bihar the raiyats needed protection against the zemindars while in Bengal the zemindars needed protection against the raiyats.[161] But the Viceroy told the zemindars, who had been encouraged to resist by the promise of support of the Conservative party given by 'that mischievous wretch Randolph Churchill',[162] that he would go through with the bill, and the result was that they were disposed to come to terms. Dufferin made it easier for them by modifying certain provisions so as to make the bill more moderate, and as finally passed it favoured the raiyat, according to Dufferin, no more than was necessary or just.[163] Ripon thought that Dufferin had made more concessions to the zemindars than he himself would have done.[164] The raiyats themselves were not satisfied, and within a few years there were the beginnings of agitation; but the government almost welcomed this, for agrarian discontent would compel the landed interests to draw closer to the authorities.[165]

There was a similar tenancy problem in Oudh. The talukdars realized the need for safeguarding the tenants from frequent ejection and would have accepted a measure of control; but, frightened by the Bengal Bill, Kimberley and the India Council vetoed the moderate proposals of the government of the North-West Provinces and substituted a scheme which was far more arbitrary and likely to frighten the landholders more.[166] Churchill who, on his visit to India in 1885, had met the leading talukdars in Lucknow, was not in favour of any legislation which was not acceptable to them. 'A moment might come when there was a great strain on India, when the irritated Talookdars might play an analogous part to that which they did in 1857.'[167] But he was willing, in this as in all matters, to let the Viceroy decide, and Dufferin was convinced that the condition of the peasantry in Oudh was intolerable and that there was need for cautious legislation such as Lyall had advocated.[168] Indeed, Lyall himself suggested revision of the Oudh Tenancy Bill in the interests of the landholders for political reasons. The talukdars still adhered to the notion that it was their duty and in their interest to obey the government, and it was expedient to give them no reasonable grounds for abandoning this notion, especially as there were many persons in Lucknow anxious to convince them that opposition was the only way of dealing with the government.[169] So compensation to be paid by the landlord for eviction of a tenant, which had originally been fixed at a year's rent, was changed, as suggested by the talukdars,[170] into a stamp duty on a notice of eviction. This, as Dufferin recognized, was a most illogical and absurd device,[171] for compensation for eviction would be paid not to the tenant concerned but to the government. But now the Oudh tenancy law fulfilled the condition of acceptability to the talukdars while it ensured fixity of tenure for seven years to tenants-at-will and entitled them on eviction to compensation for improvements made less than thirty years before.

The same eagerness to enlist the support of the conservative elements of Indian society lay behind other decisions of Dufferin. He encouraged Lyall's proposal for a legislative council in the North-West Provinces, although such a council would have little work, because it would please the landholders.[172] He did his best, in public and in private, to ensure that the Princes were treated with consideration and their administration protected from unnecessary interference. The fort of Gwalior was restored to Scindia, and the Viceroy hoped that this would impress all India as the clearest signal of his general policy.[173] He established friendly relations on a personal basis with all the leading Princes except Holkar. He believed rightly that as time passed the Princes would lean increasingly on the British as their sole protection against the flood of advancing democracy; and he thought that there was no risk involved in encouraging them, for they were never likely to act in concert except under British pressure.[174]

Dufferin's financial policy also was part of this pattern. Both the Viceroy and the home government were convinced of the dangers of over-taxation in India. It was his duty, wrote Dufferin within two months of assuming office, to protect the Indian tax-payer from unfair burdens because of the extreme poverty of the country and the instability of the financial system.[175] 'What you will have to do', wrote Northbrook,[176] 'and no one can do it better, is to keep our rule as popular as is possible in India; and this is, I believe, to be done by making as few changes as possible, and especially by avoiding fresh taxes, and of fresh taxes especially direct taxes, and of direct taxes, especially the income tax.' Kimberley too did not like the notion of increased taxation, still less of an income tax.[177]

Despite this unanimity of opinion, the Government of India had their hands forced; for there was a large increase of military expenditure, which necessarily meant increased taxation. The finance member, Colvin, disclosed ten years later that from 1885, with the establishment of Russian power in Central Asia, the balance of influence in the Viceroy's council between the finance member and the other members, more especially the military members, had been radically disturbed by the very great preponderance given to military considerations.[178] Dufferin would have preferred to retrench rather than to increase taxation[179] but the scope for this was limited; and the Viceroy, whatever his prejudices, was obliged, under the pressure of increasing expenditure and depreciation in the value of silver, to seek new sources of revenue. Aitchison, by nature cautious and conservative, advocated that the license tax, to which the people had resigned themselves, should now be expanded into an income tax. 'The abolition of the income tax, in deference to the selfish clamour of Calcutta merchants and the Government services, has always appeared to me to be one of our greatest administrative blunders.'[180] Dufferin was inclined to agree. He felt that Baring's abolition of the customs duties in 1882 had been a mistake because it had exempted a rich class which could well afford to bear its share of the public burdens. So an income tax, rather than an increase of the salt duties, to which the new Secretary of State, Churchill, was opposed, seemed the answer. Its incidence was indiscriminate in that it would affect both Indians and Europeans—an added advantage in the prevailing political atmosphere. Once Indians felt that the British in India were taxing themselves as well as the people, they would reconcile themselves to their fate.[181] The matter was discussed in council and it was decided to extend the license tax to all incomes other than those derived from land, Dufferin being still resolute in defence of landed interests. The Viceroy had much difficulty in inducing his colleagues not to recommend a high rate of tax.[182]

The proposal to extend the license tax was, to the Viceroy's great relief and surprise,[183] well received. The Chambers of

Commerce of both Bombay and Calcutta supported the government, and the Indian press was not hostile. Even with this additional revenue, the Government of India were faced in 1885 with a deficit; but the Salisbury Ministry was unwilling to approve of either a reimposition of import duties or an enhancement of the salt duties.[184] The next year, however, the financial situation grew worse. Expenditure on railway construction was about ten million pounds, the revenue from opium declined, the price of silver continued to fall and Burma and frontier defences caused a heavy drain. The net deficit was about four million pounds. Colvin and his deputy, James Westland,[185] therefore, once again urged an increase in salt duties. Westland also suggested an import duty on petroleum.[186] Cross, who succeeded Kimberley as Secretary of State in August 1886, finding that Salisbury had no objection, agreed with great reluctance to the increase in salt duties.[187] Westland calculated that the increased cost of salt to a family of man, wife and three children would not annually exceed eight annas.[188] A small duty was imposed on petroleum also. The articulate section of the public, which had expected an increase in the income tax, raised no objection to the burden being placed instead on weaker shoulders. 'I flatter myself', wrote Dufferin, 'it is not every Viceroy who could have put on an Income Tax, and after two years again increased the taxation of the country to the amount of a million and a half with so small fuss being made about it.'[189]

It was not the co-operation of the upper classes alone which Dufferin solicited; he also from the start encouraged the Moslems to regard themselves as a distinct political entity in India. On his arrival in Bombay, he stated that he had spent much of his life among Moslems and that he would watch with pleasure over the interests of the Moslems in India. In fulfilment of this pledge he took steps to mitigate the hardships of the *Haj* pilgrimage and learnt Persian in order to converse with Moslems. Wherever he went in India, he let it be known that he was anxious to promote the education of Moslems and to appoint a greater number of them in the public service.[190] The Government of India also published a resolution recommending the greater employment of Moslems.

Those who have the privilege of making appointments should realize that something more has to be considered than the convenience of the moment; that, besides the efficiency of the public service, which is always the first thing to be regarded, it is necessary also to attend to the due distribution of places of emolument, so as to prevent the depression of a numerous and influential class, and secure their co-operation for the general benefit of the administration.[191]

Of all the provincial governments, it was the government of Bengal which was the foremost in implementing this resolution.[192]

This effort to accentuate the separatist feeling among the Moslems of India and win their support for the government yielded results. One consequence of Dufferin's activity, as he himself complacently acknowledged,[193] was a recrudescence of communal rioting. The spread of education and improved prospects of public service, instead of bridging the gulf between the two communities, gradually transformed religious animosity to political rivalry among the educated classes.[194] Both the Muhammadan National Association, which represented educated Moslem opinion, and the more conservative Muhammadan Literary Society, though they disliked each other, declined in 1886 to participate in the session of the Indian National Congress. In 1888, the year Dufferin left India, Sir Syed Ahmad, the leader of the educated Moslems, wrote to Badruddin Tyabji, one of the Moslem members of the Congress, regretting that Tyabji had taken a leading part in the Congress session at Madras.

I do not understand what the words 'National Congress' mean. Is it supposed that the different castes and creeds living in India belong to one nation, or can become (one) nation, and their aims and aspirations be one and the same? I think it is quite impossible. . . . You regard the doings of the misnamed National Congress as beneficial to India, but I am sorry to say that I regard them as not only injurious to our own community but also to India at large.

Tyabji replied that the Congress was 'nothing more and should be nothing more than an assembly of educated people from all parts of India and representing all races and creeds met together for the discussion of only such questions as may be generally admitted to concern the whole of India at large'. No one, said Tyabji, regarded the whole of India as one nation; but there were some questions which touched all communities or nations in India. Hindus from all provinces and Moslems from Bombay and Madras supported the Congress.

We can no more stop the Congress than we can stop the progress of education. But it is in our power by firm and resolute action to direct the course the Congress shall take. . . . I would say to all Mussalmans, 'act with your Hindu fellow-subjects in all matters in which you are agreed but oppose them as strongly as you can if they bring forward any propositions that you may deem prejudicial to yourselves.'[195]

But Syed Ahmad was unwilling to agree to any form of co-operation with the Hindus. He later publicly declared:

Is it possible that under these circumstances two nations—the Mahomedan and Hindu—could sit on the same throne and remain equal in power? Most certainly not. It is necessary that one of them should conquer the other and thrust it down. To hope that both could remain equal is to desire the impossible and the inconceivable.[196]

Dufferin's government, having encouraged this political cleavage, protested their innocence.

The diversity of races in India, and the presence of a powerful Mahomedan community, are undoubtedly circumstances favourable to the maintenance of our rule; but these circumstances we found and did not create, nor, had they been non-existent, would we have been justified in establishing them by artificial means. It would have been a diabolical policy on the part of any Government to endeavour to emphasize or exacerbate race hatreds among the Queen's Indian subjects for a political object.[197]

No doubt there was no official pressure on the Moslem community to keep aloof from the Congress. But the Government of India could not disclaim their share in strengthening a Moslem, as distinct from an Indian, political outlook. The position was summed up in a sentence by Mackenzie Wallace: 'Without being in the least hostile or unjust to the Hindoos, Lord Dufferin is rapidly acquiring the reputation of the benevolent protector of the Moslim.'[198]

However, the political consciousness of the educated classes, once it had sprung to life, could not be extinguished by official neglect. The first session of the Indian National Congress was held in Bombay in December 1885. The same year a Bombay Presidency Association was inaugurated. There were also increased contacts between Indian political bodies and progressive opinion in Britain. The Congress recommended the formation of a standing committee of the House of Commons to consider protests by Indian legislatures against the overruling of their decisions by the executive authorities in India. The Bombay Presidency Association sent a delegation to canvass for certain candidates and oppose certain others in the general elections of 1885. Hume visited England, sought support for Congress views, and established the short-lived Indian Telegraph Union to provide news about India to British newspapers.[199] Agitation in Ireland too began to influence developments in India. O'Donnell stated in the House of Commons that English tyranny in Ireland was only a part of that general system of exploitation which made the British empire a slave empire, and the Irish people should effect a coalition with the oppressed peoples of India and other British dependencies against the common enemy.[200] Dufferin complained that all the arts of Irish agitation had come into India. Associations, sub-associations and caucuses had sprung up all over the country, and mass meetings of raiyats, who had been brought together by the organization of *tamashas* (fun fairs), were being held. 'Day after day, hundreds of sharp-witted Babus pour forth their indignation against their English oppressors in very pungent and effective diatribes.' Reports of these meetings were then given wide publicity by newspapers. In this manner animosity was excited against the government generally. For the time being, the authorities could afford to be indifferent, but Dufferin wondered how long an autocratic government, 'which everyone will admit must remain so in its main features for many a long year to come', would be able to stand this strain. The traditional policy of dignified silence in face of criticism also seemed out of place, and the Viceroy was willing to consider the grant of one of the principal demands of the Congress, the right of interpellation. For this would enable the government to correct mis-statements and thwart the efforts of the press to engender a widespread feeling of hostility to British rule.[201]

In fact, as Mackenzie Wallace, the man behind the throne, wrote,[202] 'We are at the beginning of a new chapter, possibly a new volume, in Indian history.' Kimberley, who was in 1886 back for a few months as Secretary of State, declared that he had no faith in a merely repressive policy. Apart from all other considerations, democratic Britain would never allow such a policy to be firmly and continuously pursued. 'We must go forward; to stand still and simply resist is not in our power, even if we were convinced it would be the safest course.' So some concessions

161

would have to be made, but the utmost care would have to be taken in making them. The government should not go an inch beyond what was required and should carefully avoid anything which might tend to fan the flame. A very cautious step in the direction of elected members in the legislative councils might be desirable; but to permit interpellations would be a serious innovation. There should be no interference with meetings and speeches unless they were distinctly treasonable and could be dealt with sharply and decisively.[203] Dufferin's own inclination also was to examine carefully the demands of the various political organizations, to give quickly and with a good grace whatever it might be possible to grant, to announce that these concessions should be accepted as a final settlement for the next ten or fifteen years and to forbid mass meetings and agitation.

Soon after his arrival in India it had occurred to Dufferin that reform of the legislative councils might be possible. If loyal Indians with popular support could be brought into these councils and associated with the acts of the executive, the Government of India would cease to be 'an isolated rock in the middle of a tempestuous sea, around whose base the breakers dash themselves simultaneously from all the four quarters of the heavens'. The moderate men had already lost much influence to the extremists and might be intimidated by the press; but even so Dufferin was in favour of trying the experiment of revising the constitution and powers of the provincial legislative councils, if not the central one. 'Now that we have educated these people, their desire to take a larger part in the management of their own domestic affairs seems to me a legitimate and reasonable aspiration, and I think there should be enough statesmanship amongst us to continue the means of permitting them to do so without unduly compromising our Imperial supremacy.'[204]

The Viceroy, in other words, with the mind of a landlord, seemed to look upon the political problem as on a par with land revenue questions; there should be, not a permanent settlement, but periodic settlements, and no issues should be raised during the years between, just as there could be no demands for enhancements of rent till the current land settlements had lapsed. This showed a rigidity of outlook ill-attuned to the rapid changes in India. The home rule movement, as Dufferin termed it, had already grown disillusioned with him because of the long delay in taking a decision about the recruitment of Indian volunteers and the final unfavourable answer.[205] Even Hume, by nature gullible, had lost faith in the Viceroy, while the Viceroy now wrote of Hume as 'a mischievous busy-body' whom Ripon had 'rather petted... cleverish, a little cracked, vain, unscrupulous, and, I am told, very careless of truth'.[206] Hume inspired articles in the press which were almost scurrilous in their criticism of the Viceroy and the administration, and published a pamphlet, *The Rising Tide*, which referred to Dufferin in disparaging terms. A rumour was also started that Ripon had declined to be Secretary of State because he disapproved of Dufferin's policies. Dufferin drafted two letters to Hume, asserting that all his recommendations to the India Office had been in favour of reforms and appealing to 'the patriotism of an Englishman and of a loyal subject of the Queen' not to make the Viceroy's task more difficult than it was.[207] Finally he had the good sense to act on Aitchison's advice and not to mail these letters.[208] But Mackenzie Wallace wrote to Hume refuting his allegations[209] and the Viceroy granted him an interview.[210] The result was to give Hume greater importance and to lower the dignity of the Viceroy.

The petty controversy dragged on. Hume offered to write in the newspapers asserting Dufferin's *bona fides*, and insolently demanded to see Dufferin's letters to Kimberley, as he had been told that the Viceroy had misled him. The Viceroy replied that he could not show the letters, but if Hume were to meet Dufferin again he would be convinced that his impression was erroneous. In a second letter Dufferin complained of the tone of the Indian press and sought to win over Hume and his friends once again by flattery.

Before I conclude, it is a pleasure to me to recognize the very friendly and honourable spirit in which, from the moment you knew the real nature of my sentiments and opinions, you have endeavoured to remove any wrong impressions which may have existed in regard to them among your Indian friends. Believe me they have more to gain—of course, I am now alluding to the serious and reasonable section of the reform party—by helping and trusting the Viceroy than by embarrassing him in his endeavours to serve them, their country and the Empire.

This gave Hume an opportunity to castigate the administration in general. He said its whole tone was growing rotten, and there was need 'to disinfect the insalubrious streams of the administration by turning into them the purer element of independent indigenous representation'. He was writing another pamphlet, of which he sent Dufferin the proofs, but he made it clear that he would not be bound to accept all the changes which the Viceroy might propose. There was another series of interviews and thereafter once more relations thawed. When asked how he had secured what he claimed to be copies of Dufferin's letters to Kimberley, Hume said that they had been 'precipitated by clairvoyance'. Dufferin felt that Hume's pamphlet would disperse, once and for all, misapprehension regarding him, and suggested some minor modifications. Hume replied that his friends persisted in misjudging the Viceroy, and this was to him a source of unhappiness. 'I *know* that I judged you more justly than they, and, after our yesterday's conversation, I am ready to swear it....I believe that India *will* gain materially from you, and that though the conditions of your office compel you to work slowly you will work surely....I believe in you, and I am sure that if God spares you to work out your plans, the future will endorse my faith.' He then sent the Viceroy a message received by clairvoyant methods—'I took it down just as it came'—which unfortunately has not been recorded.[211]

Hume now considered himself in partnership with the Viceroy, and was lavish with advice. He drew the Viceroy's attention to the seeming failure to depute Indian delegates to the Oriental Congress and when Dufferin replied that it was not the government who chose delegates but the Congress which sent invitations, Hume gave publicity to this explanation. 'It will help a great deal towards that throwing oil upon the waters which we have at heart.' His pamphlet, *The Star in the East*, was also published; and the Viceroy, who regretted the government's lack of convenient channels to make their views known, thanked Hume for his friendly efforts to remove misunderstandings.[212] This encouraged Hume to seek membership, for himself and some other Englishmen who were friendly with Indians, of the commission that was being appointed to consider methods of recruitment to the civil service. Dufferin, who appealed to Hume to ask his Indian friends to write and speak a little less 'like spiteful and silly school-girls', for 'you have quite convinced me of the disinterestedness and sincerity of your motives',[213] was willing to consider the suggestion and was dissuaded only by the home department and by Ilbert. 'I should myself' wrote Ilbert, 'be indisposed to put Hume on the Commission, not on account of his advanced opinions, which would, in my judgement, be rather an advantage than otherwise, but because I distrust his honesty and because he is an incorrigible mischief-maker. I would infinitely prefer Cotton, whom I believe to be both able and honest, though viewy, and, I am told, difficult to work with.'[214] This was a weighty and considered opinion, such as Dufferin was not capable of forming, but which he could not set aside. The bizarre flirtation with Hume finally ended twelve months later, with Hume accusing the Viceroy of betraying his confidences, and the correspondence was broken off.[215]

The Viceroy was shrewder in his assessment of the situation and in his proposals for reform of the legislative councils. Even while appeasing Hume, he sought to isolate the extremist Indian politicians, of whom Hume was the leader, and to secure the support of the moderates. Hume saw himself as 'the Indian Parnell',[216] but the majority of educated Indians, according to Dufferin, had no desire for home rule. They were loyal because they recognized that British Indian administration, with all its shortcomings, was just, impartial and beneficent, while the alternatives to it were the revival of Moslem tyranny or anarchy or a Russian conquest.[217] There was reason to believe that these moderates would be satisfied with the introduction of a representative element into the councils.[218] They did not even propose elections. 'Of course election is out of the question now, but I do venture to think that wiser selections could be made.'[219] Dufferin thought that there would be great difficulty in securing the services of the best men and even such men might oppose the efforts of the Government of India to improve the condition of the masses. But the gain to India, to the government and to Britain of having courageous, loyal and moderate Indians in the councils could scarcely, wrote the Viceroy, be expressed in words. 'All I can say is that I think the time has come, at all events for making the experiment in a wise, cautious and benevolent spirit, provided always that whatever we may do should be so contrived as not to lead us hereafter further than the success of our initial efforts may warrant.'[220] The Viceroy was particularly impressed with the educated classes of Bombay and wished to shift the capital from Calcutta.[221]

In London, Maine believed that as the number of educated
Indians was less than 4500, to give them any semblance of
authority over the Indian people would be to create an oligarchy;
but he agreed that there should be more provincial councils and
that some non-official members should be elected to these bodies.
The problem was to frame a suitable method of election.

And, behind all this, there is the rather melancholy consideration that
the ideal at which the educated natives of India are aiming is absolutely
unattainable. How can 180 millions of souls govern themselves? Responsible and representative government are terms without meaning
when they are applied to such a multitude. Societies of that magnitude
have seldom held together at all under the same political institutions,
but, when they have, the institutions have been sternly despotic.[222]

Northbrook also was in favour of revising the composition and
functions of the councils, and suggested the selection by municipalities of representatives who might, in turn, elect members to
councils.[223] But Kimberley was less enthusiastic. He thought that
Englishmen were too prone to believe that with quick trains, low
tariffs and a parliament based on wide suffrage and a ballot, the
millennium was at hand. More attention should be paid in India
to improving the administration than to constitutional changes.
'The one great object of our rule in India should be to produce as
much contentment with our Government as the case admits.
We can never, as foreigners, be really loved, but we may, short of
that, do much to secure acquiescence in our supremacy as the best
system possible in the circumstances.'[224]

Kimberley, however, gave way to Cross, and Dufferin pressed
his views on the second Salisbury Ministry. He affirmed that
reform of the legislative councils would terminate much of the
agitation. Not, of course, that any attention need be paid to this
agitation. The National Congress, at its annual session at Calcutta,
had functioned more like an Eton or Harrow debating society than
even the Oxford or Cambridge Union, and had passed resolutions
demanding elected majorities in the councils and the submission of
all government business to them. But though the educated class
was as yet small and uninfluential, it was above all things a growing
power. Dufferin believed he had succeeded in gaining the goodwill and confidence of almost all its influential leaders. Even the
leaders of the Congress, which was inclined when in session to

prove 'a rather hysterical assembly',[225] were as individuals sober and moderate, and the Viceroy had been able to meet most of them and, it seemed to him, satisfy them of the justice of official policies. Moreover, as a result of the extravagant demands of Congress, the Moslem community had been alienated from it and 'for the first time in the recent history of educated India, a conservative party had come into obvious existence'. So Dufferin thought the time was opportune to permit some form of diluted election for all the councils. In practice this already existed, for the central and provincial governments consulted the leading members of the local communities before nominating members. Dufferin also planned to take advantage of the formal introduction of indirect elections to impose restrictions on the Indian press, even though, in his view, it had recently become mild and reasonable.[226]

The Congress itself acknowledged the correctness of Dufferin's analysis. Nearly five hundred delegates from all parts of India attended the session of 1886, but the hereditary noblemen and the Moslems, on the whole, had kept aloof.[227] Despite its resolutions, therefore, the Congress might well have been placated with some form of indirect election to the provincial councils. But Cross, while he directed Dufferin to work out a scheme, made it clear that he was wholly opposed to it. Anything like a representative assembly seemed to him absurd, and he warned the Viceroy against paying heed to a noisy and educated few. There was no desire in India for the ascendancy of any one race; 'the masses of the people do not want to be ruled by Baboos, and it is our duty, as well as our interest, and still more the interest of the people, that there is to be English rule and English justice and English consideration for the wants, the prejudices, and the habits, religious as well as social, of all classes'. Any form of election would, therefore, according to Cross, be fatal; and no reforms should affect official majorities in the councils.[228]

Dufferin, who was aware that Northbrook was also bringing his influence to bear on Cross in favour of the Viceroy's proposals, assured the Secretary of State that he would not suggest any hasty or ill-considered changes. He had only brought forward his proposals when the idea of a parliamentary commission to report on Indian affairs had been abandoned, and he was willing to give up his scheme if the home government so desired. But it was not merely the Bengalis but all educated India, inclusive of the Moslems, who wished to be more freely consulted in the management of internal affairs. To authorize the chief municipalities, universities, Moslem associations and such other bodies to send up names from which the government could select a few for nomination, might have a conservative effect. It would not endanger the ascendancy of British justice and the efficiency of the administration, but it would weaken the associations organized by the more radical section. As an additional argument the Viceroy now reported, in contrast to his conclusions but two months before, that the Indian press was again causing much mischief; but it would only be possible to place restrictions on this press without rousing an outcry if responsible opinion could find expression in the councils.[229]

The Viceroy let it be known in India that he was formulating a scheme for introducing an element of representation in the councils and was willing to receive suggestions. Raja Peary Mohun Mookerjee, a leading landholder of Bengal, proposed that local boards and public bodies of over ten years' standing should select electors who would in turn submit panels of names to the government. Maharaja Jyotindra Mohun Tagore, another well-known citizen of Calcutta, believed that any such scheme would be too cumbrous, but he could think of no plan which would be acceptable to both the people and the government. Among the officials, Cotton suggested that all Maharajas and Nawabs should be made members for life, and forty members should be elected by local boards and universities. MacDonnell was of the view that the local bodies, as constituted, were unlikely to be able to provide suitable electors. Peile, the retiring home member, requested the Viceroy to restrict the right of election to representatives of the Princes and of the landed and commercial interests, and thereby reduce the importance of the politicians.

Above all let us not be democratic or go in for numbers either in the electorate or the elected body. Let us rather follow the spirit of the country, which is in favour of the reservation of high place and power to a select and dignified few, and of individual and personal influence, and is inclined to rest satisfied with the privilege of advising and being heard, leaving the subsequent action cheerfully enough to the Government, of which the people have no reason to feel distrust.[230]

Such advice, which was in accordance with Dufferin's views during his early years in India, was no longer fully acceptable to him. For there had been a growth in Dufferin's understanding of the educated classes. Unlike Lyall, who was timid in mind, pessimistic with regard to 'the grand enterprise of civilizing India' and inclined to believe that India might become the sport of the stronger Indians and the rougher political forces,[231] the Viceroy realized by 1887 that the educated classes were a significant element in the Indian scene.

India [he wrote to the Master of Trinity][232] is daily becoming a more difficult country to govern. It has ceased to be an isolated territory, and is now a Continental Power with a strong and aggressive neighbour at its gates. On the other hand, a highly educated, and in certain respects a very able and intelligent native class has come into existence during the last thirty years, and naturally desire [*sic*] to be admitted to a larger share in the conduct of their own affairs.

There was now a greater maturity in Dufferin's judgment of this section of Indian society. He considered its ambitions natural, and was amused rather than alarmed at 'the instinctive way in which our feather-headed Bengali Baboos have coalesced with the Irish Home Rulers'.[233] For he was by 1887 more than ever convinced of the loyalty of India.

Of course, as time goes on, and education spreads among the people of India, their inclination to criticize the Government through the public press and to demand changes in the Indian constitution, which it may not always be convenient or possible to grant, will continually increase, but however unreasonable may be some of their demands, and however violent, irritating, and annoying may be the language in which they are put forward, it would be very incorrect to regard them as symptoms of disloyalty. Lord Dufferin believes that the most extravagant Bengali Baboo that ever 'slung ink' as the expression is, cherishes at heart a deep devotion to your Majesty's person and a firm conviction that it would be destruction to him and his if ever English rule in India were replaced by that of any other Power.[234]

He believed that an alien government, exercising absolute dominion through a small number of officials over a population of more than 250 millions in a distant country, should expect discontent to be rife and active and be always in a position to control and suppress a party disaffected to their rule;[235] but he did not suspect the Congress of being such a party. All that its formation indicated was that the educated class, which had been created under British auspices, was beginning to take an interest in public affairs and felt that it should be allowed to know more and to have ampler opportunities of expressing its opinions on the administrative acts of the government.[236] The Governor of Madras, where the Congress met in 1887, reported that its leaders seemed 'a very loyal and harmless set of people'; and the Viceroy agreed.[237] When the Maharaja of Mysore subscribed to Congress funds, he was informed that it was not desirable for the Princes to interest themselves in political activities outside their states; but the Viceroy added that the government had no objection to subscriptions being paid by anyone living in British India. That this reprimand was not inspired by animus against the Congress was proved later by his censure of the Nizam for contributing to anti-Congress funds.[238] Dufferin has often been given the credit for creating the Congress. This is undeserved. But he certainly, towards the end of his term, had gauged its measure and let it be; and that, in the then climate of Anglo-Indian opinion, was in itself worthy of recognition.

This growing understanding on Dufferin's part of the Indian scene did not, however, extend to the problem of recruitment to the civil service. At the outset, Kimberley made it clear that there was no possibility of his revising Salisbury's decision on the age-limit for recruitment. The primary object of the examinations in England was to secure the best recruits, the great majority of whom had necessarily to be Englishmen; so there was no justification for framing the rules with the object of facilitating the admission of Indians. The statutory civil service had been created for Indians, and this should be improved to satisfy the demand of the educated classes in India. To remove their dissatisfaction altogether was probably out of the question. 'We must however face the educated Baboo, and whilst we give him reasonable opportunities to enter our service, not from fear of him impair the efficiency of our European bureaucracy, on which we must after all mainly depend.'[239] An official despatch to the same effect was sent.

Dufferin was inclined to raise the age-limit, but had no strong views on the subject and, in view of Kimberley's attitude, was willing to turn his attention to improvement of the statutory service.[240] In India too the despatch roused little public comment, though there was considerable disappointment in Bombay[241] and no doubt elsewhere. But sharp opposition came from Ripon, who considered the refusal to raise the age-limit not only a most serious error but politically a singularly foolish act, and he threatened to oppose it in Parliament with the support of the great majority of the Liberal party.[242] In face of this, Kimberley hinted to the Viceroy that he might reply that the whole subject was under consideration.[243] Churchill, on succeeding Kimberley, took an even more liberal view, and directed the Viceroy to consider both liberalizing the rules of admission to the statutory service and raising the age-limit for the covenanted service.[244]

Kimberley, back again in office in a few months, gave much thought to this problem for on no issue did he feel more strongly than on the need to keep the Indian element in the administration subordinate. He was willing to recognize the growing desire and increasing fitness of Indians to participate in government only in so far as it was consistent with the maintenance of the foundations of British supremacy in India. 'To decry our own civil service is simply to condemn our own rule.'[245] The existing system of recruiting Indians into official service was clumsy, ill-conceived and obviously unsatisfactory in practice. Any modification of the statutory service would not by itself placate Indian opinion; but the demand for simultaneous examinations in London and in India had to be considered carefully, if only because Bengalis, 'quite unfit to rule', would benefit the most.[246] Kimberley, therefore, suggested a commission to inquire into the whole question. This would enable full reconsideration and inspire confidence in India, especially as the scheme for a parliamentary commission to inquire into Indian affairs had had to be abandoned. Ripon, Northbrook and Gladstone were all in favour of such a commission with Indian members to report on the civil service.[247] Dufferin agreed, though his council disliked the idea of Indian participation.[248]

A commission with Sir Charles Aitchison as president and both English and Indian members was appointed. Aitchison believed that the statutory service should be entirely recast to form a parallel cadre to the covenanted service, and should be recruited entirely in India.[249] But he was a weak chairman, and his colleague, Sir Charles Crosthwaite, had an outlook which was reactionary even for an English civil servant of those years. Crosthwaite held the inquiry itself to be risky. An English education was no guarantee of loyalty. What educated Indians wanted was to create by competitive examination an intellectual aristocracy which would eventually oust all Englishmen. 'I think all this talk about the just claims and inherent rights of the Natives of India to a large share in the governing body of the British Empire, which is the creation of the British people, can easily be blown up.' In the interests of the enormous aggregate of differing races and creeds in India, and of the English people whose money had been taken to build railways, wage wars and suppress insurrections, the Government of India should stand firm and maintain unimpaired the English character of their rule.[250]

The report of the commission, which was presented to the government in January 1888, bore in most respects the impress of Crosthwaite rather than of Aitchison and the few other members of like mind. Very few changes were suggested, and a meagre number of responsible posts was proposed to be made accessible to Indians. But on one, perhaps the most important, point, Aitchison prevailed. No direct recommendation regarding the age-limit was made; but the commission indicated its views by proposing that the age for Indians should be raised and that all candidates should be treated uniformly. 'The raising of the age is the one cardinal feature in our Report, and if it is not accepted, the Report had better be tossed aside altogether, for evil, and not good, will come of it.' The alternatives were differential treatment, which would create universal dissatisfaction, and examinations in India 'from which may God deliver us'. Besides, the raising of the age-limit was required not solely to benefit Indians but to enable Englishmen to come out at a maturer age; for the commission had everywhere heard complaints that English officers arrived in India at too young an age.[251] Aitchison was not exaggerating; for the heads of local governments had all made similar reports to the Viceroy. Even Roberts, by no means an Indophile, was for raising the age-limit.[252]

In India the report, when published, was received with little enthusiasm, while many junior English officials disliked it heartily as planning to deprive them of a monopoly of the senior posts. The Viceroy's council was unanimous that the statutory service should be abolished and certain posts transferred from the imperial to the provincial services,[253] but by the time of Dufferin's departure, nothing had been done.

It was in December 1888 that Dufferin left India; but the announcement was made at the beginning of the year. The news was received in India with not so much regret as indignation at what seemed an escape from decision.[254] The conservative Indian Association and the British and Moslem communities of Calcutta arranged, with the encouragement of the Viceroy,[255] a public meeting at which fulsome tributes were paid to him and his wife. Dufferin flaunted these as proof that he had won the confidence of all his subjects, British and Indian.[256] In fact, as if to repudiate these claims, meetings at which the Viceroy was criticized were held in the mofussil, and the press in Bengal adopted an attitude which led so experienced an observer as Lyall to conclude that it was 'becoming permanently irreconcilable'.[257] Indeed, Dufferin had never been generally popular, it being felt that he was too preoccupied with foreign policy.[258] But he chose to see advantage even in this hostility, for he asserted that it put his admirers on their mettle, with the result that he was leaving Bengal amid loud acclaim. 'The consequence was a larger and more enthusiastic demonstration than has ever been known in Calcutta.'[259]

This sentence was wide of the truth; but it throws light on the secret ambition of Dufferin. Throughout he saw himself in rivalry with Ripon, and was eager to be bade farewell by India as an even greater hero than his predecessor. So his last year in India saw Dufferin affable to the educated Indians and to the Congress. He declined to act on Colvin's advice and take notice of a catechism issued by the Congress, drawing a distinction between the home government and the British people on the one hand and the Government of India on the other. Dufferin argued that it would be best to leave the Congress to rouse opposition against itself among the conservatives and the non-Hindus, while the government modified the provincial councils to such an extent as to make all reasonable Indians feel that a constitutional channel had been provided for expressing their wishes and grievances.[260] Colvin replied that it was not the annual sessions of Congress which gave him concern, and he did not recommend interference with them. But as a prelude to the sessions a great variety of agents of unknown character and antecedents toured the districts preaching hostility to the local authorities; and the leaders of the Congress exploited the courtesies extended to them by members of the government to claim official sympathy with their views. Every political reform would be made to appear as a concession to their demand. 'One must be careful not to excite the thought that by yielding to agitation step by step one may give hopes of being led to yield to being agitated out of our supremacy.' Agitation, if not genuine and broad-based, seemed good reason for postponing rather than for granting concessions.[261]

Colvin was among the ablest of Indian civilians, and his views, based on local experience rather than theoretical premises, merited serious consideration. Indeed, Dufferin claimed to be in broad agreement with this assessment of the unrepresentative character of the educated classes. 'Western civilization, education, and the progress of modern ideas have as yet scarcely had any effect upon the great masses of the people'; and parts of India still represented the Stone Age.[262] But he continued to ignore Colvin's counsel and repeatedly urged the home government to authorize him, before his departure, to take steps to introduce council reforms.[263] Cross finally agreed;[264] and the Viceroy's council considered the question and, being unanimously of opinion that the time had come for enlarging and liberalizing the councils, appointed a sub-committee to formulate the details.[265] Dufferin proposed the publication of a formal announcement on the subject before he left India.[266]

Dufferin's haste was not so much, as he avowed,[267] because it would be easier for him than for an inexperienced successor to supervise the enactment of such changes as because it would make it easier for him to collect applause. The editor of *The Statesman* appears to have been the Viceroy's agent for this purpose. 'Lord Dufferin will yet leave India', the editor promised Mackenzie Wallace,[268] 'amid acclamations, despite the Native "irreconcileables" in this city.' It is also alleged that Dufferin made a covert approach to two leaders of the Congress, W. C. Bonnerjee and Manmohun Ghose, to organize a farewell for him at Calcutta which would surpass that given to Ripon four years before[269]—an allegation that would be unbelievable of any Viceroy of that century except Dufferin. That his attitude during these months was one of wooing the Congress there can be little doubt. When the Chief Commissioner of the Central Provinces complained that officials in his province were helping to organize political associations and to collect funds, he was authorized to terminate such activity; but the Viceroy would not permit any resolution of the Government of India on this subject to be published.[270] The explanation given was that suppression of the Congress would raise such a cry in England that the Secretary of State would veto the measure; but once the provincial councils had been reconstituted, it would be considered 'in what way the happy despatch may be best applied to the Congress'.[271]

By the middle of October, however, it became clear even to Dufferin that Indian plaudits could not be manufactured; and his bonhomie was soured to bitterness. 'The fact is', he wrote to an Indian correspondent in a letter which was not despatched,[272] 'you are a very unreasonable, inexperienced, and not very sensible set of people, and if you were left to follow your own devices, you would find yourselves in a far less satisfactory situation than you are at present.' Colvin, at long last, received unqualified support, and the Viceroy suggested that copies of a letter Colvin had written to Hume should be sent to all members of Parliament. 'The only remark I have to make is that you have treated that silly impostor with too great courtesy and indulgence.'[273] Dufferin himself sent a copy of the letter to the Secretary of State. He contended that the Congress was venting on him its disappointment at its failure to secure the support of the Moslems, and protested that he had never tried to stir up hostility between the two races.[274] 'One little word' from him in public, that the time had come for council reforms, might still, in his opinion, have made a difference; but such a statement had not been authorized by the home government.[275]

As it was, even the Corporation of Bombay refused to present a farewell address; and the words which Dufferin spoke in public were not to announce a decision to introduce changes in the councils but to criticize sharply the Congress and Hume. He declared that of a population of 200 millions, those with a university education numbered less than eight thousand and not more than half a million had passed out of the schools with a good knowledge of English. 'I would ask, then, how any reasonable man could imagine that the British Government would be content to allow this microscopic minority to control their administration of that majestic and multiform empire for whose safety and welfare they are responsible in the eyes of God and before the face of civilization?' Large sections of the people were already becoming alarmed at the thought of such self-constituted bodies intervening between themselves and the august impartiality of British rule. The Congress should devote its attention to such problems as over-population and sanitation and not put forward political demands and disseminate propaganda to excite hatred against public servants. Hume's 'silly threat' that the Congress held the keys not only of a popular insurrection but of a military revolt was also not calculated to restore confidence in this organization. The ambition of the educated classes to be more largely associated in the conduct of affairs was a very natural one, and the Viceroy had officially submitted to the home government some personal suggestions in this respect. But Britain could never abdicate her supreme control, and in any reforms due regard should be paid to the circumstances of the country and the conditions under which India was administered.[276]

V

The eight years from 1880 witnessed the Liberal experiment in India. It was started by Ripon and petered out under Dufferin. Ripon was a man of no high intellectual or administrative ability, and there was little in his Indian record which raised him above the ranks of mediocrity. Yet paradoxically his term has become one of the great peaks of British Indian history. Thinking Indians were persuaded by the events of those four years that there were men in high places in Britain who regarded dominion as a trust and were willing to exert themselves to fulfil that trust. Of the Viceroys of the nineteenth century, Canning alone, in his first phase, can compare with Ripon in this regard; and the fact that Ripon's contribution was for the most part unplanned did not make it any the less enduring.

The drama of the Ilbert Bill controversy gave prominence to the Viceroy's views. The situation so developed that Ripon was compelled to clarify his ideas as to the objectives of British rule and the ways in which he hoped to attain them. The tradition of the pre-Mutiny days, that the purpose of the British in India was to prepare India for their departure, was revived after a long pause of over twenty years; and Ripon was sure in his mind that it was the growing class of educated Indians to whom responsibility should gradually be transferred. 'To overlook and despise these men, to regard them as people to be "kept down" is to me the height of political folly.'[277] The unspectacular expansion of local self-government and plans to raise the age of recruitment to the civil service were his methods of increasing the participation of these educated Indians in government; and neither proved fruitful. But the tension created by the careless decision to grant powers of criminal jurisdiction to Indian judges over European British subjects in the country districts floodlighted the political ideas and beliefs of the Viceroy, and did more than any other event after 1857 to make British rule acceptable to politically conscious Indians. They realized too that British statesmen by themselves could achieve little, for they would always be confronted by the blind yet powerful antagonism of the British community in India. If Indians were some day to be free, they would themselves have to strike the blow. 1883 saw the beginnings of Indian political organization and nationalist endeavour. But even in the years of most bitter conflict between the British rulers and the Indian people, the conviction that the attainment of Indian freedom was a co-operative task of India and Britain was never wholly lost; and it was the memory of Ripon's years which, more than any other factor, kept this conviction alive in India. The testimony which Ripon had borne, however involuntarily, to the ultimate logic of the British effort in India was the prime achievement of his viceroyalty.

The only point in common between Ripon and his successor was that they both belonged to the Liberal party. Adept in the language and manners of the Court—his letters to the Queen were more flowery than those of any Viceroy before or since[278]—Dufferin was himself vain and susceptible to flattery. He had the charm and the 'well-conditioned' appearance,[279] but also the demerits, of the Sheridan race. Smug, frivolous,[280] even slightly vulgar, leading a life of cheerful ease, he left the details of policy and administration to others. The official records of these four years contain little; and the letters to the Secretary of State rarely ran into any length.[281] The Viceroy himself—and his wife[282]—thought he worked very hard. Perhaps he worked harder than he had ever done before. 'It is', he wrote to Churchill, 'the greatest grind I have ever experienced.'[283] But he worked less than any other Viceroy. Of systematic and absorbed dedication he was incapable. 'I doubt', wrote Granville with prophetic discernment in 1872, when Dufferin's name was first considered for the viceroyalty, 'his having sufficient stamina either of mind or body.'[284] Dufferin was the only Viceroy to whom his own definition, that 'a Viceroy can scarcely be said to exist outside his business',[285] did not apply. But long before his term was over, Dufferin had begun to tire of the social whirl. 'It is an odd thing to say', he wrote after three years, 'but dulness [*sic*] is certainly the characteristic of an Indian Viceroy's existence. All the people who surround him are younger than himself; he has no companions or playfellows; even the pretty women who might condescend to cheer him, it is better for him to keep at a distance; and, except occasionally, the business he has to deal with is of a very uninteresting and *terre à terre* description. . . .'[286]

There was no room in India, however, for a dilletante Viceroy. The central government during these four years lacked a firm helmsman; and both the members of council and the local governments were willing to take advantage of this. No man in his station had a greater opportunity to leave his personal impact on India; for frequent changes in the home government during his term led to delegation of responsibility to the Viceroy. Even an assertive personality like Randolph Churchill, when he became Secretary of State in 1885, though he had personal knowledge of India and views of his own, wrote to Dufferin of his general policy: 'I can give them in a sentence. As long as you remain Viceroy, my intention and desire is to support to the utmost whatever you may recommend.'[287] Yet the only trophies of the Viceroy—and one of them a tarnished one—were avoidance of war with Russia and the annexation of Burma. In internal affairs Dufferin had little to his credit. He had been eager only to be popular, as popular in India as he was reputed to be in Europe.[288] But as Dufferin reluctantly recognized, even this trivial objective he had failed to attain. All that he himself claimed as his achievement was that he had driven the administration at a low and steady pressure and had made no blunders.[289] 'When I consider the many dangers we have run and the innumerable mischances which might have overtaken us, even without any fault of our own, I am truly grateful to be able to escape out of India under these tolerable conditions, and without any very deep scratches on my credit and reputation.'[290] He left India with relief that he had got safe past the finishing post without 'having a cropper'.[291]

The fact was that Dufferin was unequal to the task of governing India. 'I never', he complained,[292] 'saw such a country as this. One is no sooner out of one kettle of boiling water than one is up to the neck in another.' His old friend Lord George Hamilton, writing of him many years after, did not allow his affection to cloud his judgment. 'He has never long held any post in which he has

not more or less been found out.'[293] In India he began by placating
the Princes, the landholders and the upper strata of Indian society,
then was attracted by the idea of pleasing the educated classes
and finally left India without having taken any decisions on any
major issues. His was 'the spontaneous dishonesty of weakness',[294] and in his time the Liberal experiment ran out into the
sands.

CHAPTER 4

RETURN TO CAUTION, 1888-98

I

Indian policy was now once more marked by caution; and the ten years after the departure of Dufferin formed a period of marking time. The two Viceroys, Lansdowne and Elgin, though they belonged to opposite parties, were both suited to this mood. For neither was outstanding in ability or in character. Lansdowne, by tradition a Whig, had left the Liberal party in protest against Gladstone's land legislation for Ireland and was Salisbury's choice for the Governor-Generalship, first of Canada and then of India. Lord Randolph Churchill had desired the Indian appointment;[1] but Salisbury had preferred a staider character and offered it to the person whom Milner described as 'a good average man'.[2] But even Lansdowne was abler than his successor, who was selected by the Gladstone Government—after a soldier with experience of India, Sir Henry Norman, had declined[3]—solely on the grounds that his father had once been Viceroy and that he was Lord Rosebery's friend. Elgin too at first had declined, and was only persuaded with great difficulty by Rosebery to accept.[4] Rosebery had no high opinion of Elgin's abilities,[5] and presumably urged him to go to India because no one better suited was available.[6] Elgin had been convinced that he lacked the ability that would justify the appointment. History has provided us with no reason to differ from his estimate of himself.

In fact, during the tenure of these two acquiescent, unimaginative men, the viceroyalty reached its lowest ebb in the nineteenth century. There was a flicker of viceregal influence in the early years of Lansdowne's term, but this soon died out and all important decisions were taken in London. The Viceroys did not even exercise fully their authority in India; they echoed the opinions of their subordinates and assumed responsibility for their actions. This decade marked the heyday of official rule in India. The tendency was particularly noticeable under Elgin, whose five years formed, in his successor Curzon's phrase, the 'apotheosis of bureaucracy'.[7] Elgin himself regarded this as worthy of commendation. 'It is all very well to talk of a strong Viceroy overruling this or that Member. That is not the way to do business; at any rate I am thankful to say it is not the way it has been done in my time. I should have considered myself to have failed miserably were it so. What India wants is a strong and united *Government*.'[8] The result was almost chaos in the executive council. The members acted as they pleased. Indeed, on one occasion the law member openly dissociated himself from the policy of a measure which it was his duty to introduce; and even with the support of the home government Elgin was unable to exercise control. Finally the Cabinet had to assert that if any member of council opposed the government and refused to resign, he would be dismissed immediately.[9]

If the home government could for the most part impose their views on the Government of India, they themselves were obliged to take note of opinions in Parliament. The Indian National Congress had emerged as a pressure group in British politics;[10] and the Liberal and Irish members of the House of Commons took an interest in India and insisted on attention being given to Indian demands. Sir John Gorst, the Under-Secretary of State for India, therefore warned Lansdowne, soon after the latter's arrival in India, that the Government of India could only retain the confidence of the House of Commons by maintaining the reputation of a progressive and reforming government. As the Government of India were no freer from the potential control of Parliament than they were 'from war, famine, pestilence, fall in the value of silver, or any of the other evils with which you have to cope', they should profess the utmost readiness to investigate and rectify any deficiency in the administration and promote 'wise and gradual development' so that the progress which was achieved from time to time did not bear the appearance of having been extorted as a concession to agitation. 'Nothing could be more mischievous than the crude application of British democratic maxims to India, which was the unhappy policy of one of your Lordship's predecessors. But between Scylla and Charybdis there is a safe passage, avoiding on the one side stupid resistance to all change, and on the other weak surrender to fantastic theories.'[11]

II

In accordance with this advice, Lansdowne supported Dufferin's proposals to permit interpellations and discussion of the budget in the central legislative council and to provide a measure of elections to the provincial councils. The total abandonment of proposals which Dufferin was known to have made would cause considerable disappointment. There was a general feeling in favour of such changes, which would give to the public a legitimate means of obtaining information about questions of general interest and to the government opportunities for announcing their intentions and correcting misapprehensions. As it was, the administration was in danger of becoming too Olympian, with Indian opinion acting as not a stimulant but an irritant. The Viceroy's legislative council, wrote Mackenzie Wallace,[12] 'rather resembles an extremely well-conducted but moribund jelly-fish'; and if it could be given a backbone and a more highly developed nervous organism, it would tend to improve the executive, which was 'in danger of being infected with the flaccidity of its consultative ornamental appendage'. Such reforms would also establish that the government were not adopting an attitude of uncompromising resistance even to the demands for a moderate advance in the direction of more representative institutions. 'A timely concession of this kind would, I believe, take a great deal of the wind out of the sails of the Congress, whereas, if the reform is delayed too long, it will be assuredly regarded as having been extorted from us.'[13]

Dufferin also continued, from the embassy in Rome, to urge acceptance of his proposals. Unless some of the members were elected, the provincial councils would always have more or less of an artificial character. 'For my own part, I am convinced that our position in India is, and will continue to be, so strong and unassailable that there would be no danger in the partial introduction of an elective principle, which, however, is a totally different thing from the representative principle.' It would be safer to do this than to continue to give any semblance of official recognition to 'the various political self-elected associations whose nominees it has hitherto been usual to accept.'[14]

However, both Salisbury and Cross were unwilling to have these proposals discussed in Parliament or even to place them before the Cabinet; and the Viceroy was requested not to circulate Dufferin's scheme to the provincial governments. The objection was not to interpellations or to the discussion of the budget, but to the principle of election. It was asserted that, while the membership of all the councils could be increased on the initiative of the governments concerned, elections seemed impractical. 'I do not see where the constituency is to be. The *ryot* cannot be represented. The other classes are against the *ryot*, whose sole protector is the British Government. Nor would the Mahomedan for a moment consent to be outvoted by the Hindu. It is the justice of British rule which contents them.'[15] Nor did the home government regard as feasible the introduction of the principle of election for the provincial councils, while maintaining the central council unaltered.

A further difficulty was created by the fact that the ministry was so hard-pressed in Parliament that even legislation permitting interpellations and discussion on the budget, which had been approved by the Cabinet, seemed out of the question. The Liberals, under Ripon's guidance, supported council reforms; but Northbrook advised against legislation lest Indian and Irish politics get mixed and Gladstone use language which would be 'dangerous' in India.[16] Lansdowne too felt there might be some advantage in avoiding legislation, for rights conferred by statute could not be subsequently withdrawn.[17] He was, therefore, prepared to act on the suggestion of the home government and promulgate an executive order permitting interpellation and discussion of the budget.[18]

However, Lansdowne continued to urge the introduction of the elective principle for the provincial councils. The Indian press was strongly in favour of it and to exclude it from any scheme of reforms would only encourage agitation. Indeed, unless the scheme included a modicum of elections, it would be better to leave the whole subject alone. There was no reason why elections should not be introduced for the provincial councils without altering the composition of the central council. It seemed to the Viceroy the only way of securing in these councils a certain number of members who would reflect public opinion with knowledge and authority. Municipal corporations, whose members were elected by the ratepayers, could serve as constituencies for the provincial councils which would then, while not representative in the fullest sense, express the opinions of different sections of the community. Even if all the elected members formed an opposition, the government would still gain more than they would lose by affording their critics an opportunity of expressing their views. It might also not be an unmixed misfortune to have one or two 'wire-pullers' elected so that their pretensions could be promptly exposed. There was little risk of these reformed councils oppressing the raiyats or the Muhammadans. The government would always have a majority;

and adequate representation would be given to the conservative landowning families as against the educated classes.[19]

Despite these arguments the Cabinet, to whom Salisbury and Cross, because of the Viceroy's persistence, referred the matter, rejected the proposals. Lansdowne then suggested that the Government of India be authorized to make rules from time to time for the selection of additional members of the councils so that some form of election could be tried as an experiment in any district in which conditions were favourable.[20] Even Lansdowne's colleagues in the executive council were not in favour of increasing the number of members of the central legislative council; but it was unanimously recommended that there should be provision for the appointment of additional members of the provincial councils by nomination or otherwise.[21]

The Cabinet, however, remained unanimous against the principle of election; and Cross believed that its extension at any time, even if not under Lansdowne's scheme, to the central council would be fatal to British rule in India.[22] Lansdowne feared that even the limited, permissive concession of elections to the provincial councils would be denied; and he pointed out that the right of interpellation also would lose much of its significance if it were exercised only by officials and nominees.[23] Despite this, the home government, now willing to legislate, were prepared to sanction only discussion of the budget and interpellations. But when the bill was introduced Northbrook moved a general amendment enabling elections; and the Salisbury Government, with a surprising *volte-face*, accepted it without disclosing that the Government of India themselves had proposed elections. Lansdowne was disappointed that he had not been given the credit[24] but urged that the amended bill be enacted quickly. He wrote to the Prime Minister, as suggested by Cross,[25] that if the bill were not passed that year, agitation in India was bound to continue.[26] But domestic reforms in India held no interest for Salisbury, and he shrank from provoking a debate in the House of Commons and a speech by Gladstone on the subject.[27] Lansdowne had to content himself with the introduction of elections in the Calcutta University. The graduates of the University were asked to submit a panel of names from which the Viceroy, as Chancellor, made the final selection of two Fellows.[28]

When, by March 1891, the bill had made no further progress, Lansdowne again urged the Prime Minister to act. A poor impression would be created in India if it were thought that the British government were not in earnest and the introduction of the bill had been a mere formality. Moreover, if the Salisbury Ministry fell, it was impossible to say how a Gladstone government would deal with it. Circumstances in India were also favourable for a moderate measure; and Lansdowne was anxious to set the new machinery in motion before he left India.[29] But it was only in 1892 that the bill was introduced in the House of Commons, and Gladstone made a speech[30] which proved Salisbury's fears to be baseless. The Indian Councils Act enlarged both the size and the functions of the legislative councils. It provided for nomination of non-official members on the basis of recommendations and empowered the government to make rules authorizing the discussion of the annual budget and the asking of questions; but no member could submit or propose any resolution or divide the council in respect of any such discussion or the answer to any question.[31]

Rules had now to be framed for securing recommendations of non-officials for appointment by the government to membership of the central and provincial councils; for despite the home government's earlier reluctance the Act made no distinction between the Viceroy's council and the provincial legislatures. Much, of course, depended on these rules; for if the recommendations were made by non-official organizations and normally accepted by the government, they would be 'elections' in all but name. Lansdowne decided to draft the rules in very general terms and to proceed experimentally in accordance with the circumstances in each province.[32] But the provincial authorities showed little inclination to co-operate. The Governor of Bombay thought that elections would never result in fair representation of all classes and interests. Either the Hindus on account of their numbers or the Parsis because of their organization and intelligence would win every seat; and the government would be obliged virtually to reserve for Englishmen and Muhammadans all such seats as were to be filled by nomination without recommendations.[33] This resistance to introducing a representative element in the councils was mainly due to a desire to keep the executive insulated from criticism. The governments of Bombay, Madras, Bengal and the North-West Provinces all urged the Viceroy to restrict even the right of interpellation and to forbid questions on certain subjects[34]—advice which was not accepted.

In the matter of elections also, Lansdowne was not discouraged by the emphasis laid by the provincial governments on the practical difficulties and decided to 'puzzle out' an election system with local variations but with a common objective.[35] His hands were strengthened by the return to office of the Liberal party and the warm support of Kimberley.[36] The Governors of Bombay and Madras were assured that no harm would be done by the election of Congressmen. 'I am inclined to think that it is a distinct advantage that politicians of the type of Surendranath Banerjea should find their way into the re-constituted Councils. They can do just as much harm outside the Councils as they can inside them, and their presence in the Councils will have the effect of considerably discounting external agitation.'[37] When the Chief Commissioner of the Central Provinces wrote that the introduction of elections and representation into a country in every respect unfitted and unripe for it would 'end in disaster and lead to bloodshed before long',[38] Lansdowne replied firmly that he was perfectly convinced that the change was inevitable and the good results would outweigh the bad.[39] Rules were framed, taking into account the special circumstances of each province and providing for nominations on the advice of selected bodies.[40] The results, on the whole, justified Lansdowne. The new elements in the reconstituted provincial councils enabled the government to maintain contact, however tenuous, with the educated classes, while the right of interpellation provided the authorities with the only means of answering charges made in the Indian press.

Lansdowne's views on council reform had for him the added advantage that it enabled him to start off well in his relations with Congress, which was still sore at Dufferin's parting attack. Lansdowne declined to receive a deputation from the Congress, as it might be regarded as a repudiation of Dufferin's views and an implied rebuke to Colvin, in whose province the Congress had held its annual session and who had declared himself strongly opposed to it.[41] The leaders of the Congress accepted this decision 'with the utmost loyalty and without even the thought of resentment', and hastened to assure him of their *bona fides*.

At our public meetings you would hear every reference to our Sovereign, every allusion to the Supreme Government, cheered with an enthusiasm which has no parallel in any other part of the Queen's Dominions—cheers, every one of them, charged with the utmost sincerity. We all are working for the consolidation of British supremacy in India in such a way that supremacy may rest, not as now, on force, but be carried on with the consent and co-operation of the governed. Under the blessing of God we are invoking a feeling in every Presidency and Province which, as it filters down into the masses of the population, will—if only our rulers are a little sympathetic and yield some at least of the moderate requests preferred—make this great Empire to rest upon love and deep affection, will broad-base it upon goodwill.[42]

In fact, the Congress sought no more with regard to the councils —and this was their main demand—than what Lansdowne was planning to do. Hume, it is true, informed the various provincial Congress committees that while they were all as firmly convinced as ever that the country was not yet fit for representative government as it obtained in Britain, half the number of the members of the councils should be elected. Hume himself was in favour of electoral colleges, three-fourths of whose members would be elected, from territorial constituencies, and of reservation of seats in the councils for minorities and elections to these seats from 'sectional' constituencies.[43] But Charles Bradlaugh, in the bill which he introduced on behalf of the Congress in the House of Commons,[44] proposed elections to the provincial councils by local bodies, chambers of commerce, trade and planters associations and similar organizations, and elections to the central council by the members of the provincial councils—a scheme which was identical, except for elections to the central council, with that of Lansdowne.[45]

The Congress, therefore, took kindly to the new Viceroy, who believed that his reform proposals would enable the large majority of its leaders 'to shake themselves clear of Mr Hume and all his works'.[46] The government could then afford to treat its academic discussions with good-humoured indifference, while making sure that its adherents throughout the country were keeping within proper limits,[47] for it was in quasi-secret bye-meetings in the small, provincial towns, at which the government were criticized wildly, that the real danger seemed to lie.[48] Lansdowne was, on the whole, inclined to be tolerant of the Congress organization and even to ignore the payment to it of contributions by the Princes.[49] He was uneasy at the possibility of their making a political issue of the permanent settlement—the Irish agrarian question was never far from his mind; but he refused to join Cross in regarding this as an additional reason for not introducing elections.[50] He also declined to take Hume, and his gloomy forebodings of general discontent and an imminent national revolt, seriously, as Hume claimed to have reached his conclusions by occult means.[51] Lansdowne believed that he need only strengthen the tame, moderate leadership of the Congress and reach an understanding with it.

Therefore, when the home department of the Government of India commended to all provincial administrations the order of the Madras government prohibiting their officials from participating in any meetings and demonstrations at which official measures or policies were likely to be discussed, Lansdowne ordered the directive to be cancelled. Instead, it was laid down as a general rule that no official should attend a political meeting where his presence was likely to be misconstrued or to impair his usefulness as an official and that no official should take part in the proceedings of a political meeting or in organizing or promoting a political meeting or agitation.[52] The Bengal government extended this order to prohibit even the presence of officials at the annual session of the Congress in December 1890.[53] Pherozeshah Mehta,[54] the President of the Congress, wrote to Lansdowne to inquire if this interpreted the orders of the Government of India correctly.[55] The Lieutenant-Governor of Bengal acknowledged that the letter had been carelessly worded and had failed to explain that the reason for the government order was not hostility but the desire that officials should keep aloof from political agitation.[56] So when Mehta pressed the Viceroy, as 'the immediate Representative of our beloved Queen-Empress, to whom all India alike looks for justice and the redress of grievances',[57] for an answer, Lansdowne admitted that the Bengal government had gone 'somewhat beyond' the orders of the Government of India.[58]

The courage shown by Lansdowne in making this retraction surprised even the Congress. Hume, who had written that as a former official he clearly understood that the Government of India could not disavow the Bengal government,[59] declared that Lansdowne's admission 'absolutely knocks me down'.[60] When Lansdowne informed Hume, in amplification, that the original order of 18 March 1890 had no special reference to the Congress movement, which the government regarded as a perfectly legitimate movement representative in India of what in Europe would be called the more advanced liberal party,[61] Hume published the correspondence. He then wrote to the Congress committees to give the widest publicity to Lansdowne's letter which assured the Congress of the neutrality of government. A close watch should be maintained by the committees to see that these orders were loyally carried out by officials, and any violation should be brought to the notice of the provincial governments.[62]

It looked indeed as if Lansdowne were determined to build on the Ripon inheritance; and it was in this hope that Hume, who was granted several interviews by the Viceroy, appealed to him to meet the Congress half-way and rule India in co-operation with it. 'Be another witch of Atlas, kneading fire and snow together, and tempering the repugnant mass with "liquid love".'[63] Lansdowne replied that though he had never underestimated the power of sentiment as a political factor, Hume's commendable objective should be attained without departing from an attitude of strict impartiality to all.[64]

Lansdowne realized that he would be criticized for being too conciliatory and granting too distinct a recognition of the Congress. But he was convinced that his attitude was the only sensible one. With a free press and the right of public meeting some such organization as the Congress was inevitable; and

I doubt whether it could, upon the whole, assume a more innocuous shape than that which it now takes. So long as it is allowed to hold its meetings under the nose of the Government of India, and so long as these meetings are frequented by Members of the Viceroy's Legislative Council, Judges of the High Court, and other functionaries of position, it is useless either to ignore its existence, or to endeavour to procure its suppression by indirect methods. Nothing will so well serve to keep the movement alive as exhibitions of hostility or timidity on the part of the Government of India.[65]

That Lansdowne was right there is no doubt. The Congress of the early years required no more than friendly and courteous treatment. But of its demands Lansdowne was willing to grant only the reform of the councils. He was neither attracted by Hume's invitation to immortality[66] nor alarmed by his warning that if the hopes of Congress were killed, it would be seen at some unforeseen crisis 'how much the wretched dare'.[67] Lansdowne ignored the various suggestions, such as the separation of the executive and judicial powers and the recruitment of Indian volunteers, which were recommended every year by the Congress.

Hume was disappointed; and the result was what Lansdowne termed an 'abominably wicked concoction'.[68] In a circular letter to every Congressman Hume declared that the cup of the misery of scores of millions of the Indian masses was well nigh full, and day by day 'Poverty, the mother of Anarchy' was pressing with a heavier hand upon an ever-growing portion of the population. The result would be a general agrarian rising, and the government would be powerless to protect anyone or themselves. The only way to prevent this was to rouse the British public to the need for radical reforms in the Indian administration. So all Congressmen —who were 'the creation of Great Britain—of British learning, history and literature, and with British rule you stand or fall'— should provide ample funds for deputations to England and for an unbroken series of public meetings there.[69]

This was the end of Lansdowne's flirtation with the Congress. He was only dissuaded by Cross from taking legal action against Hume.[70] He then was rebuked by Kimberley for objecting to recognition being given to the London committee of the Congress by a reference to it in an official despatch from the Secretary of State.[71] Assured by his officials, the vast majority of whom had instinctively disliked his early tolerance of the Congress, that the party had collapsed,[72] his thinking reverted to the traditional grooves of strengthening the conservative, landed classes as against the educated middle classes; and a bill permitting the endowment of hereditary titles was drafted. 'At one time', he wrote to Kimberley,[73] 'it was our policy to cut off the tall poppies. In the present day I am inclined to think that we should endeavour to gain for ourselves adherents amongst the large landowners, and there is no more certain mode of securing their gratitude than to meet their wishes where they are desirous of founding a family.'

How far apart Lansdowne and the Congress had drawn became clear when the House of Commons passed a resolution in June 1893 recommending that examinations for recruitment to the Indian civil service be held simultaneously in England and India. This was one of the regular demands of the Congress and a resolution advocating it was passed at every annual session; but the government, fortified by the report of the Public Service Commission of 1888, had refused to consider it. All that they had been willing to do to benefit Indian candidates was to raise the age limit for the examinations in England;[74] and the home government had agreed. As regards simultaneous examinations, even when faced with a House of Commons resolution Lansdowne refused to yield. He was supported in this attitude by Kimberley, who felt that the basis of British supremacy in India would be endangered if there were not a sufficient number of British civil servants to enable effective control of the administration.[75] Gladstone suggested that the reply should not be 'a simple *non possumus*';[76] and since there was a strong feeling on the subject in the Liberal party, the resolution was referred to the Government of India.[77] Kimberley advised Lansdowne to take his time and then reject it, while couching his objections in language of sympathy 'with desire of natives'.[78]

The Viceroy was willing to play his part in what can only be described as a dishonest transaction. It was not the Lansdowne of the early years, who had looked on the Congress almost as an ally and dealt with it fairly. He rebuked the law member, Sir Arthur Miller, for writing in an Indian journal under a thinly disguised pseudonym that the resolution of the House of Commons would have no effect whatever.[79] A despatch was sent to the Secretary of State, firmly rejecting the proposal; and the Cabinet agreed. Lansdowne's successor, Elgin, saw no reason to change the decision. He too was convinced that there was a point at which the British should reserve to themselves the control of the civil administration, if they were to remain in India; and he justified his attitude on practical grounds as well, with the assertion that Indians were as yet unfit for the higher ranks of the administration.[80] Indian opinion then placed its hopes in the Welby Commission, appointed by Parliament in 1895 to suggest improvements in the Indian administration. 'I hope', Dadabhai Naoroji, a member of the commission, wrote to its chairman, 'you will be the means of wiping off this black spot on the British character. The iniquity is, in fact, at the bottom of all our woes and misery. If England redresses her honour and honesty in this most vital matter, everything will fall into its natural condition—finances, and loyal satisfaction of the people upon which British rule rests.'[81] But again the hopes were denied.

However, in one matter Lansdowne, while not working in accord with the Congress, went much further than a considerable section of that party would perhaps have approved. Malabari, a social reformer of Bombay, urged that the law should be amended to render infant marriages culpable under civil law, to prohibit social persecution of widows who remarried and to raise the age of consent for the consummation of marriages from ten to twelve in the case of girls.[82] These practices, which darkened the face of Hinduism, were no part of the Hindu faith; but an alien government was naturally chary of dealing with them. However, an outrageous instance in July 1890, when a child wife in Bengal died as the result of premature consummation, seemed to the law member to provide an opportunity for what was really a minor reform of amending the law relating to the age of consent.[83] Lansdowne agreed that if the court found itself unable to deal with the case in question, the law should be amended.[84] The court in fact declared its helplessness, and the Indian press generally was in favour of raising the age of consent. Lansdowne thought this was best done without interfering with the age for marriage or requiring ratification of marriage on the attainment of the age of consent.[85]

The problem, though one which mainly concerned Bengal, divided the Congress. W. S. Caine, a visiting British member of Parliament, urged the Congress at its annual session to pass a resolution supporting the Viceroy's efforts; and the Congress leaders realized that this was an issue on which their sympathizers in Britain could be expected to feel strongly. On the other hand, support of the bill would have weakened their influence not only with the orthodox Hindus but also with the Muhammadans, who were prone to take alarm at any infringement of marriage customs. The result was half-hearted attempts to criticize the bill, not on its merits but either on the general principle that the government should not interfere in social and religious matters or on the ground that legislation would be inoperative and liable to abuse.[86] Such criticism, justified to some extent by loose drafting,[87] petered out, especially after Hume gave public expression to his unqualified support.[88] Even orthodox Hindu opposition outside the Congress, though it was led by a former Chief Justice of Bengal, Romesh Chandra Mitter, failed to muster wide support, and the passage of the bill into law was smooth.

The Congress, it will be seen, did not seek to collect support by framing a Hindu slogan, but was, to its credit, striving to evolve a political identity that transcended the different religions. It was a sophisticated movement, in keeping with its representation of the educated classes. But it did not, unfortunately, have the political field to itself. Islam was securing articulation through the Aligarh movement, while Hindu revivalism found voice in politics mainly through the Arya Samaj. This organization was reinforced by the Theosophical movement. In 1878 its founders, Madame Blavatsky and Colonel Olcott, reached an understanding with Dayanand Saraswati, the leader of the Arya Samaj, even though theosophy preached a vague eclecticism much wider than Hinduism. The movement received a great impetus with the arrival in India in 1891 of Mrs Annie Besant, perhaps the only one of its leaders who was not wholly a charlatan. A woman with a record of varied achievement even in England,[89] a companion of Bradlaugh, whose last thoughts had been of the 'inarticulate, misunderstood' people of India,[90] and an impassioned orator, Mrs Besant won wide popularity in India; but always more as a political than as a spiritual leader. For a time, in later years, her path coincided with that of Congress; but in the nineteenth century she identified herself with those who sought to build nationalism on a Hindu foundation. 'The Indian work is, first of all, the revival, strengthening, and uplifting of the ancient religions. This has brought with it a new self-respect, a pride in the past, a belief in the future, and, as an inevitable result, a great wave of patriotic life, the beginning of the rebuilding of a nation.'[91]

The dark side of this emphasis on religious approaches in politics was an increasing animosity in north India between the adherents of the two faiths who had for centuries lived amicably though disparately. By the time Lansdowne came out to India considerable tension had developed; and the political significance of this tension was not lost on the officials. 'The theory of a "national" movement' wrote Colvin,[92] 'is necessarily absurd in India. The Muhammedans, as a body, will not adopt a movement initiated by Hindus, and they detest the claim of the Hindu, whom they dispossessed centuries ago, to return, in whatever guise, to power.' It was the view of the home department that an explosion could be caused easily at any time in the towns of the North-West Provinces and the Punjab.[93] What usually aroused feeling was the killing of cows by Moslems, a practice which seemed to become more widespread in proportion to the Hindu agitation against it.[94] The British officials were not disposed to sympathize with the Hindu viewpoint,[95] and though cow-killing was not an essential part of any Moslem ritual and could easily have been proscribed, the Government of India, after considering the matter, declined to do so[96] and contented themselves with blaming both sides for endangering the public peace.[97] The futility of such airy exhortations was shown the next year, when there was communal rioting in Calcutta itself. It is not easy to exonerate the government for their indifference, for they knew that there was no basic cleavage between the two communities—'the Indian Mahomedan', wrote the Viceroy's private secretary, 'is merely a Hindu in disguise,'[98]—and that cow-killing was prompted by the anti-Hindu political factions among the Moslems.[99]

The Hindu reply to cow-killing was the formation of Cow-Protection Associations. By 1893 the movement had gained considerable strength. It had its epicentre in the North-West Provinces and Bihar,[100] but its influence spread even as far as Burma.[101] In July 1893 there was a widespread Hindu uprising in the Azamgarh, Ballia and Ghazipore districts, in the eastern part of the North-West Provinces. Most of the zemindars, despite their vested interest in law and order, joined the agitation. The Commissioner reported that all authority was in abeyance[102] and British troops were sent to the area to quell the disturbances. But soon there were similar riots in Bombay. The problem, in fact, required solution at a deeper level. MacDonnell alone, of the senior civil servants, realized this. He reported that while the propaganda preached by Hindu emissaries was to some extent responsible for this immediate excitement, the Moslems also had given cause for offence. 'There is a bias in favour of Mahomedans on the part of my officers which must not be allowed to appear. The Hindus are so vastly in the majority that any bias against them would be productive of the worst effects, even if it were not so bad in itself. The strength of our position lies in our impartiality at present.'[103] The serious implications of this report were not lost on Lansdowne. 'I have always had an uneasy feeling that the Hindus might, after all, have good cause for complaint, and what you have said as to the bias in favour of Muhammadans exhibited by some of your officers, increases my misgivings. We ought to deal in an exemplary manner with anyone whom we find taking sides, or making mischief.'[104] But he did not allow this to alter his basic policy and still insisted on regarding, with the majority of his officials, the agitation as organized by disloyal men who were inspired solely by anti-British motives.[105]

Indeed, Lansdowne alleged that the Congress was behind the

agitation.[106] There was no evidence of this, and is significant only in showing the Viceroy's refusal to comprehend the real elements of the situation.[107] The result, not surprisingly, was the growth of the cow-protection movement to alarming proportions. It was a popular movement, far more than the Congress at this time could ever hope to be, and, considering the paucity of British civilian and military personnel, it was a potentially explosive one. Crosthwaite of the North-West Provinces reported that the Cow-Protection Associations held trials in imitation of British law courts substituting 'Gao-Maharani'—Cow-Empress—for the Queen-Empress. 'If it [the movement] is allowed to grow, it will become a Hindu Government beneath, or supplanting, the British Government.'[108]

Though Lansdowne was alarmed,[109] he did not, as advised by Crosthwaite, resort to repressive legislation.[110] The laws against seditious writing and conspiracy were already wide and any further extension was not only unnecessary but would have roused sharp criticism in Britain.[111] Indeed, as Lansdowne himself recognized,[112] the movement was by itself legal and blameless; and even if the Cow-Protection Associations were outlawed and the 'scoundrelly preachers'[113] arrested, the sentiment inspiring the movement would survive.

In 1894, while all was quiet on the surface, there were rumblings below, particularly in Bombay. As on the eve of the revolt of 1857, *chapatis* were in circulation, and there had been at least one effort to incite Indian troops.[114] Towards the end of March there were reports from the northern districts of Bihar that trees were being daubed with mud and hair; and thereafter the practice spread to the southern districts and to the North-West Provinces, Oudh and even the Punjab. Though the markings were largely due to the chance rubbing of animals against trees, some of them were effected by human agency. The fact that the smearings began from the Nepal border and followed the roads supported the theory that they had their origin at the Janakpur shrine in Nepal and were intended to attract pilgrims. Moreover, analysis of the hair showed that it had been taken from a great variety of animals, including pig; so there seemed to be no close connexion with the cow-killing agitation. The Government of India were, therefore, disinclined to attach much importance to the smearing or to regard it as a serious political danger.[115] But the provincial authorities took a more serious view. The Lieutenant-Governor of Bengal saw in it alarming evidence of the power of combination and conspiracy and of the government's lack of close relations with the people. Crosthwaite of the North-West Provinces reported an explanation provided to him that the smearing of trees signified a complaint that the Hindu religion was being polluted by failure to protect the cow. The Governor of Bombay wrote that the Hindus in his presidency were getting nastier every day and compelling even European merchants to subscribe to cow-welfare organizations.[116] But the *Bakr Id* festival in June, which was usually the occasion for slaughter of cows and consequent rioting, passed off quietly; and the new Viceroy, Elgin, reported that while hidden fires undoubtedly existed, there was no reason to believe that relations between Hindus and Moslems were more dangerous than before.[117] But he advised the Secretary of State against any severity at this stage in dealing with the Indian Princes,[118] and refused, on MacDonnell's advice, to cause any provocation of orthodox Hindus by interfering with the management of Hindu religious endowments.[119] By August, the tree-smearing practice had ceased. Its only significance was, as a petty chieftain of the Punjab observed, that the British regarded rebellion as possible, and thereby recognized that cause for rebellion existed.[120]

The provincial governments were also concerned at what they regarded as an increase in seditious writing. Crosthwaite wished to prosecute the writer of a pamphlet which hinted that the government were encouraging the Hindus to quarrel with the Moslems and then influencing the judges to punish the Hindus unjustly. To tell the Indian people, who by and large believed in British justice and impartiality, 'that the Government is against them and their religion, and is plotting to destroy both, can have only one effect'; and Crosthwaite proposed that if the law could not deal with such writing it should be altered.[121] A majority in the Viceroy's council agreed; but Elgin advised against prosecution as likely to defeat its object. Moreover, while 96 per cent of the population was illiterate and secret agencies defied detection, it was worthwhile not to drive all expression of opinion under the surface by adopting repressive methods alien to British constitutional practice.[122] Crosthwaite then suggested that opportunities for education be limited. That seemed to him the only way of preventing the educated classes, 'and especially the half-educated boys' who were faced with unemployment, from being indoctrinated with 'grumbling sedition'.[123]

The Bombay government also complained frequently about the virulence of the newspapers published in Indian languages. But Sir Henry Fowler, the Secretary of State in the Rosebery Ministry, did not think it feasible to re-enact any law similar to Lytton's Vernacular Press Act. He directed the Government of India to deal with any clear case of seditious libel under the existing law, though there was the danger of any such prosecution providing advertisement for a newspaper of limited circulation.[124]

So both Elgin and Fowler were agreed on the need for forbearance—a policy which was justified by the lull of the next two years. The Bakr Id festivals gave rise to no serious disturbances and though there was considerable tree-smearing in 1896, law and order remained inviolate. The Indian press provided no cause for anxiety. The worst motives were often imputed to the government and the officials, but there was little expression of desire to replace the British government by an Indian, far less another foreign, government. Famine, which some regarded as the worst of the century,[125] spread over the country in 1896 but did not deepen discontent. Rather, the efforts of the authorities to alleviate famine seemed to emphasize their 'true benevolent character, and, come what may, the political good of this cannot be easily eradicated'.[126] Communal violence in Poona in September 1894 and at Dhulia twelve months later showed that feelings were still inflamed in Bombay presidency; and there was indefatigable activity to organize public opinion in a militant manner on the basis of Shivaji commemoration functions, Ganapati festivals, the cow-protection movement and agitation against the Famine Code. The Governor of Bombay complained even in 1894 that the Hindu extremists were behaving in a most truculent manner, and thought it was 'monstrous that the whole of Maharashtra should be convulsed by the machinations of a few fanatical Brahmins'.[127] But it proved difficult to take any action against either the men considered responsible for this uneasy situation or the journals which voiced extremist opinion. And this seemed a provincial rather than a national malaise. The country, wrote the new Secretary of State, Lord George Hamilton, was 'wonderfully quiet'.[128]

Yet the unrest in Bombay developed into a crisis of major proportions, and spilt over communal limits into an offensive on the authority of government. The occasion was early in 1897, when there were cases of plague in the cities of Bombay and Poona. Apart from the loss of life, the epidemic affected British trade, for foreign countries seized the opportunity to boycott exports from India. The Bombay government were reluctant to take stringent measures such as compulsory segregation, as these might alienate local opinion and deprive the government of the services of sanitary and hospital workers. Lord Sandhurst, the new Governor of Bombay, feared that even riots might break out in Poona, and require shooting—'a curious way of curing people of a disease'.[129]

The outbreak of plague at Bombay caused a panic throughout India, and the Government of India were vehemently criticized for not enforcing adequate quarantine measures. The Europeans in Calcutta grew almost hysterical, and there were threats of an agitation similar to that against the Ilbert Bill.[130] The Salisbury Government reacted to pressures from Europe and urged that the annual Haj pilgrimage of Indian Moslems to Mecca should be suspended. The Prime Minister was strongly of opinion that the inconvenience and discontent caused by suspension should be faced, as the alternative of sanctioning the pilgrimage with restrictions would create even more serious dangers and difficulties.[131] The Lieutenant-Governor of Bengal was also for cancellation, as one case in the harbour at Calcutta would mean a great loss of trade and measures of control for the whole city.[132] MacDonnell, on the other hand, was apprehensive of the effect of any such general prohibition of the Haj on the Moslem community, and especially on the Moslem Princes. 'In India you *cannot foresee* what will come from interfering with religious observance.'[133] Elgin agreed that the consequences might be serious, but felt he could not withstand the British government on this issue.[134] The pilgrimage for 1897 was cancelled. It was suggested that, to placate Moslem opinion, the gate of the Juma Masjid at Delhi, which had been kept closed for sixty years, might be opened.[135]

In fact, except for a few cases in the hilly district of Garhwal in the United Provinces, the plague was isolated in Bombay and Poona. In those two cities the Bombay government enlisted the co-operation of the army to ensure effective control. In Poona there was a house-to-house inspection, and those suffering from plague or likely to have been contaminated by it were removed to segregation camps. In Lucknow, where MacDonnell introduced precautionary measures of a similar type, the Moslem nobles made it clear that in their view plague was a far less evil than segregation; but MacDonnell summoned a meeting of the leaders of both communities and persuaded them to formulate segregation rules which would be acceptable to them.[136] The result was unbroken peace. Sir Syed Ahmed's warning, that the Plague Rules were creating more ill-will against the British among the Moslems than anything he had known since 1857,[137] proved baseless. Similar tact on the part of the government of Bombay might have eased the tension at Poona, whose predominantly Hindu population was less hostile than the Moslems to segregation. The sense of emergency was, of course, greater at Poona than at Lucknow, where plague had not broken out; but even so, the civil and military officials acted in Poona in a way which MacDonnell regarded as calculated to drive men to desperation.[138]

The tension reached flash-point on 22 June, when Rand, the civil servant in charge of plague operations, and Ayerst, an army officer, were shot in their carriages on their way home from the Jubilee celebrations at Government House. Ayerst died instantaneously, and Rand on 3 July. Ayerst had been murdered either by mistake or to prevent him from offering any assistance to Rand; and Rand had been killed perhaps in private vengeance but more probably in protest against the government's plague operations. Marathi newspapers had been for months demanding that the people should revolt against the interfering activities of the authorities. The *Poona Vaibhav* had written that history recorded no instance of such oppression, violence and lack of consideration on the part of any ruler towards his subjects;[139] and the *Kesari* had reported Bal Gangadhar Tilak, the leader of Maratha opinion and the editor of the paper, as having said that according to Hinduism no blame attached even to killing if it were disinterested and as having called on his listeners to 'get out of the Penal Code'.[140]

The murders took the Bombay government by surprise and induced in them a state of angry panic. A punitive police force was sent to Poona, a large collective fine to cover the cost was levied, disarming of the whole city was considered and an amendment of the law of sedition was recommended to the central government.[141] Lord George Hamilton, unlike his predecessor, also favoured a renewal of the Vernacular Press Act.[142] Elgin replied that the executive had sufficient summary powers under the 1827 Regulations.

All the provincial governments agreed with the central government that there was no need for a Vernacular Press Act.[143] As for the sedition law, Tilak should be prosecuted under the law as it stood and only in case of failure to obtain a verdict should revision be contemplated.[144] For the time being, it seemed necessary only to tighten the procedure of prosecution in sedition cases; and legislation to this effect was enacted in March 1898.

Meanwhile the Bombay government, unable to trace the murderers or even to obtain evidence more tangible than 'cumulative suspicion', detained without trial Balwant Natu and Hari Natu, two well-known sirdars of Poona, one of whom at least was alleged to have been a leading instigator of the riots in 1894,[145] and prosecuted Tilak.[146]

These brothers with Mr Tilak are the backbone of the party who are by common consent credited with seditions and revolutionary opinions and with great activity in the dissemination thereof. The opinion as far as it has been ascertained of loyal and educated native gentlemen in Poona who had no connection with or personal knowledge of the conspiracy to murder also points with singular unanimity to the Natu family having been directly or indirectly concerned in the actual crimes and the local officials hold that the removal of the above three men from Poona will probably lead to obtaining information.[147]

These were very flimsy grounds for depriving men of their liberty. Tilak himself, however fiery his speeches, was innocent of complicity in the murders. Throughout he remained calm, asserting that he had nothing to fear as long as the government were just;[148] and the police officer investigating the case reported that Tilak had nothing to do with the crime.[149] Even his speech reported in the *Kesari* was not, according to Sandhurst,[150] seditious, though the Court, defining sedition not as disaffection but as want of affection, sentenced him to eighteen months imprisonment.[151]

How utterly wrong the Bombay government were in arresting the Natus and in prosecuting Tilak was shown soon after, when a young man, Damodar Chapekar, confessed to the crime and was tried and hanged for it. The government recognized that there was no trace of conspiracy and that Chapekar had 'developed dislike into hatred by his own fierce enthusiasm'.[152] The most that can be held against Tilak, in the light of all the evidence available now, is that he knew the identity of the murderer and sought to aid and protect him.[153] Tilak was released before the expiry of his full term, but despite Elgin's promptings[154] the Bombay government failed to release the Natus.

The unrest in Bombay presidency led the authorities to examine once more the whole question of the stability of British rule in India and to consider the political attitudes of the Hindu and Moslem communities. The Bishop of Madras suggested republication of the Proclamation of 1857 on the occasion of the Queen's Jubilee; but the Viceroy thought it would be misunderstood, and Sir Arthur Godley, the Permanent Under-Secretary at the India Office, agreed that it was hardly the moment to remind the world that the Queen had promised to make no distinction of race. 'The less said about it the better.'[155] As for any concession to the Moslems in particular on the occasion of the Jubilee, the Lieutenant-Governor of the Punjab warned that relations between the communities were so unsatisfactory that any favour shown to one community was likely to be misrepresented by the other.[156] This did not worry Hamilton unduly. 'One hardly knows what to wish for. Unity of ideas and action would be very dangerous politically, divergence of ideas and collision are administratively troublesome. Of the two the latter is the least risky, though it throws anxiety and responsibility upon those on the spot where the friction exists.'[157] When, in fact, relations between the communities began to improve and even in Bombay, for the first time since communal differences began, the Hindus joined freely with the Moslems in celebrating *Mohurram*,[158] the Government of India suspected that the improvement of Hindu-Moslem relations might be associated with a joint conspiracy against the government.[159]

Nevertheless, Elgin was able to assure the home government that there was no evidence for connecting the Poona murders with any widespread movement, that the country was much more peaceful than in 1894, and that there were no reasons for suspecting the loyalty of Indian troops.[160] In Calcutta, Turkey's victories over Greece caused excitement among the Moslem population and there were local riots; but the situation never got out of control.[161] In Assam, Burma, the Central Provinces and Madras there was no agitation of any kind, and in the North-West Provinces the tension had subsided. MacDonnell believed that the Hindu masses, under the leadership of their landlords, were not discontented. Indeed, by October 1897 they began to draw closer to the government as a reaction to the feeling, akin to an Islamic revival, which was agitating the Moslems. Though this unrest among the Moslems had by no means attained the dimensions of a conspiracy, MacDonnell proposed precautions such as guarding the railways, as there might be sudden, unexpected developments. In the Punjab, too, while Hindu-Moslem antagonism had lessened, the Lieutenant-Governor feared that the masses might at any time be incited by the press, whose editors were recruited from the discontented educated classes.[162]

The Viceroy informed the home government, on the basis of these various reports, that while they should ever be on the watch, there was no imminent danger. The difficulties of administration were due 'to a movement that they can no more stop than Canute could restrain the waves, to progress of education and the acquisition of knowledge'.[163]

Hamilton agreed that there was no immediate anxiety, but said that 'the far future' filled him with apprehension; for if both the North-West Provinces and the Punjab became disaffected, the retention of India would become an almost impossible military and financial task. Further, if Britain were to suffer a major reverse inside or outside India, there would be serious disturbances in many of the large towns and a general weakening of authority.[164] So Hamilton was willing to consider deliberate efforts to thwart Hindu-Moslem harmony. 'The solidarity, which is growing, of native opinion and races and religion in antagonism to our rule frightens me as regards the future. Education and the press will enhance that bad feeling and we ought to leave no stone unturned to counteract this dangerous tendency.'[165] No such *rapprochement*, however, was evident to Elgin. The Bengali babu had nothing in common with other Indians; the intense jealousy felt by the Moslems of the cleverer Hindus was notorious; and there was no increase in religious harmony sufficient to threaten British rule. In all his travels in India since 1894, Peshawar was the only place where Elgin had felt himself in the midst of a hostile population.[166] But as a measure of caution and in accordance with Hamilton's suggestion, Elgin sent a subscription and a testimonial to the college at Aligarh, whose purpose was to advance Moslem separatism. This action of the Viceroy encouraged the Moslem community to support the Aligarh movement and the Principal described Elgin as 'the saviour of our college'.[167]

It was not, however, in the North-West Provinces or the Punjab that the uneasy peace was broken. In March 1898 there was once again an outbreak of plague in the city of Bombay, and an attempt to remove a patient to hospital led to serious rioting. Sandhurst's Government had by now lost grip of the administration. Plague operations were slack and confused, while knowledge of public feeling was almost non-existent.[168] MacDonnell reported from the North-West Provinces that the incidents in Bombay had become known and had produced a general disquieting effect. He urged that 'we must not let the sanitary end blind us to the importance of political considerations'. The extent to which the government could carry the people with them should be the measure of their programme of plague control. Instead of the forcible removal of patients to hospitals, there should be a more liberal licensing of private dwelling-houses as hospitals. This would increase the danger of the spread of the plague and might well prolong its incidence; but MacDonnell believed this to be a less serious evil than the danger of popular disturbances.[169]

This surprisingly defeatist opinion of MacDonnell was shared by Mackworth Young of the Punjab.[170] Elgin, at first inclined to reject the advice,[171] soon, as usual, gave way and permitted the local governments to use their discretion in departing from the Plague Rules.[172] His excuse was that the plague had reached Calcutta, whose inhabitants, both European and Indian, were 'as inflammable as touchwood, and though timid, with a recklessness, due perhaps in part to timidity, that has a dangerous side'.[173]

Tree-smearing and the plague disturbances pushed into the background the government's relations with the Congress. Elgin had declared in 1894 that he was not afraid of cultivating friendly relations with this organization, and he even spoke of holding the scales as evenly as possible between the Bombay government and their critics in Poona.[174] However, in consultation with MacDonnell, he declined to receive a deputation of the Congress as it would give colour to the assertion that he wished to dissociate himself from his predecessors, and as, according to practice, he would be unable to reply to any speeches made.[175] Some officials warned that the educational system was training too many graduates who later became unemployed and joined the ranks of the discontented. The remedial measures suggested were higher fees in schools and colleges and the diversion of Indians to industrial occupations.[176] But Elgin, who claimed to be unafraid of the Congress,[177] showed no concern.

Indeed, the Viceroy seemed anxious to encourage the Congress, whose opposition was articulate, if only because he was baffled by what he described as the other 'great, silent, indefinite and impalpable' movement. How best to cope with such unrest was a problem yet to be solved; but it was clearly not by granting peerages to leading Indian Princes—Salisbury's favourite scheme[178]—or by seeking the support of the landed classes, as suggested by Crosthwaite,[179] and stifling criticism.

Elgin did take steps to strengthen the landed aristocracy in India. The Secretary of State was approached for sanction of legislation enabling the talukdars of Oudh to render their estates inalienable in whole or in part and declaring the ancient zemindaries of Madras impartible and inalienable.[180] But Elgin preferred to strengthen the government by inviting free discussion and by disclosing and justifying the acts of the government and of the officials. To further this objective he recommended the establishment of legislative councils in the Punjab and Burma. The Indian members of the councils in other provinces had proved to be able men who had applied themselves to the practical work of legislation with assiduity and in a spirit of loyalty. Moreover, to justify themselves with their supporters, they were obliged to speak out; and this provided the government with information which otherwise it was most difficult to obtain.[181]

The Secretary of State believed that in India the Congress was in decline as a political force, while its committee in London only irritated him. 'They are all of them a thankless, ungrateful venomous crew, and Wedderburn ought to know better than head the gang.' Yet he agreed with Elgin that it was judicious to select Congressmen for the councils. If they were earnest, contact with reality would sober them; if they were dishonest, it would be easier to expose them. Hamilton felt that the dishonest element was powerful enough not to be ignored. 'The more I see and hear of the National Congress party the more I am impressed with the seditious and double-sided character of the prime movers of the organisation.'[182] But Elgin mildly pointed out that though the Congress frequently trespassed on the borderland of what was permissible and perhaps included men who would go much further if they dared, no responsible man would ever consider banning the organization.[183] Indeed, the evidence given before the Welby Commission by the prominent leaders of the Congress left no doubt of their basic loyalty.[184]   Naoroji summed up their position in a sentence:

I gladly recognise the benefits of British rule, especially as regards law and order, education and freedom of the press and public meeting; but I believe that British power and influence are much weakened by the refusal to administer expenditure in a way so as to give the people justice and a voice in their own affairs, by the consequent 'extreme poverty' of the masses, and by the non-fulfilment of the solemn pledges given by Parliament and the Crown, of equal opportunity in the public service to all subjects of Her Majesty; and I sincerely desire to see British rule strengthened on the lines most beneficial to the people both of India and of Britain.[185]

The Congress functioned also in a way that seemed to belie Hamilton's fears. The annual session at Amraoti in 1897 had, according to official reports, been attended mostly by schoolboys.[186] There was some agitation regarding the revision of the sedition law, but as Elgin himself disliked it, he saw no reason to object.[187]

III

During these ten years, failure to exercise with wisdom the initiative and decision that goes with ultimate responsibility became increasingly prominent. Lansdowne was much more of a Viceroy at the commencement than at the end of his term; he was not corrupted but weakened by power. The man primarily responsible for securing the introduction of the elective principle into India was also driven by alarmist officials into virtually a panic over the cow-protection agitation. Confronted in 1891 with a crisis in the small hill-state of Manipur, he displayed courage and fairness, but neither quality was to be seen in his handling of internal issues but a few months later. A palace revolution in Manipur had led to the deposition and exile of the Maharaja and his replacement by a kinsman.[188] There was a confusion of counsels among the British. Lansdowne wished to restore the old Maharaja; Quinton, the Chief Commissioner of Assam, was for accepting the change but deporting the commander-in-chief, also a member of the ruling family, who had been responsible for the *coup*; Grimwood, the Political Agent, was a close friend of the commander-in-chief;[189] the Lieutenant-Governor of Bengal expressed the widely held view that this opportunity be utilized to annex Manipur.[190] Lansdowne, however, refused to annex Manipur even after Quinton and Grimwood, who had set out rashly to arrest the commander-in-chief, had been murdered.[191] All he did was to execute—despite the Queen's protests[192]—the men considered responsible for the crime and to install a junior member of the family on the throne.

Lansdowne was not always as clear-sighted and was often, as he himself realized, out of his depth. 'The more I see of it, the more I am impressed by the difficulty of measuring the strength of the currents which flow beneath the apparently quiet waters surrounding us.'[193] He believed that the Indian press was systematically rendering public opinion disloyal and even Cross could not dissuade him from repressive action.[194] On the eve of Lansdowne's arrival in India, a sub-committee of the Viceroy's executive council had recommended that council reforms should be coupled with a more effective criminal law against libellous and seditious writing which had recently, according to the sub-committee, been on the increase.[195] Lansdowne decided to confirm the inadequacy of the existing law before seeking further statutory powers.[196] He directed the government of Bengal to institute a prosecution against a conservative Bengali newspaper, the *Bangabasi*, which had impugned the partiality of the British government, even though the lawyers were not certain of a favourable verdict and the Lieutenant-Governor was hesitant.[197] However, Lansdowne's luck held; the Indian editors, as a whole, lost courage,[198] and the Chief Justice pronounced the *Bangabasi* guilty, though he confided to the Lieutenant-Governor that he did not think the articles had exceeded fair criticism.[199] In view of this, and the disowning by the law member in public of responsibility for the prosecution,[200] Lansdowne decided not to press for a sentence from the jury. The defendants were informed that if they apologized and promised good behaviour a lenient view would be taken.[201] Such an apology was received[202] and published, and the prosecution withdrawn. Lansdowne was satisfied with his achievement. The Indian press had realized that the government were not afraid to prosecute and consequently formed an association to censor their own writings. Thereafter criticism of the government was less vehement, and informal warnings served to keep the press under control.[203]

Curbing the Indian editors of newspapers was much easier than modifying the institution of trial by jury; for this was calculated to rouse opinion in Britain. Yet it was such a modification that Lansdowne's Government attempted in 1893. It had frequently been alleged that in India the jury system had favoured the escape of criminals, for in some parts of the country juries could not be relied upon, whatever the weight of evidence, to convict in cases involving capital punishment. It was true that in such instances the judge could refer the case to the High Court; but the judges also often hesitated to do so, and the High Courts had taken different views as to their right to interfere with the verdicts of juries. In May 1890 the government requested the provincial governments and the Calcutta High Court to report on the working of the system and to suggest possible improvements.[204]

There was no uniformity in India, of prevalence or of practice, with regard to the right of trial by jury. It was to be found in all the High Courts. There was no trial by jury in the mofussil areas of the Punjab, Burma and the Central Provinces. It existed in all the districts of Madras, five districts of Bombay, eight districts of Bengal, six districts of Assam, and three districts of the North-West Provinces. But even where it existed there were many variations. In Madras and the North-West Provinces only selected offences, not punishable with death, could be tried by juries whereas in Bengal, Assam and Bombay even cases of murder and culpable homicide came before juries. The Madras government thought the system unsuited to the country; the Bombay government considered it was popular and useful but did not wish to extend it to other districts; Bengal condemned it as a failure and proposed to limit the cases triable by jury; Sir Auckland Colvin thought the system had worked well and was willing to extend it to other districts of the North-West Provinces. The Chief Commissioner of Assam also stated that the system had worked well.[205] The Government of India realized that any alterations in the practice of jury trials would raise political issues, for the Congress annually suggested its extension to the whole country, and the problem was closely linked with memories of the Ilbert Bill agitation.[206] It was, therefore, decided to avoid legislation, but to invite local governments to consider revision of the lists of offences triable by jury.[207]

Thus far Lansdowne had made no mistake. But thereafter, believing it to be a matter more of routine than of policy, he sanctioned the withdrawal in Bengal from the cognizance of juries of cases of murder and culpable homicide.[208] The notification was issued by the Bengal government on 20 October.[209] At once, to

the surprise of the Government of India and the Bengal government, there was agitation in Calcutta. Even the Chief Secretary
to the Bengal government, Henry Cotton, who was in close touch
with Indian opinion,[210] was taken by surprise. The British Indian
and Zemindars Associations took the lead, and the non-official
British community did not conceal its sympathy. It was suggested,
as a compromise, that along with the reduction of the number of
offences triable by juries, the system should be extended to new
districts.[211] Lansdowne, even though he had been aware that the
principle of trial by jury was a sensitive political issue, was inclined to ignore this agitation, and rashly asserted that the government would not retrace their steps.[212] Indeed he asked the
government of Bombay to strengthen the hands of the Government
of India by following Bengal's example; but the Bombay government were not willing to oblige. When they finally did, it was too
late.[213]

Moreover, Lansdowne had not taken sufficiently into account
the change of ministry in Britain. The Liberals were now in office
and had strong views on the subject. Ripon wrote to Kimberley
that the Lansdowne Government had mismanaged the whole
question from the start,[214] and the Secretary of State warned the
Viceroy to expect a sharp attack and to take no further steps without his approval.[215] Lansdowne, in reply, threatened resignation
and pointed out the consequences of such an event.

The difficulty of governing this country would, I believe, be greatly
increased if a Bengali agitation were to be allowed to bring about the virtual recall of a Viceroy and the resignation of the Lieutenant-Governor
of the Presidency. You may depend upon my bearing this in mind
and doing nothing inconsiderately or without a previous interchange of
ideas with you. On the other hand, if you will put yourself in my place
you will readily understand that the case is not one in which a Viceroy
could retain his office after anything equivalent to a public reprimand
by H.M.'s Government.[216]

Lansdowne also—an unusual and questionable step for a Viceroy
—canvassed his friends in the Conservative party. Goschen and
Curzon were told[217] that the change was a minor one resented not
on its merits but as a 'slap in the face to Babudom', that the
agitation was not deep-seated and that the home government
should not interfere with the actions of a provincial government.

However, the despatch of the Government of India seeking to justify their policy carried no conviction.[218] The statistics by themselves refuted the government's position. During the previous five years, the Calcutta High Court had set aside jury verdicts in only 13 out of 203 murder cases—6·4 per cent, a low figure which justified the working of the jury system. Kimberley therefore proposed the withdrawal of the notification of the Bengal government and the forwarding of schemes to reform the jury system for the consideration of the home government. Lansdowne now saw that a retreat was inevitable: and as immediate withdrawal of the notification would be regarded as a severe public censure and leave him no option but to resign, he suggested instead an expression of the home government's objections to the notification and the immediate appointment of a commission to consider the whole question. Kimberley agreed to a commission but insisted on withdrawal of the notification.[219] Lansdowne pleaded that, with the Bengali press proclaiming its triumph and boasting of the success of Congress,[220] 'the decent interment of the Notification meant a great deal. You are ordering us to throw its corpse to the dogs.'[221] Finally, the home government decided to be merciful. Though they stated that they disapproved of the withdrawal of certain cases from juries, they did not insist on cancellation of the notification and directed the immediate appointment of a commission.[222]

On 23 February the Government of India appointed a commission to consider the working of the jury system in Bengal. It included two Indians, Jyotindra Mohun Tagore and Romesh Mitter, who had been opposed to the notification.[223] The commission reported promptly, by the end of March, suggesting various amendments of the law of criminal procedure. It recommended withdrawal of the notification; but while the majority were silent regarding the types of offences triable by juries and the extension of the jury system, the two Indian members wrote a separate note supporting the development of the jury principle in both respects. The notification was quietly withdrawn and the governments of Bengal and India examined the proposals of the commission. The government of Bengal even advocated, after Lansdowne's departure, the strengthening and extension of the jury system. They said they had not changed their views, but 'events have shown that this Government underrated the popularity of the system among the educated classes, and the political value which should be set upon it as a training for these classes and an admission of them to a share in the power of the Courts'.[224] It was a disarming way of accepting defeat.

If the first half of these ten years disclosed an increasing lack of vision in internal affairs, the second half witnessed a startling lack of consideration of Indian interests in economic matters. In 1893 the finance member proposed import duties in order to meet the deficit, even though the home government would not like them.[225] Lansdowne wrote to Kimberley that these were the taxes which would find most favour in India, for they would be considered a practical protest against what was regarded as the regulation of Indian finance to suit the interests of British manufacturers. Import duties would yield about ten lakhs of rupees if piece-goods and yarns were exempted, and double that amount if they were not.[226] The Secretary of State replied that British public opinion would never permit their levy; nor would the British government admit that Indian finance had been regulated to suit British manufacturers. The British government still adhered to the principles of free trade and believed that free imports were of benefit to the community as a whole.[227]

Lansdowne thereupon abandoned the idea of import duties, and the deficit in 1894 rose to Rs 35 million. It began to be realized in Britain that some action would have to be taken. Godley informed Elgin that while an import duty on cotton goods seemed at the moment impossible, it might appear feasible if the situation in India did not mend, and no one in the India Office had the smallest doubt as to its justice and expediency. However, the initiative should come from India. If the Indian government urged again the reimposition of cotton duties, the Cabinet would incur a great responsibility if it refused; but it could not be expected to propose their levy.[228] Elgin at first rejected all proposals for duties on cotton goods as out of the question in view of the opposition in Britain, but later he came round to the view that once the principle of import duties was accepted, the exclusion of cotton goods was indefensible. No one in the Government of India, however, not even Sir James Westland, the finance member, at this time shared this view;[229] the thinking among British civilians in India was determined by British interests rather than Indian requirements. So Elgin characteristically requested the home government to decide.[230] If Lansdowne had gradually lost his nerve, Elgin never showed signs of having any. Gladstone, Ripon and Kimberley were anxious to support the Government of India,[231] but in view of the latter's indecision, vetoed the imposition of cotton duties.[232]

The Viceroy dutifully introduced legislation imposing a 5 per cent duty on imports other than cottons, but pleaded with the home government for reconsideration. There was an unusual consensus of opinion in India against the exemption of cottons, which was interpreted as a concession to British interests at the cost of those of India.[233] But the Gladstone Ministry saw no prospect of changing the decision once it had been taken. It would require overwhelming proof of financial pressure to overcome opposition in Britain, as the cotton manufacturers, irrespective of party, would fight to the death against such duties.[234] For the British cotton industry had begun to suffer from Indian competition. Indian yarn exports exceeded imports from the early 1880's, and a few years later British exports of cheap cottons started to decline.[235]

So the tariffs bill was passed. But both Fowler, Kimberley's successor, and Godley held out hopes that cotton duties would be sanctioned if a countervailing excise duty were also imposed on Indian cottons to rid the measure of any protective character.[236] Though Elgin was at first attracted by the proposal,[237] he pleaded on reflexion that the government should encourage India's sole great modern industry.[238] But Fowler insisted that the principle of a countervailing duty should be recognized as vital and levied on the higher counts of Indian yarn and the better class of Indian piece-goods. There should not be the shadow of a doubt as to the comprehensive nature of the excise duty to cover all cases in which competition between Lancashire and India existed or was likely to arise.[239] It was 'absolutely *essential* that the Excise Duty should be so fixed as to eliminate any possibility of protection. The Government are absolutely pledged that they will not, without the consent of Parliament, assent to any protective duty.'[240]

In the winter of 1894, fresh tariff legislation was undertaken on these lines by the Government of India. The Secretary of State, under pressure from Lancashire interests, further stiffened the terms, and urged that even coarse cotton goods from Britain should be exempted from customs duties or alternatively that an excise duty should be levied on coarse Indian yarn.[241] The latter course

was adopted and an excise duty was levied on all yarn 'above 20'—
that is, yarn requiring over twenty bundles of a specific length to
weigh one pound—even though the Government of India had
wished to exempt all yarn up to 24.[242] The result was that manufacture of yarn in India above 20 ceased, and the average percentage of British cotton exports to India in the first ten months of 1894
and of 1895 taken together was slightly in excess of that of the first
ten months of 1892 and of 1893 taken together.[243] Even this,
however, did not satisfy British commercial interests. 'The fact is
that the present arrangement is a rough and ready one, which can
only exist by the help of goodwill and a spirit of compromise; and
in Lancashire there is neither the one nor the other.'[244] There was
moreover a change of government in Britain, and the Salisbury
Ministry had extreme views on this subject of cotton duties.
Salisbury himself had played a prominent role at the time of the
repeal of the cotton duties in 1879; Cross represented Lancashire's
interests; and the new Secretary of State, Lord George Hamilton,
was an outspoken and extreme protagonist of free trade. He was
convinced that the cotton duties, even as they stood, were protective and therefore indefensible.[245] The argument was that in
coarse yarn and in bleached, dyed, woven and printed goods India
secured advantages.[246] Elgin pointed out—but not forcefully
enough—that by placing an equal duty on Indian yarns, the Government of India were in fact protecting Manchester against
India.[247] But with Lancashire suffering from a depression[248] the
Viceroy's plea was ignored and he was instructed to take advantage
of the increased revenue gained from the fluctuating exchange
value of the rupee to reduce the duties to $3\frac{1}{2}$ or 3 per cent *ad
valorem* on all piece-goods, whether manufactured in Britain or
India, and to exempt yarn of all counts.[249]

Once again Elgin agreed to set aside India's interests and cloaked
his weakness in dissimulation. 'I saw', he wrote to the Secretary
of State,[250] 'that you and Her Majesty's Government, in face of
difficulties I appreciated, intended to deal sympathetically with
our financial difficulties, and it seems to me we could do no less
than endeavour, so far as we could, to diminish the strain upon
you.' The bill was enacted in defiance of considerable opposition in
India. Elgin anticipated that this agitation would soon die down.[251]
He had indeed by now persuaded himself that the opposition was
unreasonable.[252] As for Hamilton, he was elated that with the

removal of the 'shadow of protection', 'the grave political danger of two hostile industrial camps arrayed against one another inside the same Empire, and fighting over a tariff question, is gone, I hope, for ever'.[253]

The tariff legislation of 1896 served its purpose of protecting British cotton exports to India. Indeed they even registered an increase.[254] But on the iniquity of the acts passed in Elgin's term there can be no two opinions. Romesh Dutt, writing a few years later, described the tariff acts as 'an instance of fiscal injustice... unexampled in any civilized country in modern times'.[255] A British scholar of our own times has commented, 'A more unsympathetic and selfish act of policy it would be hard to imagine'.[256]

No single measure during the years of the Crown's administration of India in the nineteenth century cast a greater stain on its honour; and nothing could have been better calculated to prove the charge that India was administered in Britain's interests. Advantage had been taken of a timid and hesitant Viceroy to impose brazenly a series of decisions and enactments, framed not merely to avoid protection or even to benefit Lancashire but almost to destroy an infant industry in India. The only difference in this matter of cotton duties between the Gladstone and the Salisbury Governments was that while the former would have preferred to avoid the decision, the latter were shameless in their insistence.

The scheme [wrote Sir Charles Pritchard, a member of the Viceroy's council],[257] as has been admitted, lacks a solid foundation of principle; the only justification to be offered for it must be based on considerations of expediency and the orders of the Home Government.... Such taxation would not be possible in England. I fear that, if it is persevered with, the Government of India will give its opponents for the first time a strong foot-hold for their agitation.

Pritchard's fear proved to be well-founded. The Congress, at its annual session in 1894, put on record its firm conviction that the interests of India were being sacrificed to those of Lancashire;[258] and for the next two years similar protests were received from political and commercial organizations all over India.[259] Even non-official Englishmen spoke in the same vein in the legislative council. The agitation, far from subsiding, gave a powerful impetus to Indian discontent by justifying it. Ten years later, Curzon reported that everyone in India knew that if it came to a question of Lancashire or Dundee, India would never be allowed to safe-guard herself as if she were a self-governing colony. The feeling roused by the manner in which India had been exploited for the benefit of Lancashire was very strong and entirely legitimate. 'This consciousness is one of the things that makes the native party in India, in particular, bitter about the Empire.'[260]

Tariff legislation was not, however, the sole Indian achievement of Lancashire interests. There was also a demand by them for Indian factory legislation uniform with that in Britain, as the rela-tively less stringent provisions of the Act of 1881 were deemed by Lancashire to amount to protection of Indian trade. The home government wished the Act to be amended so as to provide four holidays a month for women; and Lansdowne consulted the pro-vincial governments as to how this could best be done without closing the factories on the chosen days. Indeed, it was believed by some sectors of Indian opinion that factory legislation was in-tended to crush Indian industry by preventing women from work-ing in the mills.[261] This was, however, unfair to the Governments of India and Britain, whose main purpose, whatever the pressures, was to safeguard the health and lives of women and child em-ployees.

On the basis of the opinions of the local governments the central government drafted a bill, and even tried, on the suggestion of the home government, the novel experiment of appointing a commis-sion to ascertain the views of the operatives.[262] But the report of this commission was disappointing and shed little light on the problem. Cross suggested that only a comprehensive measure would satisfy the humanitarian and manufacturing interests in Britain; and as Gorst, the Under-Secretary, had participated in the recent Berlin Conference on the subject, it would be almost im-possible for the British government to deviate from its recom-mendations.[263] But the Government of India felt that circum-stances in India were very different from those in Europe. For instance, without children, factories would have to close down.[264] Even the restriction on hours of work for women had led to the dismissal of a large number employed in the mills at Ahmedabad.

The Factory Act of 1891 raised the minimum age for the employment of children from 7 to 9 years and reduced their working time from 9 to 7 hours, limited the hours of employment of women to 11 hours a day, insisted on proper intervals for food and rest during the day and provided for at least four holidays in every month for both women and children. This did not satisfy opinion in Britain where employment of children and women was restricted to 10 hours during the day. The Dundee Chamber of Commerce, for example, falsely complained that as a result of the want of adequate inspection by officials in India, machinery was worked for 22 hours by women and for 15 hours by children.[265]

Regulation of working conditions and of the employment of women was also sought to be enforced in the mines. But after collecting information from the local governments, the Government of India felt there was no strong case. The government of Bengal advised against legislation, and elsewhere the mines were mostly under official control. Much of the work in the mines was done on the family system, the wife and children helping the father; explosions and accidents were relatively unknown; and a needlessly stringent Act might smother a promising national industry.[266]

IV

In foreign affairs the major objective of these years was the strengthening of British influence in Afghanistan and Persia. Lansdowne was keen on establishing telegraph communications with Kabul, asserting British authority over the Amir's foreign relations and moderating his internal rule which was reputed to be savagely cruel.[267] The Viceroy was also too much under the influence of Roberts, who wished to commit the home government to an occupation of Afghanistan up to the Kabul–Kandahar line in the event of a fresh menace from Russia. Only by demonstrating their willingness to undertake permanent occupation could the British secure Afghan loyalty. Roberts favoured the construction of railways to Kandahar and Jalalabad and through the Gumal to the Zhob valley and Pishin, and the stationing of troops at Kandahar and Jalalabad. But he realized that the British government were unlikely to agree to the advance of troops and limited his plans to railway construction. This he thought essential for the defence both of Afghanistan and of India. Otherwise there would be no barrier to the gradual occupation by Russian troops of the whole of Afghanistan, followed by an effort, in overwhelming numbers and with the support of Afghans and the 200,000 tribesmen on the border, at the invasion of India.[268] Sir Robert Sandeman in Baluchistan broadly agreed with this analysis and suggested another railway from Lahore to Ghazai.[269]

All such schemes, however, required the acceptance not only of the British government but what was even more difficult to obtain, that of the Amir, Abdur Rahman. The Salisbury Government feared Russian interference in Afghanistan in the event of Abdur Rahman's death and thought in terms of strengthening British influence by supporting his son Habibulla's succession to the throne;[270] but Abdur Rahman showed no signs of dying, and Roberts predicted catastrophe if the British government waited on events.

My firm belief is that we shall some day lose India unless the Home authorities recognize the extreme danger of having Russia as a near neighbour, and determine, after making suitable arrangements for the protection of England and our Colonial possessions, to put forth the whole of our strength for the defence of this country whenever the occasion arises.

He was convinced that Indian troops could not be depended upon, that 280 million Indians would be ready to revolt on the first signs of defeat and that ten thousand miles of land and sea frontier would be threatened.[271] Lansdowne too urged immediate action, and thought advantage could be taken of a friendly letter from the Amir inviting a British mission to Kabul to arrange a direct interview with the Viceroy and to secure agreement on the establishment of telegraph and railway communications.[272]

The Salisbury Government, however, did not share this sense of urgency and the months passed with no tangible result. Meantime Abdur Rahman became, from the British point of view, increasingly undependable. He took no action regarding Russian encroachments in the Pamir region.[273] His attitude to the Government of India ceased even to be courteous and he made it clear that he preferred to deal directly with the British government.[274] Lansdowne toyed with the idea of sending Roberts to meet the Amir; but in fact the Government of India did no more than tighten their control over the frontier tribes.[275]

The Liberal Government of 1892 were even less impressed than their predecessors with the alarmist ideas of Roberts; and Lansdowne's new plan to coerce the Amir by threatening to withhold the subsidy[276] did not appeal to them. Their attitude had been summed up by Northbrook the previous year:

We English are quite satisfied with our own perfect right and justice when we annex anything. For instance, we have pushed on to near Kandahar, we have exercised greater control over Kashmir, and I believe have a garrison at Gilgit, we have annexed Upper Burma, and yet some of us seem to think the Russians are unscrupulous villains if they cast a sheep's eye on Shignan and certain other tracts which can produce little or nothing but heads of the *ovis poli*.[277]

The Cabinet overruled the Government of India and instructed them that no more should be done than keeping the Amir in good humour, if possible by an interview, and defining the north-west frontier of India. The Amir's complaints of Russian acts of aggression were to be ignored. Even the strengthening of control over the tribes was discouraged, and Lansdowne's remonstrances against the Amir's cruelties were considered to be unwarranted interferences in the internal affairs of Afghanistan.[278]

Though still of the view that the Amir was being treated with excessive forbearance, the Viceroy loyally accepted the home government's policy. He was even willing, if it became necessary, himself to go to Kabul to convince the Amir that the British sought only to support him and to respect his independence.[279] However, after much procrastination, the Amir consented to receive a mission under Sir Mortimer Durand.[280] These negotiations led to an agreement that the Amir would evacuate all the districts held by him north of the Oxus river in exchange for the districts lying to the south of the river. He also promised not to interfere with the frontier tribes and consented to a definition and demarcation, whenever practicable and desirable, of the Indo-Afghan frontier by a joint commission. He retained Aswar and the Birwal tract but renounced his claims to the rest of Waziri territory, Dewer and Chageh. The Government of India withdrew all restrictions on the purchase and import by the Amir of ammunition, promised assistance in arms and ammunition and increased his annual subsidy from 12 to 18 lakhs of rupees.[281]

With the conclusion of this agreement, Lansdowne became anxious that British authority should be extended up to the settled boundary. The administration should be taken over by the Government of India from the Punjab government, roads constructed and posts established.[282] But the British government were satisfied with the existing position. Godley wrote that he could 'hardly believe that we are within sight of a time when we shall have a defined frontier all round our Indian possessions';[283] and though Kimberley was not so optimistic as to believe that 'a millenium of peace' had arrived, he warned the Government of India against pushing forward, under one pretext or another, with the intent of bringing the territory up to the frontier directly under British rule.[284] Elgin was in full agreement. He vetoed the punitive expeditions which had been recommended by the Punjab government as he regarded such campaigns as making directly for annexation, and he agreed to posts on the new boundary only when informed that they had been suggested by the Amir in the interests of tranquillity on the border.[285] While British control of the border area between Quetta and the Khyber Pass should be ensured, there should be no interference in Baluchistan; and all that was required in Chitral and Gilgit in the north was the exclusion of Russian influence.[286] Fowler, in hearty accord in condemning 'the costly hunger for constant annexation', warned Elgin that even the limited objective of preventing Russian intrigue in Chitral and Gilgit allowed no relaxation of effort.[287]

The frontier itself was, for the most part, demarcated by joint commissions between the years 1894-6. Though the agreement of 1893 had not stated that the 'Durand Line' formed the boundary between India and Afghanistan, the joint demarcation agreements of 1895 and 1896 explicitly declared that it was the boundary between the territories of the Government of India and those of the Amir of Afghanistan which was being demarcated. But hopes that, with a known frontier with Afghanistan and the settlement with Russia in 1895 regarding the Pamirs, a policy of 'sitting still with little interference' could be followed, were soon belied. Abdur Rahman soon ceased to be friendly, and there were grounds for suspecting his connivance at the disturbances which broke out in Chitral. The Viceroy thought that if the frontier were to serve as the limit not only for the Amir's territories but also of his sphere of influence, it might be necessary to construct a road from Peshawar to Chitral.[288] The home government, advised by Lyall,[289] were inclined to withdraw altogether from Chitral and rely on Afghanistan and Russia abiding by their treaty commitments; but Elgin now argued against it. Chitral had great strategic value, and the Pamirs Agreement, by bringing Russia nearer the Hindu Kush mountains, had increased the necessity of the British holding Chitral. Elgin believed that military withdrawal would also weaken

British influence with the tribes. 'I hesitate to use the word prestige, but depend upon it, it goes for a good deal; and if it is damaged by a withdrawal from Chitral it is by no means certain where the mischief may stop.' India, according to Elgin, could only be governed by maintaining the fact that the British were the dominant race. Unless Russia were checked by placing a detachment in this forward position, circumstances might develop when the whole frontier would be ablaze, while dangers in the rear paralysed British efforts.[290] That even Elgin, in principle in agreement with the Liberal Government and by nature prone to translate subordination into subservience, should have expressed his dissent in the language of Roberts, proves strikingly the powerful contagion of the forward policy. There was much truth in Curzon's observation that 'the usual Viceroy is a mere puppet in the hands of his military advisers. The tunes to which my two predecessors were induced to dance would constitute a page of history that I hope for their sakes may never be written.'[291]

The Rosebery Government, however, were unanimous and firm on Chitral. The Prime Minister wrote that he differed with the greatest reluctance from the Viceroy, mainly because of the double danger to which India was exposed. 'While you are guarding against Russia on every peak of the Hindu-Kush, a great military, and in these matters most unveracious and unscrupulous, government is about to establish a conterminous frontier with you—I mean France.' There should be no dispersal of force such as was involved in the occupation of Chitral while France, in alliance with Russia, menaced India. If, after a British withdrawal from Chitral, Russia still adopted a threatening posture, reoccupation could be considered.[292]

The decision to withdraw was supported, although perhaps for differing reasons, by the Liberal party as a whole.[293] Indeed, Northbrook was reported to be in favour of withdrawal from Gilgit as well.[294] But before the withdrawal from Chitral had been implemented, the Rosebery Ministry fell. In the new Conservative Government, Lansdowne and Curzon supported the retention of Chitral,[295] and the decision to withdraw was reversed.[296] The Liberals, in opposition, charged the Government of India, to Elgin's chagrin,[297] with breach of faith of a proclamation of March 1895, which had promised the tribes that their territory would not be occupied.

The thrust of British influence right up to the frontier revitalized the problem of relations with the Amir. Apart from his suspected role in the Chitral disturbances, there were allegations of ill-treatment of British sepoys and employees on furlough in Afghanistan, while his attitude to the British agent at Kandahar was rude and even hostile. 'At present he asks us to treat him as the responsible Governor of a civilized state, whilst he treats us in an offhand and treacherous manner quite incompatible with the comity of civilized countries.'[298] But the Government of India who, as his proposal for an envoy in London had been rejected,[299] continued to deal directly with the Amir, were in no position to show their resentment. On the contrary, when the Amir sought a renewal of assurances of support against Russia, they were willing to reiterate Ripon's statement of 4 October 1880.[300] But they were dissuaded by Salisbury, who, after the Tsar's visit to London in October 1896, concluded that there was nothing to fear from Russia and that therefore a firm line could be taken with the Amir.[301]

The Government of India, however, preferred to do nothing so long as Abdur Rahman was Amir.[302] The Viceroy gave little credence to the reports, widely current, that the Amir had inspired the general disturbances in the Malakand area in 1897.[303] Some elements in the army clamoured for an advance on Kabul, but as there was no positive proof of the Amir's complicity, Elgin curbed them. 'Honestly I feel that an incautious word or act on my part might land us in an Afghan war.'[304] It was not the Amir's activities but the growing discontent at the incessant encroachment into tribal territory which was the major cause for the outbreak.[305] Indeed the disturbances had established that the Amir, while capable of very unfriendly acts, did not intend to sever his relations with Britain; for if he did, he could scarcely hope to get a better chance.[306]

The other bastion, Persia, had also for a time seemed in danger from Russian encroachments. Drummond Wolff, the British envoy in Teheran, reported that Russia was 'gripping up' the whole country, and suggested a direct railway connexion from Persia to India through Baluchistan.[307] Both his earlier schemes, to co-operate with Russia in Persia and to bolster Persian rule, had failed.[308] Wolff, therefore, planned to visit India to discuss with the Viceroy the railway project, which had the support of Salisbury; but in November 1890 the Shah signed an agreement with

Russia promising to reject all schemes to construct railways in Persia, from whatever quarter they might emanate, for the next ten years, and thereafter to give Russia five years for consideration of such schemes.[309]

With this major rebuff to British plans, Salisbury began to consider the protection of British interests in south Persia only and to accept the northern part of the country as a Russian sphere of influence.[310] He urged the Government of India to construct a railway from Quetta, Karachi or Gwadar, whereby Persia could be assisted against Russia.[311] But to the foreign department in Calcutta Persia seemed less important than Afghanistan. The answer to any Russian encroachments would have to be given in Afghanistan. With the resources available to the Government of India and the amount of support likely to be received from Britain Persia could not be sustained, and the mere construction of a railway to Seistan without having any troops to send by it would not only be a waste of money but a direct incentive to the construction of railways by Russia in northern Persia.[312] Rosebery, Salisbury's successor as Foreign Secretary, was inclined to agree. While Britain should do all she could to keep the 'rickety concern' in Persia going, it was to her an item only in the second order of priority.[313] So for the remainder of these years Persia ceased to loom large on the horizon of Indian policy. It was left to Curzon to bring it back to prominence.

CHAPTER 5

CURZON:
THE APOGEE OF ADMINISTRATION

I

All the characteristics of British rule in India in the forty years after the revolt of 1857 found their full, and even exaggerated, development in the seven years of Curzon's viceroyalty. The wave rose to a crescendo and broke, with almost explosive force, on the shore, carrying India to the second and final phase of British effort and achievement. India had become in 1858 a British dependency in the full sense, had been safeguarded, and had, after some years, even been cherished; but to Curzon it was not merely the central piece of the British empire but the focus of British interests. For perhaps the last time British policy in Asia was initiated not from Whitehall but from Calcutta; and a vigorous Viceroy laid down lines of policy and took crucial decisions, while the home government, in the early years, acquiesced with often little more than a mild and private reservation. Within India, efficient administration, on which a premium had been laid ever since the Crown assumed responsibility, now became an end in itself. Curzon was determined to administer well and, sparing neither himself nor his subordinates, succeeded in doing so; but so much effort was spent in perfecting the methods of administration that its objectives were lost from view.

For it was not sufficient to give the people what Curzon thought was best for them and to promote their material interests in ways which he considered most suitable. It was also necessary to bear in mind their feelings and impulses and to recognize, as so many British statesmen before Curzon had done, that the noblest purpose of an alien administration was to prepare for its own withdrawal. It was the failure to do so which flawed Curzon's rule. He returned to Britain seething with misery because of his discomfiture at Kitchener's hands. The correspondence of his last year as Viceroy was concerned almost solely with this and makes obsessional reading. It was, of course, a defeat from which he and his career never fully recovered; from then on, as Lord

Snow says of one of his characters, he was a man with his future
behind him. But it was not the root cause of his Indian failure.
What limited Curzon's achievement was his inability to take into
account the inhabitants of India. He handled India as a sculptor
his marble, chiselling to his intention what he assumed to be an
inanimate mass.

The blindness was all the more astonishing because the Indian
people were no longer quiescent. The last year of Curzon's tenure
of office saw the fervent agitation over the partition of Bengal. This
episode was a perfect sample of the qualities and defects of the
viceroyalty—a step taken solely on administrative grounds and
opposed vehemently for political and emotional reasons. Indian
nationalism, which Curzon had consistently belittled and sneered
at, showed itself to have at last attained a revolutionary stage. It
was the incapacity to recognize this and to come to grips with the
new situation and not the petty controversy with the Commander-
in-Chief that reduced Curzon's viceroyalty to a *folie de grandeur*.
Thereafter no Viceroy could afford to ignore Indian sentiment. The
viceroyalty of Curzon marked both the apogee of British Indian
administration and the beginnings of adult Indian nationalism
and the uninterrupted revolution which reached its goal in 1947.

II

The announcement in August 1898 of Curzon's appointment as
Viceroy caused no flutter of surprise in any part of the world. The
Secretary of State, Lord George Hamilton, wrote that the choice
lay between Lord Balfour of Burleigh and Curzon;[1] but in fact
there was no alternative selection which Salisbury could seriously
consider. Curzon seemed to have all the qualities and resources
which go to the making of a great Viceroy. He, who even at Eton
had written of himself in terms which were 'an enviable marvel of
self-satisfaction',[2] was captivated by the allurements and the demands of the Indian viceroyalty and believed that it was a post
which he was born to hold. It would give him scope to indulge his
taste for magnificence, while its wide range of high responsibilities
and its varied sphere of initiative seemed commensurate only with
his own genius. This was not a wildly extravagant self-delusion.
Curzon was a man of natural authority, with a clear and vigorous
mind. Its strength, which lay in application and analysis rather
than in reflexion, had been nourished by wide reading and travel.

Curzon had been not only to India but to Persia, Afghanistan and China, and had built up large reserves of encyclopaedic knowledge. Even in 1895, when offering Curzon the Under-Secretaryship for Foreign Affairs, Salisbury had acknowledged that there was no other Conservative politician who was more familiar with Eastern questions;[3] and though Curzon had not regarded that post as adequate to his powers, he had accepted it because it would enable him to watch and move amid great events. Three years later, when the succession to the viceroyalty lay open, he drew the Prime Minister's attention, without a trace of reticence, to his own claims. The announcement followed almost as a matter of course.

Apart from his mental energy and swift apprenticeship, Curzon brought two great qualities to the Indian opportunity—immense powers of work and an unswerving dedication to duty. The viceroyalty was to him essentially a stupendous task in administration, and he devoted himself to it with intense and lonely concentration. 'I get through my work', he wrote to Lord Ampthill,[4] 'a. by never doing anything else b. by sitting up into the night c. by rapidity in writing, the result of long practice d. by familiarity with most subjects. I have been studying India for years e. by invariably devoting Sunday to some big subject, in independence of the ordinary routine.' The very idea of a holiday seemed to him a remote and almost forgotten dream.[5] No matter was too trivial for his attention, and every problem was studied to the last detail. For seven years the continuous directive impulse of the Government of India came from the Viceroy. Minutes to his subordinates, despatches to the home government, resolutions to the general public and letters to a wide circle of correspondents, all drafted by Curzon himself in his brocaded, self-admiring prose, poured forth in an unceasing stream.

It would be unfair to Curzon to suggest that in these prodigious efforts he was inspired solely by personal motives. He was bursting with vanity and ambition, and was armoured in a chinkless self-confidence. But there was also a nobler strand, an unwearying sense of mission, in the Indian phase of Curzon's public life. He believed that it was the duty 'laid on Englishmen from on high'[6] to maintain the empire in India, which was 'the miracle of the world'[7] and 'the biggest thing that the English are doing anywhere in the world'.[8] But he was also honest enough to recognize that imperialism was not unselfish. 'As long as we rule India, we are the greatest Power in the world. If we lose it, we shall drop straight-away to a third-rate Power.'[9] These various reasons, taken together, made him

an Imperialist heart and soul. Imperial expansion seems to me an inevitable necessity and carries a noble and majestic obligation. I do not see how any Englishman, contrasting India as it is with what it was or might have been, can fail to see that we came here in obedience to what I call the decree of Providence, for the lasting benefit of millions of the human race. We often make great mistakes here; but I do firmly believe that there is no Government in the world that rests on so secure a moral basis, or is more fiercely animated by duty.[10]

If, after five years of grinding toil, he desired to stay at least an-other two years in India, it was not solely because he could not tear himself away from the dazzle of the office and rationalized a petty emotion.

I might be [he wrote to Ampthill][11] a member of the Cabinet at once by remaining in England. But I have declined this and other things too, feeling that it is a duty to see my work in India rather further on to-wards completion. I am well aware that there are many who do not want my return and who would like to settle down again into the muddy old rut. I doubt not that many other men could carry on the work with ability and success. But I want to ground a few more indispensable things with just sufficient firmness to prevent them from being shaken out of the soil. A good many changes for which I was most denounced there, four and five years ago are now unalterably fixed and universally accepted. I want to steer a few more into close approximity to this class and then leave them to survive or perish on their merits.

When all is said, the fact remains that Curzon was one of the great public servants of his time.

The tragedy of Curzon lay in that, with such an abundance of trained talent, he was denied the crowning qualities. He was never an administrator of the first rank. Grasp of detail, which was Curzon's great asset, is only incidental to successful administra-tion; the essence of it is an easy command of men, and of this Curzon was incapable. With a cold and grating personality, Cur-zon was unsuited to an office which ensured that he would never meet an equal. The tendency which Lord Haldane noticed in Curzon many years later, 'of treating his officials as if they were serfs',[12] first became prominent in India, and his unconcealed scorn gradually alienated almost everyone he had to work with in the central government and in the provinces. His lack of courtesy, fussiness about protocol and irascible pettiness became notorious, and friends in Britain wrote to him in warning.

Try [wrote Lord George Hamilton on the eve of laying down office as Secretary of State][13] and suffer fools more gladly; they constitute the majority of mankind. In dealing with your colleagues and subordinates try and use your rare powers of expression in making things pleasant and smooth to those whom you overrule or dominate. Cases have more than once come to my notice where persons have been deeply wounded and gone from you full of resentment in consequence of some incautious joke or verbal rebuke, which they thought was harshly administered.

But advice, however *bona fide*, cannot change character.

Such a personal deficiency had naturally, in the case of an Indian Viceroy, public consequences. Contempt for his subordinates reinforced Curzon's incapacity to delegate authority. His intellectual confidence was unassailable. There was no one with whom Curzon was willing to associate in carrying out his vast responsibilities.

Over and over again I have tried the policy of delegation, with the same deplorable results....The Government of India is a mighty and miraculous machine for doing nothing. It is worked by loyal and hard-working men. I have not one word to say against their devotion to duty and their industry. But they are so absorbed with the daily grind that their eyes are never lifted from the ground....It is, I am afraid, therefore, out of the question to expect the administration to be conducted as I am trying to do it all along the line, and at the same time to press upon me devolution.[14]

It was with the greatest reluctance that he permitted even the execution of his decisions to leave his hands, as it perforce had to do at some stage. 'It is supposed', he wrote to Hamilton, 'to be a mark of efficiency and even greatness to get your work done for you by other people. I frankly disagree. I say that if you want a thing done in a certain way, the only manner in which to be sure that it is so done, is to do it yourself.'[15] The viceroyalty was an astonishing attempt on the part of one man to run the Government of India, and it is a measure of Curzon's volcanic industry and strength of intellect that the effort did not result in an inglorious breakdown. A success, however, it could never be.

In this respect the contrast between Curzon and the other eminent proconsul of the age, Milner, was sharp. Both were endowed with keen intelligence and had equipped themselves to rule over vast dominions. They could both move rapidly to the core of a problem and handle it with equal courage and efficiency. In addition Milner, strong and humble where Curzon was insecure and vain, could raise round him a band of younger men who gave him total allegiance and implemented his principles and policies with full understanding. But a Curzon kindergarten, although Curzon had had hopes of founding a school,[16] was inconceivable.

Incapable of developing any spirit of partnership even with his fellow-countrymen whose lot it was to serve him, Curzon was not even aware that it was possible, and indeed necessary, to achieve emotional identity with the people he ruled. He spoke of Indians in tones one normally reserves for pet animals. 'They are very strange people, these natives; they have such an extraordinary respect for strength of decision and action that, if it be based upon sincere purpose, and expressed in sympathetic language, there is scarcely anything that they will not accept from their rulers, however contrary to their own previous utterances or prepossessions.'[17] His natural emphasis was on efficiency rather than on understanding, on cool application to the daily tasks rather than on furtherance of any belief or ideal. It was a viceroyalty without vision. Curzon himself claimed that he was always looking ahead. 'There is not a day of my life in which I do not say to myself, "What is going to happen in this country 20 years or 50 years hence?"'[18] But scattered throughout Curzon's correspondence is evidence of lack of discernment. His rule relied solely on externals and never plunged into the depths. Autocratic grandeur, however efficient, which was supported by no wide and imaginative sympathy was not sufficient to mesmerize India of the twentieth century; and as the clouds gathered round the viceroyalty at its sunset, the beams of Curzon's glory failed either to illumine or to warm. The best assessment of Curzon's personality as Viceroy would seem to be his own comment on his ablest civil servant, Anthony MacDonnell: 'a strange creature—by far the most capable administrator that we have in this country, but destitute of a ray of human emotion.'[19]

Foreign affairs had, till he came to India, been Curzon's chief interest, and during his term there was a foreign policy of India, in the sense that it was formulated in India by the Viceroy on the basis of what he regarded as India's interests. The foreign department of the Government of India functioned as the Asiatic branch of the British Foreign Office[20] rather than as merely its executive agent. Curzon believed that India was no longer a matter of imperial concern only but was a part of the direct conflict between the Great Powers. The Indian empire—which for this purpose included Aden and the outposts in the Persian Gulf—had common frontiers with Turkey, Russia, China and France. 'The geographical position of India will more and more push her into the forefront of international politics. She will more and more become the strategical frontier of the British Empire.'[21]

The foreign policy of India, as conceived by Curzon, had two aspects. Beyond the administrative boundaries of India lay various states over which Curzon thought it essential to extend the penumbra of British authority. He was not eager to push forward the limits of empire, but he was determined that other Powers should not gain ascendancy in these areas bordering on India. So it was necessary both to prevent rival encroachments and to establish the predominance of British influence. These dual objectives governed Curzon's policy in Arabia, Persia, Afghanistan, Tibet and even Siam.

The curbing of Turkey on the western flank and of France on the eastern one were achievements of minor interest and the Viceroy attached no great importance to them. What really possessed his whole mind was the need to exclude Russia from southern Persia, Afghanistan and Tibet. This was an *ideé fixe* which Curzon had repeatedly expounded in his books long before he came to India.[22] His experience as Viceroy only served to strengthen his fears of the Russian menace. 'As a student of Russian aspirations and methods for fifteen years, I assert with confidence—what I do not think that any one of her own statesmen would deny—that her ultimate ambition is the dominion of Asia.'[23] He believed that the desire for India and the consciousness, however mistaken or ludicrous, of a capacity to seize it were growing in Russian minds, and that an Englishman could commit no more serious mistake than to think that Russia would merely peck at India across the frontier whenever she had trouble with Britain elsewhere.[24] Russia would in such circumstances throw her whole force against India, because for the purposes of an Anglo-Russian war India rather than England was the heart of the empire.[25] 'It really seems to me as though the fear of Russia dominated like some great nightmare every phase and aspect of the Asiatic situation; and that since the South African war the fear is even greater than it was before.'[26] This was not a view which the home government (with the exception perhaps of Salisbury) shared wholeheartedly;[27] but the initiative in planning policy was assumed by the Viceroy.

Curzon viewed with serious concern Russia's advance across the Persian desert towards the southern part of the country and her possible acquisition of a port in the Persian Gulf. There were, he told the Secretary of State,[28] few things in the world upon which he felt more strongly; it was bad enough and costly enough to have to defend India against the constant threat of Russia by land, but the task would be beyond British power if Russia were also to have the power of threatening by sea. He examined the various alternative policies and, in a despatch sent on 21 September 1899,[29] advocated, though with some scepticism, his favourite project[30] of the partition of Persia into spheres of influence. It seemed to Curzon impracticable to expect Russia to join Britain in introducing reforms in Persia, while independent British action, with retaliation if need arose, was too belligerent. When forming a British sphere of influence, it was important to include in it Seistan, through which lay an important British trade route, but in which Russia was interested and where she had already posted news-writers.[31] It was not merely possible but essential to secure British interests in southern Persia. Britain could without the slightest difficulty seize and hold all important posts in the Persian Gulf; but this preponderance, 'absolutely essential for the protection and salvation of India', would be shattered if Russia were permitted to secure Kuwait, Bunder Abbas or Chahbar, in which she had begun to show interest, or to build the railway she was planning from Isfahan to the sea.[32] 'Oh, my God, English policy towards Persia throughout this century has been a page of history that makes one alternately laugh with derision and groan with despair.'[33] At least now it should be made clear to Persia and to Russia that Britain would not permit southern Persia to pass under any foreign influence other than her own.

To Curzon's annoyance the British government made no response. 'I do not suppose', wrote the Viceroy, 'that Lord Salisbury will be persuaded to lift a little finger to save Persia from her doom. . . . We are slowly—no, I think I may say swiftly, paving the way for the total extinction of our influence in that country.'[34] Meantime, Russia was strengthening her influence and, by making a large loan conditional on an undertaking that Persia would never again put herself under financial obligations to any other Power, seemed to Curzon to be binding Persia hand and foot and taking her over into perpetual slavery. 'If you do nothing now, the halter which Russia has pitched round the neck of Persia in the hour of our embarrassment will be tightened bit by bit till the last breath has been squeezed out of the body of the wretched victim.'[35]

The British government, however, remained for long of the view that no action was necessary,[36] or perhaps even possible;[37] and Curzon believed that his insistence on a Persian policy had irritated Salisbury.[38] It was only in July 1901, almost two years after Curzon's despatch, that the British government made any move in the matter. Sir Arthur Hardinge, the British Minister at Teheran, was instructed to speak to the Persian government on Seistan and explain British interest in that area. This seemed to Curzon to be most inadequate, and he now wrote to Lansdowne, the Foreign Secretary. An understanding with Russia was no longer to be thought of, as she had practically, according to the Viceroy, declared war against Britain all along the line. So Persia should be told that Britain wished her to continue as an independent buffer state but could not afford to see the buffer reduced to the thinness of a wafer.[39] At last the Viceroy's pleadings prevailed;[40] and on 6 January 1902 Hardinge was directed to inform the Persian government that Britain could not reasonably be expected to abandon a position obtained by many years of constant effort or to acquiesce in the attempts of other Powers to acquire political predominance in southern Persia. Britain could not consent to the acquisition by Russia of a military or naval station in the Persian Gulf, and if the Persian government at any time made such a concession to Russia, Britain would be obliged to take such measures in the Gulf as she might consider necessary for the protection of her interests. The British government could not tolerate the concession to Russia of any preferential political rights or advantages or of any commercial monopoly or exclusive privilege in the southern or south-eastern districts of Persia, including Seistan. If, despite these warnings, the Persian government encouraged the advance of Russian political influence and intervention in those regions, the British government would necessarily have to reconsider their policy.[41]

In the summer of 1902 the Shah visited London and Lansdowne informed him that the British government were determined, should occasion arise, to put forth the whole of their strength to prevent encroachments by other Powers in the southern parts of Persia and the Persian Gulf. Twelve months later, in May 1903, Lansdowne stated in the House of Lords that British policy in the Persian Gulf aimed at the protection and promotion of British commerce and, while the British government did not seek to exclude the legitimate trade of other Powers, they would regard the establishment of a naval base or a fortified post by any other Power as a very grave menace to British interests and would certainly resist it with all the means at their disposal.[42]

The day after he had laid down what Curzon termed a Monroe doctrine[43] for the Gulf, Lansdowne broached the question of an understanding with the Russian Ambassador. He said the British government recognized the preponderance of Russia in north Persia, but themselves had special interests in the Gulf, the southern ports and Seistan and would regard with serious apprehension any attempt on Russia's part to construct a railway from the north which would threaten India's frontiers in Baluchistan. The Ambassador replied that Russia had no intention of establishing a naval base in the Gulf, and any such railway project was most unlikely. But he doubted if the situation was ripe for any general discussion on Persia. Subsequent overtures during Curzon's term confirmed this and made it clear that the Russian government were as yet unwilling to consider any partition of Persia into spheres of influence. Curzon urged the home government to be firm. The future of the Persian Gulf was vital to the future of the British empire and it would be an act of national treachery to admit the most formidable of Britain's enemies into an area where he had no interests but those of aggression and the security of which was essential to the security of India.[44] In fact, the Viceroy's hope of a partition of Persia into spheres of influence was achieved two years after he had left India.

Curzon was also anxious to resist the strengthening of Russian influence by granting large loans to the Persian government; but the Committee of Imperial Defence regarded this as undesirable in principle, and preferred to encourage the completion of the railway from Constantinople to Baghdad, thereby bringing the Turks on the Russian flank. Curzon dissented from the suggestion that Turkish and German assistance should be utilized to further British interests, and regarded the Committee of Imperial Defence as a heterogeneous and dangerous body. 'But in respect of his pet creation Balfour was wholly unbalanced; and in his day it was quite capable of advising against the purchase of the Rokeby Velasquez for the nation.'[45]

Though Curzon was willing to consider the partition of Persia with Russia, he was determined in Afghanistan to maintain the traditional policy of excluding Russian influence and interference. Only Herat seemed to him indefensible; but he did not believe that the loss of this town would endanger India.[46] However, Russia, despite her formal pledges to regard Afghanistan as outside her sphere of influence, had continued to evince interest in that country. Within a few days of Curzon's arrival in India the Amir, Abdur Rahman, sent him evidence of efforts by Russian officials in Trans-Caspia to communicate directly on important matters with the Afghan authorities. Curzon advised the Amir not to reply to the letter of the Governor of Ashkabad, but as the Amir thought that an explicit rebuff was required, he was permitted to reply in his own words. Similar action was taken later in the year with regard to the letters of the Russian General at Kushk and the Governor at Merv.[47]

On 6 February 1900 the Russian Embassy in London sent a memorandum to the Foreign Office stating that although Russia's obligations only bound her to refrain from political action, she had, from a feeling of friendly interest towards Britain, foregone even non-political relations. Such an attitude, however, was said to be no longer possible without material loss to Russian interests, owing to the establishment in 1885 of a long common frontier between Russia and Afghanistan and the completion of the Trans-Caspian railway. Attempts to settle frontier questions by reference to the British government having proved abortive, the re-establishment of direct relations with the Afghan government was indispensable. But the Russian government asserted that these relations would have no political character and that Afghanistan would remain outside the sphere of Russian influence.[48]

The Amir also received a message in March 1900 from the Russian agent at Bokhara expressing the friendly sentiments of the Russian government towards Afghanistan and their wish to facilitate trade;[49] and there were reports of friendly relations between Russian and Afghan officials in north and north-western Afghanistan, of the prompt grants of reparation for border offences committed by Afghans against Russian subjects and of an improvement in commercial relations. Curzon advised the home government to stand firm. If re-establishment of direct relations meant a Russian envoy at Kabul, it was open to the gravest objections; for no such envoy, despite the Russian disclaimer, could avoid political matters, and the inevitable result of his presence would be, if not predominant Russian influence, the growth of a condominium at Kabul. But if the Russians wished to have an agent not at Kabul but at Herat or elsewhere to communicate with the Governor on trade and frontier matters, the British government could offer to bring the proposal to the Amir's notice.[50] Salisbury agreed with the Viceroy but thought the time inopportune for further communication with Russia.

So nothing was done till October 1901, when Abdur Rahman died and was succeeded by his son Habibulla. Lansdowne informed the Russian Ambassador that both British policy and the situation in Afghanistan remained unaffected by the change of rulers.[51] In January 1902 the Russian government were told that with a new Amir some time would have to be allowed before any change in the management of Afghanistan's relations with neighbouring states could be discussed.[52] But the British government, who had believed that the Amir would countenance no direct relations without their permission, were alarmed by reports in the autumn of 1902 that a Russian mission was about to visit Kabul, especially as the Amir had stated publicly that if Britain objected to his import of arms and machinery there were other means of getting them and that he was making arrangements with Russia for the maintenance of Afghan commercial interests.[53] Curzon thought it possible—'surprising but not incredible'—that Habibulla had made an appeal to Russia.[54]

In December 1902 Russia proclaimed her intention of entering into direct relations with Afghanistan,[55] and two months later Britain was informed that these relations would be straightforward and open. But it was not intended to give them a political character and the despatch of agents was not contemplated for the time being.[56] Curzon inquired if the Foreign Office intended to take any action on this memorandum which, if literally interpreted, was a repudiation of Russia's existing engagements regarding Afghanistan. Local correspondence, though not free from danger, might be permitted with the Amir's consent; but the Government of India deprecated any admission of Russia's right to send agents into Afghanistan.[57] However, the Amir, terminating any flirtation he might have indulged in with Russia, protested at the despatch of letters by the Governor of Ashkabad and stated that he would not correspond with the Russian government.[58]

The British government did not regard the Russian menace with the same seriousness as the Viceroy. It seemed to them that if Russia advanced, her difficulties of transport and commissariat would be immense. Balfour, now Prime Minister, said that for ten days he had thought of little else but Afghanistan and proposed a policy of 'sterilization'—discouragement of communications and of cultivation—in the area between Kandahar and the Russian frontier.[59] Balfour also agreed to lay down a Monroe doctrine for Afghanistan. The Russian government were informed on 25 November 1903 that Britain expected them to recognize in the most formal manner the position of Afghanistan as being entirely within the British sphere of influence and guided by Britain in regard to its external policy. Subject to this, the British government were willing to permit, if the Amir agreed, direct correspondence on local, non-political matters.

The Russian government replied on 16 December 1903 that any direct communications with Afghanistan would be restricted to frontier matters and have no political character. They assured the British government that they still abided by their declaration that Afghanistan was absolutely within the British sphere of influence, and stated that 'for the present' they had no thought of stationing a representative at Kabul or sending agents to the Amir. They clarified this qualification on 4 January 1904 to mean that Russia could not possibly make engagements of this nature binding for all time and in all circumstances.

The British government were unable, before Curzon left India, to commit Russia any further. On 5 February 1905, in response to an inquiry, Lansdowne assured the Russian Ambassador that the despatch of a British mission to Kabul denoted no change in

British policy; and the Ambassador said that Russia desired no change in her own relations with Afghanistan and wished it to remain a buffer state. But when Lansdowne suggested the exchange of official assurances the Ambassador replied that the Russian government did not wish to enter into any formal agreement.[60]

Curzon not only moved the pieces in the Great Game on the traditional squares of Persia and Afghanistan but also, for the first time, brought Tibet within its scope. Within six months of his arrival in India he mentioned the possibility of Russian influence in Tibet and thought it would be a great pity if judgment went against the British by default. He was, therefore, eager to communicate with the Tibetans directly and not through the Chinese who claimed suzerainty over Tibet.[61] But British interest was only quickened by the official announcement, on 30 September 1900, that the Tsar had received Dorjieff, one of those colourful, fraudulent characters whom Tibet periodically gives to the world. The Russian government assured Britain that the interview had no diplomatic or political significance—and this was doubtless true, at least as far as Russia was concerned; but it alarmed the British, and their attitude was justified in that the visit disclosed Tibet's desire for Russian sympathy, if not assistance.[62]

Surprisingly enough, Curzon appears to have been less agitated than the home government by Dorjieff's activity. It was only in the summer of 1901 that he again warned the Cabinet that unless the Tibetans were frightened into accepting British influence, there might well be a Russian protectorate within ten years. 'Of course we do not want their country. It would be madness for us to cross the Himalayas and to occupy it. But it is important that no one else should seize it, and that it should be turned into a sort of buffer state between the Russian and Indian Empires.'[63] Curzon wished to take military action. The Secretary of State was disposed to open negotiations with Tibet and to point out to her the disturbing effects of Russia's advance in Central Asia.[64] 'There is some resemblance between the attitude now taken up by the Government of the Dalai Lama and that adopted by the Amir Shere Ali in 1876, when he refused to receive a Mission from the British Government whilst carrying on negotiations with the Russian authorities in Central Asia.'[65] The Foreign Secretary, Lansdowne, was inclined to agree with the Viceroy, though he preferred to move more cautiously than Curzon intended.[66]

Curzon was still considering the next move when, in the summer of 1902, the situation seemed to acquire urgency. The Chinese official who was to meet the British Political Officer in Sikkim did not come; and the Government of India received a report that this was because of orders from Peking that the meeting be postponed till Russian troops had arrived at Lhasa. Independently of this, on 2 August 1902, the British Minister at Peking reported that a secret agreement was believed to have been concluded by Russia and China regarding Tibet.[67] Curzon urged the prompt despatch of a military expedition to Lhasa. 'Russia has no interest in Tibet, no subjects in Tibet, no trade with Tibet, no object in going there except one of hostility to ourselves. On that ground we are entitled to resist it in our own interest by whatever means we choose; but we are equally entitled to say to China, if she abets any such conspiracy, that we hold ourselves at liberty to retaliate upon her and to exact whatever compensation we will.'[68]

The Cabinet, however, preferred to exhaust their diplomatic resources before resorting to armed effort. The Chinese government were warned that if they concluded any agreement with Russia over Tibet, Britain would be forced to take steps to protect her own interests; and the Chinese government replied that no such transaction had ever been discussed.[69] They also, in December 1902, ordered their official to proceed at once to the Sikkim border and to negotiate amicably with the British officer.[70]

Curzon, unconvinced by these conciliatory moves, once more, on 8 January 1903, pressed the home government to permit an advance into Tibet.[71] But they still remained cautious, particularly as the Russian government declared that if a British expedition moved into Tibet they might be obliged to take steps to safeguard their own interests. Hamilton supported Curzon but the rest of the Cabinet disagreed. Lansdowne added that he was in communication with the Russian government and any military action at that stage would be regarded as sharp practice.[72]

On 8 April 1903 the Russian government stated that they had reached no agreement regarding Tibet with anyone, had no agents in Tibet and had no intention of sending any. Only if Tibet were annexed or converted into a protectorate would Russia probably seek compensation there.[73] These denials were true, but to Curzon they carried no conviction. It would probably be unfair to suggest that his declared fear of Russia was only a cloak for expansionist ambition. The Government of India had not a shadow of doubt that there was in existence some form of agreement vesting Russia with powers of intervention which would one day be used to the detriment of British interests in Tibet.[74]

Lansdowne wrote to Balfour that the Russian Ambassador had been quite straightforward and satisfactory and Hamilton would be writing to Curzon not to 'send his little army to conquer Lhasa'.[75] In fact, Hamilton interpreted the Russian answer as giving Britain a free hand short of a protectorate or annexation;[76] and Curzon was now cheerfully asked for practical suggestions. He proposed that a British representative with an escort of two hundred men should cross the border to meet Tibetan and Chinese representatives at Khamba Jong; and the Cabinet gave its general approval. It was not, however, willing to sanction any further advance into Tibet beyond Khamba Jong.[77] This, wrote Curzon was 'just funk',[78] and he instructed Colonel Younghusband, who was in charge of the Tibetan mission, to pursue a policy of imperturbable patience. Curzon and Younghusband were both of the view that a military action was inevitable, but they bided their time because the home government 'squirm badly at the idea of doing anything beyond a kick of the leg over the frontier'.[79] Curzon reported that the Tibetans were still relying firmly on Russian support. Any failure of negotiations would precipitate Russian ascendancy,[80] and have a deplorable effect on the Nepal government, whose Prime Minister had earlier told the Viceroy that as Russian presence in Tibet would be the end of Nepal's independence, the government and people of Nepal would support the British whole-heartedly.[81] On 1 October the British government reluctantly sanctioned an advance to Gyantse should the necessity arise.[82] A month later they informed the Russian and Chinese governments of this. These governments having mildly objected, Lansdowne asserted to the Russian government that the British had a right to advance into Tibet, and informed the Chinese government that further delay was impossible.[83] Younghusband prepared with glee to move forward and 'burst that bloated bubble of monkish power'.[84] Near Guru, where a Tibetan horde was massacred, the British claimed to have captured two rifles of Russian make—if true, the only evidence of even the semblance of Russian influence found by the Younghusband mission throughout its sojourn.

As it was rumoured that the Dalai Lama, after resisting to the

utmost, would flee to Russia, the British government desired that
he be informed by the Chinese government that the British did not
intend to remain in Tibet. The British Minister at Peking replied
that the Chinese government were unable to exercise any influence
in Tibet. The British government now reluctantly sanctioned an
advance to Lhasa if the Tibetans did not negotiate at Gyantse,[85]
and assured the Russian government that as long as no other Power
sought to intervene in Tibet, the British would not attempt to annex
Tibet or to establish a protectorate or in any way to control its
internal administration.[86] The Cabinet attached no importance to
Curzon's conviction that negotiations between Russia and Tibet
had taken place and had stopped little short of a veiled protectorate.[87]

Yet Curzon had prevailed to the extent that the Younghusband
mission proceeded slowly northwards. Younghusband was eager
not only to reach Lhasa but to stay there; and Curzon, in England
between his two terms, urged the Cabinet to agree to a British
agent at Lhasa. Ampthill, the acting Viceroy, did not share these
views. He wrote to the Secretary of State that it would be better to
risk the failure of the mission rather than to purchase its success at
the cost of implacable Russian hostility.[88] But Ampthill's private
letters have little in common with his official despatches, which
still had a Curzonian tone. 'Indeed', he complained to Brodrick,
'when the English mail comes in or the Indian mail goes out I
realize that I am only half a Viceroy, and I feel as if I were dealing
with two Secretaries of State.'[89] In their despatch of 30 June 1904
the Government of India argued that the Russian denial of interest
in Tibet could not remove all grounds for apprehension as proof
existed of a steady endeavour on Russia's part to cultivate political
influence by unofficial means. Russian arms and ammunition had
reached Tibet and had been used against British troops; and
Russian Buriats seemed to be aiding the Tibetans in their military
arrangements. Therefore Russia might soon say that a new situation had arisen which rendered it necessary to reconsider the
assurances of April 1903.

The Cabinet was not convinced and was anxious to rid itself of
the problem.[90] The mission should go to Lhasa to re-establish
British prestige and make it clear to Russia that Britain would not
surrender predominance in Tibet to her. The Tibetan government
should be told that no Tibetan territory should be ceded to a

foreign Power without British consent; and no such Power should be permitted to intervene in Tibetan affairs. But no agent in Lhasa was necessary.[91] The injunction against concessions to foreign Powers was incorporated in the convention signed by Younghusband at Lhasa, and thereafter the mission returned. No agent was posted at Lhasa.

Curzon was disappointed. 'His Majesty's Government's policy about Tibet is not my policy. Indeed I regard it as entirely mistaken.'[92] At the time it was widely believed that Curzon's Tibetan policy was wild adventurism, especially as references to Russia were omitted from the papers presented to Parliament. 'Any one reading the papers as they stand would wonder what the Government of India were about and whether they were not genuinely mad in going to Tibet at all.'[93] It is true that no concrete evidence of Russian presence in Tibet, to which the Government of India and Younghusband constantly made reference, has ever been produced. But the fear, at least as far as Curzon was concerned, was genuine. That the Dalai Lama looked to the Tsar for political protection has been admitted by a Russian diplomatist near the centre of these events;[94] even the Balfour Government, though it was sharply critical of the Viceroy's policy, recognized that Tibet was essentially 'a question between us and Russia';[95] the Russian government repeatedly refused to give a permanent and formal assurance of their lack of political interest in Tibet; and in 1905, a year after the convention had been signed, there were reports of Russian agents in Lhasa.[96] It was only after Japan's victory in 1905 that Russia ceased to cast her shadow over this area; but the possibility of Russian influence was still real enough to justify an arrangement regarding Tibet in the convention of 1907.

Curzon's foreign policy was essentially two-pronged; in areas from which Russian influence was excluded, British influence had to be strengthened. The second task was as important as the first, and Curzon believed he was equally qualified to undertake it. 'Downing Street', he wrote,[97] 'probably regards me, as it always has regarded experts, as a monomaniac in respect of Asia; but in Asia, on the other hand, I am regarded as the first authority. . . .' Indeed, his knowledge of these Asian countries was perhaps deeper than his understanding of Russian policy.

While, mainly because of the indifference of the home government, efforts to secure British influence in Teheran itself were both meagre and futile, Curzon continuously strengthened British interests in Seistan, southern Persia and the Persian Gulf. The British Consul at Nasratabad gained in prestige—a development which was greatly assisted by the increase in trade between Seistan and Baluchistan and by the boundary settlement achieved by the British Arbitration Commission. In the Persian Gulf, as an answer to new Russian, French and German consular posts, a vice-consulate was opened at Bunder Abbas in 1900 and raised to the status of a full consulate in 1904. The Bushire residency and consulate-general were strengthened, vice-consulates were established at Ahwaz and Kenbela, the agent at Mohammerah was made a Consul, an agent was posted at Kuwait, and in Bahrein a political agency was created by stages. Passenger, postal and telegraph communications were improved and trade was promoted.[98] Kuwait became a British protectorate in all but name and the Sheikh of Mohammerah was brought under British influence.

To render this ascendancy unshakable and to proclaim it to the world, Curzon favoured a personal visit to the area. 'A visit from the Viceroy of India in a man-of-war, with a suitable escort, would create an impression of our interests and influence immeasurably greater than any other plan that can be suggested. Neither the Russians, nor the French, could put anyone into the field who could, for a moment, compare with his prestige.'[99] But the Cabinet was not keen and let the plan lie; and it was only in 1903, when Curzon made a desperate 'Now or Never' appeal,[100] that they reluctantly consented. No political advantage seemed to them likely to accrue, while it would be distasteful to Turkey and would provoke Russia to increase pressure at Teheran. Even the British Minister in Persia would feel he had been superseded; and the Viceroy was advised to avoid an encounter with him.[101] But no lingering doubts on the part of the home government were at this stage likely to arrest Curzon's departure, to whom it was now a matter of personal achievement. His stately procession, supported by British naval might, through the Gulf—referred to in Whitehall as the Curzon lake[102]—was the climax of his Persian policy.

In Afghanistan, where the Amir, Abdur Rahman, had, during a reign of nearly twenty years, firmly established his position, the problem was whether the 1893 agreement on which British control was based should be revised. Even Curzon's critics acknowledged that no man was better fitted to deal with it.[103] When, soon after

Curzon's assumption of the viceroyalty, the Amir raised the question, Curzon proposed the development of railway and telegraph communications between India and Afghanistan, for only then would British troops be able to move rapidly to the Amir's assistance in any emergency. The Amir rejected this suggestion and implied that any such construction would endanger the independence of Afghanistan. He added that military assistance would never be sought from the British government, whose sole obligation, according to him, was to supply money, arms and ammunition.[104]

Curzon described these letters of the Amir as 'extremely ingenious, very able, not altogether honest, and exceedingly difficult to reply to'; and he thought it necessary, in the light of the Amir's interpretations of British obligations, to re-examine the policy of supplying arms and ammunition 'to which we have, as I think, foolishly pledged ourselves by the most injudicious of all the clauses included in that most injudicious agreement of Sir Mortimer Durand'.[105] Both the import of war material and its manufacture at Kabul were proceeding on a large scale and, while there was no strong reason to doubt the Amir's loyalty, it was a situation fraught with danger to British interests, particularly if his interpretations of British obligations were left unchallenged. So Curzon wrote again to the Amir, with the approval of the Cabinet, in July 1899 pointing out that the British government would assist him against any unprovoked aggression only to the extent and in the manner they considered appropriate, provided the Amir continued to abide unreservedly by their advice in regard to his external relations. The British government had, going beyond their pledges, presented him with a vast amount of ammunition during the years 1880 to 1895; and in 1893 they had agreed to the import of munitions by him. Curzon now warned the Amir to proceed cautiously and more slowly, to import only such arms as were essential and not to tempt the British government to repent of their laxity.[106]

Abdur Rahman replied in September 1899, reiterating his objections to railways and telegraphs. He said the Government of India need only send troops if the Afghans were unable to repel a Russian advance, in which case his people would, as a matter of course, consent to their entry. This firmness worried the British government. Sir Alfred Lyall, now a member of the India Council, thought the Amir might go over to Russia; but Hamilton was less pessimistic.[107] The Viceroy's assessment was that Abdur Rahman had revived the idea of consolidating Afghanistan into an independent military power which would be capable of looking both her powerful neighbours in the face. He was therefore always seeking more arms and had begun for the first time to boast about defending his country without the aid of British troops. However, he was not likely to cast his lot openly with Russia, because the price of such a friendship would be Herat; and not even the promise of Peshawar would be an adequate compensation for such a crushing blow to his prestige.[108]

While it did not seem opportune to precipitate a quarrel with the Amir, Curzon thought it necessary to arrest the conversion of Afghanistan into a vast arsenal which would be used against Britain after a few years. But Salisbury and Hamilton directed him to send a mild reply and, though Curzon believed this to be a mistake,[109] he complied. The letter of January 1900 merely stated that the British government did not intend to discuss the Amir's statements anew, as each side knew the other's view. The Amir was also aware of the friendly sentiments of the Government of India and knew that he could rely on them for the protection of his interests.

This was obviously not the end of the matter. Nothing, wrote Hamilton, could be more unsatisfactory than a state of relations where the British were powerless to do anything but give the Amir money and arms without any guarantee regarding their use. The only safeguard was that the Amir seemed more frightened of Russia than of Britain.[110] Curzon pointed out that nothing could ever have been expected from a correspondence with the Amir. 'It is about as fruitless an occupation as throwing pebbles into the ocean, but I think I know where to stand up to him and how; and the real impression if any is produced not by the policy but by the tone and manner.'[111]

Curzon, in fact, was biding his time, waiting for the death of Abdur Rahman and hoping for a personal interview with his successor. No further attempt was made to argue with Abdur Rahman and when, in March 1901, he sought to purchase thirty mountain guns from the German firm of Krupps, Curzon saw the danger but did not withhold his sanction. In no other sphere was Curzon's policy so much at the mercy of events as it was in Afghanistan during these years. Reprieve came on 3 October 1901, when Abdur Rahman died and his son Habibulla succeeded to the throne.

Curzon rejoiced that the death of Abdur Rahman, the probability of which had been one of the reasons which had induced him to accept the viceroyalty, could not have come at a more opportune moment, in the middle of his own term, at the beginning of the cold weather when if any military movements were required they could be prosecuted easily, and before he had left on his winter tour. Habibulla was his friend, and it was an advantage to Britain that there was no rival for the succession. The Viceroy hoped that Habibulla could be induced to come to Peshawar in April 1902 and to negotiate a new treaty.[112]

The home government approved,[113] and Curzon invited Habibulla to a personal discussion. He asserted that as the agreement of 1880 and the promise in 1883 of an annual subsidy of twelve lakhs of rupees were personal engagements with Abdur Rahman which had lapsed with his death, a fresh agreement should be signed.[114] The Viceroy believed that he now had the opportunity to revise the Durand Agreement in Britain's interests and to restrict the facilities for import of arms.[115] The new Amir, however, was not as pliant as Curzon had expected. He replied that the agreements of 1880 and 1883 were not personal but between governments and required no renewal; and all further efforts to convince him were of no avail. He persisted in the view that so long as he maintained a correct attitude in his external relations, the British government were bound to pay his subsidy and permit the import of arms and ammunition. Indeed, it seemed to him that it was the British government who were violating the agreements by detaining at Peshawar two million cartridges and castings for two hundred mountain guns which were on their way to Kabul. He agreed that it was a 'necessary matter' to visit his friends but committed himself to no date; and he dissented from the view that personal discussions of the measures required to oppose the Russian advance would be of advantage.[116]

Curzon claimed to discern in this adamant attitude the hand of Russia and advocated firm action in a serious situation. Russia was nibbling at Tibet and 'steadily swallowing the Persian artichoke leaf by leaf'; but 'looking over the whole surface of the political world with which I have to deal, the spot where the clouds seem to me to cluster most menacingly is in the direction of Afghanistan'.[117] If Habibulla went over openly to Russia, an advance on Kabul would be rash, but Kandahar should be taken and

16-2

probably retained, and the frontiers should be pushed forward to Girishk and the Helmund.[118] The Cabinet, however, had long ceased to be enthusiastic about revising the agreements or pressing the Amir hard lest he be pushed over completely to Russia's side, and it advised the Viceroy to avoid war.[119] Joseph Chamberlain, then in South Africa, stated what was the essence of the Lawrence policy. 'You are quite right about Afghanistan. For Heaven's sake do not let Curzon get us into a row there. Remember that it ruined Dizzy's government. It would be much better to wash our hands of the whole business leaving the Ameer to go to Russia or the Devil—and making all necessary preparations for the defence of our own border.'[120] It was this assessment—and not Curzon's— which was the correct one. There was varied evidence to show that the Amir was not a Russian client but sought only to maintain the independence which he had inherited. He consented towards the end of 1902 to the appointment of a British arbitrator to deter- mine his border with Persia in Seistan, and permitted Sir Henry McMahon to proceed to the area through Afghanistan. Early the next year he authorized the co-operation of British and Afghan commissioners for settling disputes in the border areas of Kurram and Waziristan. He also admitted British representatives for a short while into Herat. Even the Viceroy was obliged to change his views about the Amir and to acknowledge that he was now 'running quite straight'.[121]

Curzon was permitted by the home government to seek to per- suade the Amir to come down to India, though they believed that no revision of the agreement with Abdur Rahman seemed likely.[122] The Viceroy agreed that the Amir was seeking by dilatory tactics to force Britain to leave the treaty unmodified; but he would 'go on pegging and pegging away' at Habibulla. He might not obtain the ideal solution but of a satisfactory settlement he had little doubt.[123] He wrote repeatedly to the Amir, assuring him that the British government had no desire to treat him less liberally than his father and renewing the invitation to a personal discussion. But the Amir abided by his interpretation of the agreements and said that while the Afghans would fight the Russians if need be, they would never fight with foreigners as allies—a reiteration of the position taken up by his father that British troops would not be allowed to enter Afghanistan.[124] Curzon wished in answer to state that the Amir's attitude was endangering friendly relations between the two countries. No one on India's frontiers believed in British strength while the Russian nightmare obsessed all. Even Russia's reverses in the war with Japan had only increased the fear that she would turn her attention southwards. The attitude of the British government, that so long as the Amir was generally loyal to his obligations matters could be allowed to drift, only seemed to the Viceroy to postpone the evil day; but a firm stand would force the Amir, who was essentially a weak man, to commit himself to the British.[125] However, the Cabinet had no desire to create a crisis; and after much consultation[126] and the receipt of a message from Habibulla that he would never come to India,[127] Ampthill, the acting Viceroy, wrote on 10 September 1904 to the Amir, proposing the despatch of a British mission to Kabul.[128]

In other words, Habibulla had had his way. Ampthill and Kitchener in India still stressed that the official chosen for this mission, Sir Louis Dane,[129] should inform the Amir that unless he agreed to accept active British military help from the commencement of any war with Russia, the British government would be obliged to make their own arrangements for the defence of India without any further reference to him. A firm guarantee that he would abstain from political relations with foreign Powers other than Britain should be sought and a new agreement, supplemented by a secret military convention, should be signed.[130] But the home government, after consulting Curzon, decided that Dane should seek only a renewal, in the form of a personal treaty, of the engagements with Abdur Rahman. No more should be sought than absolute control of foreign relations, assurances that arms would not be despatched to the frontier tribes and prior information regarding import of arms.[131]

Dane arrived at Kabul on 12 December 1904. The Amir, who doubtless regarded—and with good reason—Dane's presence as in itself a personal triumph, hinted that the Russo-Japanese war provided a good opportunity to expel Russia from Asia, and brought forward a detailed plan of military co-operation as well as a draft treaty incorporating his requirements.[132] Dane replied that he had not been authorized to consider an attack on Russia[133] and, on instructions from Curzon and the home government,[134] reserved examination of defence proposals till a treaty had been settled. Curzon, who would have preferred Sir Hugh Barnes to have led the mission and had in fact informally invited him to do so,[135] blamed Dane for allowing the negotiations to develop on these lines. He was not sure if the Amir were serious or bluffing or joking, and wished Dane to conclude a treaty and leave Kabul as soon as possible.[136] But the Amir, who is said to have been informed of the home government's views by his spies in the offices of the Government of India, persisted in his contention that the old engagements were valid without renewal and, in face of the British attitude, withdrew his defence plan.[137] Curzon wished Dane to stand firm and fix a date for his departure. If the Amir realized that the British 'limit of squeezability' had been reached, he would give in. But the home government were advised by the India Council that any such withdrawal without an agreement might result in the Amir turning to Russia and they favoured an agreement on the Amir's terms.[138] In their view, as Curzon observed, any treaty would be better than no treaty and the certainty of humiliation was a preferable alternative to the risk of rupture.[139] In vain did the Viceroy storm that this would be to surrender to the Amir on every point.[140] The treaty drafted by the Amir, declaring that the old engagements would continue, was signed on 21 March 1905.

It was a defeat for Curzon. 'The Home Government', he wrote to Ampthill,[141] 'has allowed the Amir to dictate to us his own terms. Dane has been ordered to sign a ridiculously worded document drawn up by the Amir in his own language. This is all he brings back. I should have resigned over this had not the nature of the case rendered it impossible that I could ever with due regard to the public interest give a public explanation.' It seems, of course, at first sight absurd that the British government, so immensely superior in strength, should have tolerated the whims, suspicions and discourtesies of a semi-barbarous potentate whose very existence was guaranteed by the British. But in the context of Central Asian politics in the early twentieth century, the friendship of Afghanistan was the most important factor; and this Curzon, with all his local knowledge, failed to discern.

His achievement in Tibet was more spectacular but hardly more solid. Finding that the Chinese government had not even a shadow of real authority in this country, Curzon decided, with the home government's approval, to seek direct contact with the Tibetans themselves. He wrote to the Dalai Lama but could find no one who would deliver the letters. A Bhutanese agent, the monks

at Shigatse, the provincial governors at Gartok, the adviser on
Chinese affairs to the Government of Burma—all were considered
and most of them approached in vain. Curzon thereupon decided
that epistolary action was inadequate. Nothing would happen
until the Tibetans were frightened; and to achieve this he proposed to move troops up to the frontier and to expel any Tibetans
in Indian territory. If they resisted he would occupy the Chumbi
valley, and if they then wished to negotiate he would agree to do
so only at Lhasa.[142] But the home government were lukewarm and
obliged him to think again; and by the end of the year the Viceroy
confessed that he was not clear as to what the next move should
be.[143] However, the reports of growing Russian influence in
Tibet which continued to reach the Government of India throughout the next twelve months led Curzon back—not, one might imagine, unwillingly—to his old position. When the Chinese government suggested in December a conference of officials, the Viceroy
favoured a tripartite conference at Lhasa, with the expectation that
the negotiations would culminate in the appointment of a permanent British representative in the Tibetan capital.

Again the Cabinet objected, and, despite Curzon's protest that
they were condemning the Government of India to 'eternal steri-
lity',[144] directed that Younghusband, whom Curzon proposed to
send to negotiate with the Chinese and Tibetans at Khamba Jong,
should deal only with local questions; the posting of a British
agent at Lhasa or Gyantse should not form part of the British
proposals. But the opportunity seemed to Curzon too good to lose
and he decided to follow his own policy, trusting to success to
exonerate his disobedience. 'I shall just go quietly on my way with
this Tibetan business, and shall not be surprised if I am able sooner
or later to present the Government with an agreement which will
make their recent attitude of suspicion look a little premature, if
not foolish.'[145] Younghusband was told of the Cabinet's views but
instructed to arrange if possible for free communication between
the Government of India and the authorities at Lhasa. Aware of
the Cabinet's opinion that if negotiations broke down the most that
should be done was to blockade or occupy the Chumbi valley,[146]
Curzon, in concert with Younghusband, utilized the Tibetan arrest
of two yokels and their attack on some yaks to accuse the Tibetans
of overt hostility, and secured permission to advance to Gyantse.[147]
Once there, a Tibetan attack on the British camp and the failure of

Tibetan negotiators to appear were made the excuse for a further advance to Lhasa. The Government of India were in command of events and dragged the home government in their wake.[148] But what should be done when the mission arrived at Lhasa? The Government of India proposed that any settlement should provide for Indian officers at trade marts and a British agent at Lhasa. The home government, dominated by memories of the fate of Burnes and Cavagnari at Kabul, vetoed the proposal for British Residents at Lhasa or elsewhere.[149]

On 2 August Younghusband reached Lhasa and the Government of India authorized him (in a telegram which was not at once despatched to the Secretary of State) to seize if necessary the Dalai Lama and the principal Tibetan officials.[150] No such drastic action proved necessary and on 4 September the convention was signed. It regulated trade relations, gave Britain the right to exclude any foreign influence and provided for the Tibetan payment of an indemnity. In defiance of express instructions, Younghusband demanded an indemnity of Rs 7,500,000, to be paid in seventy-five annual instalments, during which period the British would be in occupation of the Chumbi valley. The Cabinet wished this article to be amended and the indemnity reduced by two-thirds but Younghusband deliberately left Lhasa without doing so.[151] As the occupation of the valley contravened British assurances to Russia, the Cabinet believed that the honour of the country was involved in repudiating Younghusband.[152] The Government of India, however, upheld him, and ratified the convention with an attached declaration that as an act of grace the indemnity would be reduced to Rs 2,500,000 and the valley occupied for only three years if the money were paid regularly in annual instalments, trade marts were effectively opened for three years and the convention faithfully complied with in all other respects.

IV

Thus Curzon, though defeated in some matters of foreign policy and disappointed in others, had attained much. But the heart of his Indian achievement lay in administration. The machinery of government was overhauled at every level. Whatever was being done was sought to be done better. The same emphasis was not always given to consideration of what was being done. Indeed, when an Indian newspaper in 1905 described the aim of Curzon's term as having been 'nothing but efficiency', the home department of the Government of India saw in it not a reproach but a correct assessment.[153] Curzon too said of his work in India, 'If I were asked to sum it up in a single word, I would say "efficiency". That has been our gospel, the keynote of our administration.'[154]

In theory, Curzon was aware that the success of any administration of such a scope and on such a scale as that in India depended primarily on the men rather than on the machine. In fact he exaggerated the role of the official and asserted that

the keys of India are not in England, nor in the House of Commons. They are in the office desk of every young Civilian in this country. He, by his character and conduct, is insensibly, but materially, contributing to the future maintenance, or collapse, of the British dominion in India. If he is like the men who went before him, if he is keen about his work, has a high sense of duty, and is interested in, and likes the people, our position here will be secure for a century to come. If he is indifferent, or incompetent, or slack, if he dislikes the country and the people, and has no taste for his work then the great structure of which we are all so proud will one day break down.[155]

This raises the expectation that the Viceroy cast himself in the role of chief executive officer, the head of the Indian civil service, and made the officials in the districts and the provinces and at the capital participants in his efforts to improve the condition of India. But temperament collided with theory. The Viceroy was unwilling to allow anyone else to handle the engines. His own council was overwhelmed by his dominating mastery;[156] and Curzon became, as he claimed, the member for every department of the Government of India.[157] But with all other subordinates—provincial governors, senior officials, Indian princes—relations were strained. The result was that Curzon could hope neither to improve the tone of the services on which he believed the future of the empire to depend nor to see his reforms implemented rapidly and effectively. The personal factor ensured that the administration of Curzon was confined to the enactment of measures and the improvement of the mechanics of administration.

The first major effort, to which Curzon gave his attention from almost the day of his arrival, was the transfer of responsibility for the administration of the north-west frontier from the Punjab government to the Government of India. For the Punjab to administer the frontier areas was, as Godley remarked,[158] like the

National Gallery being managed by the householders of Trafalgar Square. The Viceroy was convinced that only by such direct assumption of authority could he ensure the success of his frontier policy of concentrating the regular forces in cantonments in the interior and leaving the forward duties to tribal levies and the militia. He believed that in this he would have the co-operation of the Governor of the Punjab, Sir Mackworth Young, 'a man upon whose loyalty, whatever our points of minor disagreement, I can absolutely rely. I should regard him as a very excellent type of the superior order of official evolved by our Indian system; not, I should think, a particularly able nor a very strong man, but conciliatory and prudent, perhaps to the point of over-caution.'[159] The comment is worth quoting because it reveals Curzon's total inability to judge men. Young opposed bitterly the reorganization of the frontier administration, showed himself wholly lacking in moderation and prudence and left India after a public quarrel with the Viceroy.

In 1900 Curzon toured the frontier area and formulated proposals for the creation of a new frontier province. The approval of the Secretary of State was received by the end of the year and in 1901 the North-West Frontier Province was created. Results soon justified this measure. The tribes acquired a sense of cohesion.[160] There was unprecedented tranquillity and for the first time in half a century the frontier was relatively free from war. As against 15,289 British troops in the forward areas in 1899, there were only 4156 at the time of Curzon's departure. Five blockades had been imposed on various tribes during his term, but no general dissatisfaction or opposition could be discerned. Indeed, Curzon believed that one of the main reasons for which Kitchener desired his departure in 1905 was an eagerness to pursue a policy of vigorous and aggressive initiative against the tribes, a policy which Curzon warned could have no other result than frontier war and disaster.[161]

The other sphere of activity, also under his immediate control, where a clash of personalities developed was the Indian states. The strains were due to Curzon's unbending expectations. He had no hesitation about the ultimate authority of the Paramount Power.

I maintain that the essential attributes of sovereignty in India are exercised by the British Crown and by it alone; and that so much of the essential attributes of sovereignty has been taken from the Native States that to continue to give them the title is not merely a misnomer, but is a political error. I deprecate the constant use of all those vague and unsatisfactory terms—the invention of constitutional lawyers—such as subordinate isolation, subordinate co-operation, protected sovereignties, subordinate allies, and the like.[162]

But the Viceroy hoped that these princelings, who exercised what little power they had by the sufferance of the British government, could be moulded into minor Curzons of native hue, endowed with the same serious-mindedness and industry. He visited almost every Indian state, lectured the rulers in private and in public on their responsibilities, vested them with imaginary virtues and even shared in their hollow pageantry.

In fact, in speaking of them constantly as his partners in administration,[163] Curzon was right to the extent, not that they responded to his call and sought to rise to his normal level, but that he often reduced himself to theirs. There is no other explanation for the gaudy Coronation Durbar which he held on 1 January 1903, with himself as the central figure. Even a year before the event he suggested that the reduction of the salt tax should be announced on the occasion of the Durbar[164]—an act in the style of old Hindu monarchs, who associated accessions with acts of royal beneficence. The Cabinet and the India Office were surprised, because earlier when Hamilton had suggested it,[165] Curzon had said that if once the salt tax were reduced it would be exceedingly difficult to increase it, that it was resented by none and that it would be 'doubtful statesmanship, even if it be sound finance' to throw away so much money which would only go to the middlemen and benefit no one else.[166] The home government now naturally opposed a reduction on these same grounds.[167] Curzon hectored, said he would sooner not hold the Durbar, hinted resignation[168] and finally secured permission to give a general promise of future relief; and in the next budget tax remissions—the first in twenty years—were announced.

In all other respects the Durbar was to Curzon's entire satisfaction. He succeeded in keeping the Prince of Wales away and made the Duke of Connaught the second figure at the 'Curzonation' Durbar. For months every minute detail received his personal attention—'the design of a railing, the width of a road, the pattern of a carving, the colour of a plaster, the planting of a flower bed, the decoration of a pole—all this alongside of big questions affecting the movement or accommodation of tens of thousands of persons'.[169] He had convinced himself that the Durbar—apart from converting the Viceroy from a constitutional formula to a personal force—had a profound political purpose and that the benefit to India and Britain would be enormous; 'from the Arab sheiks of Aden on the west to the Shan chiefs of the Mekong on the borders of China, they felt the thrill of a common loyalty and the inspiration of a single aim'.[170] In fact, such political consequence as the Durbar had was adverse, it being regarded by the discerning as self-glorification and ostentatious waste. Curzon himself described it as 'the greatest series of shows that have been seen for hundreds of years in Asia, extending over a fortnight of time and involving the participation of enormous numbers of persons and troops'.[171]

The Viceroy believed that the Princes in particular had been deeply impressed and had departed 'proud of their honourable position as partners and pillars of the Empire'.[172] But events showed that the Durbar marked no turning-point in their lives and had not transformed them into conscientious rulers. Within twelve months of his arrival in India, Curzon had told the Princes that the throne was not 'a divan of indulgence but the stern seat of duty'.[173] To encourage a sense of responsibility he removed, without weakening paramountcy, unnecessary trammels on their administration. A few Princes on their part humoured the Viceroy but the majority of them did not pretend to respond either before or after the Durbar. Representative was the behaviour of one young Maharaja, who so disgusted the Viceroy that he wrote 'the best thing that he [the Maharaja] could do would be to die'.[174]

But the case of the Gaekwar of Baroda was the best known. There was a political tinge to the Gaekwar's resistance. For long he had sought to assert his rights and to shake off as much as he could of British supervision. This led him to claim in 1902 full powers of civil and criminal jurisdiction over Europeans resident in Baroda and in 1904 the right to prohibit Europeans and Americans from acquiring immovable property in his state. Both claims were rejected as contravening the prerogative of the Paramount Power. The Gaekwar then declined to proceed with plans for railway construction if this involved a cession of jurisdiction over the territory across which the railway would run;[175] and he

conversation'.[187] But surprisingly, within a week of this letter, Curzon managed to secure a pledge of good government from the Nizam;[188] and this establishment of direct contact enabled the Viceroy to take up the main question the next year, when he considered the circumstances favourable. Curzon had by now modified his proposals and favoured a perpetual lease rather than a cession of territory. In practice there was no difference. 'But to an Oriental there is all the difference in the world. The one saves his face, the other sacrifices his honour.'[189] The Nizam was told that there was no possibility of the Berars being restored to him and that his prestige would be enhanced by the status of a lessor.[190] The Nizam declined the offer.[191] Then Curzon went in person to Hyderabad and awed the Nizam into agreement.[192] The Berars were leased in perpetuity to the Indian government on payment of an annual rent of Rs 2.5 millions. Curzon boasted that he had added to the empire an entire province with two to three millions of inhabitants without the firing of a single cartridge.[193] The Nizam received in token of his surrender the Grand Cross of the Bath. Some Indian newspapers suggested that the general application of this policy would reduce all the Princes to pensioners; but it must be said for Curzon that this was never his intention. In fact, he tended to exalt rather than to minimize their role in the Indian system.

In British India Curzon probed into every cranny of administration, set up numerous investigating commissions and increased the number of specialist officials. His activities constitute a long catalogue of detail, but fall into three broad categories: the enforcement of governmental authority and the promotion of economic progress and of cultural development. The major measure in the first category was police reform. The gross corruption and inefficiency of the Indian police had become 'the great internal scandal of India',[194] and there had been a sharp increase of serious crime. Curzon set up in 1902 a commission which included two Indian non-officials to examine the problem and to make detailed suggestions for improvement. As the commission in its report sharply criticized the police force, the Secretary of State was against publication; but on Curzon's insistence the report was released in March 1905 along with a resolution announcing the government's decisions on the subject. The village agency would be developed and the methods of selection and training improved.

A draft bill consolidating the police law was also circulated. The publication of the report itself excited little comment.

In economic affairs, the chief preoccupation of Curzon was with famine. All his efforts and schemes stemmed from this. Scarcity was a constant threat and, whenever it materialized, the blight was widespread. Before policy could be re-examined on the basis of the report of the Lyall Commission of 1898, which had advocated more generous relief in times of famine, there was another crisis. The famine which deepened in August 1899 and lifted only in October 1900 was, said Curzon,[195] the greatest and the most appalling any Indian government had ever had to face. The loss of crops was estimated at seventy crores of rupees, and nearly six million persons were recipients of state relief. But the crisis was handled with efficiency—an achievement all the more creditable as much of the famine area lay in the Indian states. Another commission, under Sir Anthony MacDonnell, was appointed, and on the basis of its report the Government of India in March 1903 formulated new principles of famine policy, providing for both anticipatory measures of relief and precautionary measures against undue liberality.

Curzon also considered measures for minimizing the impact of famine. It was as a medium of famine relief rather than as a means of passenger traffic that railway development assumed importance. Curzon improved the management of railways, ordered examination of the whole problem by an expert from Britain and sanctioned expenditure of about sixty crores of rupees on the construction of 6110 miles—the greatest expansion under any viceroyalty. He evolved a policy for improving agriculture on the triple basis of experiment, research and education. In 1901 an inspector-general of agriculture was appointed and an expert staff was gradually recruited. In 1905 a private donation was utilized to establish an Institute of Agricultural Research at Pusa. Proposals were also made for the development of colleges and research institutes of agriculture in the provinces. In September 1901 the Viceroy appointed a commission to examine the whole problem of irrigation. There was much loose thinking on this subject, it being widely held that if irrigation were sufficiently developed it would cancel famine. In fact, given the stage of technological development of those times, there was no prospect of indefinite expansion of irrigation. But Curzon increased the expenditure on such protective public works and accepted the suggestions of the commission for a greater outlay on both productive and protective works, development of minor irrigation works and encouragement of private enterprise in the construction of wells and tanks. A post of inspector-general of irrigation was also created.

In the winter of 1900, Romesh Dutt, in his presidential address to the National Congress and in a series of open letters to the Viceroy, contended that the intensity and frequency of famines were largely due to the poverty caused by over-assessment of land revenue.[196] The India Office was inclined to agree that assessments in certain parts of India, particularly in Bombay, were too high;[197] but Curzon was unwilling to leave the Dutt thesis unchallenged. It was the kind of controversy, involving much didacticism and detail, in which his mind delighted; and the unique spectacle was seen of a Viceroy writing and publishing a book in the form of a Government of India resolution[198] and rebutting arguments in terms normally to be found in the pages of academic journals. He studied the question till he had secured what he termed 'a fair layman's grasp',[199] drafted the reply to Dutt and published it after it had been checked by MacDonnell.[200] The Viceroy asserted that famines were caused by want of rain, and improvements in assessment could at most mitigate and not prevent distress. It was historically inaccurate to say that a permanent settlement was in any way a protection against the occurrence or consequences of famine. The temporary assessments had been moderate and every effort was made to avoid harassment at the time of settlements. So over-assessment was not a general and widespread source of poverty and indebtedness and could not fairly be regarded as a contributory cause of famine. While Curzon did not carry conviction to all, his resolution was the best possible defence of the government's position; and Indian opinion both appreciated that the Viceroy had taken the criticisms seriously and recognized that his contentions had some merit.

Curzon, however, in March 1905, promulgated rules providing for elasticity of collection in times of distress and enacted laws which limited transfers of land from agriculturists to money-lenders and others in the Punjab, Bundelkhand and Bombay. To replace the money-lender as a source of cheap capital, a statute of March 1904 enabled the formation of mutual loan societies which would receive assistance from the government and be subject to official audit and supervision. Proposals providing for the formation of agricultural banks were forwarded to the Secretary of State. To relieve pressure on the land, emigration of labour to plantations in Assam was facilitated by legislation raising the minimum level of contract wages and prohibiting unlicensed recruiting. The Government of India also sought to promote emigration to the Transvaal and Natal, but with no success, as these governments refused to ensure even the minimum terms. 'The name of South Africa stinks in the nostrils of India.'[201]

Other avenues of employment were also sought to be developed. At the time of the Durbar, an exhibition of Indian art was held to give a stimulus to handicrafts. It was recognized for the first time that as there was great scope for industrial development, encouragement should be given by the government. Conditions for mineral prospecting and mining were improved, a department of mines was set up and legislation for protecting labour in mines was introduced. Indeed the Viceroy, on his own responsibility, informed Sir Ernest Cassel that Jubbulpore district, which was believed to contain iron ore, was being reserved for him, and there would be no rigid insistence on mining rules if he were willing to invest a large sum of money in order to develop the steel-making industry.[202] Cassel ordered the area to be surveyed and concluded from the report that there was not enough ore to justify a steel-making plant. A separate department of commerce and industry was constituted in March 1905. The new department was entrusted with the tasks of promoting good relations between the government and the mercantile community and encouraging trade and commercial enterprise. The reduction of taxes too served to give an impetus to commerce and private enterprise, though Curzon's motives in this matter had been more sentimental than calculating.

Sentimental too, but in a better sense, was Curzon's determination to preserve India's ancient monuments which for want of attention were fast falling into decay. He was shocked to find how little was known of, and how few people cared for, these buildings.[203] 'Beautiful remains are tumbling into irretrievable ruin, all for the want of a directing hand, and a few thousand rupees.'[204] When on one occasion the Government of India directed the Madras government to consult their archaeologist, the Madras government replied that they had never heard of this official in their employ.[205] Curzon improved the working of the provincial surveys, gave financial assistance to the provincial governments and secured the services of the distinguished archaeologist, Sir John Marshall,[206] as director-general of the department. The government also assumed by legislation extensive powers to protect monuments in private possession. Curzon took a personal interest in the preservation of these historic buildings. He gave orders on every detail regarding Agra and supervised progress elsewhere. That he should have been the first Viceroy to visit the caves at Ajanta was revelatory of the nature of British administration in India in the nineteenth century.

Had Curzon been content to restore and protect these ancient works of architecture, he would, on this score alone, have earned the gratitude of India. But, unfortunately, to these monuments of the past he decided to add one of his own. He raised in the centre of Calcutta a memorial ostensibly to Queen Victoria but in fact to himself. Intended to be the British Indian government's contribution to the country's architectural tradition, it was a bizarre conception in marble—the Taj Mahal brought up to date. The building was to be ringed with statues of the Governors-General; and facing its entrance was to be that of Curzon. There is no doubt who, in Curzon's mind, was the greatest of the Queen's proconsuls in India.[207]

More important than Curzon's efforts in archaeology and architecture were his attempts at language and educational reform. He was the only Viceroy ever to appreciate the importance of Hindi. When, for administrative reasons, MacDonnell proposed to permit the presentation by the public of petitions in Hindi and the translation of the orders of government into that language,[208] Curzon approved the suggestion and authorized him to ignore the protests of the Moslems. 'The howls of the Mussulmans merely represent the spleen of a minority from whose hands are slipping away the reins of power, and who clutch at any method of arbitrarily retaining them.'[209] He later recommended to Ampthill, the Governor of Madras, that as Hindi was the language of the greater part of the Indian continent it should be officially recognized everywhere.[210] Nor did this astounding prescience—for Curzon stated a view which is only now being accepted in India—imply that he underrated the value of education in the English language.

But though the Viceroy had an awareness in theory of the importance of such education—'the future of Indian Education...

is the future of the Indian race'[211]—he never realized the practical implications of educating large numbers of Indians. His mind moved only on the surface of this question and he devoted his attention to the improvement of educational management and administration and not to the purpose and the results of education. In September 1901 he convened a conference of all senior officials dealing with educational matters at the capital and in the provinces to make recommendations for reform at every level. It was characteristic of Curzon that he ignored Hamilton's advice that he should also take evidence from Indian graduates and hear their side of the case.[212] Education was regarded as but one more subject for governmental action. University education was examined by a commission which made various proposals for raising standards and recommended that no more universities be established. The report was severely criticized in the Indian press for restricting opportunities for education. Both the Viceroy and the Secretary of State were surprised at what they regarded as distorted interpretation of a sincere endeavour[213] and decided to ignore the protests. In March 1904, brushing aside the dissent of Indian members of the legislature, a statute was enacted incorporating the commission's recommendations. School education was also reorganized by executive decree. Curzon was well pleased with these achievements and proclaimed his complacency.[214]

V

The greatest of Curzon's achievements, however, was unintended. It was the transformation of a mild, nationalist sentiment into a resentful, revolutionary movement. When he arrived in India, he found that all was tranquil except in Poona, where a few agitators had been arrested by the Bombay government. Hamilton was convinced that there was a small but deep-rooted conspiracy in Poona and that the Mahratta Brahmins were plotting and disseminating subversive propaganda throughout the Deccan;[215] but Curzon doubted the validity of detention without trial, directed the Bombay government to consider the release of the Natu brothers and did not believe that any political conspiracy existed.[216] In fact, he shocked the staid officials of the India Office by sending a telegram of congratulations to the Principal of the Fergusson College at Poona on one of its students securing the Senior Wranglership at Cambridge. Hamilton protested that this College was regarded by his advisers as the mainspring of the political conspiracies at Poona and alleged that, after reading Curzon's message, many wealthy Indians had withdrawn their offers to provide funds for publishing loyal newspapers.[217] The Viceroy, however, refused to repent. He failed to see how his telegram could be regarded as approval or condonation of any type of political activity. As for the wealthy Indians who had declined to pay, they 'must either have been very reluctant donors or great donkeys'.[218]

This incident, which was to Curzon's credit, was also characteristic of his outlook. He could appreciate intellectual achievement wherever it was to be found. He had also no racial prejudice; but this was a mental blindness and not an ethical virtue. A man who was not really aware even of the lower orders in Britain could not be expected to register the full significance of the problem of race relations in India. It was not tolerance but insensitivity which precluded discrimination on Curzon's part. He had the lowest opinion of Indians,[219] believed that as a race they were incapable of speaking the truth and saw no reason to keep his opinions to himself.[220] But he was determined that Indians should be well treated because that was part of good administration. Indians could expect no political advance. In fact, even in civil employment the highest ranks would, as a general rule, be closed to them. But otherwise the scales would be held even and strict and inflexible justice done between the two races. This—and not any preparation for self-government—was to Curzon the sole justification for British rule in India.[221] There was a job to be done, not a duty to be fulfilled.

The insistence on fair treatment of Indians brought Curzon many unhappy moments but showed him at his best. What roused him was the increasing number of cases of assault of Indians by Europeans, particularly British soldiers. One of the worst of such cases occurred in April 1899, when some soldiers of the Royal West Kent Regiment raped a Burmese woman near Rangoon. Curzon was determined to punish the guilty men severely and, if they could not be discovered or punished, to inflict disgrace and punishment on the Regiment itself;[222] for European juries, heedless of the blot on the impartiality of British rule, almost always acquitted offenders of their own community, while Indian assailants were punished with almost savage ferocity.[223] In this particular case even the evidence that would have led to the conviction of the guilty men was withheld by the Regimental authorities from the civil court; so Curzon directed that the substance of the proceedings of the military court of inquiry be communicated. He also ordered, even before the civil trial, the transfer of the whole Regiment for two years to Aden, the most unpleasant station in the Indian command, and cancelled all leave and amenities. As the courts of law would not punish the guilty, the government punished the Regiment for what the Viceroy considered a gross violation of honour and of discipline. As expected, the European jury acquitted the accused, with a rider that men of the West Kent Regiment were guilty of the offence but evidence was not available to convict the individual offenders. All that the Viceroy could do was to discharge these men from the army and censure the officers of the Regiment for obstructing justice and the local police officials and magistrates for acquiescing in such obstruction. The press in India and Britain unanimously supported Curzon, but Anglo-Indian opinion was generally in sympathy with the Regiment. This feeling even infected the Viceroy's council, and Curzon had to overrule it in order to issue an Order in Council condemning the outrage in the strongest terms.[224]

As collisions between British soldiers and Indians occurred most frequently because of the liberal grants to soldiers of shooting passes in populated areas, Curzon wished to restrict the issue of these passes and to withdraw them from regiments whose members had abused the concession. His council was again strongly opposed to this. One member believed that it would detract from 'the respect for the white skin on which our hold on India so largely depends'; and the Commander-in-Chief and the military member feared that it might produce a mutiny in India.[225] But Curzon was not to be so easily frightened. These cases, he wrote, 'eat into my very soul. That such gross outrages should occur in the first place in a country under British rule; and then that everybody, commanding officers, officials, juries, departments, should conspire to screen the guilty, is, in my judgment, a black and permanent blot upon the British name.' He asserted that he would do as much as one man could to efface this stain and that no amount of unpopularity would induce him to swerve from this task.[226] In fact, despite these brave words, Curzon was not prepared, for fear of a second Ilbert Bill agitation, to modify the jury system which enabled European accused to escape sentence; but short of this he did his utmost.[227]

In October 1900 the issue of shooting passes was curtailed, with the result that whereas in the two years ending in March 1900 there were 129 shooting pass incidents, only 45 such cases were reported during the rest of Curzon's term. But in April 1902 there was another serious case of assault by British soldiers. An Indian cook was beaten to death by two troopers of the Ninth Lancers Regiment. Both the military authorities and the civil police were apathetic and, when the Government of India urged a thorough inquiry, the Lieutenant-General Commanding reported that the evidence had failed to prove that the assailants belonged to the Ninth Lancers or indeed were soldiers at all. Curzon, in contrast to the attitude of an earlier Viceroy who had argued that the Government of India had no jurisdiction in such cases,[228] rejected the finding. This decision was later supported by the information provided by the Colonel of the Ninth Lancers that the two guilty men had confessed to their comrades. The Commander-in-Chief was instructed to punish the Regiment and to censure its commanding officer; the General Officer Commanding was told he had taken an inadequate view of the offence; and the Lieutenant-General Commanding was rebuked for special pleading. 'These soldiers, with their violence and their lust, are pulling the fabric of our dominion down about our ears; and I for one will not sacrifice what I regard as the most solemn obligation imposed upon the British race to the licence of even the finest regiment in the British army.'[229] As for the civil officials, they were all condemned—the police superintendent for failing in his duty to ensure proper investigation, the investigating inspector for culpable negligence, the district magistrate for lack of judgment and the commissioner for want of vigour in conducting the case.

Though the punishment imposed on the Regiment—sentry duty and cancellation of leave—was light, the Viceroy was regarded by the British community in India as having acted harshly and there was great pressure for an amnesty. As the Viceroy had written earlier, 'I really believe I am almost the only man in this country who at all seriously deplores the monstrous travesties of justice in acquitting soldiers who kill Indians.'[230] Much sympathy was shown for the Regiment in Britain too and even the King expressed his dislike of collective punishment.[231] But Curzon, loyally supported by Hamilton, stood firm. 'If it be known that the Viceroy, backed by the Secretary of State, will stand up even against the crack regiment of the British Army, packed though it be with dukes sons, earls sons and so on—then a most salutary lesson will be taught to the army. If we yield to military and aristocratic clamour no Viceroy will dare to go on with the work that I have begun.'[232]

At the Durbar, by a tactless arrangement unknown to Curzon, the Ninth Lancers were assigned to escort the Duke of Connaught; and as the Regiment, 'in whose ranks were most certainly two murderers',[233] rode past, the assembly, consisting mostly of British men and women, broke forth into a shattering cheer. It was intended to be a vote of censure on the Viceroy, but Curzon sat impassive on his horse, with 'a certain gloomy pride in having dared to do the right'.[234] In fact, though Curzon did not know it, this, and not the state entry into Delhi or the other glittering ceremonies he so carefully planned, was his proudest moment in India.

There were also cases, though fewer in number, of European civilians assaulting Indians and being acquitted by the courts. A particularly glaring instance was in December 1902 when Bain, a tea planter in Assam, beat a labourer to death. The sessions court sentenced him to simple imprisonment for six months. When the government appealed for an enhancement of the sentence, a single British judge of the High Court acquitted him; and the government were powerless. Curzon realized the damage done by such flagrant miscarriages of justice. 'They are so injurious to our character as Englishmen and so fatal to our predominance and prestige in this country.'[235] Curzon believed that there could be no real improvement until a British soldier was hanged for the murder of an Indian.[236] But the fact that he stamped with relentless heel on every such case that came to his notice earned the approbation of observant Indian opinion. The nationalist leader Bepin Chandra Pal wrote that the chief strength of the British government in India had always lain in the impression it had been able to create in the public mind regarding British justice and benevolence; and the deterioration, real or fancied, in the British character constituted a political danger the gravity of which could not be over-estimated. Only one man in the whole country appeared to have a proper appreciation of this problem, and that was Curzon. He alone, said Pal, had persistently sought to maintain British character in India.[237]

So Curzon built up, by his attitude in the matter of crimes involving Europeans and Indians, a large fund of goodwill on which he could have drawn in any effort to mould or influence Indian political development. He had other advantages also. He visited almost every part of his vast kingdom, listened to all complaints and saw to it that every one of them, however absurd, was investigated. 'You are the Court of Appeal against the decisions of a close and united corporation, namely the Indian Civil Service.'[238] The mystery enveloping the Government of India was dispelled as much as possible. Concealment was no part of Curzon's armour. The reports of all commissions of inquiry were published and the Viceroy, in a ceaseless round of speeches and resolutions, elucidated the government's policy and outlook in detail. But all these assets were of no avail in face of the Viceroy's total lack of political sense. He knew that there was a growing restiveness at British tutelage and that British policy itself was responsible for this. 'The leaven of our education, with all the ideas that it inculcates of individual rights and the equality of one man with another, is fermenting in the Indian mind, and cannot be expected to produce no results.'[239] Nor did he deplore this policy. 'We could no more avoid bringing our law and our education, than we could help, sooner or later, introducing umbrellas and kerosene-lamps.'[240] But that the restiveness should be reckoned with and that it could perhaps be organized and led forward, he could not see.

Curzon, let it be said, was no alarmist. He declined to strengthen the law against sedition on the ground that there was no widespread sympathy with sedition in India[241]—a view that was borne out by the general Indian reaction to the Boer War. He was not carried away by the extravagant fears of the Bombay government and the India Office regarding the allegedly treasonable activities in western India and he secured the release of the Natu brothers. As for the Congress, he was aware that some Princes were subsidizing it[242] and he spoke to the Gaekwar on the subject. When that ruler protested that the Congress was a social, and not a political, movement which was supported by the bulk of educated Indian opinion, the Viceroy replied that the Congress was in the last resort animated by hostile feelings towards the government.[243] But while Curzon disliked that organization, he attached little importance to it; 'the whole of our case against that party is this, that it is in no sense a representative national body, as it claims to be, and that, if not actually disloyal to the British Government in this country, it is, at any rate, far from friendly towards it'.[244]

That winter the annual Congress session was presided over by Romesh Dutt. He had no animus against the Viceroy and had written on Curzon's appointment appreciating the great importance seemingly attached by him to conciliating all sections of the Indian people.[245] Dutt's presidential address was a sober one, urging the government to avoid over-assessments and to take greater care to secure the co-operation of Indians. Hamilton was for a fair response; he had a shrewd, if somewhat vague, desire to appeal within the Congress to men like Dutt and thus weaken the younger elements who were likely to prove less moderate. Hamilton suggested to Curzon that, considering the great difficulty of proposing any measures or schemes which would fit in with the aspirations of 'young India', it was most advisable to encourage 'older India'.[246] Sir William Wedderburn, a retired member of the Indian civil service who was prominent in the counsels of the Congress, also suggested to the Viceroy that he establish 'a national Government' by winning for British rule the sympathy of educated Indians.[247] But the Viceroy saw no reason why he need placate Indians, old or young.[248] Curzon also pointed out to Dutt the 'political absurdity' of one of his proposals that Indians be appointed to the Viceroy's council.[249] All that Curzon was prepared to do was to appoint Indians, even those who belonged to the Congress, as judges of high courts or members of official commissions; and this too was in a sense a measure of his contempt for the organization. For he was convinced that, despite the Congress, he had gained public support. 'The people of all India are, I think, filled with more loyal sentiments, and are more favourably disposed towards the Government at this juncture than at almost any previous time.'[250] There was growing up a sort of national feeling in India, but the British could hold India permanently by convincing the mass of the people that their rule was more just and beneficent than either any other foreign rule or the rule of Indians. The real strength of British rule in India lay in the extraordinary inferiority in character, honesty and capacity of the Indians. Curzon did not believe that the Congress was the voice of India; and he saw no need, as he phrased it, for focusing so necessarily composite a public opinion as that of India and for trying to make it speak through a single megaphone.[251]

Curzon's assessment of the Congress as a weak body was justified. It was at this time more interested in seeking favours from the government than in opposing British rule. The Lucknow session of 1899 had been 'a general conspiracy of good behaviour';[252] and of the next annual session the Viceroy reported that the speakers 'seem to have spent the greater part of their time in complimenting me'.[253] What the Congress during these years most desired was the greater employment of Indians in official service. But on this Curzon was beyond persuasion. He believed not only that Indians were as a race inefficient but that the greatest peril with which British administration in India was confronted was the fact that every year an increasing number of the higher posts 'that were meant and *ought to have been exclusively and specifically reserved* for Europeans are being filched away by the superior wits of the native in the English examination'.[254] Hamilton was of the same opinion. He regarded the mention in the Proclamation of 1858 of the principle of equality of Indian and British citizens in the matter of appointments as one of the greatest mistakes ever made, and refused even to meet Wedderburn.[255]

So on this issue the Congress had no hope of securing any concession, or even a favourable hearing, from either the Viceroy or the Salisbury Government; and the result was naturally to discomfit and discredit it. Hamilton felt it was losing its popularity and influence and was waning fast, as it had been for some years in existence and had achieved nothing;[256] and he cheered the Viceroy's efforts to shatter it.[257] 'I am sure pouring ridicule on those parts of the Congress creed, which are fantastical, does a great deal of good; and if the Congress, in the course of a year or two, totally collapses, you will have the credit of being the main instrument of its extinction.'[258]

Faced for the first time with frank, unqualified hostility from the authorities, the Congress was acutely embarrassed and sought a *rapprochement*. It had developed as a body of loyalist Indian opinion and was puzzled by Curzon's refusal to treat it as such. Dinshaw Wacha, President of the Congress in 1902, appealed for consideration of the resolutions of the Congress with justice and sympathy which, Wacha said, were the two watchwords of Curzon's administration.[259] To this letter there seems to have been no reply. Wedderburn requested Curzon for a friendly if informal recognition of the Congress as a responsible body expressing the Indian view of Indian affairs, and was told that no co-operation was possible so long as the Congress tried both to guide 'the respectable reforming party, and at the same time to keep in with the extreme men', who wanted something very different.[260] But Curzon was dishonest in suggesting that the government would be willing to co-operate with the Congress if it remained a party solely of moderates. From the start, as he avowed to Ampthill, he treated it as 'an unclean thing' and was determined to reduce it to impotence by never taking any notice of it, by carrying out such reasonable reforms as would deprive it of grounds of complaint, by showing such sympathy and tolerance towards Indians as would give Congress no excuse to revive racial issues and by never in the smallest degree truckling to its leaders or communing with them.[261]

Yet the unwitting acts of Curzon were to prove in perspective more consequential than his conscious efforts. Refusal to invite Congressmen to garden parties at Government Houses and to attend industrial exhibitions organized by the Congress may have weakened the moderate elements in the party; but this was far less important than the steps taken, however unknowingly, to give the party a popular basis. Curzon was an unconscious catalyst, who did not understand, let alone desire, what the new century was about to bring forth, but who helped it to be born. It is one of the pleasant ironies of history that he who criticized his predecessors for patting infant nationalism on the back[262] left behind, in the English eighteenth century phrase, a 'formed Opposition', strong and violently stirring.

VI

The development of terrorist activity in the Mahratta districts of Bombay had almost monopolized official attention in both Calcutta and London and had been regarded as much more serious than the frothy political agitation in Bengal. The latter, indeed, was of a kind with which Curzon had no patience. He reorganized the municipal corporation of Calcutta in such a manner as to reduce the influence of the educated Indians and to give greater representation to the European mercantile community. It must be said, however, that similar political considerations did not weigh with him when he first considered the partition of the province. Whatever the motives inspiring his subordinates, to him the partition of Bengal was, at the start, essentially an administrative reform, on a par with the establishment of the North-West Frontier Province.

When the Berar affair is concluded [he wrote to Hamilton almost casually on 30 April 1902][263] the question will arise of adding the greater part of it to the Central Provinces. I am not sure that this will not be a proper occasion upon which to examine into the larger question of the boundaries of the Local Governments or some of them, in general. Bengal is unquestionably too large a charge for any single man. Ought Chittagong to continue to belong to it, or ought we to give Assam an outlet on the sea? Is Orissa best governed from Calcutta?

Hamilton agreed that Bengal was too large for the superintendence of one individual and that a seaboard district might well be added to Assam.[264]

So when the Viceroy found that his officials were already at work on a scheme to divest Bengal[265] of some of its districts, he objected vehemently to the failure to refer the matter to him.[266] But on the merits of the question, he agreed that Bengal was 'over-swollen' and Assam required 'a strong lift forward'; and, strengthened by the information that the local feeling in the Chittagong districts was in favour of separation,[267] he gave the scheme his general approval.[268] The details were approved by the Viceroy's council in October and the proposals were published, without consulting the local governments other than Bengal,[269] on 7 December 1903.[270] The three most populous districts of Chittagong, Dacca and Mymensingh and the Tippera Hills would be transferred to Assam and Chota Nagpur to the Central Provinces, while certain other areas from the Central Provinces and Madras would be added to Bengal. But the final result would be a reduction of the population of Bengal from about 78.5 millions to 67.5 millions.

There were undoubtedly certain administrative advantages in fragmenting Bengal. It would reduce the responsibilities of the Lieutenant-Governor of Bengal and enable greater contacts between the officials and the people. But to public opinion in Bengal the plan seemed to be an attempt to diminish the status of the province and to destroy the unity of the Bengali people. This was a correct assessment, if not of viceregal, at least of official thinking. The Lieutenant-Governor of Bengal anticipated a great political advantage from severing the eastern districts, which he deemed to be 'a hotbed of the purely Bengali movement, unfriendly if not seditious in character'. He thought that partition would also weaken the tyrannical character of the press and the leaders of Calcutta.[271] The home member of the Government of India believed that the preponderance of Bengal proper in provincial politics was an evil it was '*most* desirable' to diminish.[272] But it was the home secretary who developed the political argument in favour of partition most fully.

Bengal united is a power, Bengal divided will pull several different ways. That is what the Congress leaders feel: their apprehensions are perfectly correct and they form one of the great merits of the scheme. . . . It is not altogether easy to reply in a despatch which is sure to be published without disclosing the fact that in this scheme as in the matter of the amalgamation of Berar to the Central Provinces one of our main objects is to split up and thereby weaken a solid body of opponents to our rule.[273]

Opposition to the proposal was organized by the educated Indians. 'We object', wrote Surendranath Banerjee in the *Bengalee*,[274] 'to the proposed dismemberment of Bengal and we are sure the whole country will rise as one man to protest against it.' The Congress at its annual session passed a resolution condemning this 'preposterous scheme' to undo the work of welding India into one nation.[275] Meetings of protest were held throughout the province. Had Curzon been a sensitive tactician, he would have noted the storm signals. Instead, he regarded the agitation as an artificial turmoil. The speakers at the Congress session were to him 'ancient agitators' who were 'untaught and unteachable', and he described their speeches as 'a stale re-hash of belated cries and obsolete platitudes'. There seemed no reason to pay heed to the 'hysterical outcry' in Bengal at certain districts 'being torn from the maternal bosom', for in the hundreds of articles and letters published in Bengal, he could not find one single line of argument. The interests of sentiment and historical association, if applied all round, would prevent any administrative reform whatever.[276] On the other hand, the agitation impressed Curzon with the political advantages which had been delineated by his officials.

The Bengalis, who like to think themselves a nation, and who dream of a future when the English will have been turned out and a Bengali Babu will have been installed in Government House, Calcutta, of course bitterly resent any disruption that will be likely to interfere with the realization of this dream. If we are weak enough to yield to their clamour now, we shall not be able to dismember or reduce Bengal again;

and you will be cementing and solidifying, on the eastern flank of India, a force already formidable and certain to be a source of increasing trouble in the future.[277]

In February 1904 Curzon toured the eastern districts of Bengal, declared that he had not found a single argument against partition and believed that by his speeches he had changed the situation.[278] In fact, he had further confused it by appealing to Moslem sentiment. Partition, he had said, was necessary to 'invest the Mahomedans in Eastern Bengal with a unity which they have not enjoyed since the days of the old Mussulman Viceroys and Kings'.[279] No sentence could have been better calculated to convince Bengali opinion of the pernicious motives underlying partition. A vast crowd collected at the Calcutta Town Hall on 18 March 1904 to denounce the scheme; and similar meetings were held in almost every town in the eastern districts.

With Curzon's departure for England in April the idea of partition seemed to recede into the background, but it was evident that the government had not abandoned the scheme. The Congress in December 1904 once again condemned it and suggested as an alternative measure of administrative reform the conversion of the Lieutenant-Governorship of Bengal into a Governorship.[280] This was an alternative which Curzon had considered and rejected earlier in the year as a cumbrous system. He believed that only politicians sent out from Britain as Governors should be provided with executive councils.[281] That Curzon attached little, if any, importance to the agitation is clear from the fact that it finds no mention at all in his correspondence with Ampthill, the acting Viceroy; nor does he seem to have discussed it with the home government. He was the victim of what Tawney termed 'the administrator's fallacy—the belief that is to say, that efficient management, combined with public spirit and a logically unanswerable case, can hold its own against interests and ambitions wielding personal and political power'.[282] On his return in December, Curzon refused to receive officially a deputation led by Sir Henry Cotton, then President of the Congress,[283] and interpreted this as a sign that the Congress knew that it was beaten.[284]

The Government of India, who had throughout 1904 been examining the details,[285] sent their final proposals to the Secretary of State on 2 February 1905.[286] The despatch was to a considerable extent drafted by the Viceroy himself, and he requested the

Secretary of State to convey his approval soon. The necessity for relief was indisputable and the opposition of the Congress was inspired by political motives and directed to a political end. Calcutta was the centre from which the Congress party was manipulated throughout the whole of India. The perfection of their machinery and the tyranny which it enabled them to exercise were truly remarkable. So any measure which would divide Bengalis, permit the growth of independent centres of activity and influence, dethrone Calcutta and weaken the influence of the lawyer class who had the entire organization in their hands was intensely and hotly resented by them.[287]

By now, however, relations between the Viceroy and the home government were acutely strained; and the Secretary of State, while giving his approval to partition, took care to state all the criticisms and even to write sympathetically of the opposition. He agreed that the case for relief to the Bengal government had been in the main thoroughly established, but he was disposed to think that the Government of India had tended to undervalue the strength and substance of the sentiment inspiring the opposition. 'That a large and upon the whole homogeneous community of $41\frac{1}{2}$ millions, with Calcutta as their centre of culture and political and commercial life, should object to the transfer of $\frac{3}{5}$ of their number to a new administration with a distant capital, involving the severance of old and historic ties and the breaking up of racial unity, appears to me in no way surprising.' He regretted that the Government of India had not examined in greater detail the proposal to create more commissionerships in Bengal, but gave his sanction to the general principles of Curzon's scheme.[288]

The Viceroy believed that the decision should be announced and, almost simultaneously, executed. 'It is useless to attempt to persuade Bengal. The *fait accompli* is the only argument that will appeal to them. . . . The more we say the greater will be the anger and commotion.'[289] The Lieutenant-Governor of Bengal also was of the view that an early completion of partition would lead to peace.[290] The Viceroy, however, continued to treat the agitation with contempt. In his correspondence with the Lieutenant-Governor at this time there are detailed discussions regarding structural alterations in Calcutta but little reference to the partition and the excitement roused by it.

On 19 July the official resolution, which had been drafted by

Curzon himself,[291] was published. It was claimed for the new
province of East Bengal and Assam that with a population of about
31 millions it would form a clearly defined geographical, ethno-
logical, social and linguistic entity, that it 'would concentrate in a
single province the typical Muhammadan population of Bengal,
for whom Dacca would furnish a natural capital' and that it would
bring most of the tea industry and jute tracts under a single administration. Territorial redistribution could rarely be accomplished except at the cost of disruption; but when old connexions
were severed, new ones almost immediately took their place and
developed sanctity very soon. The scheme had been formulated so
as to meet every reasonable demand of those who would be personally affected; and all alternatives had been exhaustively
examined.[292]

A fortnight earlier, on 4 July, the Secretary of State had disclosed in the House of Commons that the proposal for partition
had been accepted. The resolution, therefore, was no surprise.
Indeed, even the action to be taken had been considered by the
opposition. On 13 July a Bengali newspaper had advocated the
boycott of British goods as a measure of protest.[293] So, with the
announcement of the details, the agitation quickly revived. Meetings and processions were held throughout Bengal and thousands
wore black bands as a sign of mourning. India's streets, in Lenin's
words, were beginning to uphold their own writers and political
leaders.[294] Business was almost suspended in Calcutta on 7 August,
when a meeting was held at the Town Hall, and it was resolved to
boycott the purchase of British manufactures as a protest against
the indifference of the British public to Indian affairs. The response was immediate and there was a sharp fall in the sale of
British goods, especially textiles, not only in Bengal but also in
other provinces, particularly Bombay. The *swadeshi* (indigenous)
movement had become an integral part of Indian nationalist endeavour. Even the British Chamber of Commerce had been
stirred to protest against partition by the reports in *The Statesman*
and *The Englishman*—two British-owned newspapers of Calcutta—
that the purpose of the change was to weaken the authority of the
Calcutta High Court and to deprive European British citizens of
the protection of the High Court in districts in which they were
commercially interested.[295]

Faced with this turmoil, the Secretary of State agreed to place the relevant papers before Parliament. Curzon thought that any such publication would be 'a calamity'[296] as in India it could only give rise to further newspaper agitation and recrimination and to a revival of the feelings of bitterness and rancour. The future vitality of the agitation depended solely on the amount of extraneous fuel supplied to it and upon the expectation that with a change of government in England the decision might be reversed.[297] But the home government published the papers on 10 October. They also suggested that to avoid the appearance of haste, three weeks be allowed to pass between publication and the division of the province.[298] The Government of India replied that postponement was not practicable and, even if it were, would be attended by the gravest possible consequences. Any such concession at the eleventh hour would forfeit the respect of all classes and place a premium on similar tactics in future.[299] In fact, the proclamation was published on 1 September and the partition effected on 16 October.

The result was a further intensification of the agitation. Men who had normally no interest in politics came out into the streets to participate in processions and meetings. The Viceroy was keen that the agitation should be repressed and he accused the local government of showing neither firmness nor courage; 'the spectacle that has been presented by the streets of Calcutta during the past fortnight has not in my opinion been creditable to the capital of a great Empire'.[300] But the Bengal government felt unable to take any action, as the agitators had done nothing that was punishable under the criminal law.[301] The day of partition was celebrated throughout Bengal as a day of mourning. The poet Rabindranath Tagore left his seclusion to agitate, for the first and last time, actively, and wrote songs for the occasion. As Ezra Pound said later, 'Tagore has sung Bengal into a nation'.[302]

Curzon, however, continued short-sightedly to underrate the movement. He believed that the Secretary of State, by his ill-advised speeches and weak conduct, was largely responsible for the persistence of the agitation. 'It no longer rests upon any substantial basis either of sentiment or self-interest but has been converted into a purely political movement organized by a small disloyal faction on anti-British lines. It is only saved from being formidable by having hitherto been childish.'[303] He failed to discern that Indian nationalism had ceased to be purely intellectual and had attracted emotional support,[304] that it had for the first time secured a grievance which agitated not politicians only but most men of thought and feeling and that it had evolved revolutionary techniques other than terrorism. The future lay with the type of nationalism that had now developed in Bengal. Till then national consciousness in Bengal had been tepid and was reflected in its school of painting—'hesitant, indecisive line, misty vagueness of form, sombre murkiness of colour, likings for wistful girlish stances, dainty wanness, anaemic sentimentality. . . . They are the qualities which go with a tepid shrinkage from reality, faltering distrust, a failure in courage.'[305] But in 1905 a new robustness was stung into the politics of Bengal and of India. Men, knowing what they fought for and loving what they knew, stood up as a body for the first time against the government. Indian nationalism moved away from both mendicant resolutions and stray bomb outrages to ardent, broad-based revolutionary pressure.

> All changed, changed utterly,
> A terrible beauty is born.

VII

In the midst of these seminal developments, Curzon resigned. It was thought in the bazaars of Calcutta that the Bengalis had directly effected the Viceroy's departure;[306] but in fact it was the result of a sharp conflict with Kitchener, the Commander-in-Chief, on an issue that is in history of no importance. The controversy had its root in the provision of the Indian Councils Act of 1861, which laid down that the Commander-in-Chief could be appointed an extraordinary member of the Viceroy's executive council.[307] In other words, he was not *ex officio* a member, and sometimes Commanders-in-Chief were not appointed to the council. It was the member in charge of the military department who was the regular member of council and looked after the administrative problems of the Indian army. The intention was to enable the Commander-in-Chief to devote his attention to strategy, technical matters and executive command of the army. But in practice the arrangement proved anomalous; for the military member, who was always a soldier junior in rank to the Commander-in-Chief, participated in the highest councils of the Government of India from which the Commander-in-Chief was sometimes excluded, and often vetoed proposals submitted by the army.[308] If the system worked without a major hitch for so surprisingly long, it was because the men concerned adjusted themselves to the compromises of conciliar government, and even Commanders-in-Chief like Roberts were not men of consuming, autocratic ambition.

With Kitchener, however, matters were bound to come to a head. He was a dominating personality—'tall, erect, stern, almost grim, the very incarnation of war itself'[309]—and he came to India which had, as in Curzon's case, throughout been the goal of his endeavours, with the reputation of being the empire's greatest soldier. He was also as accustomed as Curzon had become to having his own way. His massive impassivity and slow-burning energies hid a shrewd, sullen malevolence towards those who opposed him and a well-developed capacity for intrigue. 'To achieve a purpose', Lord Esher observed,[310] 'he is Ignatius Loyola and Juggernaut.' Milner wrote that all the worst points of Kitchener came out in any struggle for mastery. 'I do not think he has ever distinguished between fighting, shall we say, the Mahdi and fighting his own colleagues and countrymen.'[311] Of Curzon's many misjudgments of men, his appraisal of Kitchener was the most disastrous.

In the summer of 1899 Kitchener called on the Secretary of State to inquire about, not the post of Commander-in-Chief, but the military membership.[312] Hamilton, who had earlier thought of Kitchener for the post of Commander-in-Chief but had decided that Kitchener should commence his career in India with a regular command,[313] was not responsive to Kitchener's request. For he was sure that while Kitchener would improve military organization and transport, he would not be equally successful in dealing with the men under his control,[314] and Curzon agreed.[315] The existing situation suited him. Both the Commander-in-Chief, Sir William Lockhart, and the military member, Sir Edwin Collen, were weak men, and even when they were not feebly quarrelling with each other, they allowed the Viceroy to take the decisions.[316] So Curzon even rejected the unanimous suggestion of the India Council that the Commander-in-Chief be excluded from the Viceroy's council. He did not fear the presence of two soldiers in the council and had found that in military matters the advice of the Commander-in-Chief was more useful than that of the military member 'who, as a rule, has dangled his sword for the best part of a lifetime from an office stool'.[317]

In the spring of 1900, when Lockhart died, Curzon, anxious for reforms in the military administration and confident of his own personal superiority, changed his mind about Kitchener and requested that he be sent out.[318] Curiously, Hamilton too had begun to waver and had tentatively suggested, on his own, that it might be worth considering whether Kitchener's South African experience would be specially valuable to India and counteract his obvious disqualifications.[319] The Viceroy's enthusiasm increased, especially when he heard reports that the Duke of Connaught was being considered and realized the social problems that such an appointment would create. 'The man I would soonest have is Kitchener. He might be difficult to get on with and imperious and stubborn. But I am too firmly seated now to mind that, and here as elsewhere I say give me the best man.'[320] When Hamilton pointed out that Kitchener, with all his ability, was most unpopular with the army and might produce a mutiny, Curzon replied he did not think that 'matters one scrap'.[321]

The appointment of Kitchener as Commander-in-Chief was made in August 1900. Curzon drew Kitchener's attention to his own share in this decision but at the same time made it clear that he did not intend Kitchener to have a free hand in military affairs. For not only was the management of the North-West Frontier, which was the principal military interest of India, exclusively in the Viceroy's charge; 'you will find in myself a Viceroy who has perhaps a greater excuse than some of his predecessors for interesting himself in military questions'.[322] Within a week, the appointment was cancelled and Sir Powers Palmer appointed, Kitchener's services being required elsewhere; but the tone of condescension in the Viceroy's letter and the warning of interference could not have been lost on Kitchener. There was clearly no prospect of working with Curzon as he did with Milner in South Africa. Milner had thought it would be impossible for him to work with Kitchener, but after two years could congratulate himself that they had not quarrelled. 'No doubt he is as sick of me as I am eternally sick of him. But we manage to get on decently in our personal relations. Of course his being a strong man, makes it easier.'[323] But with Curzon it was the other way round. He began with confidence and, lacking Milner's finesse, found himself embroiled in conflict.

The news that Kitchener was being seriously considered for

India caused widespread alarm. Brodrick, Lansdowne, North-brook and Esher all warned Curzon, while Cromer, who recommended him strongly to Curzon, wrote in very different terms to Brodrick, thus suggesting that his real purpose in proposing him for India was to get him out of Egypt.[324] The Queen declared that nothing would induce her to consent to the appointment because Kitchener's manners were too ferocious.[325] In India, Collen and Palmer predicted general disaster if 'Kitchener of Chaos' were appointed.[326] But despite Brodrick's discouraging letters, Kitchener remained eager for the Indian appointment and made his representations to the Prime Minister's household; Curzon continued to press for it; and finally, in March 1901, it was decided to give Palmer the appointment only till Kitchener was ready to assume it.[327] Curzon assured Kitchener, without any justification, that his arrival in India would be welcomed with an unbroken chorus of satisfaction; and Kitchener in reply promised to serve Curzon loyally.[328]

It was, however, only over a year later, in October 1902, that Kitchener sailed for India. He told Hamilton that he was most anxious to move cautiously in India and to be on good terms with all those with whom he would serve; but he was also, ominously, concerned about his position and powers.[329] Hamilton assured him that he had never known any competent Commander-in-Chief who could not hold more than his own against the military member; 'but I quite admit the force of Kitchener's contention that the official who is the recognized head of the Military Department, and who is always at the elbow of the Viceroy, will have a more constant and, therefore, a more potent voice in determining the military policy of the Government of India'.[330] Sir Clinton Dawkins gave the Viceroy a clearer notion of Kitchener's plans. It seemed to him that Kitchener was going out to India with the sole intent of running the 'whole show'. Indeed, he quoted Kitchener as having said that he would bide his time during the remaining year of Curzon's term and thereafter use his popularity and prestige to dominate the next Viceroy.[331] A clash between Kitchener and the military member was all the more likely as Collen, who 'is mentally composed of indiarubber',[332] had been succeeded as military member in February 1901 by Sir Edmond Elles, a man whom even Curzon, no easy master, described as 'clear-headed, businesslike and not afraid of responsibility... Neither, now that he is in an independent position, does he at all mind standing up against his former superior, the Commander-in-Chief.'[333]

Thus all the elements in the situation were converging towards catastrophe. But Curzon sensed no danger. 'I feel', he wrote to Hamilton[334] after welcoming Kitchener to India, 'that at last I shall have a Commander-in-Chief worthy of the name and position. Hitherto I have dealt with phantoms.' But when Kitchener said that he appeared to have made a mistake in coming out as Commander-in-Chief and ought rather to have been military member, Curzon, instead of assuring him of his *ex officio* primacy, asked him to trust to his personality and not to be concerned by paper rules or situations; 'it was not likely that we should get in India the inestimable advantage of the presence and counsels of the first soldier of the day, and then commit the unpardonable error of not profiting by them'.[335] To Kitchener this must have seemed an answer answerless, and so it was. There appears to be no doubt that the system, which even Elles described as 'that of *divide et impera*',[336] was to Curzon's liking, and he hoped to take advantage of friction between Kitchener and Elles to establish his own decisive authority.

Kitchener was, of course, shrewd enough to realize that Curzon planned to place him in harness. He was not taken in by Curzon's insistence that, whatever the system, in practice he would be treated by the Viceroy as an equal. 'The Viceroy and the Commander-in-Chief are brought a good deal into contact with each other, and each is capable of being a powerful coadjutor to the other.'[337] Kitchener even alleged[338] that Curzon had informed him that 'if the C.-in-C. had anything to do with the machinery he would become too powerful, so to keep him down we take his power away and run another man as well; between the two the civil elements get control'. While this statement correctly reflected Curzon's attitude, it is not likely to have been made to Kitchener, and seems an instance of the latter's unscrupulous inventiveness rather than of the Viceroy's naïve frankness. But it was clear from the start that Kitchener's authority was being curbed even in practice. In February 1903 the military member modified the plan submitted by the Commander-in-Chief for the Tibet mission.[339] Kitchener, therefore, decided to resist. He was doubtless encouraged in this by his staff, most of whom were as lacking in experience of India as he was, and by the fact that

Curzon was disliked intensely by the Indian army.[340] He toured the Frontier areas almost in defiance of the Viceroy's claim that the Frontier was primarily his responsibility[341] and sought, through private correspondence, the assistance of Lady Salisbury (whose husband was the cousin of Balfour), Roberts and other friends in England.

> The position of affairs here [wrote Kitchener on 6 May] is very galling with the Military Member virtually Commander-in-Chief and supported at every turn by the Viceroy; it makes what would have been a pleasure a disagreeable duty. I hope to be able to stand it till next year; but . . . things may get critical at any time. If Elles had any military knowledge of what an army ought to be to hold its own in a big war, we might get on; but he is narrow-minded and bigoted to a degree.

So Kitchener let it be known that he did not expect his proposals to be criticized by officers of inferior rank, and weakened the military department by transferring its ablest officers to other posts.[342]

Hamilton asked Curzon to warn Kitchener that he should send proposals for reform not directly in private correspondence to the War Office but only officially through the Government of India to the India Office.[343] The chiding was taken by Kitchener in good part and Curzon was still confident of his personal control: 'I shudder to think of what he might do were not a very strong hand kept upon him.'[344] Curzon still believed that so long as he was Viceroy Kitchener would not precipitate an open quarrel.

> I know, as a matter of fact, that he has told his friends that he intends to have no quarrel with me during my time; but he looks forward eagerly, and not I think unpardonably, to the time when I will go. . . . He thinks that when I go, he will get rid of the Military Member, and with a new Viceroy, ignorant of India, and probably less strong-willed than himself, that he will be the ruler of the country in every thing but the name.[345]

Curzon was clearly relying on the report of Dawkins; he was not aware that Kitchener had also told Dawkins that even in Curzon's time he was not prepared to tolerate any criticism of his professional activities. 'While I am Commander in Chief nobody is going to have a word in criticism of my proposals and no Department which renders this possible shall exist.'[346] He was now willing to join battle with Curzon himself and was eager to be Viceroy not only in fact but in name as well. On 21 May he objected to the issue of orders by the military department to the army without his previous knowledge; and when the Viceroy pointed out that all orders were of the Government of India, Kitchener replied that the army was not on a par with the civil departments and if the military department could issue orders to the army the executive command would have passed out of the hands of the Commander-in-Chief. In that case, said Kitchener, there was no course open to him but to resign; and Curzon did not force the issue.[347]

Thereafter Kitchener quietened down and supported the Viceroy, especially in his insistence on justice being done in cases of assault of Indians;[348] and Curzon wrote with relief that 'not a cloud flecks the sky'.[349] For the rest of the year there was no open discord, perhaps to some degree because of the accident in November, when Kitchener broke his leg and was confined to his house for three months. So Curzon thought the storm had passed.[350] But Kitchener's incessant private correspondence, carried on despite the official reprimands,[351] was beginning to produce results. Balfour, now Prime Minister, wrote to Kitchener in December 1903 that his personal conviction was that the division of attributes between the Commander-in-Chief and the military member was quite indefensible;[352] and when Curzon went home in April 1904, he found the Cabinet firm in support of Kitchener. Brodrick, Hamilton's successor as Secretary of State, was even considering the exclusion of the military member from the council[353]—a reversal of the statutory position which made the Commander-in-Chief the occasional and extraordinary member. Kitchener also sent an agent to London. Kitchener's assets were his great reputation, which made it impossible for the government even to consider acceptance of his resignation which was frequently tendered, and the fear aroused by him that if war with Russia broke out the existing 'dual control' would lead to disaster.[354]

Ampthill, the acting Viceroy, was inclined to share Curzon's views on this question[355] but was no match for Kitchener, who was determined to secure control of the military department and get rid of the military member. 'I do not know', he wrote to Roberts,[356] 'how the Military Department worked in your time; but now it is the Government of India and as such the Military Member is almost *de facto* and certainly *de jure* Commander-in-Chief.' He demanded, as a first step, the transfer from the military department of supply and transport matters; otherwise he could not accept the responsibility of command in a serious war and his position became a false one. Ampthill and his council were unwilling to accept the proposal and were naïve enough to expect the support of the home government if the matter were referred to them.[357] But Kitchener had sent his memorandum directly to the Prime Minister, who circulated it among the members of the Committee of Imperial Defence and withdrew it only when Curzon protested.[358] The latter also wrote a long memorandum contesting Kitchener's arguments; but it was clear that the home government had been won over by Kitchener. A conference was held on 4 August, those present being Balfour, Brodrick, Curzon, Roberts, Sir Arthur Godley and Sir William Lee-Warner of the India Office. Balfour, Brodrick, Godley and Lee-Warner argued strongly for the abolition of the military department and the concentration of all military authority in the hands of the Commander-in-Chief, assisted by an Army Board. Their reason was that the government could not face a Russian war with two War Offices in India. They therefore suggested, as a first step, the appointment of a commission to inquire into military administration in India and to propose schemes of reorganization. Curzon, supported on the whole by Roberts, said he saw no reason to destroy the entire system in order to please Kitchener, and if this were to be done it would have to be undertaken by his successor. But he seems to have yielded to the extent of agreeing to the transfer of supply and transport matters to the Commander-in-Chief.[359]

Kitchener, however, while he was aware that Balfour and the Cabinet were on his side, was not satisfied with the pace of progress and sought to lend the question urgency by maintaining an atmosphere of tension in India. He wrote to Brodrick that 'really life is hardly worth living with all the worries caused by the Military Department'.[360] He described it as 'a baboo's office of the worst type' which gave up military interests or discipline in order to secure the Viceroy's favours.[361] On 23 September he handed in his resignation on the ground that there had been a fresh instance of his authority being impaired by Elles. 'Under the present system of dual control of the Army in India, the Military Department, and not the Commander-in-Chief, is practically the principal military adviser to the Viceroy as well as the authority that transmits the Viceroy's personal orders or issues orders in his name to the Commander-in-Chief.' He felt that although he had a seat in council he was being treated in all such matters as if he did not form part of the Government of India at all.[362] Ampthill protested to Brodrick that Kitchener's real demand was that in all matters relating to the army he should be vested with Papal infallibility;[363] but it was the Viceroy who had to give way. The Government of India put forward proposals, acceptable to Kitchener, for the transfer to the Commander-in-Chief of control of the supply and transport services.[364] Curzon, going back on what he had apparently agreed to earlier, was now against any concession and was supported by Roberts and most officials except Godley.[365] But Balfour was strongly on Kitchener's side. He thought that the separation of the executive and administrative functions of the army was indefensible in principle and he had no desire to face the possibility of war with what was admitted to be a divided administration.[366] Other determining factors in favour of Kitchener were no doubt his own unceasing, tortuous pressure and the increasing irritation with Curzon. In October 1904, when Curzon was still in Britain, Balfour had expressed his hope that Curzon would give up his post in April 1905.[367] 'Life would be tolerable', Balfour told his secretary, 'but for its Viceroys.'[368]

The Prime Minister appealed to Curzon, on the eve of the latter's return to India, to be less obstinate. He believed that for the first time a Russian invasion was practical, and if at such a time Kitchener resigned because he found it impossible to work the 'dual system', the vast weight of opinion in Britain would agree with him.[369] What the home government had in mind was a commission of inquiry; this was what Kitchener desired, and Ampthill too thought it was the right step.[370] Balfour and Curzon are then said to have finally agreed that the British government would address the Government of India on the subject, and if the latter replied that no change was required, a commission would be sent out to India to settle the issue.[371] Brodrick assured Curzon that he was not encouraging Kitchener and agreed with Curzon that Rosebery's support was probably at the root of Kitchener's bid for ascendancy; but he also warned the Viceroy that Kitchener commanded such popularity in Britain that he could not be in a stronger position for a battle as to his rights.[372] A week later Brodrick privately assured Kitchener, who was still threatening to resign and proposing the abolition of the post of Commander-in-Chief,[373] that he would do his best in support of Kitchener's cause.[374]

It is not surprising that on his return to India Curzon, as Kitchener noted,[375] appeared rather low and depressed. Further developments were not calculated to cheer his spirits. In response to a despatch from the Secretary of State calling for the views of the Commander-in-Chief, the military member, and the Government of India as a whole on the military administration,[376] Kitchener tabled a minute on 1 January 1905, proposing the abolition of the post of military member and the transfer of its functions to the 'Commander-in-Chief in India and War Member of Council'. Only such an abolition of 'divided counsels, divided authority and divided responsibility' would enable the Indian army to wage the 'fight for existence' for which there was every indication that Russia was pushing forward her preparations.[377] Elles replied on 24 January that there was nothing wrong with the system, and it was impossible for one man to supervise effectively both the army and the military department.[378] Curzon, in his minute of 6 February, also left no room for a settlement. He described Kitchener's proposal as 'in reality one not to disestablish an individual or even a department, but to subvert the military authority of the Government of India as a whole, and to substitute for it a military autocracy in the person of the Commander-in-Chief'. If the Commander-in-Chief were the sole military adviser, the Government of India would be in his hands in all military matters; and in war-time, if the Commander-in-Chief took the field, the military authority and competence of government would be perilously impaired. Curzon then held out the threat of his own resignation if Kitchener's proposal were accepted. 'Speaking for myself, I should respectfully ask to be excused from accepting any such responsibility.'[379]

The three minutes were discussed in council. Though the earlier consideration of this question in Ampthill's time had shown that some members were inclined to side with Kitchener,[380] the Commander-in-Chief now made no attempt to secure their support. Debate was not his forte;[381] and he was confident of the support of the home government as against Curzon and his 'pocket Council'.[382] So he contented himself with a minute of unqualified dissent to a despatch, obviously drafted by Curzon himself and accepted by all the other members. The arguments in the minutes of the military member and the Viceroy were accepted entirely and the Commander-in-Chief was accused of seeking to establish a 'military despotism'. His proposal was described as intended not so much to improve the efficiency of the army as to revolutionize the Government of India and to substitute for the control of the army by the Governor-General in Council control by a single individual.[383]

Clearly there was, whatever the home government's hopes, no possibility of a compromise. 'I have burnt my boats', wrote Kitchener,[384] 'and Curzon has accepted the fact that on this question I resign and has so arranged that I shall be free in May next.' In fact, Curzon believed that Kitchener would not press his resignation;[385] and he over-stated his case in the hope that he could overwhelm the home government. He had been carried away by his dominance in council and the isolation in Simla of Kitchener to ignore the Cabinet's mood of accommodation[386] and growing exasperation with the Viceroy. Brodrick believed Curzon had deliberately procrastinated so as to compel the government to abandon the idea of a commission of inquiry because Lord George Hamilton was unwilling to go to India after February.[387] Now, when they were still considering the formation of a committee representative of all parties,[388] there was fresh testimony of intransigence. Curzon wrote to the home government that three-fourths of Kitchener's contentions, born of a peevish and often puerile antagonism to the military department, had been 'knocked to pieces' by the minute of Elles and said that this was the opinion even of Kitchener's own entourage. The home government, therefore, would be preparing serious trouble for themselves if they adopted an attitude of positive unfairness to Curzon and his colleagues; and even the prestige of Kitchener would not save the Balfour Government. The issue should be judged on its merits.[389] The Viceroy added that if overruled it was not unlikely that the entire council would resign *en bloc* with him and there would be no Government of India but only a Commander-in-Chief.[390]

It was manifest that either Curzon or Kitchener would have to leave India; and as Curzon at last realized, the British government[391] had concluded that they stood to lose more by the resignation of Kitchener than by that of Curzon.[392] As Elgin and Fowler declined to serve on the proposed committee,[393] the Cabinet set up a committee of experts which included Brodrick, Roberts and Field-Marshal Sir George White (also a former Commander-in-Chief in India) to examine the matter; and this committee reported that the Commander-in-Chief had a legitimate griev-ance.[394] Fortified by this report, the home government authorized judgment in favour of Kitchener; and the Secretary of State pro-nounced it in language in which, Lord Ripon said later,[395] no Viceroy of India ought to be addressed. The existing system was described as not tending to smooth or effective working, for the military proposals of the Commander-in-Chief were checked and criticized by another expert of less standing and reputation, who submitted the result to the Governor-General in Council and then voted on equal terms with the Commander-in-Chief and conveyed to him the orders of the government. It was therefore necessary to reform and readjust the system under which military business was conducted. The military department had been intended to typify the paramount civilian control of the Governor-General in Council and not to supply a military equipoise to the authority of the Commander-in-Chief; but this had in fact developed and in many matters in which action might be urgently required the dis-cussions between the army and the military department had passed the limits of safety. The home government were not convinced that the absence of a second military expert in council would pro-duce a military autocracy. They therefore directed that all purely military services be transferred to the Commander-in-Chief and the military department reduced to a military supply department under a member whose duties were more of a civilian than of a military nature. Neither the military supply department nor its member would have the power to veto any proposal put forward by the Commander-in-Chief, who would submit his schemes direct to the Governor-General in Council.[396] Elles was also ordered brusquely to resign before 1 October.[397]

Curzon was informed that he had triumphed on the main issue in that the post of military member would not be abolished and there would continue to be two soldiers in his council.[398] Balfour, writing to Curzon at long last, acknowledged that the Viceroy's views had not been upheld in their entirety; but he felt that the compromise should be acceptable to Curzon. 'One thing I am sure it will *not* do; it will not diminish the authority which the Governor-General has, and ought to have, over matters of Army as well as of Civilian administration.'[399] And for good measure Curzon was told that King Edward was extremely anxious that the Viceroy should accept the compromise.[400]

The Viceroy, however, could not be humoured and regarded the despatch as depicting him as the chief villain in the piece. But he now found that if he resigned only two members of council, Sir Denzil Ibbetson[401] and Sir John Hewett,[402] were willing to do the same. Sir Arundel Arundel[403] thought it would be 'an act of Quixotic folly' for members of council to threaten to resign and believed they should do no more than record a respectful protest.[404] Curzon allowed himself, therefore, to be persuaded by Ibbetson to stay,[405] and induced Kitchener to agree to certain modifications of the home government's proposals, the chief of them being that the military supply member should continue to be known as military member and always be a soldier. The Commander-in-Chief, according to Curzon, even offered to resign if the home government did not accept these joint proposals.[406] That Kitchener should have agreed to this is one of the inexplicable developments in the relations between the two men. He could not have over-estimated Curzon's influence in London, being well aware that the home government were on his side. It was a momentary weakening, 'a slip of the tongue' effected by Curzon's superior intellect and emotional pressure.[407] Brodrick sought to get Curzon to modify his telegram and to ask for these concessions as though they were a mere elucidation or expansion of the Cabinet's original scheme, and finally announced them in the House of Commons as though they were such. Curzon thereupon gave his own version in the Indian legislative council, and disclaimed responsibility for the scheme even as amended. The Secretary of State replied by telegraph, blaming Curzon for revealing official secrets.[408]

The acrimony of this exchange was evidence that the viceroyalty was drawing to its close. It finally spluttered out in August 1905, over the issue of the choice of the military supply member. Curzon, after consulting Kitchener, recommended Major-General Sir Edmund Barrow as one acceptable to both Kitchener and himself.[409] But Kitchener telegraphed privately to the War Office that Barrow was unsuitable. Curzon, who was aware of Kitchener's private telegram, took, surprisingly, no objection. As Sir Winston Churchill is reported to have later said, 'Curzon ought then to have called on Kitchener to explain himself, accused him of being the liar and intriguer he was, and reported the whole thing to the India Office, when it would have been Kitchener who would have had to resign'.[410] The Cabinet, therefore, rejected Barrow and asked the Viceroy to suggest other names after consulting Kitchener.[411] Kitchener hectored Curzon when they met again to discuss the issue, 'lost all command of himself, raged and blustered and eventually stalked out of the room'.[412] Curzon, instead of focusing attention on Kitchener's double-dealing, chose to fight on the wrong issue and insisted that Barrow be appointed.[413] As the choice of members of council was the responsibility of the Secretary of State, the home government were enabled to say that they had accepted Curzon's resignation because he had sought to impose his views on the British government and to defeat their decision in implementation.[414]

So Curzon had been out-manœuvred by Kitchener and Brodrick, with Balfour a willing accomplice. He felt he had been 'jockeyed out of office by a weak-kneed Cabinet and a vindictive Secretary of State' in the interests of an 'utterly unscrupulous man...without truth or honour'.[415] Both sides sought to suggest, after the event, that the difference had been a major one of principle. Curzon insisted that the civil control of the army had been destroyed and that the home government, by accepting his resignation, had 'given a final twist to the halter round the neck of our Constitution'.[416] He also contended, on his return to London, that one of the chief motives of Kitchener's opposition to him and which made Kitchener's predominance in India such a source of danger was his desire to substitute for Curzon's cautious frontier policy one of political and military offensive against the tribes; and this could hardly have any other result than frontier war.[417] The result was a strong measure of support from the Liberal party, especially as the issue arose on the eve of elections. Haldane wrote to Curzon that his name had been cheered in the House of Commons by the Opposition, who seemed to look on him as their own man. 'Unless something quite unforeseen happens, I doubt whether there is anyone the Opposition would rather see in your great office than yourself.'[418] Sir Winston Churchill, who seven years earlier had offered to serve as Curzon's aide-de-camp, now gave enthusiastic support.

Let me say at once how heartily and entirely I agree with you in your gallant stand against what is nothing more nor less than the wholesale transference of the Government of India to the military power. People in England do not understand the vast predominance of the Army in

Anglo-Indian life. Unless the civil power is possessed of expert military information drawn from an independent and authoritative source, I do not see how a Viceroy can control finance or frontier policy—to mention only two subjects—except by a uniform threat of resignation on every question where important divergencies arise. I am quite certain that no Liberal Government which may be returned to power in the near future could possibly acquiesce in the position demanded by Lord Kitchener.[419]

Lord Ripon, a staunch Liberal and a well-informed ex-Viceroy, wrote: 'The military element is triumphant, the civil element is discredited. This is a great misfortune.'[420] This encouragement led Curzon to set aside his loyalty to the Conservative party, desire a Liberal victory in the election[421] and urge the Opposition to raise the matter in the House of Commons.[422]

The supporters of Kitchener, on the other hand, asserted that it was essentially a matter of the supremacy of the home government and the Secretary of State. Balfour told the King that Curzon had 'left no means unused, legitimate or illegitimate, to defeat' the policy of the Cabinet.[423] Godley informed Brodrick's successor as Secretary of State that 'the Curzonian doctrine, pure and simple' was that the home government should not have dared to overrule the Government of India; this raised 'a very big constitutional question, as to which I venture to think that Curzon has not a leg to stand on'.[424] Curzon, by his clumsiness in selecting the particular issue on which he resigned, lent strength to this argument. Morley was convinced by it and, despite the earlier attitude of the Liberal party when in opposition, did not revoke Brodrick's orders. Indeed, he told Brodrick that he would not have stood from Curzon for two months what Brodrick had stood for two years.[425] And over twenty years later, after the death of Curzon and the publication of the authorized biography in which Curzon's version of the controversy was expounded in detail,[426] Brodrick stated at a public meeting that he had been authorized by Balfour to disclose that Curzon's Indian career had been terminated not on account of the quarrel with Kitchener but because Curzon had claimed to direct the foreign policy of India without sufficient regard to its effect on British policy throughout the world.[427]

In fact, however, the point at issue was neither constitutional nor political. To suggest that Curzon had to be displaced because he sought to usurp the authority of the Secretary of State was to take cover behind a flimsy pretext. But for Curzon to speak of Kitchener's proposal as intended to overthrow civilian control of the army and to establish a military dictatorship[428] was to exaggerate wildly. It was no more than a minor administrative readjustment which Kitchener was justified in demanding. For the Commander-in-Chief to be a member of the Viceroy's council on sufferance and to have his proposals scrutinized and his orders revised by a member who was junior to him in military rank was a wholly irrational position. The assertion that the military member acted not on his own but on behalf of the Governor-General in Council, who was the final authority in India, was in theory correct; but in practice the military member scrutinized and pronounced judgment on the proposals of the Commander-in-Chief. The argument of Sir Alfred Lyall[429] and other civil servants with Indian experience, that criticism by junior officers was the norm wherever administration was carried on departmentally, was also not relevant. The criticism of the proposals of, for instance, the Governor of Madras by the secretary of the home department of the Government of India raised no problems; but the situation became explosive when set in the context of the discipline and hierarchical sense of the army.

The dispute cannot also sustain the general, political overtones which both parties later sought to give it. While there were differences between Curzon and Kitchener on frontier policy, they never assumed any dimension; and the allegation that this was one of the chief causes of Kitchener's animosity was unjustified. But Brodrick also was guilty of travesty when he held Curzon's foreign policy responsible for the estrangement between the Viceroy and the home government. It is true that Curzon wished to follow an energetic policy and prod 'that very slumberous lion, the Foreign Office. If only it would now and then roar, or even show its claws. But it is so very deferential and polite to all the other lions, and to many who are not even leopards.'[430] However, especially after Balfour succeeded Salisbury as Prime Minister, the British government kept a tight hand on the reins. The treaty with Tibet was revised on their instructions and the treaty with Afghanistan was signed despite Curzon's protests.

Curzon, in fact, was defeated not in any battle of principle but in personal rivalry. Two masterful men found that they could not function together. It was not a conflict of implacable convictions but a clash of seismic wills on an issue of no serious consequence, and under the stress the illogical system of military administration in India broke. As Kitchener had the greater reputation and, what was even more useful, a deftness in backstairs methods, Curzon found himself caught in the mesh. His conduct throughout the controversy illustrates what Lord Vansittart described as his 'essential helplessness'.[431]

VIII

For the rest of his life, Curzon chewed the cud of defeat. His own premonitions, and those of Lord George Hamilton,[432] had come true; and he was never the same man again. The Indian experience weakened his personality and deprived him of the poise and resilience required for the highest rungs of leadership in Britain. India had lit the fires of his nature and then quenched them for ever. Rarely has a man brought such assorted equipment to a high office, worked as hard, and departed with both his career in ruins and his efforts frustrated. Curzon was not even left the myth of the reputation with which he had come out to India to cloak the futility of his public endeavours. In the history of British India there is no more spectacular instance of the conjunction of failure and fallen greatness.

The personal tragedy is easily explained. The success of a British proconsul depended, to a large extent, on the confidence reposed in him by the home government. If he were trusted, he could be more than an agent furnishing his masters with information and executing their decisions; he could be himself the source of power. 'In the world of shadows', wrote Alfred Lyttelton, the Secretary of State for the Colonies, to Milner, 'I was called your political chief. But in the world of realities you must know that I always thought of you as mine.'[433] Of Cromer the story is told that at a moment of crisis in Egypt he telegraphed to Lord Salisbury, who was on holiday in France, for instructions, and received in reply an *en clair* telegram, 'Do as you like.'[434] Curzon, at the start, was in an even more commanding position than either Milner or Cromer had been. He alone of the three had been a member of the British government; and his relations with the Conservative ministers were cordial. Salisbury believed that Curzon was hustling matters and had a tendency to over-centralize;[435] but he never sought to curb the Viceroy. Curzon was aware that India was 'really governed by confidential correspondence between the Secretary of State and the Viceroy',[436] and he was fortunate in having as Secretary of State Lord George Hamilton, a man easy-going, tired and content to support the Viceroy.

I am beginning to feel [Hamilton wrote to Curzon][437] rather the weight of years in the sense of not caring to tackle and overcome difficult administrative questions as I used to do; and it is therefore a great delight to me to find one so keen and competent to undertake and tackle any question that may arise in connection with the Government of India, while I am left to discharge the functions of an old fogey, namely, to encourage and occasionally to put the drag on.

The initiative, therefore, lay wholly with Curzon, and it is not surprising that he found his relations with Hamilton 'delightful'.[438] In the first four years his authority was not so much viceregal as sovereign; and so accustomed did Curzon become to unquestioning assent that even a slight hesitancy roused his wrath. But then Salisbury gave way to Balfour; and soon after Hamilton was replaced by Brodrick. Balfour and Brodrick were close friends of the Viceroy, but they were not indifferent to the exercise of power or careless of their responsibilities; and the result was soon discernible. In November 1902 the Balfour Cabinet rejected Curzon's proposals for a remission of taxation on the occasion of the Durbar. Curzon found the situation novel and protested vehemently to the Prime Minister. 'I have served you well out here for four years. I have sacrificed everything in that time—health, ease, leisure, and very often popularity—for the sake of the duty imposed upon me.' But now he was being asked to throw away the results of all his labour 'and to injure the cause of binding the Indian people to the British throne, which is dearer to me than my life, by thrusting upon me the duty of announcing this great disappointment to the Indian people'. If the government were determined in their views, they should exercise their right to recall the Viceroy.[439] This was petulance; but in addition Curzon, in disregard of constitutional procedure, appealed to the King. This was naturally resented by the Cabinet,[440] and Balfour admonished Curzon gently and gave him a lesson in democratic government:

You seem to think that you are injured whenever you do not get exactly your own way! But which of us gets exactly his own way? Certainly not the Prime Minister. Certainly not any of his Cabinet colleagues. We all suffer the common lot of those who, having to work with others, are sometimes over-ruled by them. I doubt whether any of your predecessors have [*sic*] ever received so large a measure of confidence from either the Secretary of State or the Home Government.[441]

Curzon, however, would not learn the lesson the easy way. He had no high opinion of Balfour or Brodrick and long years of monopoly of power had rendered him inflexible. The Prime Minister appealed to him again: 'are you not sometimes tempted to use your extraordinary readiness of composition in a way which does not facilitate the co-operation of those who should find it specially easy to work together, since they are not only colleagues but lifelong friends?...do remember that so far as the Cabinet is concerned you have had an absolutely free hand in Indian administration.'[442] But nothing, as Brodrick noted,[443] which was urged by others affected Curzon's judgment in the slightest. He informed Godley—in a letter which was shown to Brodrick—that the new Secretary of State would have to undertake 'some change of clothes' before he could be generally recognized as the wholehearted champion of Indian interests;[444] for Curzon believed that as Secretary for War Brodrick had ignored India's claims. Curzon also wrote a condescending letter to Brodrick explaining the elements of the Indian problem as he saw it.[445] He did not, indeed, expect Brodrick to stay long in office and anticipated an agreeable and relatively tranquil regime. 'In proportion as a man is believed or alleged to have failed in one office, so he is probably reluctant to begin by changes in another.'[446]

Brodrick knew that Curzon had no high opinion of him but he promised the utmost possible support. He declared that he was probably more impartial than any one else in a comparable position, for he had no preconceived ideas about India, no particular respect for traditions and no axe of any sort to grind; and he added that Curzon's regime was 'the nearest approach to an absolute administration under the British Crown for five years'.[447] Curzon was, of course, aware that this disinterestedness and humility were not to be taken too seriously and that Brodrick had no wish to be the Viceroy's echo.[448] Godley had warned him not to count on Brodrick being ductile or malleable and had advised him to remove the impression that he was inclined to carry his protests beyond the recognized official limits. Both the responsibility and the right of control of the home government were absolute and unshared; and Brodrick was loyal to Curzon and most anxious to support him subject to the maintenance of his own opinion on those subjects on which he had decided views.[449] Yet Curzon continued to treat the Secretary of State brusquely and as an inferior.

In 1904, when Curzon came to Britain, he found the home government resistant. He attributed this at first to ignorance. 'As for the India Office, under a Secretary of State who knows little or nothing about India, and does not seem concerned to learn, things move more slowly than I have ever known. I write, write and worry worry. But I cannot get things done.'[450] But soon he was convinced that the opposition to him was inspired by malice. So certain was Curzon of the correctness of his opinions that he was sure that if others failed to share his views it was because they were his personal enemies. He accused Brodrick of deriving 'a peculiar satisfaction' from disagreeing with him,[451] and complained in July 1905 that his 'official existence has long ceased under Brodrick's treatment to be anything but a source of pain and distress'.[452]

It was, in fact, a failure in personal relations that brought Curzon's viceroyalty to its inglorious end; and this was reflected in its public posture. The first year of Curzon's second term—for which Balfour had shown no enthusiasm[453]—saw the relations between the two governments in total disarray. Acrimonious letters, despatches and telegrams were exchanged. In vain did Brodrick appeal to Curzon not always to stress the points of difference.[454] Curzon accused the India Office of desiring to drive him to resign;[455] and the constant tone of denunciation in his letters rendered their weekly receipt, said Brodrick,[456] a positive pain. 'No one here wishes you to resign.'

The Viceroy did not also hesitate to criticize the home government in his speeches and on the files. This public rift encouraged the long-suffering members of his council, who had till now so entirely obliterated themselves that even their existence seemed to have been forgotten by the public,[457] to differ from the Viceroy. It is only in 1905 that one finds for the first time a lack of unanimity, and even a note of harshness, in the minutes of the members. This doubtless weighed with Curzon in his complaint to Balfour that Brodrick's efforts to humiliate in public the head of the Government of India and to treat him as an offending schoolboy was—apart from the personal aspect—weakening the instruments of British rule and would soon react on the rule itself.[458] The Prime

Minister replied, after Curzon's resignation had been accepted, that distance and telegraphic communications had a most maleficent influence when differences of opinion had once made themselves felt.

You seem to suppose that from the moment he [Brodrick] went to the India Office down to his last telegram, his solitary ambition has been to give practical illustration of the theory that the Viceroy is, in certain respects, subordinate to the Secretary of State; and that he found a malicious pleasure in differing from the Head of the Indian Government, and in expressing those differences in harsh and discourteous terms. I can most truly assure you that no view of his conduct can be further from the facts. The last six months have, I fear, not been pleasant for *you*; but they have been unquestionably wretched for *him*; and the unhappiness on both sides has, I repeat, not been so much due to differences of opinion—important though these might have been—as to the embittering effects of written as compared with oral controversy.[459]

But Curzon was not persuaded and believed that Brodrick had, till the end, sought to harass him even in trifling matters.[460]

However, even if it had been the resignation of Kitchener and not that of Curzon which had been accepted, and the Viceroy's term had ended in normal circumstances, his efforts in India would not have had the permanent significance with which he sought to endow them. The achievements, of course, were many. His boundless ambition was served by a vast capacity for work. For over six years he toiled the whole day long and a considerable part of the night, 'habitually harassed, constantly weary and often in physical distress and pain';[461] and his secretary lived in constant fear that Curzon would die under the strain.[462] In Curzon's own phrase, he energized the government all along the line.[463] Gifted with executive talents far beyond the ordinary, he exercised them ruthlessly; and 'tranquil procrastination'[464] was replaced by intense activity. Though in theory everyone condemned one-man rule, in practice all came to him; and this suited the Viceroy and his 'policy of shove'.[465] The home government tacitly acknowledged Curzon's personal rule by making no arrangements for an acting Viceroy when he visited the Persian Gulf. It was not, as Curzon once claimed,[466] mere supervision that he exercised; he initiated and controlled even the minutest measures such as, for example, permission for visitors to zoos to carry cameras. The result was 'that a sparrow can hardly twitter its tail in India without the action being attributed to direct orders issued by the present Viceroy'.[467]

Curzon also claimed, in addition to having endowed the government with fresh initiative, to have inspired it with higher ideals.[468] This was true to the extent that he insisted on justice to all irrespective of race and sought to intimidate the British army in India into conduct which he thought more becoming to Christians and gentlemen.[469] This gained him wide unpopularity among his fellow-countrymen in India and he was generally condemned by them for coldness of nature and lack of sympathy. Such a reaction was, of course, inevitable and to be expected. As a great citizen of the world of our own times has said, the only way to be fair is to be inhuman.[470] That Curzon was prepared for and willingly accepted this dislike of his impartiality enhances the credit due to him.

However, it was essentially an administrative ideal. Curzon's government was sterile of political objectives. He altered, as he rightly claimed, the face of Indian administration and raised the standard of government in every department of public affairs;[471] but he did not vest his rule with a living and ennobling purpose. The Viceroy, according to Curzon, was to be a benevolent despot, going everywhere, seeing everything, treating his subjects with sympathetic impartiality and encouraging every man of real mark.[472] The two great dangers which faced British rule in India were the racial pride and undisciplined passions of the inferior class of Englishmen and the impression that the home government were unjust or indifferent to India's cause.[473] So he advised his subordinates to be kind to the people[474] and urged British opinion to show interest in and regard for India rather than impose terms 'that would shame the combined ingenuity of the usurer and the attorney'.[475] India should be lifted from the level of a dependency to the position which was bound one day to be hers if it was not so already, that of the greatest partner in the empire.[476] Never did Curzon falter in pleading India's case as he saw it. 'My first duty lies to my constituents, and they are the people of India. I would sooner retire from my post than sacrifice their interests.'[477]

These objectives, however commendable in themselves, were wholly inadequate to the India of these years; and Curzon knew it.

The real difficulty in India, my dear Godley, is this. I am thirsting after administrative reform in every direction. I want to infuse principle, direction, consistency, into our policy, so that we may know what we are driving at, and pursue it with consistency; my one object being to make our administration equitable, and our dominion permanent. The advanced natives care about little but constitutional reform. They want to get a larger share of the government of the country; and they count justice, equity, sympathy, the even hand, as of little account, compared with a larger control of the executive, for which they are as yet profoundly unfitted and which they will never get from me.[478]

This refusal to give consideration to the political development of India could, thought Curzon, be sustained by rallying round the government the loyal elements in the community, pursuing the path of unwavering justice, redressing grievances and anomalies wherever found, making British authority essential to the people by reason of its combined probity and vigour, insisting upon a juster and more generous recognition of India in the plans of Britain and the polity of the empire and perpetually building bridges over the racial chasm.[479]

To these tasks Curzon doggedly devoted himself and sought to ignore the demands for political advance. Nothing is more astonishing than to find, in the volumes of his correspondence, how little he cared to keep in touch with informed Indian opinion. Gopal Krishna Gokhale,[480] distinguished for his rectitude and moderation, was a member of the central legislative council; and when Curzon congratulated him on the receipt of a title, Gokhale responded with enthusiasm.

Your extremely generous terms will always be cherished by me with profound gratitude; and [they will be] a source of constant encouragement to me in the work to which my best energies have been and will always be humbly devoted—bringing the two races closer together in this land, so that the purpose of Providence in bringing India under British rule may best be realized by both.[481]

Yet Curzon never sought to utilize the services of Gokhale and rebuked the Governor of Bombay for attaching importance to Gokhale and his new Servants of India Society. One could not, wrote the Viceroy, awaken and appeal to the spirit of nationality in India and at the same time profess loyal acceptance of British rule.[482] Surendranath Banerjee he dismissed as 'that vitriolic windbag'.[483] Pherozeshah Mehta he knighted on the request of the Governor of Bombay, who stated that Mehta had frequently assisted the government in the Corporation of Bombay; but he refused, as he phrased it, 'to believe in the man'.[484]

It is not surprising that on its part educated Indian opinion grew to dislike Curzon intensely. In 1900 he reported that the press and the upper and educated sections of the Indian public were wonderfully generous and loyal to him and admired his sentiments and speeches.[485] Three years later he recorded, 'No angel from Heaven could satisfy the Native party or escape being the victim of their incessant abuse.'[486] But, as is to be seen from the correspondence of the Indian leaders, their disillusionment came only in 1904 and was expressed in revealing terms by Dinshaw Wacha to Gokhale. 'The person who said that Lord Curzon was an *Asiatic* Viceroy will prove true. He has forgotten English methods of governing India and is daily growing in love with *Asiatic* ways of ruling. What a fall is here. This Viceroy will leave the country the most odious and hated, aye, worse than Lord Lytton.'[487] 'Never', wrote Wacha a fortnight later, 'was a more hollow-sounding vessel than the Viceroy and he is as insincere as he is hollow'; and the next year Wacha congratulated Gokhale on laying low in the legislative council 'the exalted python who has been so viciously doing mischief all round'.[488]

It is in the light of these remarks that one has to consider Curzon's obviously wishful declarations that in a moment, so to speak, all India had come over to him in respect of his entire administration and men from all parts, classes and races—barring the Bengalis—had offered him on his departure such a parting tribute as no retiring Viceroy had ever received—for Ripon had obtained the applause of Indians alone. 'Perspective has been attained with a flash of surprising intuition; and the recognition which I did not expect to garner for years, is flooding in upon me from nearly every representative body or institution in India.'[489] The truth was that Curzon returned to Britain in defeat and was seen off in India, with relief, as a failure. If his term as Viceroy is of significance, it is because developments in India were not confined to his conscious efforts. 'Our actions', says one of the characters in Miss Iris Murdoch's novel *The Bell*, 'are like ships which we may watch set out to sea, and not know when or with what cargo they will return to port.' Curzon's partition of Bengal gave the unwitting initiative to events of magnitude, and returned many years later to port with the cargo of freedom.

CONCLUSION

This survey of British policy in India after 1858 enables recognition of the principles and achievements which dominate the detail. At the start, neither the Conservatives nor the Liberals had any clear ideas about India. The statute of 1858 providing for the administration of the country and the Royal Proclamation stating the intentions of British rule were the responsibility of a Conservative Government; but there was nothing in them which could be said particularly to reflect Conservative ideals. The India Act was Disraeli's second attempt—the first having been laughed out—to provide for India nothing more than a system of government which would be acceptable to Parliament; it did not incorporate any ideas as to policy. The Proclamation, as finally issued, was inspired more by the Queen than by the government. She returned the first draft and asked Lord Derby to rewrite it, 'bearing in mind that it is a female sovereign who speaks to more than a hundred million of Eastern people'.[1] A reference to British power to undermine Indian religions and customs was replaced by her with a promise of religious toleration; and it was at the instance of the Governor-General, Canning, that a general amnesty was announced.

The impact of the Liberals on the new administration of India did not, however, extend much further. Canning had been a Peelite and was a close friend of Gladstone; but in India after 1858 he formulated policies which were more akin to Conservative attitudes. He sought to buttress British rule with the support of the upper classes of Indian society, to strengthen the loyalty of the Indian Princes and to give them an interest in the maintenance of British power. At the level below that of the Princes, Canning attempted to gain the support of the hereditary landholders and he even created such a class in some areas where it was not to be found.

Canning had hoped that his efforts to foster the development of an Indian nobility would also assuage the bitterness of relations between the British and the Indians; for he believed that when the British community in India saw the government treating Indians with respect, it would be encouraged to follow this example. In fact, Canning's policy had none of the intended effects. The strengthening of feudal elements neither gained for British rule the support of Indian opinion nor improved relations between the two races. The sentiments which inspired Canning in the years of revolt formed the headwaters of the noblest Liberal thinking on India; but the ideas which lay behind his policies as Viceroy were continued in fruitless Conservative efforts.

For some years after Canning's departure, there was little movement in India. Elgin died too soon and Lawrence came too late. The parties in Britain took little interest. It was a misfortune that Gladstone was so preoccupied with first Italy and then Ireland that he could give little sustained thought to India. As for Disraeli, his imagination was still dormant and unaffected by the expectation that he would have gone out as Viceroy if a vacancy had arisen in 1858. Paradoxically, it was only when he was preparing, ten years later, to go into opposition that Disraeli took a step which led to the initiation of a positive Conservative policy towards India. The nomination to the viceroyalty of Mayo, a man firm in outlook and decisive in action, was Disraeli's greatest service to India. In Afghanistan, despite a suggestion from the Liberal Government that Lawrence's policy of not interfering beyond India's frontiers should be maintained, Mayo decided on a middle course between indifference and involvement. He met the Amir, gave him a letter declaring in general terms British friendship and support and gained considerable influence over him. These events had a considerable impact even beyond Afghanistan and enabled the Viceroy to negotiate confidently with Russia. Within India, Mayo reversed the policy of loose administrative control formulated by Lawrence and Stafford Northcote and laid great emphasis on centralized government. Of the permanence of British rule in India Mayo had no doubt; and to him the sole justification for this was efficient administration. He believed that it was the duty of Britain to administer well and that till that was done there was no scope in India for any major form of political advance. He therefore resumed the basic task which had been begun by Warren Hastings and Dalhousie; and it was the work of Mayo which Curzon undertook to complete.

Mayo's sudden death opened an opportunity to Gladstone to send out a Viceroy of his own choice who could be directed to implement a positively Liberal policy. For by now, in the intervals of business, Gladstone had begun to shape his outlook on India. His belief that all men were equal, his respect for the motives and sentiments of Indians and his acceptance of British obligations led Gladstone to the conclusion that while British rule in India was possibly permanent, it was the chief duty of the British not to ensure that permanence but to train Indians to assume responsibility for themselves. Unlike Mayo, Gladstone gave a political content to the British trust in India. But for such an effort Northbrook, with his inflexible outlook, was an unhappy choice. Even the Conservatives, when they returned to office and wished to continue Mayo's policies both beyond and within India, were disappointed with Northbrook. It was the Viceroy's refusal to maintain Mayo's policy of active influence in Afghanistan and his failure to give the required impetus to administration which led Salisbury to goad Northbrook into resignation.

However, the objectives of Mayo and Salisbury appeared to be too prosaic to the believers of the new gospel of Conservative imperialism. The security of India seemed to them too narrow an interest; they wished to make Britain a Great Power in Asia. It was a wholehearted member of this school whose appointment as Viceroy was approved by Disraeli after three other men had declined it.[2] Lytton's interest lay primarily in foreign affairs. He was eager to assert British authority in Afghanistan and to exclude Russian influence from that country. The home government supported him in his attempt to coerce the Amir but expressed alarm at his casual contemplation of a war with Russia. Salisbury brought Lytton to heel; but soon after, Salisbury gave way to Cranbrook and Lytton acted as he pleased. In contravention of instructions from London, he precipitated a campaign in Afghanistan and forced the Amir to agree to his demands. Such spectacular success clouded criticism; but within a few months the newly appointed British Resident in Kabul was murdered and another military campaign had to be undertaken.

Within India, Lytton acted more in accordance with the directives of the home government. In obedience to Salisbury he reduced tariffs on British cotton goods; and to satisfy Disraeli he held a great durbar to proclaim the Queen as Empress. He also revived Canning's policy of seeking the collaboration of the upper classes. Political status was sought to be conferred on the Princes and young men belonging to the upper classes were provided with avenues of official employment. On the other hand, Lytton treated the class of educated Indians with contempt and attempted to stifle newspapers and journals in Indian languages. He believed that absolute government, dependent on military force and the acquiescence of a docile population, was suited to India and that, if left unaltered, it had a better chance of permanence than any other government in the world. Lytton's only claim to remembrance, which can hardly be discerned beneath the wreckage of his foreign and domestic policies, was his sense of fairplay in cases concerning British and Indians.

The activities of Lytton had sharpened Gladstone's sense of responsibility for India. Speaking for the Opposition on the Royal Titles Bill in 1876, he referred to British power in India as 'that vast and curiously constructed fabric of which we are the stewards, and which it is our duty to maintain so long as any obligation connected with that power remains to be fulfilled'.[3] It was what seemed to him to be a flagrant abuse of this power by Lytton that shocked Gladstone. He asserted that in governing India the British had in good faith taken their stand upon the only ground that made British rule hopeful or possible—that India would be governed for the good of the Indian people and that no consideration of selfish interests would divert the British from their first and highest duty. Gladstone believed that Indians were aware of this and, therefore, though they had many specific complaints, showed no disposition to deny that British rule was beneficial to them. This was to him a matter of 'gratified astonishment' and he regretted the assumption underlying Lytton's regime that the masses of India were disloyal.[4] The truth as to India could not too soon be understood.

There are two policies, fundamentally different; and it is the wrong one that is now in favour. One of them treats India as a child treats a doll and defends it against other children; the other places all its hopes for the permanence of our Indian rule in our good government of India. ... Let us only make common cause with her people; let them feel that we are there to give more than we can receive; that their interests are not traversed and frustrated by selfish aims of ours; that if we are defending ourselves upon the line of the Hindoo Coosh it is them and their interests that we are defending, even more, and far more than our own. Unless we can produce this conviction in the mind of India, in vain shall we lavish our thoughts and our resources upon a purely material defence.[5]

Conclusion

So in the years from 1876 to 1880 Gladstone put forward in greater amplitude the principles that the rights of men were not limited by the boundaries of Christian civilization, that the feelings and desires of the Indian people should be given consideration and that Britain had a duty in India. These principles had become the policy of the Liberal party and formed the mandate for Ripon. He withdrew British troops from Afghanistan and reached an amicable settlement with its ruler. But within India, his major effort at promoting political education in local bodies failed to gather momentum; and in the battle which he found himself waging with the British community he was worsted by lack of resolution. Because of the personal limitations of the Viceroy, his principles suffered a reverse.

The retirement of Ripon in 1884 was not expected to be the end of the Liberal experiment. Ripon, in fact, retired prematurely after four years, in order that the Gladstone Government could, before it went out of office, choose his successor. But Dufferin's only achievements were in foreign affairs; and these were more to the liking of the Conservatives than of his own party. Within India, he first wooed the landholding gentry and encouraged the Moslems to stand apart, then sought applause from the middle classes and finally departed in a mood of irritation. If Ripon was nerveless, Dufferin suffered from lack of horizon and inertness of spirit; and together they ensured that the eight years of Liberal administration should have no immediate success. Yet, out of this defeat and frustration, came a slow victory. Ripon's term had been one not of command but of character and it revealed to Indians the possibility of working with their rulers for political and social advance.

Immediately, however, there followed a decade of uninspired rule. Both the Conservatives and the Liberals allowed their concern for India to decline. Salisbury's only positive recommendation, which was fortunately not acted upon, was that the leading Indian Princes should be raised to the peerage; and the interest of Gladstone in India had been reduced to a flicker. Nor did the British government select Viceroys with any ideas or policies of their own. Lansdowne, who succeeded Dufferin, at the start sought to keep alive the mood of response to Indian opinion but shrank back at the first obstacle and decided to deal sternly with the educated classes. This unimaginative outlook continued under Elgin, who had no firm views and was happy to leave the power to decide with the authorities in Whitehall. Their interference was for the most part in the narrow interests of Britain.

It was for Curzon, who came out as Viceroy towards the end of 1898, to give Conservatism in India a new and better face—or rather to restore the main features of the Mayo tradition: good administration and priority for Indian development in the belief that it would render British rule in India permanent. He gave a new vigour to the machinery of government, modernized it wherever necessary and extended it to cover many new spheres of economic and social life. But this executive effort, though laudable in itself, was not sufficient. Twenty five years had passed since Mayo's death and during that period there had developed in India a political self-consciousness which made the principles of Gladstone not merely virtuous but vital. Efficient administration is not a fulfilment but a process; and this was beyond the understanding of Curzon. So the Viceroy, despite all the driving force of these seven years, never attained the success of statesmanship; and his term is remembered not so much for what he achieved as for what occurred in opposition to him. Curzon was the last of the eminent administrators of British India; and the stage had been transformed even before he had departed from it. India after 1905 had new interests and objectives and compelled new lines of British policy.

NOTES

1 Gladstone to Canning 23 July 1859, Canning Papers, volume of letters from Her Majesty's Ministers, no. 28.

2 Canning to Sir Charles Wood, Secretary of State, 8 Aug. 1859, Wood Papers, India Office Library, F. 78, box 2A.

3 See M. Maclagan, *Clemency Canning* (London, 1962), p. 21.

4 Palmerston to the Chairman of the East India Company, 2 Sept. 1856, Palmerston Papers, B.M. Add. MSS 48580, pp. 272 ff.

5 Canning to Granville 19 May 1857, Granville Papers, P.R.O. 30/29, box 21.

6 Professor Asa Briggs is of the view that no single event more powerfully affected the mind of that generation in Britain than the massacre at Cawnpore in 1857. (*Victorian People* (London 1954), p. 19.) Professor W. L. Burn has stated that Cawnpore 'was written on the heart of that generation'. (*The Age of Equipoise* (London, 1964), p. 84.)

7 See Sir Keith Feiling, *In Christ Church Hall* (London, 1960), p. 164.

8 See Granville to Canning 10 Feb. 1859, Granville Papers, box 21.

9 Canning to Stanley 19 Oct. 1858, Canning Papers, volume of letters to Secretary of State, no. 127.

10 Granville to Canning 9 Nov. 1857, Granville Papers, box 21.

11 See the reports of the district officers in Foreign Department Proceedings 31 Dec. 1858, nos. 1127–1214.

12 Canning to Stanley 15 Sept. 1858, Canning Papers, volume of letters to Secretary of State, no. 119.

13 Secretary to the Government of India to Local Governments, Allahabad 8 Nov. 1858, no. 519, Home Department Public Proceedings 26 Nov. 1858, nos. 75–92.

14 See letters of Secretary to the Government of India 18 Nov. 1858, no. 549, and notes of Members of Council, *ibid.*; Minute of Canning 4 Dec. 1858, Home Department Public Proceedings 17 Dec. 1858, nos. 96–101.

15 Public Despatch of Secretary of State no. 11 dated 31 Jan. 1859 and no. 20 dated 24 Feb. 1859, Foreign Department Secret Proceedings 30 Dec. 1859, nos. 1944 and 1945.

16 Annual Report on the Administration of the Province of Oudh for 1858–9, Foreign Department Proceedings 5 Aug. 1859, no. 292.

17 *Ibid.*

18 B. 1803; entered Company's army 1819; resident at Baroda 1847–51; resident at Oudh 1855; service in 1857 campaigns; chief commissioner of Oudh 1857–8; member of Viceroy's council 1858–60; d. 1863.

19 John, first baron Lawrence, b. 1811; arrived in India 1830; service in Delhi and the Punjab; chief commissioner of the Punjab 1853–7; member of India council 1859–63; viceroy of India 1864–9; d. 1879.

20 Canning to Granville 16 March 1858, Granville Papers, box 21; Secretary to Chief Commissioner of Oudh to the Secretary to the Government of India no. 642 dated 10 July 1858, Foreign Department Secret Proceedings 27 Aug. 1858, nos. 26–45.

21 Foreign Department to Chief Commissioner Oudh no. 3502 dated 6 Oct. 1858, Foreign Department Political Secret Proceedings 5 Nov. 1858, nos. 191–5.

22 Annual Report on the Administration of the Province of Oudh for 1858–9, *op. cit.*

23 Secretary to Chief Commissioner to all Commissioners, Circular 12/577 of 1858 dated 15 Oct. 1858, Foreign Department Political Secret Proceedings 12 Nov. 1858, nos. 197–200.

24 Secretary to Chief Commissioner to Secretary to Government of India no. 1710, of 1858 dated 27 Dec. 1858, Foreign Department Proceedings 14 Jan. 1859, nos. 391–6; Canning to Stanley 19 Jan. 1859, Canning Papers, volume of letters to Secretary of State, no. 150.

25 Canning to General Low 15 Feb. 1858, Canning Papers, volume of letters to Members of Council, no. 16.

26 See J. Raj, 'The Introduction of the Taluqdari System in Oudh', in T. Raychaudhuri (ed.), *Contributions to Indian Economic History*, I (Calcutta, 1960), p. 57 ff.; Maclagan, *op. cit.* pp. 176 ff.

27 Raj, *op. cit.*; also Secretary to Chief Commissioner to Secretary to Government of India no. 461 dated 12 June 1858, Foreign Department Secret Proceedings 30 July 1858, nos. 70–5.

28 Canning to Granville 31 Jan. 1860, Granville Papers, box 21.

29 Canning to Wood 27 Feb. 1860, Wood Papers, box 2A.

30 Wood to Canning 10 Oct. 1859, Wood Papers, vol. 1, p. 174.

31 Telegram to Wood 22 Nov. 1859, Wood Papers, box 2A.

32 Canning to Wood 12 Nov. 1859, Wood Papers, box 2A.

33 W. H. Russell, *My Indian Mutiny Diary* (London, 1957 edition), p. 22.

34 Canning to Wood 6 Nov. 1859, Wood Papers, box 2A.

35 *Ibid.* 16 Oct. 1859, Wood Papers, box 2A.

36 *Ibid.* 13 June 1860, Wood Papers, box 2A.

37 Canning to Stanley 29 Jan. 1859, Canning Papers, volume of letters to Secretary of State, no. 152.

38 Canning to Wood 5 May 1860, Wood Papers, box 2A.

39 *Ibid.* 13 and 18 June 1860, Wood Papers, box 2A; Viceroy's minute on note by Governor of Madras sent to Wood 3 June 1861, Wood Papers, box 2B.

40 Wood to Canning 26 June and 26 July 1860, no. 2, Wood Papers, vol. 3, pp. 74 and 254 ff. respectively; the Queen to Wood 19 June 1860, Wood Papers, box 4A; Stanley to Wood 31 July 1860, Wood Papers, box 4B.

41 Canning to Stanley 3 April 1859, Canning Papers, volume of correspondence with Stanley, part II, p. 171.

42 Canning to Wood 31 March 1860, Wood Papers, box 2A.

43 Wood to Trevelyan 25 May 1860, Wood Papers, vol. 3, fo. 122; Canning to Wood 13 June 1860, Wood Papers, box 2A.

44 Canning to Wood 20 Aug. 1860, Wood Papers, box 2A.

45 Wood to Canning 10 Oct. 1860, no. 2, Wood Papers, vol. 4, fos. 238ff.

46 Wood to Canning 18 Aug. 1861, Wood Papers, vol. 8, fos. 224ff., and 25 Dec. 1861, Wood Papers, vol. 9, fos. 174ff.

47 Wood to Canning 10 Jan. 1862, Wood Papers, vol. 9, fo. 184.

48 Wood to Elgin 18 June 1862, Wood Papers, vol. 10, fos. 304ff.

49 Wood to Elgin 16 Aug. 1862, Wood Papers, vol. 11, fos. 60ff.

50 Elgin to Wood 17 Aug. 1862, Elgin Papers, India Office Library, MSS Eur. F. 83, letter book volume 2, fos. 144ff.

51 Wood to Elgin 24 Sept. 1862, no. 1, Wood Papers, vol. 11, fos. 156ff.

52 Wood to Elgin 18 March 1863, Wood Papers, vol. 12, fos. 136ff.

53 Lawrence to Cranborne 20 Sept. 1866, Lawrence Papers, India Office Library. MSS Eur. F. 90, letters to Secretary of State, vol. 3, no. 36.

54 Cranborne to Lawrence 19 Nov. 1866, Lawrence Papers, letters from Secretary of State, vol. 3, no. 42.

55 *Ibid.* 27 Feb. 1867, Lawrence Papers, letters from Secretary of State, vol. 4, no. 8.

56 Lawrence to Cranborne 28 March 1867, Lawrence Papers, letters to Secretary of State, vol. 4, no. 22.

57 Northcote to Lawrence 26 March, 3 April and 20 April 1867, Lawrence Papers, letters from Secretary of State, vol. 4, nos. 13, 16 and 18.

58 Lawrence to Northcote 2 May and 16 May 1867, Lawrence Papers, letters to Secretary of State, vol. 4, nos. 28 and 31.

59 Canning to Wood 2 Dec. 1859, Wood Papers, box 2A.

60 Secretary to Government North-West Provinces to Secretary to Government of India no. 2473 dated 6 July 1859, Home Department Public Proceedings 16 Sept. 1859, nos. 3–5.

61 Letter of Government of India 7 July 1860, Home Department Public Proceedings 7 July 1860, no. 17; reply of the Government of the North-West Provinces no. 1850A dated 16 July 1860, Home Department Public Proceedings 3 Aug. 1860, nos. 7–9.

62 Secretary to Government North-West Provinces to Secretary to Government of India no. 2060A dated 7 Aug. 1860, Home Department Public Proceedings 24 Aug. 1860, nos. 42–5.

63 Canning to Wood 1 July 1861, Wood Papers, box 2B.

64 *Ibid.* 8 Oct. 1861, Wood Papers, box 2B.

65 Wood to Frere 25 Dec. 1861, Wood Papers, vol. 9, fos. 168ff.

66 Lawrence to Wood 16 June 1864, Wood Papers, box 7A.

67 Wood to Lawrence 17 Aug. 1864, Wood Papers, vol. 18, fos. 40ff.

68 Lawrence to Wood 15 Sept. 1864, Wood Papers, box 7A.

69 Wood to Lawrence 31 Dec. 1864, Wood Papers, vol. 19, fos. 150ff.

70 Lawrence to Wood 4 Feb. 1865, Wood Papers, box 7B.

71 Wood to Lawrence 10 March 1865, Wood Papers, vol. 20, fos. 83ff.

72 Cranborne to Lawrence 2 Jan. 1867, Lawrence Papers, letters from Secretary of State, vol. 4, no. 1.

73 Lawrence to Cranborne 8 and 21 Jan. and 5 Feb. 1867, Lawrence Papers, letters to Secretary of State, vol. 4, nos. 4, 7 and 10.

74 Canning to Ricketts 17 Jan. 1860, Canning Papers, vol. of letters to Members of Council no. 73; Canning to Wood 27 Feb. 1860, Wood Papers, box 2A.

75 Canning to Wood 22 July 1861, Wood Papers, box 2B.

76 Wood to Canning 19 Dec. 1859, Wood Papers, vol. 2, p. 40.

77 Wood to Trevelyan 25 Dec. 1859, Wood Papers, vol. 2, p. 56.

78 Wood to Canning 3 Jan. 1860, Wood Papers, vol. 2, pp. 60ff.; Wood to Frere 1 Aug. 1862, Wood Papers, vol. 11, pp. 46ff.

79 Wood to Trevelyan 9 April 1860 and to Canning 18 April 1860 and 26 July 1860, no. 2, Wood Papers, vol. 3, fos. 8ff., 28ff. and 254ff. respectively. Wood's idea of recruitment to official service of members of the feudal classes took shape later, in 1878, as the Statutory Civil Service. See pp. 117–18.

80 Canning to Wood 5 May 1860, Wood Papers, box 2A, and 10 April and 18 Oct. 1861, Wood Papers, box 2B; Canning to Granville 3 March 1861, Granville Papers, box 21.

81 Wood to Elgin 18 July 1863, Wood Papers, vol. 13, fos. 156ff.

82 Elgin to Wood 30 Aug. 1863, Elgin Papers, section 1, part 1, vol. 5, no. 24.

83 Wood to Frere 17 Aug. 1864, and to Lawrence 1 Sept. 1864, Wood Papers, vol. 18, fos. 42ff. and 70ff. respectively; Wood to Lawrence 18, 25, 26 Jan. and 3 Feb. 1865, Wood Papers, vol. 19, fos. 240ff. Also Canning to Granville 29 May 1860, Granville Papers, box 21.

84 Lawrence to Wood 15 Sept. 1864, Wood Papers, box 7A.

85 *Ibid.* 4 Feb. 1865, Wood Papers, box 7B.

86 *Ibid.* 20 Feb. 1865, Wood Papers, box 7B.

87 B. 1820; arrived in India 1839; service in North-West Provinces; chief commissioner of Oudh 1860–5; M.P. 1868–74; d. 1892.

88 B. 1818; joined Bengal civil service 1840; secretary to government of India 1859–62; member of Viceroy's council 1862–7; lieutenant-governor of Bengal 1867–71; governor of Jamaica 1874–7; d. 1878.

89 Wingfield to Grey 19 Feb. and 19 March 1866, and Grey to Lawrence 13 Sept. 1866, Lawrence Papers, letters from Members of Council, vol. 3, nos. 7B, 20B and 81.

90 Lawrence to Grey 24 Feb. 1866, Lawrence Papers, letters to Members of Council, vol. 1, no. 32.

91 Sir R. Temple, *Men and Events of My Time in India* (London, 1882), p. 324.

92 See Maine to Lawrence 28 Sept. 1864, letters from Members of Council, vol. 1. Maine was Law Member in India from 1862 to 1869.

93 Lawrence to Halifax (Sir C. Wood) 1 Sept. 1866, Lawrence Papers, letters to Secretary of State, vol. 3, no. 32.

94 Canning to Stanley 24 June 1859, Canning Papers, volume of letters to Secretary of State, no. 195.

95 The idea is said to have been not that of Canning but of Ricketts, a member of his council. (Sir A. Arbuthnot, *Memories of Rugby and India* (London, 1910), p. 125.)

96 Canning to Stanley 13 June 1859, Canning Papers, volume of letters to Secretary of State, no. 192.

97 Minute of Sir Charles Trevelyan 13 July 1859, Home Department Public Proceedings 12 August 1859, nos. 11 and 12.

98 Canning to Wood 8 Aug. 1859, Wood Papers, box 2A.

99 B. 1815; entered Bombay civil service 1834; chief commissioner of Sind 1850–9; member of Viceroy's council 1859–62; governor of Bombay 1862–7; governor of the Cape 1877–80; d. 1884.

100 Frere to Wood 5 Sept. 1859, Wood Papers, box 5A.

101 Stanley to Wood 22 June 1859, Wood Papers, box 4B; Wood to Canning 26 July 1859, Wood Papers, vol. 1, pp. 48ff.

102 Canning to Wood 30 Sept. 1859, Wood Papers, box 2A.

103 *Ibid.* 7 June 1860, Wood Papers, box 2A.

104 *Ibid.* 25 May 1860, Wood Papers, box 2A.

105 Wood to Canning 27 Aug. 1860, no. 2 and 2 Sept. 1860, Wood Papers, vol. 4, pp. 62ff. and 110ff. respectively; Minutes of Sir B. Frere 29 Dec. 1860, Sir C. Beadon 26 Jan. 1861 and S. Laing 28 Jan. 1861. Home Department Public Proceedings 31 Jan. 1861, nos. 76–80.

106 Stanley to Wood 22 June 1859, Wood Papers, box 4B; Wood to Canning 26 Aug., to Elphinstone Governor of Bombay 31 Aug. and to Trevelyan of Madras 10 Sept. 1859, Wood Papers, vol. 1, pp. 94ff.

107 Wood to Elphinstone 2 Nov. 1859, Wood Papers, vol. 1, p. 202.

108 Canning to Wood 30 Sept. 1859, Wood Papers, box 2A.

109 Frere's minutes 16 March and 29 Dec. 1860, Home Department Public Proceedings 31 Jan. 1861, nos. 76–80.

110 Wood to Canning 27 Aug. 1860, no. 2, Wood Papers, vol. 4, pp. 62ff.

111 Canning to Wood 8 Oct. 1860, Wood Papers, box 2A.

112 *Ibid.* 6 Jan. 1861, Wood Papers, box 2B.

113 Wood to Canning 26 March 1861, no. 3 and 26 April 1861, no. 1, Wood Papers, vol. 7, pp. 74ff. and 204ff. respectively.

114 *Ibid.* 9 April 1861, Wood Papers, vol. 7, pp. 126ff.

115 Canning to Wood 10 April 1861, Wood Papers, box 2B.

116 21 July 1861, Granville Papers, box 21.

117 Canning to Wood 2 Sept. 1861, Wood Papers, box 2B; Wood to Canning 3 Aug. and to Denison 18 Aug. 1861, Wood Papers, vol. 8, pp. 142ff. and 204ff. respectively.

118 Canning to Wood 22 July 1861, Wood Papers, box 2B.

119 Wood to Canning 3 Dec. 1861, Wood Papers, vol. 9, pp. 142ff.

120 Wood to Canning and to Elgin 10 Feb. 1862, Wood Papers, vol. 10, fos. 20ff.

121 Wood to Elgin 18 March 1862, Wood Papers, vol. 10, fos. 100ff.

122 Wood to Elgin 10 and 19 May 1862, Wood Papers, vol. 10, fos. 220ff.

123 Elgin to Wood 22 July and 2 Aug. 1862, Elgin Papers, letter book vol. 2, fos. 71ff., and 9 Oct. 1862, Elgin Papers, letter book vol. 3, fos. 66ff.

124 Wood to Elgin 10 Sept. 1862, Wood Papers, vol. 11, fos. 124ff.

125 Wood to Frere 15 Sept. 1862, no. 1, Wood Papers, vol. 11, fos. 140ff.

126 See Dr B. Chowdhury, 'Growth of Commercial Agriculture in Bengal', ch. 1 in *Indian Studies*, iv, no. 3 (Calcutta, 1963), pp. 289ff.

127 Acting Secretary Indigo Planters Association to Secretary Bengal Government no. 2 dated 13 March 1860, Home Department Proceedings Judicial 19 May 1860, no. 49.

128 Petition of the Indigo Planters Association to the Lieutenant-Governor of Bengal 13 March 1860. *Ibid.*

129 See the reports of the magistrates of Nuddea and Jessore transmitted by the Commissioner of Nuddea to the Bengal Government no. 71 Ct. dated 13 March 1860. *Ibid.*

130 Secretary Bengal Government to Commissioner of Nuddea no. 926 dated 14 March 1860. *Ibid.*

131 Secretary Bengal Government to Commissioner of Nuddea no. 1053 dated 21 March 1860; telegram of Governor-General in Council to Secretary of State 26 March 1860. *Ibid.*

132 Sir Charles Trevelyan b. 1807; official service in India 1826–38; assistant secretary to the Treasury 1840–59; joint author of report on permanent civil service 1853; governor of Madras 1859–60; finance member of Viceroy's council 1862–5; d. 1886.

133 Trevelyan to Wood 13 April 1860, Wood Papers, box 3 A.

134 Commissioner of Circuit, Rajshahi, to Secretary Bengal Government no. 611 dated 18 April 1860; Secretary Bengal Government to Commissioner of Circuit, Rajshahi no. 1847 dated 21 April 1860; Commissioner of Nuddea to Secretary Bengal Government no. 109 Ct. dated 25 April 1860, Home Department Proceedings Judicial 19 May 1860, no. 49.

135 Wood to Canning 3, 10 and 18 May 1860, Wood Papers, vol. 3, fos. 62ff., 100ff. and 108ff. respectively.

136 Secretary Bengal Government to Commissioner Rajshahi division no. 3280 dated 16 June 1860 and no. 3218 dated 18 June 1860, Home Department Proceedings Judicial 2 July 1860, nos. 1–2 (B).

137 B. 1807; joined Bengal civil service 1828; secretary to government 1853; member of governor-general's council 1854–9; lieutenant-governor of Bengal 1859–62; governor of Jamaica 1866–73; d. 1893.

138 Petition of the Bengal Indigo Planters Association 26 July 1860, Home Department Proceedings Judicial 31 Aug. 1860, nos. 41–8.

139 Grant to Wood 9 Aug. 1860, Wood Papers, box 4 C.

140 Minute of Grant 17 Aug. 1860, Home Department Proceedings Judicial 31 Aug. 1860, nos. 41–8.

141 Viceroy's Minute 26 Aug. 1860. *Ibid.*

142 Secretary to Government of India to Secretary Indigo Planters Association no. 1640 dated 31 Aug. 1860. *Ibid.*

143 Secretary to Government of India to Officiating Secretary Bengal Government no. 1639 dated 31 Aug. 1860. *Ibid.*

144 Wood to Grant 24 Sept. 1860, Wood Papers, vol. 4, fo. 202.

145 Wood to Canning 24 Sept. 1860, no. 1, Wood Papers, vol. 4, fo. 174; and 9, 14 and 24 Nov. 1860, no. 3, Wood Papers, vol. 5, fos. 58 ff., 68 ff. and 104 ff. respectively.

146 Secretary Indigo Planters Association to Secretary to the Government of India 13 Oct. 1860, Home Department Proceedings Judicial (Land Revenue) 28 Dec. 1860, nos. 36–43.

147 Grant's second minute 23 Nov. 1860. *Ibid.*

148 Grant to Wood 23 Nov. 1860, Wood Papers, box 4 C.

149 Secretary to Government of India to Officiating Secretary with Governor-General no. 2707 dated 30 Nov. 1860 and Officiating Secretary with Governor-General to Secretary to Government of India no. 31 dated 24 Dec. 1860, Home Department Proceedings Judicial (Land Revenue) 28 Dec. 1860, nos. 36–43.

150 Wood to Canning 9 Jan. 1861, Wood Papers, vol. 6, fos. 12 ff.

151 Wood to Canning 4 Feb. 1861, Wood Papers, vol. 6, fo. 138; Granville to Canning 24 Feb. 1861, Granville Papers, box 21.

152 Stanley to Wood 8 Dec. 1860, Wood Papers, box 4 B.

153 Despatch to the Secretary of State no. 3 dated 29 Dec. 1860, Home Department Proceedings Judicial 27 Feb. 1861, nos. 43–50.

154 Canning to Wood 18 March 1861, Wood Papers, box 2 B.

155 Wood to Canning 18 April 1861, no. 2, Wood Papers, vol. 7, fo. 184.

156 Canning to Wood 9 May 1861, Wood Papers, box 2 B.

157 Grant's minute 19 June 1861, Home Department Proceedings Public 28 June 1861, nos. 103–5 A.

158 W. S. Seton-Karr, joined Bengal civil service 1842; president of indigo commission 1860; secretary to Bengal government 1860–1; judge of Calcutta high court 1862–8; vice-chancellor of Calcutta university 1868–9; retired 1870.

159 Secretary Landholders and Commercial Association of British India to Secretary Bengal Government 29 May 1861. *Ibid.*

160 Under-secretary Bengal Government to Secretary Landholders and Commercial Association of British India no. 1426 A dated 3 June 1861. *Ibid.*

161 Canning to Wood 23 June 1861, Wood Papers, box 2 B.

162 Seton-Karr to Secretary Bengal Government 29 July 1861, and minute of Grant 30 July 1861, Home Department Proceedings Public 8 August 1861, nos. 34–7.

163 Canning to Wood 31 July 1861, Wood Papers, box 2 B.

164 Resolution of the Governor-General in Council 8 Aug. 1861, Home Department Proceedings Public 8 Aug. 1861, nos. 34–7.

165 Landholders and Commercial Association of British India to Secretary to the Government of India 12 Aug. 1861, Home Department Proceedings Public 15 Aug. 1861, nos. 63/64.

166 Canning to Wood 9 Aug. 1861, Wood Papers, box 2 B; Wood to

Canning 26 Sept. and 18 Oct. 1861 and 10 Feb. 1862, Wood Papers, vol. 8, fos. 270ff., vol. 9, fos. 28ff., and vol. 10, fos. 20ff. respectively.

167 B. 1810; barrister of Inner Temple; law member in India 1852–9; chief justice of Bengal 1859–70; d. 1890.

168 Wood to Canning 10 June 1861, no. 1, Wood Papers, vol. 8, fos. 40ff.

169 *Ibid.* 10 Jan. 1862, Wood Papers, vol. 9, fos. 186ff.

170 Elgin to Beadon, Lieutenant-Governor of Bengal 16 Aug. 1862, Elgin Papers, section 1, part 2, vol. 13, no. 2.

171 Wood to Trevelyan 17 Sept. 1863, Wood Papers, vol. 14, fos. 28ff.

172 Wood to Elgin 1 Oct. 1863, Wood Papers, vol. 14, fos. 48ff.

173 Wood to Maine 3 Dec. 1863, Wood Papers, vol. 15, fos. 8ff.

174 Wood to Trevelyan 9 Dec. 1863, Wood Papers, vol. 15, fos. 38ff.; Lawrence to Wood 3 April 1864, Wood Papers, box 7A.

175 Lawrence to Wood 28 June 1864, Wood Papers, box 7A.

176 Lawrence to Sir Erskine Perry, cited in R. Bosworth Smith, *Life of Lord Lawrence* (London, 1883), II, 417.

177 J. Beckwith, Secretary to the Landholders and Commercial Association to F. R. Cockerell, Officiating Secretary to Bengal Government 3 May 1864, Home Department Judicial Proceedings 13 Sept. 1864, no. 21.

178 See, for example, the report of the Magistrate of Nuddea district in Bengal, 18 March 1864, Home Department Judicial Proceedings 18 June 1864, nos. 36–46.

179 Letters of J. Beckwith, Secretary to the Landholders and Commercial Association to F. R. Cockerell, Officiating Secretary to Bengal Government 14 April and 3 May 1864. *Ibid.*

180 Letter of A. Eden, Secretary to Bengal Government, to the Secretary to the Landholders and Commercial Association, no. 513T dated 4 June 1864. *Ibid.*

181 Note of W. Grey, Secretary, Home Department 13 May 1864. *Ibid.*

182 Note of Lawrence 16 May 1864. *Ibid.*

183 Maine to Lawrence 2/4 April 1864, Lawrence Papers, letters from members of council, vol. 1.

184 Note of Maine 20 May 1864, Home Department Judicial Proceedings 18 June 1864, nos. 36–46.

185 Note of Trevelyan 27 May 1864. *Ibid.*

186 Wood to Maine 2 August 1864, Wood Papers, vol. 17, fos. 212ff.

187 Trevelyan to Wood 25 July 1864, Wood Papers, box 3B. Maine, however, realized the importance of land questions and believed they were at the root of all conflicts with the masses. See *Ancient Law*.

188 Wood to Beadon 9 Aug. 1864, Wood Papers, vol. 17, fos. 234ff.; Wood to Maine 16 Aug. 1864, Wood Papers, vol. 18, fos. 6ff.

189 Wood to Maine 9 Sept. 1864, Wood Papers, vol. 18, fos. 108ff.

190 Wood to Maine 7 Jan. 1865, Wood Papers, vol. 19, fos. 188ff.

191 Lawrence to Maine 4 April 1864, Lawrence Papers, volume of letters to members of council, 1864–6, no. 3.

192 Lawrence to Wood 15 Jan. 1865, Wood Papers, box 7B.

193 *Ibid.* 18 Feb. 1865, Wood Papers, box 7B.

194 Wood to Maine 19 Feb. 1866, Wood Papers, vol. 22, fos. 189ff.

195 Ripon to Lawrence 3 June 1866, Lawrence Papers, letters from Secretary of State, vol. 3, no. 22.

196 Lawrence to Northcote 27 April 1868, Lawrence Papers, letters to Secretary of State, vol. 5, no. 29.

197 Strachey to Lawrence 24 Aug. 1868, Lawrence Papers, letters from members of council, vol. 3, no. 100. Sir John Strachey b. 1823; entered Indian civil service 1842; chief commissioner of Oudh 1866–8; member of Viceroy's council 1868–74 and 1876–80; lieutenant-governor of North-West Provinces 1874–6; member of India council 1885–95; d. 1907.

198 Lawrence to Cranborne 21 Feb. and 1 March 1867, Lawrence Papers, letters to Secretary of State, vol. 4, nos. 14 and 15.

199 Lawrence to Northcote 27 April and 29 June 1868, Lawrence Papers, letters to Secretary of State, vol. 5, nos. 29 and 45.

200 Wood to Elgin 3 May 1862, Wood Papers, vol. 10, fos. 208ff.; Wood to Maine 9 Dec. 1863, Wood Papers, vol. 15, fos. 30ff.

201 Maine to Wood 20 Jan. 1864, Wood Papers, box 7C.

202 *Ibid.* 2 April 1864, Wood Papers, box 7C.

203 Wood to Maine 25 Feb. 1864, Wood Papers, vol. 16, fos. 86ff.

204 Wood to Elgin 28 Aug. 1862, Wood Papers, vol. 11, fos. 94ff.

205 Wood to Trevelyan 24 Sept. and to Denison 10 Oct. 1863, Wood Papers, vol. 14, fos. 38ff. and 72ff. respectively.

206 Wood to Canning 8 April 1861, Wood Papers, vol. 7, fos. 112ff.

207 Sir Hugh Rose, first Lord Strathnairn b. 1801; entered army 1820; led central Indian campaigns 1858; commander-in-chief 1860–5; d. 1885.

208 Wood to Elgin 3 March 1862, Wood Papers, vol. 10, fos. 62ff.

209 *Ibid.* 10 and 19 May 1862, Wood Papers, vol. 10, fos. 220ff.

210 John, 13th baron Elphinstone b. 1807; governor of Madras 1837–42; governor of Bombay, 1853–60; d. 1860.

211 Elphinstone to Wood 15 June 1860, Wood Papers, box 4C.

212 Frere to Wood 8 July 1863, Wood Papers, box 5A.

213 Rose to Elgin 28 March and 7 June 1862, Elgin Papers, part III, vol. 29, nos. 9 and 57.

214 Elgin to Wood 17 and 22 June 1862, Elgin Papers, section I, part I, letter books, vol. 1, fo. 130A and vol. 2, fos. 1ff. respectively.

215 Wood to Maine 9 Oct. 1862, Wood Papers, vol. 11, fos. 190ff.

216 Wood to Denison 10 June 1863, Wood Papers, vol. 13, fo. 108.

217 Wood to Denison 9 Sept. 1863 and to Maine 30 Oct. 1863, Wood Papers, vol. 14, fos. 16ff. and 128ff. respectively.

218 Wood to Elgin 18 July 1863, Wood Papers, vol. 13, fos. 156ff.; Wood to Maine 27 July 1863, Wood Papers, vol. 13, fos. 192ff.

219 Lawrence to Wood 3 April 1864, Wood Papers, box 7A.

220 Wood to Lawrence 2 May 1864, Wood Papers, vol. 16, fos. 230ff.

221 *Ibid.* 3 June 1864, Wood Papers, vol. 17, fos. 60ff.

222 Lawrence to Wood 22 March 1864, Wood Papers, box 7A.

223 Wood to Frere 4 July 1864, Wood Papers, vol. 17, fos. 140ff.

224 Wood to Denison 11 July 1864, Wood Papers, vol. 17, fos. 156ff.

225 Wood to Maine 2 and 9 Sept. 1864, Wood Papers, vol. 18, fos. 90 ff.

226 Maine to Wood 4 and 9 Dec. 1864, Wood Papers, box 7 c.

227 Wood to Maine 9 Jan. 1865, Wood Papers, vol. 19, fos. 208 ff.

228 *Ibid.* 18 Jan. 1865, Wood Papers, vol. 19, fo. 236.

229 Wood to Lawrence and to Trevelyan 18 Jan. 1865, Wood Papers, vol. 19, fos. 238 and 244 respectively.

230 Lawrence to Ripon 5 March and 4 May 1866 and to Cranborne 17 July and 8 Nov. 1866, Lawrence Papers, letters to Secretary of State, vol. 3, nos. 12, 18, 27 and 49.

231 Cranborne to Lawrence 19 Nov. and 5 Dec. 1866, Lawrence Papers, letters from Secretary of State, vol. 3, nos. 42 and 45.

232 Lawrence to Cranborne 19 Dec. 1866, Lawrence Papers, letters to Secretary of State, vol. 3, no. 58.

233 *Ibid.* 4 Jan. 1867, Lawrence Papers, letters to Secretary of State, vol. 4, no. 2.

234 Northcote to Lawrence 15 Aug. 1867, Lawrence Papers, letters from Secretary of State, vol. 4, no. 36.

235 Lawrence to Northcote 18 Aug. and 18 Dec. 1867, Lawrence Papers, letters to Secretary of State, vol. 3, nos. 49 and 71.

236 Northcote to Lawrence 1 Dec. 1867 and 3 Feb. 1868, Lawrence Papers, letters from Secretary of State, vol. 4, no. 52 and vol. 5, no. 4; Lawrence to Northcote 2 March 1868, Lawrence Papers, letters to Secretary of State, vol. 5, no. 13.

237 Home Department Public June 1867, Proceedings, nos. 98–107 A.

238 Lawrence to Northcote 25 Aug. 1868, Lawrence Papers, letters to Secretary of State, vol. 5, no. 62.

239 Lawrence to Northcote 7 July 1868, Lawrence Papers, letters to Secretary of State, vol. 5, no. 47.

240 Lawrence to Northcote 25 June 1867, Lawrence Papers, letters to Secretary of State, vol. 4, no. 38. The display of arrogance was also noticed by Sir Charles Dilke who visited India at this time. 'Even a traveller, indeed, becomes so soon used to see the natives wronged in every way by people of quiet manner and apparent kindness of disposition, that he ceases to record the cases . . . I noticed in all the hotels in India the significant notice: "Gentlemen are earnestly requested not to strike the servants". . . . It is in India when listening to a mess-table conversation on the subject of looting, that we begin to remember our descent from Scandinavian sea-king robbers' (*Greater Britain* (1868), II, 222–4).

241 Northcote to Lawrence 24 June and 15 Aug. 1867, Lawrence Papers, letters from Secretary of State, vol. 4, nos. 30 and 36.

242 Lawrence to Northcote 17 Aug. 1867, Lawrence Papers, letters to Secretary of State, vol. 4, no. 48.

243 In 1868 the number of Indian officials employed by the Government of India and drawing a monthly salary of over Rs 100 was 4039, Home Department Public 26 Dec. 1868, Proceedings, nos. 65–66(A).

244 Despatch of Secretary of State no. 10 dated 8 Feb. 1868, Home Department Public 4 April 1868, Proceeding, no. 75.

245 Wood to Canning 26 July and 3 Dec. 1859, Wood Papers, vol. 1, fos. 48 ff. and vol. 2, fos. 16 ff. respectively.

246 Canning to Wood 31 Aug. 1859 and 16 Jan. 1860, Wood Papers, box 2 A.

247 Wood to Canning 23 Jan. 1861, Wood Papers, vol. 6, fos. 72 ff.

248 Canning to Wood 20 Dec. 1860, Wood Papers, box 2A, and 1 March 1861, Wood Papers, box 2B.

249 Wood to Canning 10 May 1861, Wood Papers, vol. 7, fo. 238.

250 Elgin to Wood 16 July 1862, Elgin Papers, section 1, part 1, letter book, vol. 2, fos. 47 ff.

251 Elgin to Wood 21 May 1863, Elgin Papers, section 1, part 1, letter book, vol. 4, fo. 152.

252 G. F. Edmonstone, Lieutenant-Governor of the North-West Provinces to Elgin 19 May 1862, Elgin Papers, section 1, part 2, letter book, vol. 21, no. 1.

253 Wood to Elgin 25 May, 9 Aug. and 24 Sept. 1862, Wood Papers, vol. 10, fos. 276 ff. and vol. 11, fos. 50 ff. and 166 ff. respectively.

254 Wood to Frere 2 Feb. 1863, to Elgin 18 April 1863 and to Frere 18 April 1863, Wood Papers, vol. 12, fos. 62 ff., 210 ff. and 218 ff. respectively.

255 Wood to Elgin 30 Sept. 1863, Wood Papers, vol. 14, fo. 54.

256 Wood to Maine 23 Dec. 1863, Wood Papers, vol. 15, fos. 86 ff.; Ripon to Lawrence 3 May 1866, Lawrence Papers, letters from Secretary of State, vol. 3, no. 20.

257 B. 1804; lieutenant-governor of Van Diemen's Land 1846–54; governor of New South Wales 1854–61; governor of Madras 1861–6; acting Viceroy 1863; d. 1871.

258 Lawrence to Wood 3 April 1864, Wood Papers, box 7A.

259 Lawrence to Cranborne 17 July 1866, Lawrence Papers, letters to Secretary of State, vol. 3, no. 27.

260 Cranborne to Lawrence 27 Aug. 1866, Lawrence Papers, letters from Secretary of State, vol. 3, no. 32.

261 Cranborne to Lawrence 5 and 10 Dec. 1866, Lawrence Papers, letters from Secretary of State, vol. 3, nos. 45 and 46.

262 Lawrence to Cranborne 5 Feb. and 21 March 1867 and to Northcote 21 March and 16 May 1867, Lawrence Papers, letters to Secretary of State, vol. 4, nos. 10, 19, 20 and 31.

263 See Secretary, Foreign Department, to Secretary, Punjab Government, no. 355 dated 17 April 1866 and no. 460 dated 7 May 1866, Foreign Department Proceedings April 1866, Political A, nos. 191–5 and May 1866, political A, no. 56 respectively.

264 Viceroy to Afzul Khan, Wali of Cabul, 11 July 1866, Foreign Department Proceedings July 1866, Political A, nos. 52–7.

265 Viceroy to Afzul Khan, 25 Feb. 1867, *Parl. Papers*, 1878, Afghanistan no. 1, p. 14.

266 Lawrence to Cranborne 9 Feb. 1867, Lawrence Papers, letters to Secretary of State, vol. 4, no. 12.

267 Lawrence to Northcote 9 March 1867, Lawrence Papers, letters to Secretary of State, vol. 4, no. 16.

268 Northcote to Lawrence 10 April, 26 June, 1 Oct. and 9 Dec. 1867, Lawrence Papers, letters from Secretary of State, vol. 4, nos. 17, 31, 41 and 54.

269 Report by the British Agent at Kabul of his conversation with the Amir 25 Sept. 1868, Foreign Department Proceedings December 1868, political A, nos. 31–44.

270 Lawrence to Northcote 10 Oct. and 16 Oct. 1868, Lawrence Papers, letters to Secretary of State, vol. 5, nos. 72 and 73.

271 Lawrence to Northcote 17 Aug. 1868, and Northcote to Lawrence 17 September 1868, Lawrence Papers, letters to Secretary of State, vol. 5, no. 60 and letters from Secretary of State, vol. 5, no. 45.

272 Viceroy to Shere Ali 9 Jan. 1869, *Parl. Papers*, 1878, Afghanistan no. 1, pp. 83–4.

273 Lawrence to Wood 27 May 1865, Wood Papers, box 7B; Lawrence to Ripon 20 April 1866, Lawrence Papers, letters to Secretary of State, vol. 3, no. 16.

274 Sir Henry Rawlinson b. 1810; joined Bombay army 1827; service in Persia 1833–9; service in Afghanistan 1839–42; consul at Baghdad 1844–55; minister in Persia 1859–60; member of India council 1868–95; d. 1895.

275 Wood to Lawrence, 27 Feb., 12, 28 Aug. and 16 Sept. 1865, Wood Papers, vol. 20, fos. 57ff. and vol. 21, fos. 175, 205ff. and 233ff. respectively.

276 Ripon to Lawrence 3 May and 3 June 1866, Lawrence Papers, letters from Secretary of State, vol. 3, nos. 20 and 22.

277 Lawrence to Cranborne 15 Aug. 1866, Lawrence Papers, letters to Secretary of State, vol. 3, no. 29.

278 *Ibid.* 4 Oct. 1866, Lawrence Papers, letters to Secretary of State, vol. 3, no. 39.

279 Cranborne to Lawrence 27 Aug. 1866, Lawrence Papers, letters from Secretary of State, vol. 3, no. 32.

280 *Ibid.* 2 Oct. 1866, Lawrence Papers, letters from Secretary of State, vol. 3, no. 35.

281 *Ibid.* 10 Dec. 1866, Lawrence Papers, letters from Secretary of State, vol. 3, no. 46.

282 Letters to Lawrence 10 April and 26 June 1867, Lawrence Papers, letters from Secretary of State, vol. 4, nos. 17 and 31.

283 Minute of Lawrence 3 Oct. 1867, Foreign Department Proceedings October 1867, political A, nos. 133–40.

284 Lawrence to Northcote 23 Oct. 1867, Lawrence Papers, letters to Secretary of State, vol. 4, no. 60.

285 Despatch of the Secretary of State 26 Dec. 1867, *Parl. Papers*, 1878, Afghanistan no. 1, pp. 24–6; Northcote to Lawrence 19 Nov. and 9 Dec. 1867, Lawrence Papers, letters from Secretary of State, vol. 4, nos. 49 and 54.

286 Memorandum 20 July 1868, Foreign Department Proceedings Jan. 1869, political A, nos. 50–67.

287 Despatch of the Government of India 4 Jan. 1869, *Parl. Papers*, 1878, Afghanistan no. 1, pp. 43–5.

288 Stanley to Disraeli 17 March 1859, Disraeli Papers.

289 See Stanley's letters to Canning 4, 9, 18 and 25 April 1859, Canning Papers, volume of letters from Secretary of State nos. 103, 106, 109 and 110. James Wilson b. 1805; founded *The Economist* 1843; M.P. 1847, 1852 and 1857–9; financial secretary to the Treasury 1853–8; paymaster-general 1859; finance member in India from 1859 till his death in 1860.

290 Canning to Stanley 24 June 1859, Canning Papers, volume of letters to Secretary of State, no. 195.

291 Trevelyan's minute 11 July 1859, Home Department Public Proceedings 22 Dec. 1859, no. 18; Wilson's memorandum on the financial administration of India 11 July 1859, Wood Papers, box 3D; Wood to Canning 11 July, 26 July, and 10 Aug. 1859, Wood Papers, vol. 1, pp. 18ff., 48ff., and 71 respectively.

292 Wilson to Wood 16 Dec. 1859, Wood Papers, box 3D.

293 Canning to Wood 27 Feb. 1860, Wood Papers, box 2A.

294 Wood to Wilson 3 April 1860, Wood Papers, vol. 2, pp. 262ff.

295 Wood to Canning 18 May 1860, Wood Papers, vol. 3, pp. 108ff.

296 To Wood 26 April 1860, Wood Papers, box 4C.

297 Granville to Canning 14 March 1859 and Canning to Granville 17 April 1859, Granville Papers, box 21.

298 See, for instance, Canning's minute of 18 May 1859, conveyed to the Governor of Madras: 'public functionaries, though they be so high-placed as a Governor of Madras, do wisely to confine themselves, even in their criticisms, to matters within the sphere of their own action', Home Department Judicial Proceedings 16 Sept. 1859, no. 6.

299 See Trevelyan's letters to Wood 24, 28 July and 5 Dec. 1859 and 4 Jan. and 19 Feb. 1860, Wood Papers, box 3A.

300 *Ibid.* 22 March 1860, Wood Papers, box 3A.

301 Wood to Trevelyan 26 March 1860, Wood Papers, vol. 2, pp. 254ff.

302 *Ibid.* 3 May 1860, Wood Papers, vol. 3, pp. 60ff.

303 Trevelyan to Wood 6 and 13 April 1860 and to Frere 15 April 1860, Wood Papers, box 3A.

304 *Ibid.* 5 May 1860, Wood Papers, box 3A.

305 Canning to Wood 19 April 1860, Wood Papers, box 2A; Wood to Trevelyan 10 May 1860, Wood Papers, vol. 3, p. 70.

306 Canning to Granville 17 May 1860, Granville Papers, box 21.

307 To Sir H. Ward, Trevelyan's successor in Madras, 10 July 1860, Wood Papers, vol. 3, p. 226. Nana Sahib and Tantia Topi were leaders in the revolt of 1857.

308 Wood to Canning 11 June 1860, Wood Papers, vol. 3, pp. 156ff.; Canning to Wood 20 July 1860, Wood Papers, box 2A; Canning to Granville 3 March 1861, Granville Papers, box 21.

309 Wood to Sir George Clerk 18 Aug. 1860, Wood Papers, vol. 4, p. 36.

310 Wood to Canning 16 Sept. 1860, no. 1, Wood Papers, vol. 4, pp. 152ff.

311 Sir George Cornewall Lewis to Wood 8 Oct. 1860, Wood Papers, box 4D; Wood to Canning 18 Oct. 1860, Wood Papers, vol. 5, pp. 14ff.; Gladstone to Canning 18 Oct. 1860, Canning Papers, volume of letters from Ministers, no. 41.

312   S. Laing b. 1812; fellow of St John's College, Cambridge, 1834; M.P. 1852–7, 1859, 1865–8 and 1872–85; financial secretary to the Treasury 1859–60; finance member in India 1860–2; d. 1897.

313   Wood to Canning 3 Dec. 1860, Wood Papers, vol. 5, pp. 154ff.

314   Laing to Wood 22 Jan. 1861, Wood Papers, box 3D.

315   *Ibid.* 2 March 1861, Wood Papers, box 3D.

316   Canning to Wood 5 and 19 Feb. 1861, Wood Papers, box 2B.

317   *Ibid.* 23 June 1861, Wood Papers, box 2B.

318   *Ibid.* 19 and 24 Feb. 1861, Wood Papers, box 2B.

319   Wood to Elgin 10 Feb. and 18 Feb. 1862, Wood Papers, vol. 10, fos. 28ff.

320   Laing to Wood 22 Feb. 1862, Wood Papers, box 3D.

321   *Ibid.* 8 March 1862, Wood Papers, box 3D.

322   Wood to Elgin 3 March 1862, Wood Papers, vol. 10, fos. 62ff.

323   Wood to Laing 26 March 1862, Wood Papers, vol. 10, fos. 120ff.

324   Elgin to Wood 9 April 1862, Elgin Papers, letter book, vol. 1, fos. 39ff.

325   Elgin to Wood 19 March 1862, Elgin Papers, section 1, part 1, letter book, vol. 1, fo. 13.

326   Laing to Wood 8 May 1862, Wood Papers, box 3D.

327   Wood to Elgin 26 May 1862, Wood Papers, vol. 10, fos. 286ff.

328   Elgin to Wood 14 May 1862, Elgin Papers, letter book, vol. 1, fo. 105Aff.

329   Wood to Elgin 25 June 1862, Wood Papers, volume 10, fos. 310ff.

330   Wood to Trevelyan 17 Feb. 1863, Wood Papers, vol. 12, fos. 82ff.

331   Frere to Wood 27 Jan. 1863, Wood Papers, box 5A; Elgin to Trevelyan 13 and 23 Feb. 1863, Elgin Papers, section 1, part 2, letter book, vol. 16, nos. 25 and 40; Elgin to Wood 21 Feb. 1863, Elgin Papers, section 1, part 1, letter book, vol. 4, no. 30.

332   21 Feb. 1863, Elgin Papers, section 1, part 3, vol. 30, no. 19.

333   Wood to Elgin 9 March 1863, Wood Papers, vol. 12, fos. 118ff.

334   Elgin to Sir R. Napier 30 March 1863, Elgin Papers, section 1, part 2, vol. 16, no. 159.

335   Trevelyan to Elgin 11 April 1863, Elgin Papers, section 1, part 2, vol. 23, no. 423.

336   Elgin to Wood 21 April and 6 May 1863, Elgin Papers, section 1, part 1, vol. 4, nos. 113 and 131; Wood to Frere 2 April 1863, Wood Papers, vol. 12, fos. 170ff.

337   Wood to Frere 2 April 1863, Wood Papers, vol. 12, fos. 170ff.

338   Wood to Frere 4 May 1863, Wood Papers, vol. 13, fos. 34ff.; Frere to Wood 12 May 1863, Wood Papers, box 5A.

339   Wood to Maine 25 Dec. 1863, Wood Papers, vol. 15, fos. 122ff.; Wood to Lawrence 25 Feb. 1864, Wood Papers, vol. 16, fos. 70ff.

340   Wood to Lawrence 23 March 1864, Wood Papers, vol. 16, fos. 148ff.

341   Wood to Trevelyan 17 June 1864, Wood Papers, vol. 17, fos. 104ff.; Wood to Frere 17 Aug. 1864, Wood Papers, vol. 18, fos. 42ff.

342 Lawrence to Wood 30 Aug. 1864, Wood Papers, box 7A; Wood to Trevelyan 16 Oct. 1864, Wood Papers, vol. 18, fos. 214ff.; Denison, Governor of Madras, to Wood 30 Nov. 1864, Wood Papers, box 5D; Lawrence to Wood 4 Feb. 1865, Wood Papers, box 7B.

343 Wood to Lawrence 10 March 1865, Wood Papers, vol. 20, fos. 83ff.; Wood to Massey (Trevelyan's successor) 10, 17 and 27 March 1865, Wood Papers, vol. 20, fos. 99, 109ff., and 149 respectively.

344 Lawrence to Wood, 4, 14 and 17 April, 16 May and 15 June 1865, Wood Papers, box 7B.

345 Wood to Beadon 10 May 1865, Wood Papers, vol. 20, fos. 241ff.; Wood to Massey 15 May 1865, Wood Papers, vol. 21, fos. 5ff.; Wood to Lawrence 12 Aug. 1865, Wood Papers, vol 21, fos. 163ff.

346 Wood to Frere 17 May 1865, Wood Papers, vol. 21, fos. 41ff.

347 Lawrence to Wood 15 June 1865, Wood Papers, box 7B.

348 *Ibid.* 1 Aug. 1865, Wood Papers, box 7B.

349 Wood to Massey 16 Sept. 1865, Wood Papers, vol. 22, fos. 5ff.

350 William Massey b. 1809; M.P. 1855–65 and 1872–81; finance member in India 1865–8; d. 1881.

351 Massey to Wood 22 Oct. 1865, Wood Papers, box 7B; Wood to Massey 16 Dec. 1865, and to Frere, 1 Jan. 1866, Wood Papers, vol. 22, fos. 89ff. and 127ff. respectively; Massey to Lawrence 10 and 12 Feb. 1866, Lawrence Papers, letters from members of council, vol. 2, nos. 8 and 8A.

352 Lawrence to Ripon 5 and 20 March 1866, Lawrence Papers, letters to Secretary of State, vol. 3, nos. 12 and 13.

353 Cranborne to Lawrence 27 Aug. 1866, Lawrence Papers, letters from Secretary of State, vol. 3, no. 32; Lawrence to Cranborne 16 Sept. and 18 Oct. 1866, Lawrence Papers, letters to Secretary of State, vol. 3, nos. 35 and 42.

354 Cranborne to Lawrence 3 Nov. 1866, Lawrence Papers, letters from Secretary of State, vol. 3, no. 39.

355 Lawrence to Northcote 9 and 28 March 1867, Lawrence Papers, letters to Secretary of State, vol. 4, nos. 16 and 21.

356 Northcote to Lawrence 10 April, 26 May, 9 June and 24 June 1867, Lawrence Papers, letters from Secretary of State, vol. 4, nos. 17, 27, 29 and 30.

357 Lawrence to Northcote 7 Dec. 1867 and 7 Jan. 1868, Lawrence Papers, letters to Secretary of State, vol. 4, no. 70 and vol. 5, no. 3.

358 Temple, *op. cit.* p. 337.

359 Elgin to Wood 9 Oct. 1862, Elgin Papers, letter book, vol. 3, no. 66.

360 Canning to Granville 24 Dec. 1857, Canning Papers, volume of letters to Ministers, no. 7.

361 Canning to Wood 8 Oct. 1860, Wood Papers, box 2A.

362 Canning to Wood 4 March 1862, Wood Papers, box 2B.

363 Bright to Gladstone 9 Jan. 1861, Gladstone Papers, B.M. Add. MSS 44112, fo. 33.

364 Granville to Canning 26 July 1860, Granville Papers, box 21.

365 Canning to Frere 8 Jan. 1861, Canning Papers, volume of letters to members of council, no. 117.

366 Canning to Wood 3 Jan. 1862, Wood Papers, box 2B.

367 To Granville 11 Dec. 1857, cited in Maclagan, *Clemency Canning*, p. 140.

368 'I heard an educated gentleman say, with the deepest earnestness and apparent sincerity, that he should delight in firing a pistol at Lord Canning's head, and would consider it a highly patriotic and meritorious act.' Sir Frederick Halliday, Lieutenant-Governor of Bengal, cited in R. Bosworth Smith, *Life of Lord Lawrence*, vol. II, p. 264.

369 Gladstone to Argyll 10 May 1862, Gladstone Papers, B.M. Add. MSS 44099, fo. 124.

370 To Sir A. Gordon 20 June 1862. P. Knaplund (ed.), *The Gladstone —Gordon Correspondence 1851–1896* (The American Philosophical Society, 1961), p. 41.

371 See Godley to Lord Elgin 19 Sept. 1895, Elgin Papers, India Office Library MSS Eur. F. 84, Correspondence with persons in England, vol. 2, no. 114.

372 Granville to Canning 17 July 1861, Granville Papers, box 21.

373 To Canning 24 Oct. 1857 and 10 May 1860, Granville Papers, box 21.

374 To Granville 29 May 1860, Granville Papers, box 21.

375 Col. Bruce to Sir Henry Campbell-Bannerman 9 April 1863, Campbell-Bannerman Papers, B.M. Add. MSS 41212, fos. 38–9.

376 T. Walrond, *Letters and Journals of James, Eighth Earl of Elgin* (London, 1872), p. 396.

377 Elgin to Wood 20 Jan. 1863, Elgin Papers, section I, part I, vol. 4, no. 9.

378 *Ibid.* 9 Dec. 1862, Elgin Papers, section I, part I, vol. 3, no. 197. Elgin had been a great success in Canada.

379 To Campbell-Bannerman 20 Nov. 1863, Campbell-Bannerman Papers, B.M. Add. MSS 41212, fo. 62.

380 By J. L. Morison, *The Eighth Earl of Elgin* (London, 1928), pp. 284 ff.

381 Wood to Canning 10 Aug. 1860, Wood Papers, vol. 4, pp. 8 ff.

382 Sir George Campbell, *Memories of My Indian Career* (London, 1893), vol. 2, p. 110.

383 J. Beames, *Memoirs of a Bengal Civilian* (London, 1961), p. 102.

384 Lawrence to Cranborne 18 Oct. 1866, Lawrence Papers, letters to Secretary of State, vol. 3, no. 42.

385 See Wood to Maine and to Trevelyan 3 Dec. 1863, Wood Papers, vol. 15, fos. 16 ff.

386 Trevelyan to Wood 30 June 1864, Wood Papers, box 3B.

387 Maine to Wood 5 July 1864, Wood Papers, box 7C.

388 Lawrence to Northcote 9 April 1867, Lawrence Papers, letters to Secretary of State, vol. 4, no. 25.

389 *Ibid.* 22 April 1867, Lawrence Papers, letters to Secretary of State, vol. 4, no. 27.

390 B. 1812; joined Bengal engineers 1828; agent to central Indian states 1857; foreign secretary 1861–5; military member of Viceroy's council 1865–70; lieutenant-governor of the Punjab 1870–1; d. 1871.

391 Lawrence to Cranborne 9 Feb. 1867 and to Northcote 30 July, 2 Sept. and 4 Nov. 1867 and 2 Jan. 13 and 21 March 1868, Lawrence Papers, letters to Secretary of State, vol. 4, nos. 12, 45, 51 and 62 and vol. 5, nos. 2, 16 and 19.

392 Lawrence to Northcote 13 March 1868, Lawrence Papers, letters to Secretary of State, vol. 5, no. 16.

393 *Ibid.* 17 Aug. and 10 Oct. 1868, Lawrence Papers, letters to Secretary of State, vol. 5, nos. 60 and 72.

394 Northcote to Lawrence 25 Jan. and 7 April 1868, Lawrence Papers, letters from Secretary of State, vol. 5, nos. 3 and 17.

395 Lawrence to Cranborne 21 Feb. 1867, Lawrence Papers, letters to Secretary of State, vol. 4, no. 14.

396 See Granville to Canning 10 May 1860, Granville Papers, box 21.

397 Wood to Lawrence 16 July 1864, Wood Papers, vol. 17, fos. 178 ff.

398 Minute 22 Oct. 1868, quoted in Dharm Pal, *Administration of Sir John Lawrence in India* (Simla, 1952), pp. 72–3.

399 Letters to Canning 10 and 31 Aug. 1860 and 27 May 1861, Wood Papers, vol. 4, pp. 8 ff. and 98 ff. and vol. 8, no. 1, pp. 2 ff.

400 On tenancy legislation in the Punjab, see G. R. G. Hambly, 'Richard Temple and the Punjab Tenancy Act of 1868', *English Historical Review*, LXXIX (January 1964), pp. 47–66.

401 Henry Lawrence to John Lawrence, 20 June 1853. Edwardes and Merivale, *Henry Lawrence*, vol. 2, p. 194.

CHAPTER 2, pp. 64–128

1 Diary entry 1877. See his *Journal of Events during the Gladstone Ministry*. Camden Miscellany, vol. XXI (London, 1958), part 2, p. 27.

2 Gladstone to Kimberley 24 Feb. 1884, Kimberley Papers, vol. D 20.

3 Lord Derby to Disraeli 17 Sept. 1868, Disraeli Papers.

4 Argyll to Mayo 18 Dec. 1868 and 12 Feb. 1869, Mayo Papers, C.U.L. Add. 7490, vol. 47, nos. 1 and 4.

5 Argyll to Northcote 26 Aug. 1871, Northcote Papers, 50028/106–110.

6 Mayo to Disraeli and to R. Bourke 9 May 1871, Mayo Papers, vol. 43, nos. 100 and 101.

7 Gladstone to Northbrook 15 Oct. 1872, Northbrook Papers, India Office Library MSS Eur. C. 144, vol. 20, part 1, p. 74.

8 To Salisbury 27 March 1874, Northbrook Papers, vol. 11, part 2, no. 6, pp. xii ff.

9 To Northbrook 26 June 1874, Northbrook Papers, vol. 11, part 1, no. 18, pp. 32 ff.

10 To Northbrook 28 May 1874, Northbrook Papers, vol. 11, part 1, no. 13, pp. 23 ff.

11 *Ibid.* 25 Aug. 1875, Northbrook Papers, vol. 12, part 1, no. 38, pp. 74 ff.

12 See Cromer's note, printed in B. Mallet, *The Earl of Northbrook* (London, 1908), p. 91.

13 To Disraeli 17 Nov. 1874, Disraeli Papers.

14 Salisbury to Disraeli 30 April 1875, Disraeli Papers.

15 *Ibid.* 13 Dec. 1875, Disraeli Papers.

16 Mayo to Sir Donald Macleod, Lieutenant-Governor of the Punjab, 25 Jan. 1869, Mayo Papers, vol. 34, no. 7.

17 Mayo to Argyll 7 Feb. 1869, Mayo Papers, vol. 34, no. 39; report of the British agent at Kabul 7 Feb. 1869. *Parl. Papers*, 1878, no. 1, Afghanistan no. 15, enclosure 3.

18 Mayo to Macleod 12 Feb. 1869, Mayo Papers, vol. 34, no. 43.

19 Argyll to Mayo 19 Feb. 1869, Mayo Papers, vol. 47, no. 7.

20 Mayo to Argyll and to the Duke of Cambridge 2 March 1869, to Macleod 7 March 1869, to Frere 14 March 1869 and to Argyll 16 and 25 March 1869, Mayo Papers, vol. 34, nos. 60, 62, 75, 92, 101 and 111.

21 Quoted in W. W. Hunter, *A Life of the Earl of Mayo* (London, 1876), vol. 1, p. 258.

22 Mayo to Argyll 4 April, to Lawrence 4 April, to Fitzgerald 17 April and to Argyll 18 April 1869, Mayo Papers, vol. 35, nos. 22, 25, 31 and 35; records of Viceroy's interviews with the Amir 29 March and 3 April 1869, Foreign Department Proceedings 1869, nos. 1–7 S.I.

23 Viceroy's letter to the Amir 31 March 1869, *Parl. Papers*, 1878, no. 1, Afghanistan, no. 17, enclosure 3.

24 Mayo to Argyll 4 April and to Northcote 17 April 1869, Mayo Papers, vol. 35, nos. 22 and 29.

25 Mayo to Disraeli 2 May 1869, Mayo Papers, vol. 35, no. 53.

26 Mayo to Fitzgerald 17 April 1869, Mayo Papers, vol. 35, no. 31.

27 Argyll to Mayo 23 April and 7 May 1869, Mayo Papers, vol. 47, nos. 14 and 16; despatch of the Secretary of State 14 May 1869, *Parl. Papers*, 1878, no. 1, Afghanistan, no. 18.

28 Mayo to Argyll 3 June 1869, Mayo Papers, vol. 35, no. 96; despatch of the Government of India 1 July 1869, *Parl. Papers*, 1878, no. 1, Afghanistan, no. 19.

29 To Mayo 17 June 1869, Mayo Papers, vol. 52 (bundle of correspondence. No number).

30 Argyll to Mayo 14 Aug. 1869, Mayo Papers, vol. 47, no. 23; also despatch of the Secretary of State 27 Aug. 1869, *Parl. Papers*, 1878, no. 1, Afghanistan, no. 20.

31 Mayo to Argyll 2, 9 June and 7 July 1871, Mayo Papers, vol. 43, nos. 124 and 132; and vol. 44, no. 155.

32 To Sir A. Buchanan 24 July 1871, Mayo Papers, vol. 44, no. 169.

33 To Arbuthnot 9 May and to Frere 27 May 1869, Mayo Papers, vol. 35, nos. 58 and 88; to Argyll 1 and 8 July 1869 and to Frere 8 July 1869, Mayo Papers, vol. 36, nos. 137, 153 and 154; to Rawlinson 19 May 1870, Mayo Papers, vol. 39, no. 131.

34 Mayo to Argyll 5 Jan. 1872, Mayo Papers, vol. 46, no. 1.

35 To Frere 27 May 1869, Mayo Papers, vol. 35, no. 88.

36 This was the objective of the Foreign Office. See Clarendon's despatch to the British Ambassador at St Petersburg 27 March 1869, Foreign Department Proceedings 1869, nos. 32–4 S.H.; and his despatch to the

British chargé d'affaires 17 April 1869, Foreign Department Proceedings 1869, nos. 37–9 S.H.

37 To Forsyth 19 Aug., to Frere 8 Sept. and to Buchanan 26 Sept. 1869, Mayo Papers, vol. 36, nos. 204, 235 and 254; to Rawlinson 19 May 1870, Mayo Papers, vol. 39, no. 131; to Buchanan 14 Dec. 1870, Mayo Papers, vol. 41, no. 358; despatch of the Government of India 3 June 1869, Foreign Department Proceedings 1869, nos. 63–5 S.I. Mayo's attitude was shared by informed Russian opinion. 'Besides, what force and whose influence could compel Russia or England to respect any guarantee in Central Asia if the necessity of defence in the event of war would require their violation ? The best guarantee in this case consists in the interests of each State' (*Moscow Gazette*, 26 Feb. 1869).

38 30 Jan. 1870, Mayo Papers, vol. 38, no. 40.

39 Despatch of the Government of India 3 June 1869, paragraph 8, Foreign Department Proceedings 1869, nos. 63–5 S.I.

40 To Durand 27 July 1870, Mayo Papers, vol. 40, no. 215.

41 See despatch of Sir A. Buchanan, the British Ambassador, 24 March 1869, Foreign Department Proceedings 1869, nos. 30–1 S.H.

42 B. 1827; entered service of East India Company 1848; service in Punjab 1849–57 and 1860–8; mission to St Petersburg 1869; removed from service for upholding Kuka executions 1872; envoy to Kashgar 1873; d. 1886.

43 Mayo to Sandhurst 1 Sept. 1871, Mayo Papers, vol. 44, no. 200.

44 M. de Stremounkoff, Minister of War, in a conversation with Forsyth, October 1869, Foreign Department Proceedings 1869, S.H. nos. 120–2; Mayo's Government, in reply, sent a detailed definition but Russia then delayed matters by referring it to General Kaufmann in Central Asia.

45 To the ninth Earl of Elgin 7 Oct. 1897, Elgin Papers, India Office Library, Correspondence with persons in England, vol. 4, part 1, no. 56.

46 To Argyll 24 June 1872 and to Grant Duff 8 July 1872, Northbrook Papers, vol. 9, part 2, p. xxiv, and vol. 20, part 2, pp. 10ff. respectively.

47 To Northbrook 14 Feb. 1873, Northbrook Papers, vol. 9, part 1, no. 23, pp. 36ff.

48 To Argyll 28 March 1873, Northbrook Papers, vol. 9, part 2, pp. cxiff.; also Northbrook to Strachey 7 March 1873, Northbrook Papers, vol. 21, part 2, pp. 31ff.

49 To Granville 31 Jan. 1873, Northbrook Papers, vol. 21, part 2, pp. 15ff.

50 To Argyll 9 June 1873, Northbrook Papers, vol. 9, part 2, p. cxxxi.

51 Granville to Northbrook 15 Oct. 1873, Northbrook Papers, vol. 21, part 1, pp. 279ff.

52 To Argyll 5 Feb. 1874 and to Halifax 6 Feb. 1874, Northbrook Papers, vol. 9, part 2, p. ccxxxviii and vol. 22, part 2, pp. xviiiff.

53 Salisbury to Northbrook 27 March 1874, Northbrook Papers, vol. 11, part 1, no. 4, pp. 5ff.

54 To Salisbury 30 April 1874 and to Argyll 1 May 1874, Northbrook Papers, vol. 11, part 2, no. 13, pp. xxxviiff. and vol. 22, part 2, p. lx.

55 Salisbury to Northbrook 19 June 1874, Northbrook Papers, vol. 11, part 1, no. 17, pp. 29ff.

56 *Ibid.* 22 May 1874, Northbrook Papers, vol. 11, part 1, no. 12, pp. 20ff.

57 Northbrook to Salisbury 16 June 1874, Northbrook Papers, vol. 11, part 2, no. 20, pp. lxviiff.

58 To Northbrook 10 and 17 July 1874, Northbrook Papers, vol. 11, part 1, nos. 20 and 21, pp. 36ff.

59 To Rawlinson 2 June and to Mallet 7 June 1874, Northbrook Papers, vol. 22, part 2, pp. lxxxiiiff.; to Salisbury 14 July 1874, Northbrook Papers, vol. 11, part 2, no. 24, pp. lxxviiff.

60 Salisbury to Northbrook 15 Oct. 1874, Northbrook Papers, vol. 11, part 1, no. 31, pp. 57ff.

61 Salisbury to Northbrook 30 April 1875, Northbrook Papers, vol. 12, part 1, no. 20, pp. 41ff.

62 *Ibid.* 5 and 20 Nov. 1874, Northbrook Papers, vol. 11, part 1, nos. 35 and 37, pp. 65ff. and 79ff.

63 Sir R. H. Davies to Northbrook 29 Oct. 1874, Northbrook Papers, vol. 16, part 2, p. 149.

64 Salisbury to Northbrook 3 Dec. 1874 and 7 Jan. 1875, Northbrook Papers, vol. 11, part 1, no. 39, pp. 82ff.; and vol. 12, part 1, no. 3, pp. 4ff.; despatch of the Secretary of State 22 Jan. 1875, *Parl. Papers*, 1878, no. 1, Afghanistan, pp. 128–9.

65 Northbrook to Salisbury 1, 22, 29 Jan. and 19 Feb. 1875, Northbrook Papers, vol. 12, part 2, nos. 1, 4, 6 and 9, pp. iff., xviff., xxiiiff. and xxixff.

66 Salisbury to Northbrook 22 Jan. 1875, Northbrook Papers, vol. 12, part 1, no. 5, pp. 8ff.

67 Salisbury to Northbrook 19, 26 Feb. and 5 March 1875, Northbrook Papers, vol. 12, part 1, nos. 9, 10 and 11, pp. 20ff.

68 Northbrook to Salisbury 26 March 1875, Northbrook Papers, vol. 12, part 2, no. 14, pp. xliff.

69 In fact Rawlinson published a book advocating a forward policy and made considerable use in it of secret official documents. Northbrook protested: 'I have been more annoyed by reading this chapter than by anything that has occurred since I have been in India...' (to Salisbury 1 April 1875, Northbrook Papers, vol. 12, part 2, no. 15, pp. xlivff.). But the Secretary of State made no comment and does not seem to have reprimanded Rawlinson.

70 Salisbury to Northbrook 25 March and 2 April 1875, Northbrook Papers, vol. 12, part 1, nos. 15 and 16, pp. 32ff.

71 *Ibid.* 23 April 1875, Northbrook Papers, vol. 12, part 1, no. 19, pp. 39ff.

72 Northbrook to Salisbury 20 May 1875, Northbrook Papers, vol. 12, part 2, p. lxviii.; see also despatch of the Government of India 7 June 1875, *Parl. Papers*, 1878, no. 1, Afghanistan, pp. 129–35.

73 Northbrook to Salisbury 28 June and 23 Aug. 1875, Northbrook Papers, vol. 12, part 2, nos. 32 and 43, pp. lxxxviff. and cxiiff.

74 Salisbury to Northbrook 1 Sept. 1875 and Northbrook to Salisbury 30 Sept. 1875, Northbrook Papers, vol. 12, part 1, no. 39, pp. 77 ff. and part 2, no. 49, pp. cxxiv ff.

75 Northbrook to Salisbury 12 Sept. 1875, Northbrook Papers, vol. 12, part 2, pp. clxii ff.

76 Salisbury to Northbrook 15 Oct. 1875, Northbrook Papers, vol. 12, part 1, no. 44A, pp. 100 ff.

77 Despatch of 19 Nov. 1875. The relevant extracts are published in *Parl. Papers*, 1878, no. 1, Afghanistan, pp. 147–9.

78 Salisbury to Northbrook 19 Nov. 1875, Northbrook Papers, vol. 12, part 1, no. 50, pp. 101 ff.

79 Northbrook to Salisbury 17 Dec. 1875, Northbrook Papers, vol. 12, part 2, no. 63, pp. clvi ff.

80 B. 1832; entered Indian civil service 1856; foreign secretary 1868–78; chief commissioner of British Burma 1878–81; lieutenant-governor of the Punjab 1882–7; chairman of the public services commission 1887–8; member of Viceroy's council 1888–9; d. 1896.

81 To Northbrook 17 Dec. 1875, Northbrook Papers, vol. 17, part 1, appendix.

82 Salisbury to Northbrook 14 and 26 Jan. 1876, Northbrook Papers, vol. 12, part 3, nos. 2 and 4, pp. 2 ff. and 6 ff.

83 Northbrook to Salisbury 7 Jan. and 11 Feb. 1876, Northbrook Papers, vol. 12, part 4, pp. i ff. and xx ff. respectively. 'We are convinced that a patient adherence to the policy adopted towards Afghanistan by Lord Canning, Lord Lawrence, and Lord Mayo, which it has been our earnest endeavour to maintain, presents the greatest promise of the eventual establishment of our relations with the Amir on a satisfactory footing; and we deprecate, as involving serious danger to the peace of Afghanistan and to the interests of the British Empire in India, the execution, under present circumstances, of the instructions conveyed in Your Lordship's Despatch.' Despatch of the Government of India, 28 Jan. 1876, paragraph 27, *Parl. Papers*, 1878, no. 1, Afghanistan, p. 155.

84 Salisbury to Northbrook 18 Feb. 1876, Northbrook Papers, vol. 12, part 3, no. 7, pp. 12 ff.

85 4 Feb. 1876, Northbrook Papers, vol. 12, part 3, no. 5, pp. 8 ff.

86 To enable Lytton to keep these instructions secret even from his council, the despatch of 28 Feb. 1876 was addressed (unconstitutionally) to the Governor-General and not to the Governor-General in Council, *Parl. Papers*, 1878, no. 1, Afghanistan, p. 156.

87 Lytton to Layard 2 July 1877, Lytton Papers, India Office Library MSS Eur. E. 218, vol. 518/2, pp. 556 ff.

88 Salisbury to Lytton 10, 24 March and 7 April 1876, Lytton Papers, vol. 516/1, nos. 8, 11 and 13; Lytton to Frere 26 March and to Rawlinson 28 March 1876, Lytton Papers, vol. 518/1, pp. 43 ff. and 55 ff. respectively.

89 See Lytton to Hamilton 3 Sept. 1877, Lytton Papers, vol. 518/2, pp. 785 ff.

90 To Temple 25 May 1876, Lytton Papers, vol. 518/1, pp. 186 ff.

91 Commissioner of Peshawar to Amir of Kabul 5 May 1876, *Parl. Papers*, 1878, no. 1, Afghanistan, no. 36, enclosure 6.

92 To Salisbury 25 May 1876, Lytton Papers, vol. 518/1, pp. 180ff.

93 Amir of Kabul to Commissioner of Peshawar 22 May 1876, *Parl. Papers*, 1878, no. 1, Afghanistan, no. 36, enclosure 7.

94 Lytton to Salisbury 29 May 1876, Lytton Papers, vol. 518/1, pp. 192ff.

95 To Lord George Hamilton 3 June 1876, Lytton Papers, vol. 518/1, pp. 220ff.

96 To Lytton 12 June 1876, Lytton Papers, vol. 517/1, no. 229.

97 Commissioner of Peshawar to the Amir of Kabul 8 July 1876, *Parl. Papers*, 1878, no. 1, Afghanistan, no. 36, enclosure 9.

98 Lytton to Disraeli 16 July 1876, Lytton Papers, vol. 518/1, pp. 293ff.

99 To C. Girdlestone, Resident at Khatmandu, 27 Aug. 1876, Lytton Papers, vol. 518/1, pp. 430ff.

100 To Rawlinson 5 Aug. 1876, Lytton Papers, vol. 518/1, pp. 348ff.

101 Lytton to Strachey 25 Oct. 1876, Lytton Papers, vol. 518/1, p. 572.

102 To Rawlinson 28 March 1876, Lytton Papers, vol. 518/1, pp. 55ff.

103 To Salisbury 3 Sept. 1876, Lytton Papers, vol. 518/1, pp. 443ff.

104 To Disraeli 18 Sept. 1876, Lytton Papers, vol. 518/1, pp. 470ff.

105 Amir to Commissioner of Peshawar 3 Sept., and Commissioner to Amir 16 Sept. 1876, *Parl. Papers*, 1878, no. 1, Afghanistan, no. 36, enclosures 14 and 16.

106 To Salisbury 25 Oct. 1876, Lytton Papers, vol. 518/1, pp. 562ff.

107 *Ibid.* 8 Nov. 1876, Lytton Papers, vol. 518/1, pp. 593ff.

108 Salisbury to Lytton 7 and 19 July 1876, Lytton Papers, vol. 516/1, nos. 32 and 37.

109 19 June 1876, Lytton Papers, vol. 518/1, pp. 238ff.

110 Lytton to Salisbury 30 July 1876, Lytton Papers, vol. 518/1, pp. 330ff.

111 Salisbury to Lytton 16 Feb. and 22 March 1877, Lytton Papers, vol. 516/2, nos. 3 and 9.

112 10 June 1877, Lytton Papers, vol. 518/2, pp. 475ff.

113 Lytton to Salisbury 23 June 1877, Lytton Papers, vol. 518/2, pp. 517ff.

114 Lytton to Salisbury 21 May 1877, Lytton Papers, vol. 518/2, pp. 399ff.

115 G. Waterfield, *Layard of Nineveh* (London, 1963), p. 382.

116 To Lytton 29 June 1877, Lytton Papers, vol. 516/2, no. 24.

117 B. 1823; entered civil service 1839; served under Cobden in implementing Anglo-French treaty of commerce 1860; permanent under-secretary India Office 1874–83; d. 1890.

118 To Lytton 29 June 1877, Lytton Papers, vol. 517/3, no. 94.

119 See despatch of the Government of India 10 May 1877, *Parl. Papers*, 1878, no. 1, Afghanistan, no. 36.

120 Lytton to the Lieutenant-Governor of the Punjab 23 April 1877, to Grant Duff 27 April 1877 and to Captain Cavagnari 31 May and 9 June 1877, Lytton Papers, vol. 518/2, pp. 295, 326ff., 440ff. and 464ff. respectively.

121 Lytton to Stephen 24 June 1877, Lytton Papers, vol. 518/2, pp. 524ff.; Lytton to Layard, to Salisbury, to Disraeli, to Rawlinson and to Hamilton 2 July 1877, Lytton Papers, vol. 518/2, pp. 556ff.; Lytton to Salisbury 13 and 16 July 1877, Lytton Papers, vol. 518/2, pp. 606ff.; Lytton to Temple 26 July and to Rawlinson 28 July 1877, Lytton Papers, vol. 518/2, pp. 650ff. Lytton arranged for the letter to Rawlinson to be printed and distributed indiscriminately in Britain.

122 Salisbury to Lytton 6 July, 3, 10 and 14 Aug. 1877, Lytton Papers, vol. 516/2, nos. 25, 31, 32 and 33.

123 Lytton to Salisbury 16 July 1877, Lytton Papers, vol. 518/2, pp. 609ff.; Salisbury to Lytton 14 Aug. 1877, Lytton Papers, vol. 516/2, no. 33.

124 Salisbury to Lytton 21 Sept. 1877, Lytton Papers, vol. 516/2, no. 38.

125 *Ibid.* 22 Sept. 1877, Lytton Papers, vol. 516/2, no. 39.

126 Lytton to Hamilton 3 Sept. and to Salisbury 5 Sept. 1877, Lytton Papers, vol. 518/2, pp. 785ff.

127 Lytton to Salisbury 4 Oct. 1877, Lytton Papers, vol. 518/2, pp. 876ff.

128 Lytton to Strachey 3 Nov. 1877, Lytton Papers, vol. 518/2, pp. 988ff.

129 Gathorne Gathorne-Hardy, first Earl of Cranbrook. B. 1814; M.P. 1856; president of the poor law board 1866; home secretary 1867; war secretary 1874–8; secretary for India 1878–80; lord president of the council 1885 and 1886–92; d. 1906.

130 Lytton to Cranbrook 8 April 1878, Lytton Papers, vol. 518/3, pp. 217ff.

131 *Ibid.* 25 April 1878, Lytton Papers, vol. 518/3, pp. 258ff.

132 To Lytton 11, 15, 17, 29 and 30 July 1878, Lytton Papers, vol. 516/3, nos. 34, 35 and 39.

133 Telegraphic correspondence between Viceroy and Secretary of State, *Parl. Papers*, 1878, no. 1, Afghanistan, nos. 42–7; M. Cowling, 'Lytton, the Cabinet, and the Russians, August to November 1878', *English Historical Review*, LXXVI (January 1961), p. 63.

134 Cranbrook to Lytton 30 Aug. 1878, Lytton Papers, vol. 516/3, no. 47.

135 Lytton to Cranbrook 3, 12, 17 and 31 Aug. 1878 and Lytton to Stanhope 26 Aug. 1878, Lytton Papers, vol. 518/3, pp. 531ff.

136 Strachey to Lytton 17 and 31 Oct. 1878, Lytton Papers, vol. 517/6, nos. 89 and 98.

137 Salisbury to the British Ambassador 19 Aug., and the British Ambassador to Salisbury 27 Aug. 1878, *Parl. Papers*, Central Asia, no. 1 (1878), nos. 152 and 158; Cowling, *op. cit.* pp. 65–6.

138 Lytton to Clarke 6 Sept. 1878, Lytton Papers, vol. 518/3, pp. 624ff.

139 To Lytton 8 Sept. 1878, Lytton Papers, vol. 516/3, no. 49.

140 Salisbury to Disraeli 11 Sept. 1878, Disraeli Papers.

141 Disraeli's attitude was more equivocal than that of Salisbury. He approved of Lytton's views as stated in the Viceroy's letter of 17 Aug. 1878 and agreed with his general policy (A. E. Gathorne Hardy, *First Earl of Cranbrook* (London, 1910), vol II, p. 96).

142 Cranbrook to Lytton 15 Sept. 1878, Lytton Papers, vol. 516/3, no. 50.

143 Lytton to Cranbrook 8 Sept. 1878, Lytton Papers, vol. 518/3, pp. 626ff.

144 Cowling, *op. cit.* pp. 69–71.

145 B. 1820; joined army of East India Company 1837; service in Afghanistan 1839–43; Delhi campaign 1857; Wahabi campaign 1863; Madras command 1876; Afghan mission 1878; d. 1902.

146 It is said that Shere Ali asked Russia to take Afghanistan under her wing, but the Russian government firmly declined. See article by F. Yuldashbayeva translated in *Central Asian Review* (London, 1958), p. 221.

147 Lytton to Cranbrook 23 Sept. 1878, Lytton Papers, vol. 518/3, pp. 674ff.

148 Viceroy's telegram to Chamberlain 22 Sept. 1878, Foreign Department Proceedings (Secret Supplementary) Dec. 1878, no. 456.

149 Salisbury to Disraeli 24 Sept. 1878 and Cranbrook to Disraeli 28 Sept. 1878, Disraeli Papers; Cranbrook to Lytton 27 and 29 Sept. and 6 Oct. 1878, Lytton Papers, vol. 516/3, nos. 54 and 55.

150 Cowling, *op. cit.* p. 75.

151 Lytton to Cranbrook 10 Oct. 1878, Lytton Papers, vol. 518/3, pp. 734ff.

152 *Ibid.* 11 Oct. 1878, Lytton Papers, vol. 518/3, pp. 741ff.

153 Salisbury to Disraeli 10 and 22 Oct. 1878, Disraeli Papers.

154 Lytton to Strachey 24 Oct. 1878, Lytton Papers, vol. 518/3, pp. 774ff.

155 Cranbrook to Lytton 21 and 28 Oct. 1878, Lytton Papers, vol. 516/3, nos. 59 and 61.

156 Cranbrook to Disraeli 3 Nov. 1878, Disraeli Papers.

157 See Disraeli's account of the Cabinet meeting of 25 Oct. 1878 (Cowling, *op. cit.* pp. 77–8).

158 Lytton to Cranbrook 21 Nov. 1878, Lytton Papers, vol. 518/3, pp. 835ff.

159 Cranbrook to Lytton 21 Nov. 1878, Lytton Papers, vol. 516/3, no. 69; despatch of the Secretary of State 18 Nov. 1878, *Parl. Papers*, 1878, no. 1, Afghanistan, no. 73.

160 Strachey to Lytton 28 Nov. and 11 Dec. 1878, Lytton Papers, vol. 517/6, nos. 123 and 137.

161 For a detailed account of the campaign, see *The Second Afghan War 1878–80 Official Account* (London, 1907), pp. 1–177.

162 Cranbrook to Lytton 8, 16, 19 and 24 Dec. 1878, Lytton Papers, vol. 516/3, nos. 74, 75, 76 and 77.

163 Lytton to Cranbrook 3 and 10 Jan. 1879, Lytton Papers, vol. 518/4, pp. 4ff. and 14ff. respectively; Cranbrook to Lytton 14 Jan. 1879, Lytton Papers, vol. 516/4, no. 3.

164 To Northbrook 24 Jan. 1879, Northbrook Papers, vol. 7, p. 288.

165 'We have seen India lately brought forward much more prominently than is usual. Personally, I am not reassured by this; for I have noticed as matter of experience that when Indian affairs become a great source of interest in this country, political trouble is at hand.' Lord Carnarvon's address at Edinburgh, 5 Nov. 1878, *Fortnightly Review*, new series, XXIV (July–December 1878), p. 757.

166 To Lytton 10 Feb. 1879, Lytton Papers, vol. 516/4, no. 9.

167 *Ibid.* 20 April 1879, Lytton Papers, vol. 516/4, no. 31.

168 *Ibid.* 23 March 1879, Lytton Papers, vol. 516/4, no. 24; Lytton to Cranbrook 10 April 1879, Lytton Papers, vol. 518/4, pp. 262ff.

169 Cranbrook to Lytton 11 March 1879, Lytton Papers, vol. 516/4, no. 21.

170 26 July 1879, Lytton Papers, vol. 517/8, no. 24.

171 Cranbrook to Lytton 23, 27 May and 1 June 1879, Lytton Papers, vol. 516/4, nos. 38, 39 and 41.

172 *Ibid.* 16 Aug. 1879, Lytton Papers, vol. 516/4, no. 65.

173 Salisbury to Lytton 23 May 1879, Lytton Papers, vol. 517/7, no. 74. It is probable, however, that Salisbury had in mind Lytton's insubordinate conduct in India when he made his caustic comment: 'The only form of control we have is that which is called moral influence, which in practice is a combination of nonsense, objurgation and worry. In this we are still supreme. . . . We must devote ourselves to the perfecting of this weapon.' (Salisbury to Lyons 15 July 1879, cited in R. Robinson and J. Gallagher, *Africa and the Victorians* (London, 1961), p. 85).

174 Lytton to Cranbrook 8 June 1879, Lytton Papers, vol. 518/4, pp. 423ff.

175 Lytton to Cranbrook 16 June 1879, Lytton Papers, vol. 518/4, pp. 475ff.

176 Morley to Lytton 13 Aug., and Blunt to Lytton 27 Aug. 1879, Lytton Papers, vol. 517/8, nos. 42 and 54.

177 B. 1841; son of one of Napoleon's officers; naturalized British subject 1857; joined East India Company's service 1858; service on Afghan frontier 1868–78; British resident in Kabul 1879.

178 See H. B. Hanna, *The Second Afghan War* (London, 1910), III, pp. 15–20.

179 Cranbrook to Lytton 3 Aug. 1879, Lytton Papers, vol. 516/4, no. 60.

180 Lytton to Cranbrook 31 Aug. 1879, Lytton Papers, vol. 518/4, pp. 697ff.

181 Ripon to Northbrook 7 Sept. and Halifax to Northbrook 9 Sept. 1879, Northbrook Papers, vol. 7, pp. 381ff. The Marquis of Ripon became Viceroy of India in 1880 (see chapter 3). Viscount Halifax was the ennobled Sir Charles Wood.

182 Lytton to Disraeli 6 Sept. 1879, Lytton Papers, vol. 518/4, pp. 707ff.

183 Cranbrook to Lytton 6 and 12 Oct. 1879, Lytton Papers, vol. 516/4, nos. 82 and 84.

184 *Ibid.* 22 Oct. 1879, Lytton Papers, vol. 516/4, no. 86.

185 Cranbrook to Lytton 2, 5, 12, 16, 23, 26, 30 Nov. and 4 Dec. 1879, Lytton Papers, vol. 516/4, nos. 87, 89, 90, 91, 93, 94, 95 and 96.

186 Lytton to Disraeli 19 Dec. 1879, Lytton Papers, vol. 518/4, pp. 1118 ff.

187 See despatch of R. Thomson, British Minister in Teheran, no. 64, 6 March 1880, F.O. 65, vol. 1099.

188 Despatch of the Government of India dated 31 March 1880 with enclosures, *Parl. Papers*, 1881, vol. LXX, pp. 47 ff.

189 Cranbrook to Lytton 30 Jan. 1880, Lytton Papers, vol. 516/5, no. 7; Lytton to Cranbrook 20 Jan. 1880, Lady Betty Balfour, *The History of Lord Lytton's Indian Administration, 1876–1880* (London, 1899), p. 397.

190 Cranbrook to Lytton 31 Jan. 1880, Lytton Papers, vol. 516/5, no. 8.

191 L. Griffin to Abdur Rahman 30 April 1880, despatch of the Government of India Foreign Department Secret no. 133 dated 15 June 1880, enclosure no. 3, F.O. 65, vol. 1104.

192 Mayo to Argyll 18 Jan. 1869, Mayo Papers, vol. 34, no. 3.

193 Mayo to Argyll 17 May 1869, Mayo Papers, vol. 35, no. 64; also Mayo to Sir H. Durand 14 Aug. 1869, Mayo Papers, vol. 36, no. 196.

194 Cited by Sir John Strachey, Minute on Lord Mayo's Administration, 30 April 1872, Home Department Proceedings Public May 1872, nos. 188 and 189.

195 To Argyll 19 April 1869, Mayo Papers, vol. 35, no. 39.

196 Mayo to Frere 21 June 1869, Mayo Papers, vol. 35, no. 122; Mayo to Argyll 21 July and 9 Aug. 1869, Mayo Papers, vol. 36, nos. 169 and 192.

197 Mayo to Fitzgerald 9 Aug. 1869, Mayo Papers, vol. 36, no. 191.

198 Mayo to Argyll 7 Feb. 1869, to Argyll and to Frere 16 Feb. 1869, to Argyll 21 Feb. 1869, to Frere 22 Feb. 1869, to Argyll 2 March 1869 and to Frere and to Argyll 8 March 1869, Mayo Papers, vol. 34, nos. 39, 48, 50, 54, 56, 60, 76 and 83.

199 Mayo to Argyll 26 April 1869, Mayo Papers, vol. 35, no. 43.

200 Mayo to W. H. Arbuthnot 9 March 1869, Mayo Papers, vol. 34, no. 77; Argyll to Mayo 25 March 1869, Mayo Papers, vol. 47, no. 12.

201 To Argyll 24 Aug. 1869, Mayo Papers, vol. 36, no. 216.

202 Mayo to Fitzgerald 9 Sept. 1869, Mayo Papers, vol. 36, no. 232.

203 B. 1826; entered Indian civil service 1847; various posts in the Punjab 1851–6; chief commissioner of the central provinces 1862–7; finance member of Viceroy's council 1868–74; lieutenant-governor of Bengal 1874–7; governor of Bombay 1877–80; M.P. 1885–95; d. 1902.

204 Mayo to Barrow Ellis 24 Aug. 1869, Mayo Papers, vol. 36, no. 215.

205 To Durand 29 April 1870, Mayo Papers, vol. 39, no. 107; see also letter to Sir William Muir 17 June 1870, Mayo Papers, vol. 39, no. 177.

206 Mayo to Fitzgerald 11 Nov. 1870, Mayo Papers, vol. 41, no. 308.

207 Argyll to Mayo 1 Jan. and 30 July 1869, Mayo Papers, vol. 47, nos. 2 and 21; Argyll to Mayo 27 April 1870, Mayo Papers, vol. 48, no. 13.

208 To Lord Napier, Governor of Madras, 20 Nov. 1870, Mayo Papers, vol. 41, no. 325; also Mayo to Fitzgerald, Governor of Bombay, 9 April 1871, Mayo Papers, vol. 43, no. 90.

209 To Muir, North-West Provinces, 19 Dec. 1870, and to Napier, Madras, 26 Dec. 1870, Mayo Papers, vol. 41, nos. 363 and 371.

210 Mayo to Napier, Governor of Madras, 20 Nov. 1870, Mayo Papers, vol. 41, no. 325.

211 Argyll to Mayo 12 Feb. 1869, Mayo Papers, vol. 47, no. 5; Mayo to Argyll 14 March 1869, Mayo Papers, vol. 34, no. 94.

212 To Mayo 29 Oct. 1869, Mayo Papers, vol. 47, no. 33. Such *esprit de corps* sometimes developed into silly jealousies. Sir William Mansfield told the story of a Madras officer who gave three cheers when told that the Bombay army had mutinied, Mayo to Argyll 22 March 1870, Mayo Papers, vol. 38, no. 81.

213 To Argyll 9 Sept. 1869, Mayo Papers, vol. 36, no. 234.

214 To Denbigh 7 Oct. 1869, Mayo Papers, vol. 37, no. 280.

215 Mayo to Arbuthnot 14 Feb. 1870 and to Argyll 15 March 1870, Mayo Papers, vol. 38, nos. 62 and 77.

216 Mayo to Napier, Madras, 15 May 1870 and to Argyll 16 May 1870, Mayo Papers, vol. 39, nos. 119 and 126.

217 To Frere 3 June 1870, Mayo Papers, vol. 39, no. 156.

218 See his letter to his secretary, Burne, 16 May 1869, cited in O. Burne, *Memories* (London, 1907), pp. 106–7.

219 To Lord Napier, Commander-in-Chief, Mayo Papers, vol. 40, no. 188.

220 Mayo to Muir 11 and 17 July 1870, Mayo Papers, vol. 40, nos. 199 and 205.

221 B. 1819; entered Indian civil service 1837; various posts in the North-West Provinces; lieutenant governor of the North-West Provinces 1868–74; finance member of Viceroy's council 1874–6; member of India council 1876–85; principal of Edinburgh University 1885–1905; d. 1905.

222 Mayo to Muir 22 and 29 July 1870, Mayo Papers, vol. 40, nos. 212 and 218.

223 Mayo to Argyll 29 July 1870, to Muir 4 Aug. 1870 and to Napier, Madras, 6 Aug. 1870, Mayo Papers, vol. 40, nos. 219, 222 and 225; Sir John Strachey to Mayo 7 Aug. 1870, Mayo Papers, vol. 60; Mayo to Argyll 12 Aug. 1870, to Mansfield 19 Aug. 1870 and to Argyll 19 Aug. 1870, Mayo Papers, vol. 40, nos. 229, 236 and 237.

224 Grey to Mayo 26 Aug. 1870, Mayo Papers, vol. 54; Muir to Mayo 20 Aug. 1870, Mayo Papers, vol. 56; Strachey to Mayo 19 Aug. 1870, Mayo Papers, vol. 60.

225 26 Aug. 1870, Mayo Papers, vol. 40, no. 244.

226 For the history of the Wahabi movement in India see report of T. E. Ravenshaw, Magistrate of Patna, 9 May 1865, Home Department Proceedings Judicial 27 Sept. 1865, nos. 70–4A; and W. W. Hunter, *The Indian Musalmans* (London, 1871).

227 Letter of Officiating Deputy Commissioner Ambala to the Commissioner and Superintendent Simla 16 Sept. 1864 and letters of Commissioner Patna Division to Secretary to Government of Bengal 4 Nov. 1864 and 1 March 1865, Home Department Proceedings Judicial 7 June 1865, nos. 9 and 10A; notes of Sir John Strachey 22 Nov. 1868 and of

Sir John Lawrence 23 November 1868, Home Department Proceedings Judicial 27 March 1869, nos. 30–3; report of the Deputy Inspector General Special Bengal Police 12 March 1869, Home Department Proceedings Judicial 24 April 1869, nos. 15–19; letter of Secretary to Government of Bengal to Secretary to Government of India 22 April 1869, Home Department Proceedings Judicial 19 June 1869, nos. 60–2 A; note of Mayo 12 Aug. 1869, Home Department Proceedings Judicial 21 Aug. 1869, nos. 39–41; reports of the Deputy Inspector General Special Bengal Police 16 and 19 Feb. 1869 and of the Acting Commissioner of Police, Madras, 23 Nov. 1865, Home Department Proceedings Judicial 9 Oct. 1865, nos. 10 and 11 B; letter of Acting Under-Secretary to Government of Bombay to Secretary to Government of Bengal 4 Dec. 1869, Home Department Proceedings Judicial 1 Jan. 1870, no. 21; report of Deputy Inspector General Special Bengal Police 7 Dec. 1869, Home Department Proceedings Judicial 12 Feb. 1870, nos. 28 and 29.

228 To Grey 1 Sept. 1870 and to Argyll 2 Sept. 1870, Mayo Papers, vol. 40, nos. 253 and 257.

229 To Argyll 9 Sept. 1870, to Napier, Madras, 13 Sept. 1870 and to Arbuthnot 20 Sept. 1870, Mayo Papers, vol. 40, nos. 265, 268 and 273; Fitzgerald to Mayo 18 Sept. 1870, Mayo Papers, vol. 53. (Bundle of correspondence. No number.)

230 To Fitzgerald 11 Nov. 1870 and to Lord Napier of Magdala 25 Nov. 1870, Mayo Papers, vol. 41, nos. 308 and 332.

231 To Argyll 9 Nov. 1870, Mayo Papers, vol. 41, no. 300.

232 To Argyll 30 Nov. 1870, Mayo Papers, vol. 41, no. 339.

233 To Argyll 8 and 22 March 1871, Mayo Papers, vol. 42, nos. 62 and 78.

234 See memorandum of the Government of India no. 1894 P dated 8 Nov. 1870, note of E. C. Bayley, Secretary, Home Department, 17 Nov. 1870 and note of B. H. Ellis, Home Member, 19 Nov. 1870, Home Department Proceedings Judicial 19 Nov. 1870, nos. 18–20.

235 To Argyll 18 Jan. 1871, to John Fowler 24 Jan. 1871, to Northbrook 8 Feb. 1871 and to Argyll 15 March 1871, Mayo Papers, vol. 42, nos. 24, 30, 39 and 72; to Argyll 7 July 1871, Mayo Papers, vol. 44, no. 156.

236 Mayo to Argyll 22 Nov. 1871, Mayo Papers, vol. 45, no. 263.

237 To Sandhurst 28 May 1871 and to Argyll 16 June 1871, Mayo Papers, vol. 43, nos. 117 and 138. Hunter (*Mayo*, vol. II, p. 87) stated that Mayo, on his voyage to the Andaman Islands, was considering the total abolition of the income tax. Northbrook also declared that to the best of his knowledge, Mayo had determined before his death to get rid of the income tax. To Sir R. Temple 4 April 1873, Northbrook Papers, vol. 14, part 2, pp. 43 ff. This is not borne out by the Mayo correspondence: see Mayo's letter to Argyll 24 Jan. 1872, Mayo Papers, vol. 46, no. 18.

238 See reports of the Inspector General of Police, Punjab, for 1867, 1868 and 1869, and note of E. C. Bayley, Secretary, Home Department, 17 July 1872, Home Department Proceedings Judicial August 1872, nos. 273–84; K. Singh, *The Sikhs* (London, 1953), pp. 90–7.

239 See letter of L. H. Griffin, Officiating Secretary, Punjab Government to E. C. Bayley, Secretary to the Government of India 9 Sept. 1871, Home Department Proceedings Judicial 13 Jan. 1872, nos. 52–63.

240 Mayo to Argyll 28 July 1871, Mayo Papers, vol. 44, no. 173.

241 Mayo to R. H. Davies 6 Aug. 1871, Mayo Papers, vol. 44, no. 179.

242 8 Aug. 1871, Mayo Papers, vol. 44, no. 181.

243 Mayo to Governor of Madras 29 May 1871 and to Argyll 2 June 1871, Mayo Papers, vol. 43, nos. 119 and 124.

244 To Argyll 30 June 1871, Mayo Papers, vol. 43, no. 149. It was, of course, the siege of Paris in the Franco-Prussian war which Mayo had in mind.

245 Mayo to Argyll 26 Sept. 1871, to Mr Justice Jackson 29 Sept. 1871 and to the Lieutenant-Governor of Bengal 30 Sept. 1871, Mayo Papers, vol. 44, nos. 219, 221 and 224; Mayo to Argyll 3 Oct. 1871 and to the Lieutenant-Governor of Bengal 8 and 10 Oct. 1871, Mayo Papers, vol. 45, nos. 229, 235 and 236.

246 See Mayo to Campbell 8 Oct. 1871, Mayo Papers, vol. 45, no. 235.

247 *The Indian Musalmans* (London, 1871), especially pp. 1, 42 and 145–6.

248 Mayo to John Strachey 22 Sept. 1871, Mayo Papers, vol. 44, no. 214.

249 Quoted in G. R. G. Hambly, 'Unrest in Northern India during the Viceroyalty of Lord Mayo 1869–72; the Background to Lord Northbrook's Policy of Inactivity', *Journal of the Royal Central Asian Society* (Jan. 1961), pp. 37–55.

250 Mayo to Argyll 15 Oct., to Lawrence 20 Oct., to Sandhurst 28 Oct., to Argyll 22 Nov. and to the Queen 8 Dec. 1871, Mayo Papers, vol. 45, nos. 239, 243, 255, 263 and 284.

251 Telegrams of the Punjab Government 15 and 16 Jan. 1872, Home Department Proceedings Judicial 20 Jan. 1872, nos. 55–71.

252 Telegram of the Punjab Government 16 Jan. 1872. *Ibid.*

253 Telegram of the Punjab Government 18 Jan. 1872, Home Department Proceedings Judicial 20 Jan. 1872, nos. 55–71; and telegram of the Punjab Government 19 Jan. 1872, Home Department Proceedings Judicial Feb. 1872, nos. 7–20.

254 Telegram 19 Jan. 1872, Home Department Proceedings Judicial 20 Jan. 1872, nos. 55–71; Mayo to Davies 23 Jan. 1872, Mayo Papers, vol. 46, no. 14; E. C. Bayley, Secretary, Home Department, to the Secretary, Punjab Government, 24 Jan. 1872, Home Department Proceedings Judicial Feb. 1872, nos. 7–20.

255 See letter of Secretary, Punjab Government, 19 Jan. 1872, Home Department Proceedings Judicial Feb. 1872, nos. 7–20; and letter of Secretary, Punjab Government, 7 Feb. 1872, Home Department Proceedings Judicial June 1872, nos. 112–32.

256 Mayo to Argyll 24 Jan. 1872, Mayo Papers, vol. 46, no. 17; E. C. Bayley, Secretary, Home Department, to Secretary Punjab Government 8 Feb. 1872, Home Department Proceedings Judicial Feb. 1872, nos. 232–6. Bayley himself, however, was inclined to agree with the Punjab government; see his note of 25 Jan. 1872, Home Department Proceedings Judicial Feb. 1872, nos. 59–65.

257 See memorandum of the officiating Deputy Commissioner, Ludhiana, forwarded by the Secretary, Punjab Government 9 Feb. 1872, Home Department Proceedings Judicial June 1872, nos. 107–11.

258 Telegram of Secretary, Home Department, to Secretary of State, 19 Feb. 1872, Home Department Proceedings Public March 1872, nos. 559–86.

259 19 Aug. 1871, quoted in Hambly, *op. cit.*

260 B. 1829; Q.C. 1868; law member of Viceroy's council 1869–72; judge of high court 1879–91; d. 1894.

261 Quoted in Hambly, *op. cit.* p. 50.

262 Viceroy's telegram to Lieutenant-Governor Punjab 1 May 1872, Home Department Proceedings Judicial June 1872, nos. 112–32. These decisions of the government of the officiating Viceroy, Lord Napier, were in fact taken by Stephen and Strachey, who both felt strongly about the brutality of blowing men from guns (see Stephen's letters, quoted in Hambly, *op. cit.* and Strachey's note 3 July 1872: 'A more revolting and horrible spectacle can hardly be conceived. This renders it terrible to the bystanders, but also repugnant to humanity, and a punishment unfit to be inflicted by civilised men', Home Department Proceedings Judicial July 1872, nos. 208–11).

263 E. C. Bayley to Secretary Punjab Government 30 April 1872, Home Department Proceedings Judicial June 1872, nos. 112–32.

264 Northbrook to Argyll from Bombay 29 April 1872, Northbrook Papers, vol. 9, part 2, no. 2, pp. iiff.; Hobart, Governor of Madras, to Northbrook 27 May and 1 June 1872, Northbrook Papers, vol. 13, part 1, pp. 15ff.; Northbrook to Wodehouse 29 May 1872, Northbrook Papers, vol. 13, part 2, pp. 12ff.; Northbrook to Argyll 17 June 1872, Northbrook Papers, vol. 9, part 2, no. 9, pp. xxiff.; Secretary Punjab Government to Secretary Foreign Department 2 April 1872, Home Department Proceedings Judicial June 1872, no. 11. Sir George Campbell b. 1824; entered service of East India Company 1842; service in North-West Provinces and the Punjab; judge of the Bengal high court, 1862–6; chief commissioner of Central Provinces 1867–8; lieutenant-governor of Bengal 1871–4; M.P. 1875–92; d. 1892.

265 To Argyll 10 May 1872, Northbrook Papers, vol. 9, part 2, no. 3, pp. vff.; to Hobart 19 May 1872, Northbrook Papers, vol. 13, part 2, pp. 8ff.

266 Northbrook to Muir 21 May 1872 and to Lord Napier of Magdala 1 July 1872, Northbrook Papers, vol. 13, part 2, pp. 9ff. and 35ff. respectively.

267 Campbell to Northbrook 22 June 1872 and Strachey to Northbrook 26 June 1872, Northbrook Papers, vol. 13, part 1, pp. 48ff. and 56ff. respectively; Northbrook to Campbell 3 June, to Strachey 26 June and to Campbell 20 July 1872, Northbrook Papers, vol. 13, part 2, pp. 16, 31 and 48ff. respectively.

268 5 July 1872, Northbrook Papers, vol. 13, part 2, pp. 38ff.

269 Northbrook to Grant Duff 9 Sept. 1872, Northbrook Papers, vol. 20, part 2, p. 30. This was, however, by no means true; of the provincial authorities, for example, the Governor of Madras alone favoured repeal of the tax.

270 Northbrook to Argyll 8 July 1872, Northbrook Papers, vol. 9, part 2, no. 13, pp. xxix ff.; Northbrook to Grant Duff 8 July and to Mallet 15 July 1872, Northbrook Papers, vol. 20, part 2, pp. 10ff.; Northbrook to Wodehouse 30 Dec. 1872, Northbrook Papers, vol. 13, part 2, pp. 124ff.

271 Kimberley to Northbrook 20 June 1872, Northbrook Papers, vol. 20, part 1, appendix, pp. xlviiff.; Argyll to Northbrook 29 June 1872 and 7 Feb. 1873, Northbrook Papers, vol. 9, part 1, nos. 6 and 22, pp. 6ff. and 35ff.; Gladstone to Northbrook 15 Oct. 1872, Northbrook Papers, vol. 20, part 1, p. 74.

272 Northbrook to Argyll 21 March 1873, Northbrook Papers, vol. 9, part 2, no. 51, pp. cviiff.; Northbrook to Halifax 21 March 1873, to Delane 28 March 1873 and to Mallet 31 March 1873, Northbrook Papers, vol. 21, part 2, pp. 36ff.

273 Northbrook to Mallet 4 May 1873, and to Argyll 22 May 1873, Northbrook Papers, vol. 21, part 2, pp. 69 and vol. 9, part 2, pp. cxxixff.; Northbrook to Wodehouse 25 Aug. 1873, Northbrook Papers, vol. 14, part 2, pp. 150ff.

274 Argyll to Northbrook 25 April, 23, 28 May and 27 June 1873, Northbrook Papers, vol. 9, part 1, nos. 33, 35, 36 and 37, pp. 51ff.

275 Public Works Despatch of Secretary of State no. 51 dated 22 May 1873.

276 Northbrook to Argyll 16 and 23 June 1873, Northbrook Papers, vol. 9, part 2, nos. 62 and 64, pp. cxxxiv and cxxxixff. respectively.

277 Northbrook to Mallet 31 May 1874, Northbrook Papers, vol. 22, part 2, pp. lxxviiff.

278 Salisbury to Northbrook 19 June 1874, Northbrook Papers, vol. 11, part 1, no. 17, pp. 29ff.

279 Northbrook to Salisbury 27 March 1874 and Salisbury to Northbrook 28 May 1874, Northbrook Papers, vol. 11, part 2, no. 6, pp. xiiff. and part 1, no. 13, pp. 23ff. respectively.

280 Salisbury to Northbrook 19 June and 2 Sept. 1874, Northbrook Papers, vol. 11, part 1, nos. 17 and 28, pp. 29ff. and 51ff. respectively.

281 Northbrook to Salisbury 15 May 1874, and Salisbury to Northbrook 12 June 1874, Northbrook Papers, vol. 11, part 2, no. 15, p. 1 and part 1, no. 15, pp. 26ff. respectively.

282 Salisbury to Northbrook 30 July 1874, Northbrook Papers, vol. 11, part 1, no. 23, pp. 42ff.

283 For the Baroda episode in general, see Mrs M. P. Kamerkar, *A Study in British Paramountcy: Baroda 1870–1875*, Indian History Congress Proceedings 1961, and R. P. Masani, *Dadabhai Naoroji* (London, 1939), pp. 131–78. The actions of the Government of India are reviewed in detail and defended in Northbrook's minute of 29 April 1875, Foreign Department Political A, Proceedings July 1875, nos. 290–6. Dadabhai

Naoroji b. 1825; resident in Britain 1855–74; chief minister of Baroda 1874; M.P. 1892–5; president of Indian national congress 1886, 1893 and 1906; member of commission on Indian expenditure 1895; d. 1917. On attitude to Bombay and Indian governments, see Northbrook to Argyll 24 Jan. 1873, Northbrook Papers, vol. 9, part 2, no. 43, pp. lxxxviii ff.

284 Sir Robert Phayre, b. 1820; joined army of East India Company 1839; resident at Baroda 1873–4; d. 1897.

285 Wodehouse to Northbrook 24 July and 29 Aug. 1873, Northbrook Papers, vol. 14, part 1, pp. 301 ff. and 367 ff. respectively. For Phayre's reports from Baroda and the letter of the Bombay government of 29 Aug. 1873, see Foreign Department Secret Aug. 1874, Proceedings 95–126 B.

286 Northbrook to Governor of Bombay 15 Sept. 1873, Northbrook Papers, vol. 14, part 2, pp. 162 ff.; letter of the Government of India to the Bombay Government 19 Sept. 1873, Foreign Department Secret Aug. 1874, Proceedings 95–126 B.

287 'It should of course be our effort to effect the reforms as much as possible *ab intra*, the Resident merely encouraging, stimulating, advising, helping, but *not* directly interfering except as a last resource. Here is the key-stone of the whole. This is what distinguishes between a good and a bad Political Officer. I fear that with a Resident of Col. Phayre's temperament we shall never bring things round at Baroda. There will be interference and denunciation in plenty, but of encouragement and gentle silent influence nil.' Note of C. U. Aitchison 11 March 1874, Foreign Department Secret Aug. 1874, Proceedings 136–93.

288 Northbrook to Argyll 21 Sept. 1873, Northbrook Papers, vol. 9, part 2, no. 78, pp. clxviii ff.; Northbrook to Salisbury 27 March 1874, Northbrook Papers, vol. 11, part 2, no. 6, pp. xii ff.

289 Salisbury to Northbrook 24 April 1874, Northbrook Papers, vol. 11, part 1, no. 8, pp. 12 ff.

290 Wodehouse to Northbrook 21 and 26 April 1874, Northbrook Papers, vol. 15, part 1, pp. 195 ff. and p. 204 respectively.

291 Northbrook to Major-Gen. H. Daly 20 June 1874, Northbrook Papers, vol. 15, part 2, p. 158.

292 See notes of General Daly, 7 March 1874 and A. C. Lyall 19 May 1874, Foreign Department Secret Aug. 1874, Proceedings 136–93.

293 Viceroy to the Gaekwar 25 July 1874, Foreign Department Secret August 1874, Proceedings 136–93.

294 Northbrook to Sir George Clerk 16 June 1874, Northbrook Papers, vol. 22, part 2, p. xc; also Northbrook to Salisbury 16 June 1874, Northbrook Papers, vol. 11, part 2, no. 20, pp. lxvii ff.

295 Governor of Bombay to Northbrook 19 Aug. and B. H. Ellis to Northbrook 11 Sept. 1874, Northbrook Papers, vol. 16, part 1, pp. 51 ff. and 69 ff. respectively.

296 Governor of Bombay to Northbrook 8 and 23 Nov. 1874, Northbrook Papers, vol. 16, part 1, pp. 158 ff. and 185 ff. respectively.

297 Northbrook to Governor of Bombay 12 Nov. 1874, Northbrook Papers, vol. 16, part 2, pp. cv ff.; Northbrook to Salisbury 12 and 27

Nov. 1874, Northbrook Papers, vol. 11, part 2, nos. 41 and 45, pp. cxxi ff. and cxxx ff. respectively.

298 Northbrook to Salisbury 11 Dec. 1874, Northbrook Papers, vol. 11, part 2, no. 47, pp. cxxxix ff.

299 Pelly to Northbrook 24 Dec. 1874, Northbrook Papers, vol. 16, part 1, pp. 225 ff.

300 Northbrook to Pelly 5 Jan. and Pelly to Northbrook 7 Jan. 1875, Northbrook Papers, vol. 17, part 2, pp. iii ff. and part 1, pp. 3 ff. respectively.

301 Northbrook to Salisbury 1 Jan. 1875, Northbrook Papers, vol. 12, part 2, pp. i ff.

302 To Northbrook 14 Jan. 1875, Northbrook Papers, vol. 12, part 1, no. 4, pp. 6 ff.

303 To Northbrook 12 Feb. 1875, Northbrook Papers, vol. 12, part 1, no. 8, pp. 18 ff.

304 Northbrook to Pelly 20 Feb. 1875, Northbrook Papers, vol. 17, part 2, pp. xxxvi ff.; Northbrook to Salisbury 4 March 1875, Northbrook Papers, vol. 12, part 2, no. 11, pp. xxxiv ff.

305 To Salisbury 26 Feb. 1875, Northbrook Papers, vol. 12, part 2, no. 10, pp. xxxii ff.

306 This alliance gave much concern to Theodore Hope, one of the ablest civil servants of Bombay: 'To play the two [Mahrattas and Gujeratis] off against each other I look upon as one of the chief means of security for this Presidency at some future, and I hope distant, day.' Letter to Evelyn Baring, Private Secretary to the Viceroy, 17 March 1875, Northbrook Papers, vol. 17, part 1, pp. 124 ff.

307 To Northbrook 16 April 1875, Northbrook Papers, vol. 23, part 1, p. 75. Sir Erskine Perry b. 1806; judge of the Bombay high court 1841–7; chief justice 1847–52; member of India council 1859–82; d. 1882.

308 Report of Sir Richard Meade, Chairman of the Commission, to Northbrook, 31 March 1875, Northbrook Papers, vol. 17, part 1, pp. 136 ff.

309 Halifax to Northbrook 15 April 1875, Northbrook Papers, vol. 23, part 1, pp. 73 ff.

310 Salisbury's telegram to Northbrook 15 April 1875, Northbrook Papers, vol. 12, part 1, supplement no. 7, p. 3; Perry to Northbrook 16 April 1875, Northbrook Papers, vol. 23, part 1, p. 75; Salisbury to Northbrook 16, 23 April and 11 June 1875, Northbrook Papers, vol. 12, part 1, nos. 18, 19 and 26, pp. 38, 39 and 53 respectively.

311 Minute of 29 April 1878, Foreign Department Political A, July 1875, Proceedings, 290–6.

312 See A. Hobhouse, Law Member, to C. U. Aitchison 15 Jan. 1875 and Aitchison to Sir Lewis Pelly 15 Jan. 1875, Foreign Department Political A, Jan. 1875, Proceedings, 252–83.

313 Salisbury to Northbrook 7 May and 4 June 1875, Northbrook Papers, vol. 12, part 1, nos. 21 and 25, pp. 43 ff. and 51 ff. respectively.

314 Northbrook to Sir George Clerk 27 Feb. 1874, Northbrook Papers, vol. 22, part 2, pp. xxx.

315 To Northbrook 2 and 27 Oct. 1874, Northbrook Papers, vol. 22, part 1, pp. 222 ff. and 263 respectively.

316 To Mallet 2 and 29 Oct. 1874, Northbrook Papers, vol. 22, part 2, pp. cxxxvii ff. and cxliv ff. respectively.

317 Salisbury to Northbrook 1 and 27 Jan. 1875, Northbrook Papers, vol. 12, part 1, nos. 1 and 6, pp. 1 ff. and 10 ff. respectively.

318 To Salisbury 2 Aug. 1875, Northbrook Papers, vol. 12, part 2, no. 40, pp. cv ff.

319 Financial Department Proceedings, Separate Revenue (Customs), Nov. 1875, Part A, no. 19.

320 Salisbury to Northbrook 6 Aug. 1875 and telegram to Northbrook 7 Aug. 1875, Northbrook Papers, vol. 12, part 1, no. 34, pp. 68 ff., and supplement no. 16, p. 6.

321 Northbrook to Salisbury 9, 16 and 30 Aug. 1875, Northbrook Papers, vol. 12, part 2, nos. 41, 42 and 45, pp. cviii ff., cxx ff. and cxviii ff. respectively.

322 See letter of the Secretary to the Government of India Financial Department to the Chief Secretary, Bombay Government 14 Oct. 1875, Financial Department Proceedings, Separate Revenue (Customs), Nov. 1875, Part A, no. 3.

323 Northbrook to Mallet 6 Sept. 1875, Northbrook Papers, vol. 23, part 2, pp. cxix ff.

324 See Mallet to Northbrook 27 March 1874, Northbrook Papers, vol. 22, part 1, pp. 66 ff.; Salisbury to Disraeli 13 May 1876, Disraeli Papers.

325 Salisbury to Northbrook 1, 7 and 15 Sept. 1875, Northbrook Papers, vol. 12, part 1, nos. 39, 40 and 41, pp. 77 ff.

326 Salisbury to Northbrook 29 Sept. and 5 Nov. 1875, Northbrook Papers, vol. 12, part 1, nos. 43 and 48, pp. 88 ff. and 97 ff. respectively.

327 Salisbury to Northbrook 29 Sept. and telegram to Northbrook 30 Sept. 1875, Northbrook Papers, vol. 12, part 1, no. 43, pp. 88 ff. and supplement no. 18, pp. 6 and 7 respectively; Mallet to Northbrook 17, 24 Sept. and 1 Oct. 1875, Northbrook Papers, vol. 22, part 1, pp. 246, 250 ff. and 257 ff. respectively.

328 Northbrook to Salisbury 7 Oct. 1875, and telegram to Salisbury of same date, Northbrook Papers, vol. 12, part 2, no. 52, pp. cxxxvi ff. and supplement no. 22 respectively.

329 Gladstone to Northbrook 20 Sept. and Mallet to Northbrook 8 Oct. 1875, Northbrook Papers, vol. 23, part 1, pp. 246 ff. and 268 ff. respectively.

330 Mallet to Northbrook 1 Dec. 1875, Northbrook Papers, vol. 17, part 1, pp. 460 ff.

331 Northbrook to Salisbury 25 Oct. 1875, Northbrook Papers, vol. 12, part 2, no. 55, pp. cxliii ff.

332 Frere to Salisbury 9 Oct. 1875, Salisbury Papers, Christ Church Library, Oxford.

333 Salisbury to Northbrook 26 Nov. 1875, Northbrook Papers, vol. 12, part 1, no. 53, pp. 106 ff. The reference is clearly to the Indian Treasury.

334 11 Nov. 1875, Financial Department Proceedings, Separate Revenue (Customs), March 1876, part A, Proceeding no. 23.

335 Mallet's telegram to Salisbury 14 Jan. 1876, Northbrook Papers, vol. 12, part 4, supplement, p. ii.

336 Northbrook to Salisbury 14 and 21 Jan. 1876, Northbrook Papers, vol. 12, part 4, nos. 4 and 5, pp. vii ff.

337 Salisbury to Northbrook 21 Jan. 1876 and telegram of same date, Northbrook Papers, vol. 12, part 3, no. 3, pp. 4 ff. and supplement no. 2 respectively. So Salisbury's later statement (letter to Lytton 17 March 1876, Lytton Papers, vol. 516/1, no. 10) that he would probably have withdrawn the despatch if Mallet had informed him that Northbrook had been personally wounded by it was clearly made in a mood of forgetfulness.

338 Northbrook to Salisbury 25 Feb. and 3 March 1876, Northbrook Papers, vol. 12, part 4, nos. 10 and 11, pp. xxiv ff.; also despatch of the Government of India 25 Feb. 1876, Financial Department Proceedings, Separate Revenue (Customs), March 1876, part A, no. 24.

339 Northbrook to Salisbury 17 March 1876, Northbrook Papers, vol. 12, part 4, no. 13, pp. xxxii ff.

340 See, for example, Eden to Northbrook 19 Feb. 1876, and Halifax to Northbrook 25 Feb. 1876, Northbrook Papers, vol. 18, part 1, pp. 62 ff. and vol. 23, part 3, p. 24 respectively.

341 Despatch of the Secretary of State 31 May 1876, Financial Department Proceedings, Separate Revenue (Customs), Part A, Aug. 1876, no. 1.

342 See letter from the Secretary, Department of Revenue, Agriculture and Commerce to the Secretary, Bengal Chamber of Commerce, 1 Sept. 1876, Financial Department Proceedings, Separate Revenue (Customs), Part A, Sept. 1876, no. 11.

343 To Salisbury 12 March 1876, Lytton Papers, vol. 518/1, pp. 17 ff.

344 Lytton to Salisbury 9 March 1876 and Salisbury to Lytton 17 and 24 March 1876, Lytton Papers, vol. 518/1, pp. 16 ff. and vol. 516/1, nos. 10 and 11.

345 Salisbury to Lytton 12 May 1876, Lytton Papers, vol. 516/1, no. 17.

346 Lytton to Mallet 12 June 1876, Lytton Papers, vol. 518/1, pp. 236.

347 To Mallet 14 March 1877, Lytton Papers, vol. 518/2, pp. 196 ff.

348 To Lytton 19 Oct. 1877, Lytton Papers, vol. 516/2, no. 42.

349 Lytton to Disraeli 16 July 1876, Lytton Papers, vol. 518/1, pp. 293 ff.; Lytton to Salisbury 1 Nov. 1877, Lytton Papers, vol. 518/2, pp. 978 ff.

350 Lytton to Strachey 3 Nov. 1877, Lytton Papers, vol. 518/2, pp. 988 ff.

351 Despatch of 30 Aug. 1877, Financial Department Proceedings, Separate Revenue (Customs), Part A, Oct. 1877.

352 4 Feb. 1879, Lytton Papers, vol. 516/4, no. 8.

353 To Cranbrook 7 Feb. 1879 and to Mallet 28 Feb. 1879, Lytton Papers, vol. 518/4, pp. 88 and 151 ff. respectively.

354 Lytton to Cranbrook 20 March 1879, Lytton Papers, vol. 518/4, pp. 186 ff.

355 See his letter to the Queen 24 June 1858 (Buckle, *Disraeli*, IV, 166).
356 To Disraeli 13 Dec. 1875, Disraeli Papers.
357 *Ibid.* 10 Jan. 1876, Disraeli Papers.
358 To Lytton 7 April 1876, Lytton Papers, vol. 516/1, no. 13. Robert Lowe declared in Parliament that it was the Queen who had initiated the proposal for the title of Empress and only succeeded on the third attempt in persuading a Prime Minister to take the necessary steps. When challenged he withdrew his allegation. There is nothing in the Lowe papers at Hinton Charterhouse that throws any light on Lowe's statement.
359 To Northbrook 11 April 1876, Northbrook Papers, vol. 7, p. 8.
360 To Corry, Private Secretary to Disraeli, 21 April 1876 and to Disraeli 30 April 1876, Lytton Papers, vol. 518/1, pp. 104ff. and 120ff. respectively.
361 To the Queen 4 May 1876, Lytton Papers, vol. 518/1, pp. 134ff.
362 For the proposed list of members, see Foreign Department Proceedings, Secret Political A, Dec. 1877, no. 296.
363 To Salisbury 25 May 1876, Lytton Papers, vol. 518/1, pp. 180ff.
364 To Disraeli 7 June 1876, Disraeli Papers; to Lytton 9 June 1876, Lytton Papers, vol. 516/1, no. 26. The passages cited in the text are from the latter.
365 To Lytton 7 July 1876, Lytton Papers, vol. 516/1, no. 32.
366 *Ibid.* 13 July 1876, Lytton Papers, vol. 516/1, no. 35.
367 *Ibid.* 30 Aug. 1876, Lytton Papers, vol. 516/1, no. 44.
368 Disraeli to Salisbury 3 Sept. 1876 and Salisbury to Lytton 12 and 18 Sept. 1876, Lytton Papers, vol. 516/1, nos. 48 enclosure, 49 and 50.
369 Lytton to Mallet 11 Jan. 1877, Lytton Papers, vol. 518/2, pp. 22ff.; Salisbury to Lytton 9 Feb. 1877, Lytton Papers, vol. 516/2, no. 2.
370 Despatch of Secretary of State 20 Nov. 1876, Foreign Department Proceedings, Secret Political A, Dec. 1877, no. 310.
371 Salisbury to Lytton 10 and 17 Nov. 1876, Lytton Papers, vol. 516/1, nos. 63 and 65.
372 Lytton to Salisbury 15 Nov. 1876 and to the Queen 15 and 22 Nov. 1876, Lytton Papers, vol. 518/1, pp. 605ff., 608ff. and 623 respectively.
373 Speech at Birmingham 18 July 1903. *The Times*, 20 July 1903.
374 To Arbuthnot 4 May 1877, Lytton Papers, vol. 518/2, p. 345.
375 Lytton's note 5 June 1876, Home Department Judicial July 1876, Proceedings 43–6.
376 Lytton to Salisbury 30 July 1876, Lytton Papers, vol. 518/1, pp. 315ff.; notes of Members of Council, Home Department Judicial July 1876, Proceedings 43–6.
377 Letter from Officiating Secretary to the Government of India to the Secretary of the Government of the North-West Provinces 7 July 1876, *Parl. Papers*, 1877, vol. 63, pp. 351ff.
378 14 Aug. 1876, Lytton Papers, vol. 518/1, pp. 381ff.
379 Lytton to Salisbury 28 Sept. 1876, Lytton Papers, vol. 518/1, pp. 487ff.
380 22 July 1876, Lytton Papers, vol. 516/1, no. 38.

424 To Hunter, cited in Hunter, *Mayo*, vol. 2, p. 226.
425 See E. Stokes, *The English Utilitarians and India* (Oxford, 1959), pp. 283 ff.; J. Roach, 'Liberalism and the Victorian Intelligentsia', *The Cambridge Historical Journal* XIII, no. 1, pp. 58–81.
426 Roach, *ibid.* p. 64.
427 2 May 1869, Mayo Papers, vol. 35, no. 53.
428 To Lord Bradford 13 Oct. 1869, Mayo Papers, vol. 37, no. 282.
429 To Col. Reilly 17 June 1869, Mayo Papers, vol. 35, no. 114; to John Fowler 30 Nov. 1870, Mayo Papers, vol. 41, no. 340.
430 Mayo to Argyll 13 Dec. 1871, Mayo Papers, vol. 45, no. 288.
431 Note of Mayo Home Department Judicial Proceedings 15 Jan. 1870, nos. 29–31A; Mayo to Napier of Magdala 24 Aug. 1871, Mayo Papers, vol. 44, no. 194; A. O. Hume (Home Secretary in Mayo's government) to Lord Dufferin 15 May 1885, Dufferin Papers (microfilm copy), India Office Library, reel 528.
432 To the Governor of Madras 3 Oct. 1869, Mayo Papers, vol. 37, no. 267.
433 The warmest remark that was ever made about Northbrook was by his old friend Edward Lear: 'He is an extremely luminious and amiable brick.' See R. Murphy (ed.), *Edward Lear's Indian Journal* (London, 1953), p. 34. The cruellest assessment was that of Dilke, after a few months with Northbrook in the Gladstone Government of 1880: 'just a nice idiotic banker's clerk'. R. Jenkins, *Sir Charles Dilke* (London, 1958), p. 149.
434 See for example, the letter of Toru Dutt 13 Jan. 1876. H. Das, *Life and Letters of Toru Dutt* (Oxford, 1921), p. 121.
435 Hume to Northbrook 1 Aug. 1872, Northbrook Papers, vol. 13, part I, pp. 109 ff. A. O. Hume b. 1829 son of Joseph Hume; joined Indian civil service 1849; service in North-West Provinces 1849-70; secretary to the government of India 1870-9; retired 1882; one of the founders of the Indian national congress; d. 1912.
436 Chief of the Intelligence Department to Northbrook 8 Oct. 1872, Northbrook Papers, vol. 13, part I, pp. 177 ff.
437 Home Department Police Proceedings Oct. 1873, nos. 14 and 15.
438 R. H. Davies to Northbrook 3 Feb. 1875, Northbrook Papers, vol. 17, part I, p. 36.
439 See Minute by Sir Richard Temple, Lieutenant-Governor of Bengal, 16 March 1875 and letter of the Bengal Government 24 March 1875, Home Department Judicial Proceedings April 1875, no. 89.
440 To Maurice Drummond 13 June 1875, Northbrook Papers, vol. 23, part II, pp. lxviii ff.
441 To Dufferin 15 May 1885, Dufferin Papers, reel 528.
442 Letter to Lytton 28 Feb. 1876, Lytton Papers, vol. 517/1, no. 180.
443 Grant Duff to Lytton 31 Jan. 1876, Lytton Papers, vol. 517/1, no. 69.
444 Northbrook to Argyll and to S. Whitbread 14 April 1876, Northbrook Papers, vol. 7, part II, pp. 1 ff.
445 To Fitzjames Stephen 7 March 1877, Lytton Papers, vol. 518/2, pp. 183 ff.

446 To Salisbury 27 April 1876, Lytton Papers, vol. 518/1, pp. 114ff.
447 To Salisbury 4 Oct. 1877, Lytton Papers, vol. 518/2, pp. 874ff.
448 Lytton to Cranbrook 30 April 1878, Lytton Papers, vol. 518/3, pp. 277ff.
449 H. M. Kisch 7 April 1880. See E. A. Waley Cohen, *A Young Victorian in India* (London, 1957), p. 173.
450 Lytton to Aitchison 8 March 1879, Lytton Papers, vol. 518/4, pp. 176ff.
451 Lytton to Cranbrook 30 June and 31 Aug. 1879, Lytton Papers, vol. 518/4, pp. 507ff. and 697ff. respectively; Cranbrook to Lytton 3, 10, 28, 31 Aug. and 29 Dec. 1879, Lytton Papers, vol. 516/4, nos. 60, 64, 68, 69 and 103.
452 Salisbury to Disraeli 10 Jan. 1876, Disraeli Papers; Auckland was the governor-general who had been responsible for the disaster of the first Afghan war.
453 Gladstone to Northbrook 2 Nov. 1878, Northbrook Papers, vol. 7, pp. 207ff.
454 Salisbury to Disraeli 10 Oct. 1878, Disraeli Papers.

CHAPTER 3, pp. 129–179

1 Gladstone to Kimberley 24 April 1880, Kimberley Papers, vol. D 20.
2 For a detailed study of Ripon's viceroyalty, see the author's earlier publication, *The Viceroyalty of Lord Ripon* (Oxford, 1953). The analysis in this chapter is broadly that in the book, but much new documentation has been utilized.
3 Gladstone to Granville 9 Sept. 1884, Gladstone Papers, Add. MSS 44177, fo. 98.
4 Lyall, *Life of Dufferin* (London, 1905), vol. 1, p. 134.
5 Argyll had strongly supported him, but Gladstone had preferred Northbrook. See Gladstone's correspondence with Argyll, Gladstone Papers, B.M. Add. MSS 44102; also A. Ramm, *The Political Correspondence of Mr Gladstone and Lord Granville 1868–1876* (London, 1952), vol.2, p. 301.
6 24 Dec. 1880, Gladstone Papers, B.M. Add. MSS 44151, fo. 149.
7 Diary of Ripon 2 Dec. 1878, B.M. Add. MSS 43591. The Ripon Papers were consulted by the author over ten years ago, and the numbers of the manuscripts cited here are as of that date.
8 Diary of Ripon 7 Sept. 1879, Add. MSS 43592.
9 Cf. Sir Donald Stewart, Commander at Kabul, to his wife 14 April 1880: 'every word Lord Lytton has written to me might have been written by the Opposition'. G. R. Elsmie, *Field Marshal Sir Donald Stewart* (London, 1903), p. 329.
10 Memorandum to Hartington 9 May 1880, Add. MSS 43610, no. 1.
11 See Earl Granville to R. Thomson no. 57, 18 May 1880, F.O. 65, vol. 1101.
12 Ripon to Sir Nevile Chamberlain 27 May 1880, Add. MSS 43600, no. 2.

99 Crosthwaite to Lord Lansdowne 25 Nov. 1890, Lansdowne Papers, India Office Library, MSS Eur. D. 558, Correspondence with persons in India, vol. 4, part 1, no. 375.

100 Note 4 Sept. 1883, Home Department Proceedings 1883, Add. MSS 43628, pp. 719 ff.

101 3 March 1882.

102 This, of course, was not the general opinion of the British unofficial community. The British-owned newspaper of Allahabad, *The Pioneer*, complained as early as 30 May 1883 that the repeal had been amply illustrated to have been a mistake.

103 Gladstone to Ripon 13 March 1882, Add. MSS 43552, no. 43.

104 Evelyn Baring, first earl of Cromer b. 1841; private secretary to Northbrook 1872–6; service in Egypt 1876–80 and 1883–1907; finance member of Viceroy's council 1880–3; d. 1917.

105 See opinions of W. R. Pratt, Collector of Satara, 9 Jan. 1882, and A. Cumine, Acting Collector of Ratnagiri, 4 June 1882, *Parl. Papers*, 1883, vol. 51, part 2, Bombay Reports. Most Bombay officials were of the same viewpoint.

106 Resolution of the Government of Bombay 25 March 1882, *Parl. Papers*, 1883, vol. 51, p. 34.

107 B. 1835; entered Indian civil service 1856; home secretary 1873–4; foreign secretary 1878–81; lieutenant-governor of the North-West Provinces 1882–7; member of India council 1887–1902; d. 1911.

108 Sir Mortimer Durand, *Life of Sir Alfred Lyall* (London, 1913), p. 268.

109 Ripon to Grant Duff 4 Oct. 1882, Add. MSS 43605, no. 203. Sir M. E. Grant Duff b. 1829; Liberal M.P. 1857–81; under-secretary for India 1868–74; Governor of Madras 1881–6; d. 1906.

110 Viceroy's Minute on Local Self-Government in India 10 Nov. 1884, Add. MSS 43639, Appendix no. 1.

111 Ripon to W. E. Forster 26 March 1883, Add. MSS 43598, no. 36.

112 Ripon to T. Hughes 12 June 1882, Add. MSS 43597, no. 82.

113 Ripon to Gladstone 24 March 1883, Add. MSS 43598, no. 33.

114 Gladstone to Ripon 24 Nov. 1881, Add. MSS 43551, no. 151.

115 Ripon to W. E. Forster 26 May 1881, Add. MSS 43596, no. 56.

116 Cited in Lord Zetland, *Lord Cromer* (London, 1932), p. 76.

117 Sir William Hunter to H. W. Primrose 28 Sept. 1882, Add. MSS 43564, no. 282 A. A Member of Parliament touring India during 1881–2 had also heard high praise of Ripon 'from persons of all political opinions and religious creeds'. W. E. Baxter, *A Winter in India* (London, 1882), p. 82.

118 Letter to Ripon 8 Feb. 1882, Add. MSS 43561, no. 89.

119 Ripon to the Law Member 8 Feb. 1882, Add. MSS 43604, no. 74.

120 Ripon to Sir Ashley Eden 7 May 1883, Add. MSS 43598, no. 57.

121 'Sir Alfred Lyall', *Quarterly Review* (July, 1913), p. 190.

122 Lord Cromer, *Political and Literary Essays* (London, 1913), p. 97.

123 Ripon's memorandum to Halifax 6 March 1883, Add. MSS 43598, no. 26.

124 *The Times,* 5 Feb. 1883.

125 Ripon to Gladstone 24 March 1883, Add. MSS 43598, no. 33; also Ripon to Northbrook 19 March and to Halifax 26 March 1883, Add. MSS 43598, nos. 31 and 35.

126 Speech of 9 March 1883, Proceedings of the Legislative Council of the Governor-General of India 1883, vol. XXII, pp. 222 ff.

127 Indian Legislative Consultations 28 March 1836, no. 13.

128 9 March 1883, Proceedings of the Legislative Council of the Governor-General of India 1883, vol. 22, pp. 220 ff. Sir Augustus Rivers Thompson b. 1829; joined Bengal civil service 1850; secretary to Bengal government 1869–75; chief commissioner of Burma 1875–8; member of Viceroy's council 1878–82; lieutenant-governor of Bengal 1882–7; d. 1890.

129 For the opinions of the officials and judges, see *Parl. Papers,* 1884, vol. 60.

130 Kimberley to Ripon 13 Sept. and 9 Nov. 1883, Add. MSS 43574, nos. 56 and 70.

131 Quoted by Ripon to Rivers Thompson 20 May 1883, Add. MSS 43606, no. 206.

132 Despatch to the Secretary of State 10 Aug. 1883, *Parl. Papers,* 1884, vol. 60, pp. 687 ff.

133 Ripon to Grant Duff 20 Aug. 1883, Add. MSS 43607, no. 66.

134 17 April 1883, Add. MSS 43553, no. 50 A.

135 11 May 1883, *Hansard,* 3rd series, vol. 279, col. 568.

136 Viceroy's telegram to Secretary of State 8 Aug. 1883, and telegrams of Secretary of State to Viceroy 8 and 24 Aug. 1883, Add. MSS 43615, nos. 1760, 1761 and 1786; Gladstone to Granville 28 Sept. and Granville to Gladstone 1 Oct. 1883. A. Ramm, *The Political Correspondence of Gladstone and Granville 1876–1886* (Oxford, 1962), vol. 2, nos. 1106 and 1107; Kimberley to Gladstone 12 Oct. 1883, Gladstone Papers, Add. MSS 44228, fo. 120; Kimberley to Ripon 18, 24 and 26 Oct. 1883, Add. MSS 43574, nos. 64, 65 and 66; telegram of Secretary of State to Viceroy 25 Oct. 1883, Add. MSS 43615, no. 1831.

137 *The Englishman,* 14 Dec. 1883.

138 Baring had by this time left India for Egypt.

139 Minute of Sir Steuart Bayley 15 Dec. 1883, Add. MSS 43614, no. 1, enclosure.

140 B. 1838; entered Indian civil service 1858; seconded to Egypt 1878–83; finance member of Viceroy's council 1883–8; lieutenant-governor of North-West Provinces 1888–92; d. 1908.

141 Sir James Fergusson, Governor of Bombay, to Dufferin 22 Dec. 1884 and Grant Duff to Dufferin 3 Jan. 1885, Dufferin Papers, reel 528.

142 To Dufferin 3 Jan. 1885, *ibid.*

143 To Dufferin 8 Jan. 1885, Kimberley Papers, D/22*b*, fo. 29.

144 Dufferin to Kimberley 15 Dec. 1884, Kimberley Papers, D/22*a*, fos. 1 ff.

145 See his replies to the addresses from the Municipal Corporations of Bombay 8 Dec. 1884 and Calcutta 13 Dec. 1884, *Speeches Delivered in India 1884–8* (London, 1890), pp. 21 and 26.

146 Dufferin to Kimberley 3 Feb. 1885, Kimberley Papers, D/22*a*, fo. 31.

147 Kimberley to Dufferin 1 and 15 May 1885, Kimberley Papers, D/22*b*, fos. 148 and 190 respectively.

148 To Dufferin 26 April 1885, Dufferin Papers, reel 528. James Gibbs b. 1825; joined Bombay civil service 1846; member of Bombay council 1874–9; home member of Viceroy's council 1880–5; d. 1886.

149 Lyall to Dufferin 13 May 1885, Dufferin Papers, reel 528.

150 Dufferin to Ripon 11 June 1885, Dufferin Papers, reel 525; Dufferin to Ilbert 30 July 1885, Dufferin Papers, reel 529.

151 Dufferin to Hume 5 May 1885, Dufferin Papers, reel 528; Dufferin to Ripon 8 July 1886, Dufferin Papers, reel 525.

152 See Hume's circular enclosed with his letter to Dufferin 12 June 1885, Dufferin Papers, reel 528.

153 Dufferin to Reay 17 May 1885, Dufferin Papers, reel 528.

154 See letters to Dufferin from Aitchison (the Punjab) 17 June, Griffin (Central India) 21 June, Reay (Bombay) 22 June, Grant Duff (Madras) 24 June, Ward (Assam) no date, Crosthwaite (Central Provinces) 2 July, Cordery (Hyderabad) 3 July, Bradford (Rajputana) 4 July, Bernard (Burma) 7 July, Rivers Thompson (Bengal) enclosing a note by Mac-Donnell 15 July and Girdlestone (Mysore) 8 Aug. 1885, Dufferin Papers, reel 528.

155 Dufferin to Ilbert 30 July 1885, Dufferin Papers, reel 529; Ilbert's note 25 Aug. 1885, Dufferin Papers, reel 528; and Dufferin to Churchill 28 Aug. 1885, Dufferin Papers, reel 517. Churchill, curiously enough, was in favour of the scheme. Letter to Dufferin 28 Aug. 1885, Dufferin Papers, reel 517.

156 Hume to Dufferin 12 June and 12 July 1885, Dufferin Papers, reel 528.

157 *Ibid.* 4 July 1885, Dufferin Papers, reel 528.

158 Dufferin to Sir Fitzjames Stephen 28 July 1885, Dufferin Papers, reel 525.

159 Dufferin to Reay 17 May 1885, Dufferin Papers, reel 528; see also Reay to Kimberley 5 March 1886, Kimberley Papers, D/26*b*.

160 Dufferin to Kimberley 15, 23 and 30 Dec. 1884, Kimberley Papers, D/22*a*. Sir Anthony, first baron MacDonnell b. 1844; entered Indian civil service 1865; home secretary 1886–9; member of Viceroy's council 1893–5; lieutenant-governor of the North-West Provinces 1895–1901; chairman Famine Commission 1901; permanent under-secretary in Ireland 1902–8; d. 1925. James O'Kinealy b. 1837; joined Indian civil service 1861; judge of Calcutta high court 1883–99; d. 1903.

161 To Mackenzie Wallace 22 Jan. 1885, Dufferin Papers, reel 528.

162 Dufferin to Kimberley 13 Feb. 1885, Kimberley Papers, D/22*a*, fos. 42ff.

163 Dufferin to Kimberley 17 March 1885, Kimberley Papers, D/22*a*, fos. 65ff.

164 To Dufferin 17 April 1885, Dufferin Papers, reel 525.

165 See Sir Steuart Bayley, Lieutenant-Governor of Bengal, to Mackenzie Wallace 1 May 1887 and Mackenzie Wallace to Bayley 10 May 1887, Dufferin Papers, reel 531.

166 See Dufferin to Churchill 10 July 1885, Dufferin Papers, reel 517; Lyall to Dufferin 16 July 1885, Dufferin Papers, reel 528.

167 Churchill to Dufferin 16 Sept. 1885, Dufferin Papers, reel 517.

168 Dufferin to Churchill 12 Oct. 1885, Dufferin Papers, reel 517.

169 Lyall to Dufferin 8 May 1886, Dufferin Papers, reel 529.

170 Lyall to Dufferin 12 Sept. 1886, Dufferin Papers, reel 530.

171 Dufferin to Cross 20 Sept. 1886, Dufferin Papers, reel 517.

172 Dufferin to Churchill 17 July 1885, Dufferin Papers, reel 517; Dufferin to Stephen 28 July and an unposted letter to Northbrook 30 July 1885, Dufferin Papers, reel 525; Lyall to Dufferin 12 July 1885, Dufferin Papers, reel 528.

173 Dufferin to Cross 18 Nov. 1888, Dufferin Papers, reel 518.

174 Dufferin to Churchill 28 Aug. 1885, Dufferin Papers, reel 517.

175 To Kimberley 13 Feb. 1885, Kimberley Papers, D/22a, fos. 42ff.

176 To Dufferin 14 March 1885, Dufferin Papers, reel 525.

177 To Dufferin 17 April 1885, Kimberley Papers, D/22b, fos. 130ff.

178 See evidence before the Indian Expenditure Commission 15 Nov. 1895, vol. I, p. 120.

179 To Rivers Thompson 5 May 1885, Dufferin Papers, reel 528.

180 Aitchison to Dufferin 7 May 1885, Dufferin Papers, reel 528.

181 Dufferin to Churchill 7 Aug. 1885, Dufferin Papers, reel 517; Mackenzie Wallace to Godley 7 Aug. 1885, Dufferin Papers, reel 525; Churchill to Dufferin 7 Aug. 1885, Dufferin Papers, reel 517.

182 Dufferin to Northbrook 7 Sept. 1885, Dufferin Papers, reel 525.

183 See Dufferin to Northbrook 10 Jan. and 3 Feb. 1886, Dufferin Papers, reel 525.

184 Godley to Mackenzie Wallace 13 Aug. 1886, Dufferin Papers, reel 525; Cross to Dufferin 19 Aug. 1886, Dufferin Papers, reel 516; Colvin to Dufferin 27 Aug. 1886, Dufferin Papers, reel 530; Mackenzie Wallace to Godley 3 Sept. 1886, Dufferin Papers, reel 525.

185 B. 1842; entered Indian civil service 1861; finance secretary 1886; acting finance member of Viceroy's council 1887–8; finance member 1893–9; member of India council 1899–1903; d. 1903.

186 Colvin to Dufferin 15 Nov. 1887 and Westland to Dufferin 4 Dec. 1887, Dufferin Papers, reel 532.

187 Cross to Dufferin 5 and 19 Jan. 1888, Dufferin Papers, reel 518; Godley to Dufferin 20 Jan. 1888, Dufferin Papers, reel 526.

188 To Dufferin 24 Jan. 1888, Dufferin Papers, reel 532.

189 To Cross 6 Feb. 1888, Dufferin Papers, reel 518.

190 *Speeches delivered in India*, pp. 23–4; Dufferin to Meredith Townsend 28 May 1888, Dufferin Papers, reel 527.

191 Resolution 7–215–25 dated 15 July 1885 of the Home Department of the Government of India.

192 See Resolution of the General Department Education 8 Oct. 1886.

Government of India Home Department Education Proceedings 15 and 16, November 1886, part B.

193 Dufferin to Cross 11 Oct. 1886, Dufferin Papers, reel 517.

194 See letter of Lyall 9 July 1887, and note of MacDonnell 23 July 1887, Home Department Public Proceedings, August 1887, Proceedings 205 and 206.

195 Syed Ahmad to Tyabji 24 Jan. 1888 and Tyabji's reply 18 Feb. 1888, Tyabji Papers, National Archives of India.

196 Sir Syed Ahmad, *The Present State of Indian Politics* (Allahabad, 1888), p. 37.

197 Dufferin to George Allen, editor *The Pioneer*, 1 Jan. 1887, Dufferin Papers, reel 531. See also Dufferin to Cross 4 Jan. 1887, Dufferin Papers, reel 518 and Dufferin to Northbrook 11 Jan. 1887, Dufferin Papers, reel 526.

198 To Sir George Birdwood 30 March 1887, Dufferin Papers, reel 526.

199 M. Cumpston, 'Some early Indian Nationalists and their Allies in the British Parliament 1851–1906', *English Historical Review*, LXXVI, no. 299 (April, 1961), p. 292.

200 15 March 1884. *Ibid.* p. 297 n.

201 Dufferin to Stephen 6 March 1886, Dufferin Papers, reel 525; Dufferin to Kimberley 21 March 1886, Kimberley Papers, D/22d, fos. 19ff.

202 To Godley 23 March 1886, Dufferin Papers, reel 525.

203 Kimberley to Dufferin 22 April and 21 May 1886, Kimberley Papers, D/22c, fos. 75 and 101 respectively.

204 Dufferin to Kimberley 26 April 1886, Kimberley Papers, D/22d, fos. 56ff.

205 Dufferin to Kimberley 17 May 1886, Kimberley Papers, D/22d, fos. 90ff.

206 Dufferin to Sir Henry Maine 9 May 1886, Dufferin Papers, reel 525.

207 See the draft letters of Dufferin 18 and 19 (?) June 1886, Dufferin Papers, reel 529.

208 See Aitchison to Dufferin 22 June 1886, Dufferin Papers, reel 529.

209 Wallace to Hume 26 June 1886, Dufferin Papers, reel 529.

210 Dufferin to Northbrook 23 June and to Ripon 8 July 1886, Dufferin Papers, reel 525; Dufferin to Hume 29 June 1886, Dufferin Papers, reel 529.

211 See Hume to Dufferin end of June, Dufferin Papers, reel 529; Hume to Dufferin 31 July, 2, 13, 27 29, 30 (?) and 31 Aug. 1886 and Dufferin to Hume 2, 7, and 28 Aug. (two letters), Dufferin Papers, reel 530; Dufferin to Ripon 9 Sept. 1886, Dufferin Papers, reel 525.

212 Hume to Dufferin 16, 20 Sept. and 25 Oct. 1886, Dufferin to Hume 20 and 25 Sept. 1886, Wallace to Hume 4 Oct. 1886, Dufferin Papers, reel 530.

213 Dufferin to Hume 27 Oct. 1886, Dufferin Papers, reel 530.

214 Hume to Dufferin 28 Oct. 1886; Dufferin's telegrams to Mac-Donnell 2 and 3 Nov. 1886; Peile to Dufferin 3 Nov. 1886; MacDonnell's telegram to Dufferin 3 Nov. 1886; Ilbert to Dufferin 4 Nov. 1886.

Dufferin Papers, reel 530. Sir Henry Cotton b. 1845; entered Indian civil service 1867; home secretary 1896; chief commissioner of Assam 1896–1902; president of Indian national congress 1904.

215 Hume to Dufferin 26 June, and Dufferin to Hume 29 June 1887, Dufferin Papers, reel 531; Hume to Dufferin 2 July, 26 Sept. and 9 Oct., and Dufferin to Hume 3 July, 25 Sept. and 8 Oct. 1887, Dufferin Papers, reel 532.

216 Wallace to A. Mackenzie 11 May 1886, Dufferin Papers, reel 525.

217 Dufferin to Kimberley 9 July 1886, Kimberley Papers, D/22d, fo. 127.

218 R. Knight, editor *The Statesman*, to Wallace 1 Nov. 1886, Dufferin Papers, reel 530.

219 P. C. Mozoomdar, a leader of the Brahmo Samaj in Bengal, to H. S. Cunningham 21 July 1886, Dufferin Papers, reel 530.

220 To Northbrook 16 Oct. 1886, Dufferin Papers, reel 525.

221 To Northbrook 16 Oct. 1886, Dufferin Papers, reel 525; to Cross 27 Sept. 1886, 23 Nov. 1886 and 8 March 1887, Dufferin Papers, reel 518.

222 Maine to Dufferin 15 April and 2 June 1886, Dufferin Papers, reel 525.

223 To Dufferin 30 July and 18 Nov. 1886, Dufferin Papers, reel 525.

224 Kimberley to Reay 30 July 1886, Kimberley Papers, D/26a.

225 Presumably Dufferin considered this an apt description of the Eton and Harrow debating societies as well.

226 Dufferin to Cross 4, 18 Jan. and 1 Feb. 1887, Dufferin Papers, reel 518; Dufferin to Ilbert 15 Jan. 1887, Dufferin Papers, reel 526.

227 Report of the Second Indian National Congress (Calcutta, Dec. 1886), pp. 1–10.

228 Cross to Dufferin 3 Feb. 1887, Dufferin Papers, reel 516; and 17, 25 Feb., 25 March and 14 April 1887, Dufferin Papers, reel 518.

229 To Northbrook 11 March 1887, Dufferin Papers, reel 526; to Cross 15, 20, 29 March and 9 May 1887, Dufferin Papers, reel 518.

230 See note of Mookerjee 1 June, Tagore to Dufferin 6 June, H. J. S. Cotton to Dufferin 9 June, MacDonnell to Wallace 14 June and Peile to Dufferin 2 Oct. 1887, Dufferin Papers, reel 531. Sir James Peile b. 1833; entered Indian civil service 1856; various posts in Bombay government 1859–86; home member of Viceroy's council 1886–7; member of India council 1887–1902; d. 1906.

231 Lyall to Dufferin 20 Nov. 1887, Dufferin Papers, reel 532.

232 8 April 1887, Dufferin Papers, reel 526.

233 To Cross 13 Nov. 1887, Dufferin Papers, reel 518.

234 Dufferin to the Queen 31 March 1887, Dufferin Papers, reel 516, no. 64.

235 Dufferin to Roberts 28 Sept. 1887, Dufferin Papers, reel 532.

236 Dufferin to Cross 13 March 1888, Dufferin Papers, reel 518.

237 Lord Connemara to Dufferin 28 Dec. 1887, Dufferin Papers, reel 532; Dufferin to Connemara 2 Jan. 1888, Dufferin Papers, reel 533. The presidential addresses of Naoroji in 1886 and Tyabji in 1887 justified this assessment. Naoroji spoke of India's 'good fortune' in being under

British rule, which alone enabled the Congress to meet; and Tyabji said that educated Indians were 'in our own interests the best, and staunchest supporters of the British Government in India'.

238 See note of Dufferin 27 Dec. 1887, Dufferin Papers, reel 532; Dufferin to Cross 8 Oct. 1888, and Mackenzie Wallace to Cunningham, Officiating Foreign Secretary, 26 Jan. 1888 (enclosure 7 of letter to Cross 8 Oct.), Dufferin Papers, reel 518.

239 Kimberley to Dufferin 8 Jan. 1885, Kimberley Papers, D/22*b*, fos. 33ff.

240 Dufferin to Kimberley 2 March 1885, Kimberley Papers, D/22*a*, fos. 61ff.; Dufferin to Churchill 28 Aug. 1885, Dufferin Papers, reel 517.

241 See G. H. R. Hart, Private Secretary to Governor of Bombay, to Mackenzie Wallace 18 July 1885, Dufferin Papers, reel 528.

242 Ripon to Dufferin 17 April 1885, Dufferin Papers, reel 525.

243 Kimberley to Dufferin 17 April 1885, Kimberley Papers, D/22*b*, fos. 130ff.

244 To Dufferin 22 Sept. 1885, Dufferin Papers, reel 517.

245 To Reay 19 March 1886, Kimberley Papers, D/26*a*.

246 Kimberley to Dufferin 22 April, 21 and 28 May 1886, Kimberley Papers, D/22*c*.

247 Kimberley to Dufferin 4 and 11 June 1886, Kimberley Papers, D/22*c*; Kimberley to Gladstone 8 June 1886, Kimberley Papers, D/30.

248 To Kimberley 11 June and 2 July 1886, Kimberley Papers, D/22*d*.

249 Letter to Dufferin 18 Dec. 1885, Dufferin Papers, reel 529.

250 Crosthwaite to Mackenzie Wallace 17 Jan. 1887, Dufferin Papers, reel 531.

251 Aitchison to Mackenzie Wallace 4 May 1888, Dufferin Papers, reel 533.

252 Dufferin to Cross 27 Dec. 1887, Dufferin Papers, reel 518; Roberts to Mackenzie Wallace 4 May 1888, Dufferin Papers, reel 533.

253 Dufferin to Cross 10 Aug. 1888, Dufferin Papers, reel 518.

254 P. C. Mozoomdar to Mackenzie Wallace 16 Feb. 1888, Dufferin Papers, reel 532; Dufferin to Cross 20 Feb. 1888, Dufferin Papers, reel 518.

255 Knight to Mackenzie Wallace 16 March and Mackenzie Wallace to Knight 17 March 1888, Dufferin Papers, reel 533.

256 Dufferin to the Queen 26 March 1888, Dufferin Papers, reel 516, no. 76.

257 To Mackenzie Wallace 9 March 1888, Dufferin Papers, reel 526.

258 Cf. the account of I. P. Minayeff of his conversation with W. C. Bonnerjee, 2 Jan. 1886 in *Travels in and Diaries of India and Burma* (Calcutta, no date), p. 120.

259 Dufferin to Cross 26 March 1888, Dufferin Papers, reel 518.

260 Colvin to Dufferin 25, 27 April and 24 May, and Dufferin to Colvin 16 May and 6 June 1888, Dufferin Papers, reel 533.

261 Colvin to Dufferin 10 June 1888, Dufferin Papers, reel 533.

262 Dufferin to Cross 22 June 1888, Dufferin Papers, reel 518. Cf. Minayeff: 'In the Congress there are no representatives of the people at all. . . . The National Congress is a fancy which is not understood by the people.' 11 March 1886, *op. cit.* p. 195.

263 To Cross 17 and 30 Aug. 1888, Dufferin Papers, reel 518.

264 Cross to Dufferin 11 and 27 Sept. 1888, Dufferin Papers, reel 518.

265 Note of the Viceroy 21 Sept. 1888, Dufferin Papers, reel 534.

266 Chesney to Dufferin 22 Sept. 1888, Dufferin Papers, reel 533.

267 To Cross 30 Aug. 1888, Dufferin Papers, reel 518.

268 27 Aug. 1888, Dufferin Papers, reel 533.

269 See note of Eardley Norton, a barrister who was in close touch with Indian opinion, dated 27 March 1904. This note, which is in a library in Calcutta, has been cited in H. and U. Mukherjee, *The Growth of Nationalism in India 1857–1905* (Calcutta, 1957), p. 99 n.

270 Mackenzie to Mackenzie Wallace 5 Sept. 1888, Dufferin Papers, reel 533; Dufferin to Cross 24 Sept. 1888, Dufferin Papers, reel 518.

271 Dufferin to Colvin 9 Oct. 1888, Dufferin Papers, reel 534.

272 To Sambhu Chander Mookerjee 15 Oct. 1888, Dufferin Papers, reel 534.

273 To Colvin 28 Oct. 1888, Dufferin Papers, reel 534. For the Hume–Colvin correspondence, see *Audi Alteram Partem* (London, 1888). In fact, at this time Hume was doing his best for the Viceroy, and wrote a spirited defence of Dufferin's administration in *The Indian Mirror*, 11 Nov. 1888. 'Moreover, it is felt that he is in a high degree entitled to the respect and esteem, and in many matters even to the gratitude of the people of India.' But Hume could not convince his Indian associates.

274 To Grattan Geary 27 Oct. 1888, Dufferin Papers, reel 534; to Cross 29 Oct. 1888, Dufferin Papers, reel 518.

275 To Cross 17 Sept. and 4 Nov. 1888, Dufferin Papers, reel 518.

276 Speech at St Andrew's Dinner, Calcutta, 30 Nov. 1888, *Speeches Delivered in India*, pp. 229–48.

277 Ripon to J. K. Cross 3 April 1884, Add. MSS 43614, no. 17.

278 For example: 'In conclusion, Lord Dufferin hopes that he may be allowed to lay at your Majesty's feet the expression of his deep sense of your Majesty's constant and unwearied kindness towards him.' 18 June 1886, Dufferin Papers, reel 516, no. 45.

279 The phrase is Granville's: letter to Gladstone 13 Feb. 1872. Ramm, *op. cit.* vol. 2, p. 301.

280 Of his visit to Hardwar he wrote to Lytton, the only other Viceroy who was equally sensitive to feminine charm, that they had been 'very much interested in seeing the gentlemen, and especially the ladies, bathe. I was told they were all *purdah* women, but their principle seems to be "in for a penny, in for a pound". They might just as well have been quite naked, their only garment being a thin muslin robe, which became invisible the moment it was wet.' 16 April 1887, Dufferin Papers, reel 526.

281 'Our mutual letters are becoming shorter and shorter, which is a good sign, for happy is the country without annals.' To Cross 17 Jan. 1888, Dufferin Papers, reel 518.

282 See the entries in her diary 21 Jan. and 18 March 1885. Marchioness of Dufferin and Ava, *Our Viceregal Life in India* (London, 1889), vol. 1, pp. 43 and 85 respectively.

283 To Churchill 14 Aug. 1885, Dufferin Papers, reel 517.

284 To Gladstone 13 Feb. 1872, Ramm, *op. cit.* vol. 2, p. 301.

285 To Lord Arthur Russell 26 July 1887, Dufferin Papers, reel 526.

286 To Sir W. H. Gregory 1 Jan. 1888, Dufferin Papers, reel 527.

287 7 Aug. 1885, Dufferin Papers, reel 517.

288 Cf. Lord Esher's opinion that Dufferin 'certainly is charming, and I suppose the most popular man in Europe'. 8 June 1879, *Journals and Letters*, vol. 1 (London, 1934), pp. 61–2.

289 To Salisbury 5 Feb. 1888, Dufferin Papers, reel 522; to Salisbury 17 Sept. 1888, Dufferin Papers, reel 527; to Cross 17 Sept. 1888, Dufferin Papers, reel 518.

290 To Cross 3 Dec. 1888, Dufferin Papers, reel 518.

291 To Granville 6 June 1887, Dufferin Papers, reel 526.

292 To Sir Ashley Eden 24 April 1886, Dufferin Papers, reel 525.

293 To Curzon 3 Jan. 1901, Lord George Hamilton correspondence. India Office Library, vol. C/26/3, fos. 1 ff.

294 Richard Pares on the Duke of Newcastle: *War and Trade in the West Indies* (Oxford, 1936), p. 45.

CHAPTER 4, pp. 180–221

1 R. Rhodes James, *Lord Randolph Churchill* (London, 1959), p. 328.

2 E. Crankshaw, *The Forsaken Idea* (London, 1952), p. 135.

3 Kimberley to Gladstone 9 and 10 Aug. 1893, Kimberley to Norman 31 Aug. 1893, and Norman to Kimberley 22 Sept. 1893, Kimberley Papers, vol. E/10. Sir Henry Norman b. 1826; joined army of East India Company 1844; secretary to the government of India in the military department 1862–70; member of Viceroy's council 1870–7; member of India council 1878–83; governor of Jamaica 1883–9; governor of Queensland 1889–95; d. 1904.

4 See Gladstone to Kimberley 11 Aug. and Elgin to Kimberley 25 Aug. 1893, Kimberley Papers, vol. E/10; speech of Rosebery May 1899.

5 See R. Rhodes James, *Rosebery* (London, 1963), p. 290 n.

6 Rosebery even considered accepting the viceroyalty himself as a refuge from Cabinet dissensions, but was dissuaded with no great difficulty. R. Rhodes James, *Rosebery*, p. 290. Edward Grey also was considered. Kimberley to Gladstone 21 Sept. 1893, Gladstone Papers, Add. MSS 44229, fol. 159. For a day to day account of the negotiations which ended with the choice of Elgin see the *Private Diaries of Sir Algernon West* (London, 1901), pp. 185 ff.

7 Curzon to Lord George Hamilton 26 Oct. 1902, Hamilton correspondence, D 510/12, fos. 121 ff.

8 Elgin to Collen 6 Jan. 1898, Elgin Papers, India Office Library, MSS Eur. F. 84, Correspondence with persons in India, vol. 9, part 2, no. 15.

9 See Fowler, Secretary of State, to Elgin 20 July, 12 Oct., 23 and 30 Nov. 1894 and Elgin to Fowler 14 Aug. 1894 and 9 Jan. 1895, Wolverhampton Papers, India Office Library, MSS Eur. C/145, vol. 2, vol. 1 and vol. 3 respectively. No numbers.

10 See M. Cumpston, 'Some early Indian Nationalists and their Allies in the British Parliament, 1851–1906,' *English Historical Review*, LXXVI, no. 299 (April, 1961), pp. 294ff.

11 Gorst to Lansdowne 23 Nov. 1888. Lord Newton, *Lord Lansdowne* (London, 1929), pp. 60–2.

12 To Godley 8 Jan. 1889, Lansdowne Papers, India Office Library, MSS Eur. D. 558, series VIII, vol. 1, part 2, no. 15. Mackenzie Wallace remained in India for a few months after Dufferin's departure as private secretary to Lansdowne.

13 Lansdowne to Cross 11 and 24 Dec. 1888 and 1 Jan. 1889, Lansdowne Papers, series IX, vol. 1, part 2, nos. 1, 3 and 5.

14 Dufferin to Cross 6 Jan. 1889, Cross Papers, B.M. Add. MSS 51277.

15 Cross to Lansdowne 7 Dec. 1888 and 3, 18, 25 and 30 Jan. 1889, Lansdowne Papers, series IX, vol. 1, part 1, nos. 3, 8, 10, 11 and 12.

16 Godley to Lansdowne 22 Feb. and Northbrook to Lansdowne 1 March 1889, Lansdowne Papers, series VIII, vol. 1, part 1, nos. 37 and 42; Cross to Lansdowne 8 March 1889, Lansdowne Papers, series IX, vol. 1, part 1, no. 17.

17 To Cross 2 April 1889, Lansdowne Papers, series IX, vol. 1, part 2, no. 20.

18 See Cross to Lansdowne 24 April 1889, Lansdowne Papers, series IX, vol. 1, part 1, no. 24.

19 Lansdowne to Cross 12 and 27 Feb. 1889, Lansdowne Papers, series IX, vol. 1, part 2, nos. 12 and 14; Lansdowne to Lieutenant-Governor of Bengal 12 April 1889, to Governor of Madras 22 April 1889 and to Governor of Bombay 1 May 1889, Lansdowne Papers, series VII, vol. 1, part 2, nos. 214, 224 and 242; note of the Viceroy 4 May 1889, Lansdowne Papers, series XIII, pp. 31ff.

20 Cross to Lansdowne 28 June 1889 and Lansdowne to Cross 5 July 1889, Lansdowne Papers, series IX, vol. 1, part 1, no. 33 and part 2, no. 38.

21 Despatch of the Government of India no. 70 dated 24 Dec. 1889, Home Department Public Proceeding Jan. 1890, no. 51; also Lansdowne to Cross 12 July and 23 Dec. 1889, Lansdowne Papers, series IX, vol. 1, part 2, nos. 40 and 66.

22 Cross to Lansdowne 16 and 23 Jan. 1890, Lansdowne Papers, series IX, vol. 2, part 1, nos. 3 and 4.

23 Lansdowne to Cross 17 Feb. 1890, Lansdowne Papers, series IX, vol. 2, part 2, no. 9B.

24 See letters to Cross 11, 18 March and 28 April 1889, Lansdowne Papers, series IX, vol. 2, part 2, nos. 12, 13 and 20.

25 Cross to Lansdowne 11 April 1890, Lansdowne Papers, series IX, vol. 2, part 1, no. 15.

26 Lansdowne to Salisbury 3 May 1890, Lansdowne Papers, series VIII, vol. 2, part 2, no. 26.

27 Salisbury to Lansdowne 27 June 1890, Newton, *op. cit.* pp. 73–4; Cross to Lansdowne 21 Aug. 1890, Lansdowne Papers, series IX, vol. 2, part 1, no. 35.

28 See Lansdowne to G. Banerji, Vice-Chancellor of Calcutta University, 17 Dec. 1890, Lansdowne Papers, series VII, vol. 4, part 2, no. 297.

29 Lansdowne to Salisbury 26 March 1891, Lansdowne Papers, series VIII, vol. 3, part 2, no. 37.

30 28 March 1892. 'I am not at all disposed to ask from the Governor General or the Secretary of State . . . at once to produce large and imposing results. What I wish is that these first steps shall . . . be genuine, and whatever amount of scope they give to the elective principle shall be real. . . . It is to the Governor General's wisdom we must trust to do the very best and to make the most out of the materials at his disposal. . . .'

31 Ilbert, *The Government of India* (Oxford, 1922), p. 107.

32 Lansdowne to Cross 24 May 1892, Lansdowne Papers, series IX, vol. 4, part 2, no. 25.

33 To Lansdowne 4 May 1892, Lansdowne Papers, series VII, vol. 7, part 1, no. 327. Also, for this paragraph generally, see Home Department Public Proceedings Aug. 1892, nos. 237–52.

34 See Note of Lansdowne 16 June 1892, sent to Kimberley 23 Aug. 1892, Kimberley Papers, E/18c.

35 To Harris 29 July 1892, Lansdowne Papers, series VII, vol. 8, part 2, no. 54.

36 See Kimberley's letter to Lansdowne 22 Sept. 1892, Lansdowne Papers, series IX, vol. 4, part 1, no. 41.

37 Lansdowne to Harris 12 June 1893, Lansdowne Papers, series VII, vol. 9, part 2, no. 345; also Lansdowne to Wenlock 22 July 1893, Lansdowne Papers, series VII, vol. 10, part 2, no. 35. Surendranath Banerjee b. 1848; entered Indian civil service 1871; services terminated 1874; leader of nationalist opinion in Bengal; twice president of Indian national congress; d. 1925.

38 Crosthwaite to Lansdowne 13 Sept. 1893, Lansdowne Papers, series VII, vol. 10, part 1, no. 246.

39 Lansdowne to Crosthwaite 17 Sept. 1893, Lansdowne Papers, series VII, vol. 10, part 2, no. 192.

40 See despatch with enclosures to the Secretary of State no. 68 dated 26 Oct. 1892, Home Department Public Proceedings, Oct. 1892, nos. 167–72.

41 Col. Ardagh, Private Secretary to Viceroy, to William Digby 29 Dec. 1888, and Lansdowne to Cross 1 Jan. 1889, Lansdowne Papers, series VII, vol. 1, part 2, no. 39 and series IX, vol. 1, part 2, no. 5.

42 William Digby to Col. Ardagh 31 Dec. 1888. Lansdowne Papers, series VII, vol. 1, part 1, no. 70.

43 A. O. Hume to Provincial Congress Committees 26 Feb. 1889, Home Department Public Proceedings 154 B, April 1890, appendix A.

44 See Bradlaugh's bill and memorandum of 11 Oct. 1889, *ibid.* appendix C.

45 Gladstone also favoured municipal bodies and local authorities, Speech in the House of Commons, 28 March 1892.

46 Lansdowne to Northbrook 13 Jan. 1889, Lansdowne Papers, series VIII, vol. 1, part 2, no. 18.

47 Lansdowne to Cross 13 March 1889, Lansdowne Papers, series IX, vol. 1, part 2, no. 17.

48 Colvin to Lansdowne 6 Jan. 1890 and Lansdowne to Colvin 17 Jan. 1890, Lansdowne Papers, series VII, vol. 3, part 1, no. 16 and part 2, no. 44.

49 Lansdowne to Reay 13 Dec. 1889, and to Cross 21 Jan. 1890, Lansdowne Papers, series VII, vol. 2, part 2, no. 306, and series IX, vol. 2 part 2, no. 4.

50 Lansdowne to Reay 18 Dec. and to Cross 31 Dec. 1889; and Cross to Lansdowne 23 Jan. 1890, Lansdowne Papers, series VII, vol. 2, part 2, no. 326; series IX, vol. 1, part 2, no. 67; and series IX, vol. 2, part 1, no. 4. In fact, the Congress was not committed to a permanent settlement, and wished to examine its working in detail, see Hume to Secretary, Home Department, Jan. 1890, Home Department Public Proceedings March 1890, nos. 180–4.

51 Reay to Lansdowne 15 Feb., and Lansdowne to Reay 20 Feb. 1890, Lansdowne Papers, series VII, vol. 3, part 1, no. 148 and part 2, no. 110. It is a sobering thought that to Hume the Theosophical Society was at least of as much importance as the Congress, and he wrote as many letters to Koot Hoomi Lal Singh, the Mahatma in Tibet, as he did to the secretaries of Congress committees and graduates of Indian universities. See J. Symonds, *Madame Blavatsky* (London, 1959), p. 148.

52 See Madras Government Order 20 Nov. 1889, Home Department Circular 31 Jan. 1890, note of Lansdowne 22 Feb. 1890 and Home Department Circular 18 March 1890, Home Department Public Proceedings April 1890, nos. 54 and 55.

53 R. C. Lyon, Private Secretary to the Lieutenant-Governor of Bengal, to the Secretary, Congress Reception Committee 26 Dec. 1890, Home Department Public Proceeding Jan. 1891, no. 3.

54 B. 1845; barrister at Bombay; president of Indian national congress 1890; d. 1915.

55 31 Dec. 1890, Lansdowne Papers, series VII, vol. 4, part 1, no. 468.

56 2 Jan. 1891, Lansdowne Papers, series VII, vol. 5, part 1, no. 7.

57 2 Jan. 1891, Lansdowne Papers, series VII, vol. 5, part 1, no. 7A.

58 Col. Ardagh, Private Secretary to Viceroy, to P. Mehta 3 Jan. 1891, Lansdowne Papers, series VII, vol. 5, part 2, no. 8.

59 To Col. Ardagh 4 Jan. 1891, Lansdowne Papers, series VII, vol. 5, part 1, no. 15.

60 To Lansdowne no date, Lansdowne Papers, series VII, vol. 5, part 1, no. 65.

61 Ardagh to Hume 19 Jan. 1891, Lansdowne Papers, series VII, vol. 5, part 2, no. 61.

62 Hume to Secretaries of Congress Committees 21 Jan. 1891, Lansdowne Papers, series VII, vol. 5, part 1, no. 84 enclosure.

63 Hume to Lansdowne 9 Jan. 1891, Lansdowne Papers, series VII, vol. 5, part 1, no. 40.

64 Lansdowne to Hume 16 Jan. 1891, Lansdowne Papers, series VII, vol. 5, part 2, no. 50.

65 Lansdowne to Cross 28 Jan. 1891, Lansdowne Papers, series IX, vol. 3, part 2, no. 5B.

142 Hamilton to Elgin 8 and 23 July 1897, Hamilton Correspondence, C 125/2, fos. 321ff. and 351ff. respectively.
143 See the correspondence in Home Department Public Proceedings May 1898, nos. 329–44.
144 Elgin to Hamilton 6, 13 and 20 July 1897, Hamilton Correspondence, D 509/6, fos. 1ff., 47ff. and 87ff. respectively.
145 See the report of the District Superintendent of Police, Poona, 21 Sept. 1894, Home Department Public Proceedings, Feb. 1895, nos. 142–55.
146 See despatches of the Bombay Government 16 July and 29 July 1897, Home Department Public Proceedings 111–16, September 1897; and 11 Aug. 1897, Home Department Public, no. 57, Oct. 1897, part B.
147 Despatch of 29 July 1897, *ibid.*
148 See the confidential deposition by an unnamed Inamdar of position, Bombay Government despatch 11 Aug. 1897, enclosure 6.
149 T. V. Parvate, *Bal Gangadhar Tilak* (Ahmedabad, 1958), p. 505.
150 To Elgin 12 July 1897, Elgin Papers, Correspondence with persons in India, vol. 8, part 1, appendix no. 32. The European community in Bombay is reported to have threatened to boycott Sandhurst socially if he failed to prosecute Tilak. D. V. Tahmankar, *Lokamanya Tilak* (London, 1956), p. 85.
151 For an account of the trial, see S. L. Karandikar, *Bal Gangadhar Tilak* (Bombay, 1957), pp. 150ff.
152 Sandhurst to Hamilton 3 Oct. and to Elgin 4 Oct. 1897, Elgin Papers, Correspondence with persons in India, vol. 8, part 1, appendix nos. 67 and 73, enclosure. Chapekar's confession has been printed in *Source Material for a History of the Freedom Movement in India* (published by the Bombay Government 1958), vol. 2, pp. 347–52.
153 See S. A. Wolpert, *Tilak and Gokhale* (University of California Press, 1962), pp. 89–97.
154 Elgin to Sandhurst 30 April 1898, Elgin Papers, Correspondence with persons in India, vol. 9, part 2, no. 221.
155 Elgin to Hamilton 14 April 1897, and Godley to Hamilton 3 May 1897, Hamilton Correspondence, D 509/4, fos. 394ff. and 413ff. respectively. J. A. Godley, first baron Kilbracken. B. 1847; assistant private secretary to Gladstone 1872–4; fellow of Hertford college 1874–81; private secretary to Gladstone 1880–2; permanent under-secretary at India Office 1883–1909; d. 1932.
156 Lieutenant-Governor of the Punjab to Private Secretary to Viceroy, 12 April 1897, Elgin Papers, Correspondence with persons in India, vol. 7, part 1, no. 297.
157 To Elgin 7 May 1897, Hamilton Correspondence, C 125/2, fos. 185ff.
158 Sandhurst to Elgin 23 June 1897, Elgin Papers, Correspondence with persons in India, vol. 7, part 1, no. 471.
159 Elgin to Mackworth Young 11 July 1897, Elgin Papers, Correspondence with persons in India, vol. 8, part 2, appendix no. 5.

160 Telegram to Secretary of State, Private and Confidential, 4 July 1897, Hamilton Correspondence, D 508.

161 C. C. Stevens, Officiating Lieutenant-Governor of Bengal, to Elgin 8 July 1897, sent by Elgin to Hamilton 14 July 1897, Hamilton Correspondence, D 509/6, fos. 83ff.; C. W. Bolton, Chief Secretary Bengal Government, to J. P. Hewett, Home Secretary 1 Aug. 1897, Home Department Public Proceedings Oct. 1897, nos. 124–57.

162 See letters of C. S. Bayley, General Superintendent of Operations for the Suppression of Thagi and Dakaiti, 12 July, Mackworth Young 15 July, MacDonnell 16 July, 22 Aug. and 3 Oct., C. J. Lyall 17 July and Barnes 18 July 1897, Elgin Papers, Correspondence with persons in India, vol. 8, part 1, no. 235 and appendix nos. 31, 35, 36, 53, 39 and 40.

163 Elgin to Hamilton 27 July 1897, Hamilton Correspondence, D 509/6, fos. 137ff.

164 Hamilton to Elgin 19 and 26 Aug. 1897, Hamilton Correspondence, C 125/2, fos. 397ff.

165 Hamilton to Elgin 10 Dec. 1897, Hamilton Correspondence, C 125/3, fos. 45Aff.

166 To Hamilton 30 Dec. 1897, Hamilton Correspondence, D 509/8, fos. 347ff.; to Crosthwaite, Member of the India Council, 28 Nov. 1897, Elgin Papers, Correspondence with persons in India, vol. 8, part 2, no. 247.

167 See letters of Private Secretary to Viceroy to Officiating Lieutenant-Governor of the North-West Provinces 15 June 1898 and of the Principal, Aligarh College, to Private Secretary to Viceroy 26 July 1898, Elgin Papers, Correspondence with persons in India, vol. 9, part 2, no. 299 and vol. 10, part 1, no. 45.

168 See Sandhurst to Elgin 10 March and Elgin to Sandhurst 19 March 1898, Elgin Papers, Correspondence with persons in India, vol. 9, part 1, no. 129 and part 2, no. 136; Hamilton to Elgin 11 and 18 March, and Elgin to Hamilton 17 March 1898, Hamilton Correspondence, C 125/3, fos. 161ff., 179ff. and 183ff.; and D 509/10, fos. 207ff.

169 MacDonnell to Elgin 6 and 29 April 1898, Elgin Papers, Correspondence with persons in India, vol. 9, part 1, nos. 200 and 233.

170 Young to Elgin 13 April 1898, Elgin Papers, Correspondence with persons in India, vol. 9, part 1, appendix no. 34. Sir Mackworth Young b. 1840; joined Indian civil service 1863; secretary to the Punjab government 1880–7; Resident in Mysore 1895–7; lieutenant-governor of the Punjab 1897–1902; d. 1924.

171 See letter to Hamilton 11 April 1898, Hamilton Correspondence, D 509/11, fos. 89ff.

172 See, for example, Private Secretary to Viceroy to A. H. T. Martindale, Agent to the Governor-General Rajputana, 27 May 1898, Elgin Papers, Correspondence with persons in India, vol. 9, part 2, no. 280.

173 To Sandhurst 30 April 1898, Elgin Papers, Correspondence with persons in India, vol. 9, part 2, no. 221; to Hamilton 26 May 1898, Hamilton Correspondence, D 509/11, fos. 189ff.

174 Elgin to Elliott 18 July 1894, Elgin Papers, Correspondence with persons in India, vol. 2, part 2, no. 22; Elgin to Reay 19 Dec. 1894, Elgin Papers, Correspondence with persons in England, vol. 1, part 2, no. 65.

175 Elgin to Fowler 16 Jan. 1895, Wolverhampton Papers, vol. 3, no number.

176 Crosthwaite to Elgin 12 Jan. and Sir Edward Buck to Elgin 12 Sept. 1895, Elgin Papers, Correspondence with persons in India, vol. 3, part 1, no. 38 and vol. 4, part 1, no. 156A.

177 Elgin to Lord Wenlock, Governor of Madras, 11 Nov. 1895, Elgin Papers, Correspondence with persons in India, vol. 4, part 2, no. 237.

178 See Hamilton to Elgin 26 Nov. and Elgin to Hamilton 16 Dec. 1896, Hamilton Correspondence, C 125/1, fos. 437ff. and D 509/3, fos. 429ff. respectively.

179 To Elgin 23 Sept. 1897, Elgin Papers, Correspondence with persons in England, vol. 4, part 1, no. 55A.

180 See despatch of the Government of India Home Department Judicial no. 43 dated 27 Oct. 1898, Home Department Judicial Proceedings Oct. 1898, nos. 505–34.

181 Minute of Elgin 24 Aug. 1896 and Elgin to Hamilton 25 Aug. 1896 and 21 April 1897, Hamilton Correspondence, D 509/2, fos. 827ff. and D 509/4, fos. 445ff. Sandhurst of Bombay agreed with Elgin: 'Mr Tilak is like a red rag to many, while I think him as merely a tedious bore.' Letter to Elgin 28 Sept. 1896, Elgin Papers, Correspondence with persons in India, vol. 6, part 1, no. 126. However, as we have seen, Sandhurst changed his mind soon after.

182 Hamilton to Elgin 5 June and 11 Dec. 1896 and 5, 12 Feb., 2 April, 14 May and 24 June 1897, Hamilton Correspondence, C 25/1, fos. 283ff. and 447 ff.; and C 125/2, fos. 28ff., 33ff., 128ff., 211ff. and 289ff. Sir William Wedderburn b. 1838; entered Indian civil service 1860; various posts in Bombay 1860–87; president of Indian national congress 1889 and 1910; M.P. 1893–1900; d. 1918.

183 Elgin to Hamilton 27 July 1897, Hamilton Correspondence, D 509/6, fos. 137ff.

184 See the evidence given in the summer of 1897 by Dadabhai Naoroji, Dinshaw Wacha, G. K. Gokhale, G. Subramania Iyer and S. N. Banerjee, Indian Expenditure Commission, vol. III, *Minutes of Evidence* (London, 1900).

185 *Ibid.* p. 155.

186 Elgin to Hamilton 27 Jan. 1898, Hamilton Correspondence, D 509/9, fos. 155ff.

187 To James Westland 17 Feb. 1898, Elgin Papers, Correspondence with persons in India, vol. 9, part 2, appendix no. 22.

188 For a detailed account of the Manipur crisis, see R. C. Majumdar, 'The Manipur Rebellion of 1891', *Bengal Past and Present* (January–June 1959), pp. 1–29. Also proceedings of a Court of Enquiry held to investigate the occurrences and narrative despatch to Secretary of State, Foreign Department Proceedings, October 1891, Secret—E, nos. 296–300.

189 See Lansdowne to Cross 25 Feb. 1891, Lansdowne Papers, series IX, vol. 3, part 2, no. 10.

190 To Col. Ardagh 30 March 1891, Lansdowne Papers, series VII, vol. 5, part 1, no. 304; also Lansdowne to Cross 15 April 1891, Lansdowne Papers, series IX, vol. 3, part 2, no. 20A.

191 Lansdowne to Cross 26 May 1891, Lansdowne Papers, series IX, vol. 3, part 2, no. 28.

192 See Cross to Lansdowne 19 and 26 June, and 12 Aug. 1891, Lansdowne Papers, series IX, vol. 3, part 1, nos. 26, 27 and 34.

193 To W. E. Neale, Commissioner Agra Division, Aug. 1892, Lansdowne Papers, series VII, vol. 8, part 2, no. 66.

194 Note of Lansdowne 31 May 1891, Home Department Public Proceedings, Oct. 1891, nos. 260–86; Cross to Lansdowne 17 July 1891, Lansdowne Papers, series IX, vol. 3, part 1, no. 30.

195 Report of November 1888, Home Department Public Proceedings Jan. 1890, nos. 318–23.

196 To Cross 6 May 1889, Lansdowne Papers, series IX, vol. 1, part 2, no. 25.

197 Sir John Edgar, Chief Secretary to Bengal Government to Home Secretary, Government of India 28 July 1891, Home Department Public Proceedings October 1891, nos. 260–86; Elliott to Lansdowne 27 July, and Lansdowne to Elliott 27 July and 1 Aug. 1891, Lansdowne Papers, series VII, vol. 6, part 1, no. 47A and part 2, nos. 29 and 41.

198 J. Wilson, editor *Indian Daily News*, to Ardagh 9 Aug., and Elliot to Lansdowne 17 and 23 Aug. 1891, Lansdowne Papers, series VII, vol. 6, part 1, nos. 73, 88 and 100.

199 Elliott to Lansdowne 28 Aug. 1891, Lansdowne Papers, series VII, vol. 6, part 1, no. 116.

200 Miller wrote to the *Times of India*. See Lansdowne to Miller 6 Sept. 1891, Lansdowne Papers, series VII, vol. 6, part 2, no. 83.

201 Ardagh to Wilson 1 Sept. 1891, Lansdowne Papers, series VII, vol. 6, part 2, no. 79.

202 Letter of 4 Sept. 1891, sent by Bengal Government 9 Sept., Home Department Public Proceedings Oct. 1891, nos. 260–86.

203 Lansdowne to Cross 15 Sept. 1891 and to Elliott 10 and 17 Sept. 1891, Lansdowne Papers, series IX, vol. 3, part 2, no. 46 and series VII, vol. 6, part 2, nos. 91 and 109.

204 Home Department circular to Provincial Governments, 31 May 1890, Home Department Judicial Proceedings Jan. 1893, nos. 272–428.

205 See letters of the Madras Government 29 Dec. 1890, the Bombay Government 19 Dec. 1890, the Bengal Government 22 June 1891, the North-West Provinces Government 2 Feb. 1891 and the Assam Government 14 Jan. 1891, Home Department Judicial Proceedings Aug. 1892, nos. 249–371.

206 See notes of C. J. Lyall, Home Secretary, 31 Oct. 1891, and of Lansdowne 31 Jan. and 9 June 1892, *ibid.*

207 Order in Council 30 June 1892, *ibid.*

208   C. J. Lyall to the Chief Secretary to the Bengal Government no. 1107 dated 25 Aug. 1892, *ibid.*

209   Home Department Judicial, Jan. 1893, Proceedings nos. 272–428.

210   He was later President of the Congress.

211   Elliott to Lansdowne 24 Nov., 1 and 5 Dec. 1892, Lansdowne Papers, series VII, vol. 8, part 1, nos. 386, 394 and 403.

212   See letter to Maharaja Sir J. M. Tagore 8 Dec. 1892, Lansdowne Papers, series VII, vol. 8, part 2, no. 290.

213   Lansdowne to Harris 12 Dec. 1892, and Harris to Lansdowne 19 Dec. 1892, and 25 and 26 Jan. 1893, Lansdowne Papers, series VII, vol. 8, part 2, no. 296, and part 1, no. 466, and vol. 9, part 1, nos. 78 and 82; also Home Department Judicial, Feb. 1893, Proceedings nos. 102–50.

214   11 Dec. 1892, Kimberley Papers, vol. E/13.

215   Telegrams nos. 20 and 36, 12 and 24 Dec. 1892, Kimberley Papers, vol. E/19.

216   To Kimberley 20 Dec. 1892, Kimberley Papers, vol. E/18*c*.

217   27 Dec. 1892, Lansdowne Papers, series VIII, vol. 4, part 2, no. 106. Only extracts of this letter were sent to Godley.

218   No. 32 of 1892 dated 21 Dec. 1892, Home Department Judicial Proceedings Jan. 1893, nos. 272–428.

219   See exchange of telegrams 12, 13, 14 and 16 Jan. 1893, Kimberley Papers, vol. E/19.

220   The *Indian Mirror* reported on 15 Jan. 1893 that there was reliable information from the India Office that the Government of India were being overruled.

221   To Kimberley 18 Jan. 1893, Private and Personal, Kimberley Papers, vol. E/18*c*.

222   See telegrams of Kimberley 16 Feb. 1893, Kimberley Papers, vol. E/19.

223   Home Department Judicial Proceeding March 1893, no. 9.

224   Chief Secretary to the Bengal Government to the Home Secretary, Government of India, no. 1350 J dated 5 March 1894, Home Department Judicial Proceedings Sept. 1894, nos. 129–64.

225   Sir David Barbour to Lansdowne 7 March 1893, Lansdowne Papers, series VII, vol. 9, part 1, no. 226A.

226   To Kimberley 3 May 1893, Lansdowne Papers, series IX, vol. 5, part 2, no. 28.

227   Kimberley to Lansdowne 25 May 1893, Lansdowne Papers, series IX, vol. 5, part 1, no. 29.

228   To Elgin 9 and 16 Feb. 1894, Elgin Papers, Correspondence with persons in England, vol. 1, part 1, nos. 5 and 7.

229   Elgin to Kimberley 14 and 20 Feb. 1894, Kimberley Papers, vol. E/18*e*, no numbers.

230   Private telegram to Kimberley 16 Feb. 1894, Kimberley Papers, vol. of telegrams, no numbers.

231   Godley to Babington Smith 16 Feb. 1894, Elgin Papers, Correspondence with persons in England, vol. 1, part 1, no. 7*a*; Gladstone to Kimberley 21 Feb. 1894, Kimberley Papers, vol. E/6*b*, no number;

Ripon to Kimberley, 22 Feb. 1894, Kimberley Papers, vol. E/17, no number.

232 Godley to Kimberley 22 Feb. 1894, Elgin Papers, Correspondence with persons in England, vol. 1, part 1, no. 8; Kimberley's private telegram to Elgin 27 Feb. 1894, Kimberley Papers, volume of telegrams, no number.

233 Elgin's private telegrams to Kimberley 5 and 6 March 1894, Kimberley Papers, volume of telegrams, no numbers.

234 Kimberley's private telegrams to Elgin 5 and 8 March 1894, Kimberley Papers, volume of telegrams, no numbers; Kimberley's letters to Elgin 2 and 9 March 1894, Elgin Papers, volume of letters from Kimberley, no numbers.

235 S. B. Saul, *Studies in British Overseas Trade 1870–1914* (Liverpool University Press, 1960), p. 189.

236 Fowler to Elgin 16 March 1894, Wolverhampton Papers, vol. 2, no number; Godley to Elgin 2 March 1894, Elgin Papers, Correspondence with persons in England, vol. 1, part 1, no. 12.

237 To Godley 21 March 1894, Elgin Papers, Correspondence with persons in England, vol. 1, part 2, no. 13; to Fowler 21 March 1894, Wolverhampton Papers, vol. 1, no number.

238 To Fowler 24 July 1894, Wolverhampton Papers, vol. 1, no number.

239 Fowler to Elgin 17 Aug. and 9 Nov. 1894, Wolverhampton Papers, vol. 2, no numbers.

240 Fowler to Elgin 30 Nov. 1894, Wolverhampton Papers, vol. 2, no number.

241 Fowler to Elgin 15 and 22 Feb. 1895, Wolverhampton Papers, vol. 2, no numbers.

242 See telegram from Secretary of State to the Government of India 11 Dec., telegram from the Government of India to Secretary of State 17 Dec., and telegram from Secretary of State to Viceroy 19 Dec. 1894, Finance and Commerce Department Proceedings Feb. 1895, Statistics and Commerce, nos. 60, 71 and 76.

243 Westland's note of 27 Nov. 1894, Finance and Commerce Department Feb. 1895, Statistics and Commerce, Proceedings nos. 59–140; communication of the Secretary Bombay Millowners' Association 7 Jan. 1896, Paragraph 71, Finance and Commerce Department July 1896, Separate Revenue, Proceedings nos. 740–929.

244 Godley to Elgin 22 Aug. 1895, Elgin Papers, Correspondence with persons in England, vol. 2, part 1, no. 107.

245 See his note Aug. 1895, Hamilton Correspondence, C 125/1, fos. 27 ff.

246 See despatch from Secretary of State no. 99 (Revenue) dated 5 Sept. 1895, and enclosures, Finance and Commerce Department July 1896, Separate Revenue, Proceedings nos. 740–929.

247 Elgin to Hamilton 16 Oct. 1895, Hamilton Correspondence, D 509/1, fos. 187 ff.

248 Output per operative was also declining. See E. H. Phelps Brown and S. J. Handfield Jones, *The Climacteric of the 1890's* (Oxford Economic Papers, 1952), p. 275.

249 See Hamilton to Elgin 31 Oct., 29 Nov. and 13 Dec. 1895, and note of 20 Dec. 1895, Hamilton Correspondence, C 125/1, fos. 79ff., 105 ff., 121ff., and 133ff. respectively.

250 22 Jan. 1896, Hamilton Correspondence, D 509/2, fo. 467.

251 Elgin to Hamilton 5 Feb. 1896, Hamilton Correspondence, D 509/2, fos. 469ff.

252 To Wenlock 16 Feb. 1896, Elgin Papers, Correspondence with persons in India, vol. 5, part 2, no. 123. Some members of his council were slightly less malleable. 'I do hope', wrote the Law Member, Sir Arthur Miller, to the Finance Member on 28 Jan. 1896, when it seemed likely that the Secretary of State would demand further concessions on points of detail, 'that they will not push us to the wall; personally I have so little to lose that a trifle would make me rebel, but I will not—I need hardly say—separate myself from the rest.' Finance and Commerce Department, July 1896, Separate and Revenue, Proceedings nos. 740–929. K.W.

253 To Elgin 31 Jan. 1896, Hamilton Correspondence, C 125/1, fos. 177ff.

254 *Import of Cottons into India (95% from Britain) in million yards*

	Grey	White	Coloured printed or dyed
1889–90—1893–4	1223	369	374
1899–1900—1903–4	1204	470	451

Saul, *op. cit.* p. 190.

255 *The Economic History of India in the Victorian Age* (London, 1906), p. 543.

256 Saul, *op. cit.* p. 198.

257 Note of 29 Jan. 1896, Finance and Commerce Department July 1896, Separate and Revenue, Proceedings nos. 740–929. K.W.

258 P. C. Ghosh, *The Development of the Indian National Congress 1892–1909* (Calcutta, 1960), p. 32.

259 See Proceedings 378–411B of the Finance and Commerce Department May 1896, Statistics and Commerce.

260 Curzon to St John Brodrick 23 Feb. and 10 March 1904, Curzon Papers, India Office Library, MSS Eur. F. 111, vol. 163, part 2, nos. 10 and 12.

261 See Reay's report of his conversation with Hume, letter to Lansdowne 15 Feb. 1890, Lansdowne Papers, series VII, vol. 3, part 1, no. 148.

262 Lansdowne to Cross 4 Aug. 1890, Lansdowne Papers, series IX, vol. 2, part 2, no. 35.

263 Cross to Lansdowne 12 Feb. 1891, Lansdowne Papers, series IX, vol. 3, part 1, no. 7.

264 See Lansdowne to Cross 22 April 1891, Lansdowne Papers, series IX, vol. 3, part 2, no. 22A.

265 Resolutions of the Dundee Chamber of Commerce 27 Dec. 1894, enclosed with despatch of the Secretary of State (Revenue) no. 18 dated 31 Jan. 1895, Home Department Judicial Proceedings April 1895, nos. 277–81.

266 Lansdowne to Cross 18 May 1892, Lansdowne Papers, series IX, vol. 4, part 2, no. 24.

267 To Cross 27 March and 2 April 1889, Lansdowne Papers, series IX, vol. I, part 2, nos. 19 and 20.

268 Lansdowne to Roberts 13 July 1890 and Roberts to Lansdowne 18 July 1890, Lansdowne Papers, series VII, vol. 4, part 2, no. 22 and part I, no. 54A.

269 To Lansdowne 17 Sept. 1890, Lansdowne Papers, series VII, vol. 4, part I, no. 195.

270 Cross to Lansdowne 6 March 1891, and Lansdowne to Salisbury 26 March and to Cross 8 April 1891, Lansdowne Papers, series IX, vol. 3, part I, no. 10; series VIII, vol. 3, part 2, no. 37; and series IX, vol. 3, part 2, no. 17.

271 Roberts to Lansdowne 20 April 1891, Lansdowne Papers, series VII, vol. 5, part I, no. 454.

272 Lansdowne to Durand 15 Sept. 1890 and to Cross 25 Feb. 1891, Lansdowne Papers, series VIII, vol. 2, part 2, no. 66 and series IX, vol. 3, part 2, no. 10; also Foreign Department, Jan. 1891, Secret F, Proceedings nos. 90–4.

273 In the summer of 1891, Russian troops arrived in the Pamir area, and their commander informed Captain Younghusband that he had been sent by the Governor-General of Turkistan to annex the Pamirs, Foreign Department, Aug. 1891, Secret F, Proceedings nos. 261–82.

274 See his proclamation, bonds taken from his subjects to be loyal during his absence, and letters to Salisbury and Gorst, Foreign Department, March 1892, Secret F, Proceedings nos. 72–98.

275 Lansdowne to Jowett I April, and to Cross 19 July 1892, Lansdowne Papers, series VIII, vol. 4, part 2, no. 31 and series IX, vol. 4, part 2, no. 33. Also Viceroy's letter to the Amir 23 July 1892, Foreign Department, Aug. 1892, Secret F, Proceeding no. 230.

276 Lansdowne to Godley 17 July 1892, Lansdowne Papers, series VIII, vol. 4, part 2, no. 56; despatch no. 155 dated 16 Aug. 1892, Foreign Department, Aug. 1892, Secret F, Proceeding no. 575; and Lansdowne to Kimberley 23 Aug. 1892, Kimberley Papers, vol. E/18c.

277 To Lansdowne 30 Nov. 1891, Lansdowne Papers, series VIII, vol. 3, part I, no. 133.

278 Kimberley to Lansdowne 26 Aug., I, 16 Sept. and 28 Oct. 1892, Lansdowne Papers, series IX, vol. 4, part I, nos. 36, 37, 40 and 49. Also Kimberley's despatch no. 42 dated 18 Nov. 1892, Foreign Department, April 1893, Secret F, Proceeding no. 70.

279 To Godley 6 Sept. and to Fitzpatrick 8 Sept. 1892, Lansdowne Papers, series VIII, vol. 4, part 2, no. 64, and series VII, vol. 8, part 2, no. 129.

280 B. 1850 son of Sir Henry Durand; joined Indian civil service 1873; served in foreign department 1874–85; foreign secretary 1885–94; mission to Kabul 1893; minister in Teheran 1894–1900; ambassador in Madrid 1900–3; ambassador in Washington 1903–5; d. 1924.

281 Agreements of 12 Nov. 1893. Aitchison, *Treaties, Engagements and Sanads*, XIII (Calcutta, 1933 edition), pp. 255–7.

282 Note of 13 Jan. 1894, Lansdowne Papers, series XIII, pp. 712ff.

283 To Elgin 26 Jan. 1894, Elgin Papers, Correspondence with persons in England, vol. 1, part 1, no. 4.

284 To Elgin 9 and 16 Feb. 1894, Elgin Papers, volume of letters from Kimberley, no numbers.

285 Elgin to Fowler 10 July 1894, Wolverhampton Papers, vol. 1, no number.

286 *Ibid.* 31 July 1894, Wolverhampton Papers, vol. 1, no number.

287 To Elgin 24 Aug. 1894 and 2 Jan. 1895, Wolverhampton Papers, vol. 2, no numbers.

288 Elgin to Fowler 20 Feb. and 13 March 1895, Wolverhampton Papers, vol. 3, no numbers.

289 See Reay to Elgin 22 March and Godley to Elgin 25 April 1895, Elgin Papers, Correspondence with persons in England, vol. 2, part 1, nos. 34 and 49.

290 Elgin to Fowler 10, 24 April and 8 May 1895, Wolverhampton Papers, vol. 3, no numbers; also Elgin to Rosebery 7 July 1895, Elgin Papers, Correspondence with persons in England, vol. 2, part 2, no. 51.

291 Curzon to Selborne 9 April 1900, Curzon Papers, vol. 181, part 2, no. 81.

292 Rosebery to Elgin June 1895, Elgin Papers, Correspondence with persons in England, vol. 2, part 1, no. 76.

293 See Godley to Elgin 25 April 1895, Elgin Papers, Correspondence with persons in England, vol. 2, part 1, no. 49.

294 See Elgin to Fowler 4 June 1895, Wolverhampton Papers, vol. 3, no number.

295 Brackenbury to Elgin 1 July 1895, Elgin Papers, Correspondence with persons in India, vol. 4, part 1, no. 1; Lansdowne to Elgin 22 July 1895, Elgin Papers, Correspondence with persons in England, vol. 2, part 1, no. 93; Hamilton to Elgin 2 Aug. 1895, Hamilton Correspondence, C 125/1, fos. 17ff.; Curzon to Sir Crawford Chamberlain 28 June 1902, Curzon Papers, vol. 182, part 2, no. 92.

296 Hamilton to Elgin 9 Aug. 1895, Hamilton Correspondence, C 125/1, fo. 21.

297 Elgin to Hamilton 28 Oct. 1897, Hamilton Correspondence, D 509/7, fos. 320ff., and 2 Dec. 1897, Hamilton Correspondence, D 509/8, fos. 145ff.

298 Hamilton to Elgin 19 Sept. 1895, Hamilton Correspondence, C 125/1, fo. 49.

299 Hamilton to Elgin 2 Aug. 1895, Hamilton Correspondence, C 125/1, fos. 17ff.

300 See above p. 134.

301 See Hamilton to Elgin, 14, 20 Aug. and 8 Oct. 1896, Hamilton Correspondence, C 125/1, fos. 347ff., 353ff., and 393ff. respectively; and 19 March 1897, Hamilton Correspondence, C 125/2, fos. 107ff.

302 Elgin to Hamilton 6 July 1897, Hamilton Correspondence, D 509/6, fos. 29ff.

303 C. C. Davies, *The Problem of the North-West Frontier* (Cambridge, 1932), pp. 91–8 and 164–6.
304 Elgin to Hamilton 10 Aug. 1897, Hamilton Correspondence, D 509/6, fos. 227 ff.
305 Davies, *op. cit.* p. 98.
306 Elgin to Col. Wylie, Officiating Agent to the Governor-General Baluchistan 3 June 1898, Elgin Papers, Correspondence with persons in India, vol. 9, part 2, no. 292.
307 To Lansdowne 12 July and 23 Aug. 1890, Lansdowne Papers, series VII, vol. 4, part 1, nos. 40A and 131A.
308 R. L. Greaves, *Persia and the Defence of India 1884–1892* (London, 1959), chapters VIII and XI.
309 A. P. Thornton, 'British Policy in Persia, 1858–90', part III, *English Historical Review*, LXX, 67–8.
310 Greaves, *op. cit.* p. 181–2.
311 Salisbury to Lansdowne 21 Oct. 1891, Lansdowne Papers, series VIII, vol. 3, part 1, no. 115. Part of it cited in Greaves, *op. cit.* p. 204–5.
312 Lansdowne to Salisbury 16 Dec. 1891, Lansdowne Papers, series VIII, vol. 3, part 2, no. 153.
313 Lascelles, Minister in Teheran, to Lansdowne 2 March 1893, Lansdowne Papers, series IX, vol. 9, part 1, no. 214A.

CHAPTER 5, pp. 222–298

1 To Elgin 24 Aug. 1898, Hamilton Correspondence, C 125/3, fo. 417.
2 Lord Vansittart, *The Mist Procession* (London, 1958), p. 30. Of the many assessments of Curzon that have been written, those of Vansittart and of Sir Winston Churchill (in his essay in *Great Contemporaries*) come closest to grasping the essence of the man.
3 See letter cited in L. Mosley, *Curzon the End of an Epoch* (London, 1960), p. 60.
4 10 April 1901, Ampthill Papers, India Office Library, MSS Eur. E. 233, vol. 15. Arthur Russell, second baron Ampthill, b. 1869, second son of Lord Odo Russell, first baron Ampthill; private secretary to Joseph Chamberlain 1897; governor of Madras 1900–6; acting viceroy 1904; d. 1935.
5 Curzon to Arthur Hardinge 11 June 1902, Curzon Papers, vol. 182, part 2, no. 86.
6 Curzon to Ibbetson 26 April 1904, Curzon Papers, vol. 209, part 2, no. 122*a*.
7 Curzon to Younghusband 19 Sept. 1901, Curzon Papers, vol. 182, part 2, no. 23.
8 Curzon to Balfour 31 March 1901, Curzon Papers, vol. 181, part 2, no. 211.
9 *Ibid.*
10 Curzon to John Morley 17 June 1900, Curzon Papers, vol. 181, part 2, no. 119.

11 Letter written from London 19 Oct. 1904, Ampthill Papers, vol. 37, no. 65, fos. 144 ff.

12 D. Sommer, *Haldane of Cloan* (London, 1960), p. 400.

13 16 Sept. 1903, Hamilton Correspondence, C.126/5, fo. 329.

14 To Hamilton 9 April 1902, Hamilton Correspondence, D 510/10, fos. 383 ff.

15 13 Jan. 1903, Hamilton Correspondence, D 510/13, fos. 29 ff.

16 See Curzon to Godley 13 Dec. 1900, Curzon Papers, vol. 159, part 2, no. 76.

17 To Hamilton 25 Jan. 1900, Hamilton Correspondence, D 510/4, fos. 73 ff.

18 To Hamilton 29 Aug. 1900, Hamilton Correspondence, D 510/5, fos. 361 ff.

19 *Ibid.* 22 April 1901, Hamilton Correspondence, D 510/8, fos. 3 ff.

20 Speech on the Budget, 25 March 1903, T. Raleigh ed. *Lord Curzon in India, Being a Selection from his Speeches as Viceroy* (London, 1906), p. 407.

21 *Ibid.* pp. 407–8.

22 See, for example, the chapter on the Anglo-Russian Question in his book *Russia in Central Asia*, published in 1889.

23 Minute 28 Oct. 1901, Foreign Department Proceedings Secret E, Nov. 1901, no. 61.

24 Curzon to Hamilton 4 Jan. 1900, Hamilton Correspondence, D 510/4, fos. 3 ff.

25 Curzon to Hamilton 15 Oct. 1902, Hamilton Correspondence, D 510/12, fos. 97 ff.

26 Curzon to Hamilton 8 Jan. 1903, Hamilton Correspondence, D 510/13, fos. 1 ff.

27 Indeed, Hamilton wrote at the commencement of the viceroyalty that he looked forward to the day when the frontiers of Russia and Britain were conterminous, letter to Curzon 16 Feb. 1900, Hamilton Correspondence, C 216/2, fos. 47 and 48. But Salisbury agreed with the Viceroy's assessment of Russian ambitions. He thought that when her Siberian railway was ready, she would want to be mistress of the greater part of China; and if Afghanistan were unprotected she could force Britain to give way in China by advancing upon India. 'She won't try to conquer it. It will be enough for her if she can shatter our Government and reduce India to anarchy. These things will not concern me—but my successor of I know not what degree.' Salisbury to Lord Northcote 8 June 1900, cited in Greaves, *op. cit.* pp. 16–17.

28 26 April 1899, Hamilton Correspondence, D 510/1, fos. 341 ff.

29 The relevant paragraphs have been published in Gooch and Temperley, *British Documents on the Origins of the War, 1898–1914* (London, 1929), IV, 356–63.

30 Curzon had suggested this even in 1889: 'There is no need to speak of a territorial partition of Persia, because I imagine that neither Power desires such an issue or would welcome so serious an increase to its burdens. A partition of control and influence in Persia is a different thing, and with a decrepit people and an expiring regime, is inevitable in the future'

(*Russia in Central Asia*, p. 379). The scheme was examined in great detail three years later, in *Persia and the Persian Question*. But by 1899 Curzon had become doubtful of its success. R. Kumar, 'Curzon and the Anglo-Russian Negotiations over Persia', *Indian Historical Records Commission Proceedings* XXXVI, part 2, p. 25.

31 Minute accompanying despatch of 21 Sept. 1899.

32 To Hamilton 14 Dec. 1899 and 4 Jan. 1900, Hamilton Correspondence, D 510/3, fos. 329ff., and D 510/4, fos. 3ff.

33 Curzon to Godley 15 March 1900, Curzon Papers, vol. 159, part 2, no. 13.

34 To Hamilton 1 Feb. 1900, Hamilton Correspondence, D 510/4, fos. 85ff.

35 *Ibid.* 8 Feb. 1900, Hamilton Correspondence, D 510/4, fos. 101ff.

36 See Hamilton's despatch 6 July 1900, Gooch and Temperley, *op. cit.* vol. IV, pp. 363–5; Salisbury to Curzon Aug. 1900, Curzon Papers, vol. 159, part 1, no. 59.

37 'I do not see how ultimately we can prevent Russia from getting into the Persian Gulf.' Hamilton to Curzon 23 Nov. 1899, Hamilton Correspondence, C 126/1, fos. 409ff. Salisbury and Goschen were said to be of the same view, *ibid.* 14 Dec. 1899, Hamilton Correspondence, C 126/1, fos. 435ff. 'I think our trouble with Persia—setting aside questions of manner and personal antipathy—arises from a fundamental and immovable cause. Other nations can lend money: and we cannot. The House of Commons, which never would guarantee the debt of India, would positively refuse any advance to an impecunious Oriental Ally. Other nations will give it. It is hopeless to struggle against that disadvantage. The real friend is the friend from whom one can borrow.' Salisbury to Currie 8 June 1900, cited in J. A. S. Grenville, *Lord Salisbury and Foreign Policy* (London, 1964), pp. 300–1.

38 See Curzon to Sir Clinton Dawkins 12 June 1900, Curzon Papers, vol. 181, part 2, no. 117.

39 Curzon to Lansdowne 5 April and 15 June 1901, Curzon Papers, vol. 160, part 2, nos. 25 and 40.

40 Lansdowne to Curzon 16 Feb. 1902, Curzon Papers, vol. 161, part 1, no. 17.

41 Gooch and Temperley, *op. cit.* vol. IV, pp. 369–71.

42 Hansard, 4th Series, vol. 121, p. 1348.

43 To Hamilton 17 June 1903, Hamilton Correspondence, D 510/13, fos. 115ff.

44 Curzon to Brodrick 16 Feb. 1905, Curzon Papers, vol. 164, part 2, no. 19.

45 Curzon to Morley 28 Dec. 1905, Morley Papers, India Office Library, MSS Eur. D 555. Curzon was right to the extent that Balfour was a keen participant in the proceedings of this Committee, and the scope of its work was not rigidly defined. It was an instrument of the Prime Minister and not a Committee of the Cabinet. F. A. Johnson, *Defence by Committee* (Oxford, 1960), pp. 74–5; J. Ehrman, *Cabinet Government and War* (Cambridge, 1958), pp. 29–30.

46 To Hamilton 26 Nov. 1899, Hamilton Correspondence, D 510/3, fos. 251 ff.

47 Amir's letter 9 Jan. 1899 and Viceroy's reply 15 Feb. 1899, Foreign Department Proceedings Secret F, April 1899, nos. 1–5; Amir's letter 4 April 1899, Foreign Department Proceedings Secret F, May 1899, nos. 334–9.

48 Foreign Department Secret F, May 1900, Proceedings 145–74.

49 Foreign Department Secret F, May 1900, Proceedings 141–4.

50 Viceroy's telegram 19 Feb. 1900 and despatch of Government of India 17 May 1900, Foreign Department Secret F, May 1900, Proceedings 145–74; Curzon to Lyall 15 March 1900, Curzon Papers, vol. 181, part 2, no. 73.

51 Foreign Department Secret F, Jan. 1902, Proceeding 274.

52 British Ambassador in St Petersburg to Lansdowne 3 Feb. 1902, Foreign Department Secret F, July 1902, Proceeding 80.

53 Foreign Department Secret F, Sept. 1902, Proceedings 25–40.

54 To Hamilton 1 Oct. 1902, Hamilton Correspondence D 510/12, fos. 67 ff.

55 *Novoe Vremya*, 19 Dec. 1902.

56 Memorandum 5 Feb. 1903, Foreign Department Secret F, Aug. 1903, Proceeding 103, enclosure.

57 Telegrams 23 March and 1 April 1903, Foreign Department Secret F, Aug. 1903, Proceedings 104 and 107.

58 Letter to Viceroy 27 June 1903, Foreign Department Secret F, Aug. 1903, Proceeding 156.

59 Godley to Curzon 23 April 1903, Curzon Papers, vol. 162, part 1, no. 23; Hamilton to Kitchener 5 June 1903, Kitchener Papers, Public Record Office; Hamilton to Curzon 5 June 1903, Hamilton Correspondence, C 126/5, fos. 196 ff.

60 See Lansdowne to Benckendorff, the Russian Ambassador, 17 Feb. 1905 and to Sir C. Hardinge, 8 March 1905, Gooch and Temperley, *op. cit.* IV, 520–1.

61 Curzon to Lord George Hamilton 24 May 1899, Hamilton Correspondence, D 510/1, fos. 405 ff. See also P. Fleming, *Bayonets to Lhasa* (London, 1961), p. 39.

62 'The acting Russian Ambassador during the Great War told me that he was a Secretary in the Russian Foreign Office during my Mission to Tibet and could assure me that the Russian Government were in no kind of communication with the Dalai Lama. What, he said, did happen was that the Dalai Lama's tutor, Dorjieff, through Rasputin, got in personal touch with the Tsar and Tsarina. There was an interchange of presents between the Tsar and the Dalai Lama. The Tsar seemed to acknowledge some kind of spiritual guidance from the Dalai Lama; and the latter thought he was under the political protection of the Tsar.' Sir Francis Younghusband to the Marquis of Zetland 21 April 1939, cited in Fleming, *op. cit.* p. 43. Sir Francis Younghusband b. 1863; service in Indian army from 1882; explorations in the Himalayas and China 1885–91; joined Indian foreign department 1889; political agent in Hunza and Chitral

1891–4; led mission to Tibet 1903–4; Resident in Kashmir 1906–9; d. 1942.

63 To Hamilton, 11 June 1901, Hamilton Correspondence, D 510/8, fos. 101 ff.

64 To Curzon 11 July 1901, Hamilton Correspondence, C126/3, fos. 305 ff.

65 Note of the India Office to Foreign Office 25 July 1901, Foreign Department Proceedings Secret E, March 1902, nos. 1–77.

66 Hamilton to Curzon, 29 Nov. 1901, Hamilton Correspondence, C 126/3, fos. 487 ff.

67 A. Lamb, *Britain and Chinese Central Asia* (London, 1961), pp. 268–77.

68 To Hamilton 20 Aug. 1902, Hamilton Correspondence, D 510/11, fos. 399 ff.

69 Telegram from British Minister in Peking to Foreign Secretary 8 Sept. 1902, Foreign Department Secret E, Feb. 1903, Proceeding 40, enclosure.

70 Telegram from British Chargé d'Affaires in Peking to Viceroy 6 Dec. 1902, Foreign Department Secret E, Feb. 1903, Proceeding 62.

71 Despatch 4C of 1903, Foreign Department Proceeding Secret E, Feb. 1903, no. 82.

72 Hamilton to Curzon 20 Feb. 1903, Hamilton Correspondence, C 126/5, fos. 48 ff.

73 Foreign Office to British Ambassador in St Petersburg 8 April 1903, Foreign Department Secret E, July 1903, Proceedings 38–95.

74 See A. Lamb, 'Some Notes on Russian Intrigue in Tibet', *Journal of the Royal Central Asian Society*, XLVI (1959), 58 ff.

75 12 April 1903, cited in G. Monger, *The End of Isolation* (London, 1963), p. 116.

76 Hamilton to Curzon 15 April 1903, Hamilton Correspondence, C 126/5, fos. 122 ff.

77 Telegram from Secretary of State 29 April 1903, Foreign Department Proceedings Secret E, July 1903, nos. 38–95.

78 To Hamilton 17 June 1903, Hamilton Correspondence, D 510/14, fos. 115 ff. But, as Mr Lamb points out, once the Cabinet had permitted the crossing of the border, Curzon was in a strong position; if the talks failed, the only direction in which the Mission could possibly move was forward (*op. cit.* p. 290).

79 Curzon to Younghusband 24 Sept. 1903, Curzon Papers, vol. 208, part 2, no. 83.

80 To Hamilton 12 Aug. 1903, Hamilton Correspondence, D 510/14, fos. 241 ff.

81 Note of Viceroy's interview with Maharaja of Nepal 31 Dec. 1902, Foreign Department Proceeding Secret E, Feb. 1903, no. 79; despatch of 3 Nov. 1903; Curzon to Hamilton 1 Jan. 1903, Hamilton Correspondence, D 510/12, fos. 508 ff.

82 Telegram from Secretary of State 1 Oct. 1903, Foreign Department Proceedings Secret E, Nov. 1903, nos. 159–234.

83 Accounts of Lansdowne's interviews with Russian Ambassador 17

Nov. and Chinese Minister 18 Nov. 1903. Foreign Department Secret E, Feb. 1904, Proceedings 244 enclosure 3 and 245 enclosure 3.

84 Letter and telegram to Curzon 8 Oct. 1903, Curzon Papers, vol. 208, part 1, nos. 115 and 117.

85 Telegram from Secretary of State 12 May 1904, Foreign Department Proceeding Secret E, July 1904, no. 310.

86 See Lansdowne to Sir C. Hardinge 2 June 1904, *Parl. Papers*, 1905, Tibet, no. III, no. 43.

87 Curzon to Brodrick 1 Dec. 1903, Curzon Papers, vol. 162, part 2, no. 90.

88 16 June 1904, cited in Fleming, *op. cit.* pp. 196–7.

89 13 July 1904, Ampthill Papers, vol. 37, fos. 103 ff. St John Brodrick first earl of Midleton b. 1856; M.P. 1880–1906; financial secretary to the War Office 1886–92; under-secretary for war 1895–8; under-secretary for foreign affairs 1898–1900; secretary for war 1900–3; secretary for India 1903–5; d. 1942.

90 Curzon to Ampthill 1 July 1904, Ampthill Papers, vol. 37, fos. 54 ff. Indeed, such was the Cabinet's ignorance of the whole position that the Prime Minister, Balfour, could not spell Lhasa correctly, despite three different efforts. See Fleming, *op. cit.* p. 211 note.

91 Brodrick to Ampthill 1 July 1904, Ampthill Papers, vol. 37, fos. 50 ff.; telegram of Secretary of State 6 July 1904.

92 To Ampthill 4 Aug. 1904, Ampthill Papers, vol. 37, fos. 93 ff.

93 Curzon to Ampthill 8 Jan. 1905, Ampthill Papers, vol. 18.

94 See above, p. 377, note. 62.

95 Brodrick to Ampthill 1 July 1904, Ampthill Papers, vol. 37, fos. 50 ff.

96 Telegram to Secretary of State 10 July 1905, Foreign Office Confidential Print on Tibet 1905, no. 49 enclosure.

97 To Hamilton 29 Jan. 1903, Hamilton Correspondence, D 510/13, fos. 69 ff.

98 However, Curzon did not support Salisbury's favourite scheme for a railway from Quetta to Seistan.

99 To Hamilton 22 May 1901, Hamilton Correspondence, D 510/8, fos. 73 ff.

100 *Ibid.* 17 June 1903, D 510/14, fos. 115 ff.

101 Hamilton to Curzon, 9 and 23 July 1903, Hamilton Correspondence, C 126/5, fos. 245 ff. and 260 ff. In fact Curzon met Sir Arthur Hardinge and blamed him for being too courteous and diplomatic with the Persians. See Hardinge to Lansdowne, Feb. 1904. Newton, *Lansdowne*, p. 243.

102 Brodrick to Curzon 17 Dec. 1903, Curzon Papers, vol. 162, part 1, no. 89.

103 'Curzon has perhaps a greater knowledge of the Afghan problem than anyone alive.' Brodrick to Ampthill 20 Oct. 1904, Ampthill Papers, vol. 37, fos. 146 ff.

104 Amir's letter 4 April 1899, Foreign Department Proceedings Secret F, May 1899, nos. 334–9.

105 To Hamilton 19 April 1899, Hamilton Correspondence, D 510/1, fos. 307ff. 'Never a week passes, but in some form or other, I have cause to regret that unfortunate agreement.' *Ibid.* 31 May 1899, Hamilton Correspondence, D 510/1, fos. 427ff.

106 Letter of 27 July 1899, Foreign Department Proceedings Secret F, Aug. 1899, nos. 76–83.

107 Hamilton to Curzon 15 Nov. 1899, Hamilton Correspondence, C 126/1, fo. 402.

108 Curzon to Hamilton 22 Nov. 1899, Hamilton Correspondence, D 510/3, fos. 205ff.

109 Curzon to Hamilton 21 Dec. 1899, Hamilton Correspondence, D 510/3, fos. 375ff.

110 Hamilton to Curzon 16 Feb. and 23 March 1900, Hamilton Correspondence, C 126/2, fos. 47–8 and 97ff.

111 Curzon to Hamilton 2 May 1900, Hamilton Correspondence, D 510/5, fos. 55ff.

112 Curzon to Hamilton 9 and 16 Oct. 1901, Hamilton Correspondence, D 510/9, fos. 57ff. and 67ff.

113 Hamilton to Curzon 7 Nov. 1901, Hamilton Correspondence, C 126/3, fos. 459ff.

114 Viceroy's letters to the Amir 7 Feb. and 6 June 1902, Foreign Department Secret F, June 1902, Proceedings 95–103.

115 Curzon to Lansdowne 16 March 1902, Curzon Papers, vol. 161, part 2, no. 22.

116 Amir to the Viceroy 9 March 1902, Foreign Department Proceedings Secret F, June 1902, nos. 95–103 and 27 Nov. 1902, Foreign Department Proceedings Secret F, Jan. 1903, nos. 1–35.

117 Curzon to Hamilton 3 Sept. 1902, Hamilton Correspondence, D 510/11, fos. 415ff.

118 *Ibid.* 27 Nov. 1902, Hamilton Correspondence, D 510/2, fos. 307ff.

119 See Hamilton to Curzon 9 Jan., 4, 11 Dec. and 19 Dec. 1902, Hamilton Correspondence, C 126/4, fos. 13, 439, 445ff., and 451ff.; also telegram of the Secretary of State 19 Dec. 1902, Foreign Department Secret F, Jan. 1903, Proceedings 1–35.

120 J. Chamberlain to Austen Chamberlain 9 Jan. 1903, cited in Monger, *op. cit.* p. 91.

121 Curzon to Lyall 9 April 1903, Curzon Papers, vol. 182, part 2, no. 178.

122 Hamilton to Curzon 9 July and 15 Sept. 1903, Hamilton Correspondence, C 126/5, fos. 245ff. and 319ff.

123 Curzon to Brodrick 21 and 28 Oct. 1903, Curzon Papers, vol. 162, part 2, nos. 78 and 81.

124 See correspondence between the Viceroy and the Amir, Foreign Department Proceedings Secret F, Feb. 1904, nos. 23–32, and May 1904, no. 33.

125 Curzon to Brodrick 7 Jan., 17, 31 March and 5 April 1904, Curzon Papers, vol. 163, part 2, nos. 1, 13, 17 and 18.

126 Curzon arrived in London in April 1904 and had frequent meetings with the Cabinet on this subject.

127 The message was given to H. R. C. Dobbs, a British official on a visit to Kabul.

128 Foreign Department Secret F, Oct. 1904, Proceeding 238.

129 B. 1856; joined Indian civil service 1876; service in the Punjab; foreign secretary to the Government of India 1903–8; led mission to Kabul 1904; lieutenant-governor of the Punjab 1908–13; d. 1946.

130 Minute by Kitchener 7 Oct. 1904, Foreign Department Secret F, Oct. 1904, Proceeding 271; Minute by Ampthill 18 Oct. and telegram to Secretary of State 21 Oct. 1904, Foreign Department Secret F, Jan. 1905, Proceedings 43 and 45.

131 Despatch of Secretary of State enclosing aide-memoire for Dane 21 Oct. 1904, Foreign Department Secret F, Jan. 1905, Proceeding 74 and enclosure.

132 Memoranda of the Amir 18 Dec. 1904, and 1 Jan. 1905, Foreign Department Secret F, May 1905, Proceedings 1–141.

133 Memorandum of Dane 22 Dec. 1904, Foreign Department Secret F, May 1905, Proceedings 1–141.

134 Telegram of Foreign Secretary 16 Jan. 1905, Foreign Department Secret F, May 1905, Proceedings 1–141.

135 Curzon to Barnes 8 April 1904, Curzon Papers, vol. 209, part 2, no. 101. Sir Hugh Barnes b. 1853; joined Indian civil service 1874; joined foreign department 1879; foreign secretary to the government of India 1900–3; lieutenant-governor of Burma 1903–5; member of India Council 1905–13; d. 1940.

136 Curzon to Ampthill 8 Jan. 1905, Curzon Papers, vol. 210, part 2, no. 33.

137 Amir's letter to Dane 31 Jan. 1905, Foreign Department Secret F, May 1905, Proceedings 1–141.

138 Telegrams of Secretary of State 3 and 21 Feb. 1905, Foreign Department Secret F, May 1905, Proceedings 1–141; Brodrick to Curzon 10 and 17 Feb. 1905, Curzon Papers, vol. 164, part 1, nos. 20 and 22.

139 Minute of the Viceroy 3 Feb. 1905, Foreign Department Secret F, May 1905, Proceedings 1–141.

140 Balfour to the King 16 Feb. 1905, B. E. C. Dugdale, *Arthur James Balfour* (London, 1936), vol. 1, pp. 402–3; Curzon to Brodrick 26 Jan., 2, 9 and 16 Feb. 1905, Curzon Papers, vol. 164, part 2, nos. 13, 15, 17 and 19; telegrams of Viceroy 10 and 27 Feb. 1905, Foreign Department Secret F, May 1905, Proceedings 1–141.

141 2 April 1905, Ampthill Papers, vol. 18.

142 To Hamilton 11 June 1901, Hamilton Correspondence, D 510/8, fos. 101 ff.

143 To Hamilton 26 Dec. 1901, Hamilton Correspondence, D 510/9, fos. 371 ff.

144 To Hamilton 12 March 1903, Hamilton Correspondence, D 510/13, fos. 161 ff.

145 To Hamilton 4 June 1903, Hamilton Correspondence, D 510/14, fos. 65 ff.

146 Hamilton to Curzon 28 May 1903, Hamilton Correspondence, C 126/5, fos. 183 ff.

147 For a vivid description of the Tibetan expedition, see Fleming, *Bayonets to Lhasa.*

148 'I am afraid that Lord Curzon is right, that Home Government have to be treated like a pack of children.' Younghusband to his father Feb. 1904, cited in Fleming, *op. cit.* p. 181.

149 Despatch of Government of India 30 June 1904, and Secretary of State's telegram in reply to summary 6 July 1904.

150 See notes 12 Aug. 1904, Foreign Department Proceedings Secret E, Feb. 1905, nos. 578–726.

151 Brodrick thought that if he had written directly to Younghusband the latter might have appreciated that the Cabinet was in earnest on this issue; but for fear of offending Curzon Brodrick refrained from communicating direct with the Viceroy's subordinates. See Brodrick to Curzon 24 Feb. 1905, Curzon Papers, vol. 164, part 1, no. 24.

152 Balfour to Curzon 4 Oct. 1904. Fleming, *op. cit.* p. 272.

153 *Summary of the Administration of Lord Curzon of Kedleston in the Home Department* (Simla, 1905), p. 1.

154 30 Sept. 1905, Raleigh, *op. cit.* p. 564.

155 To Hamilton 21 May 1902, Hamilton Correspondence, D 510/11, fos. 181 ff.

156 'It was very interesting seeing the Council. I fancy from what I saw and have heard that nobody says much against the Viceroy. He does not so much invite discussion as lay down the law and almost defiantly ask if anyone has any objection. If anyone *has* he is promptly squashed.' Younghusband after attending a meeting of the council, cited in Fleming, *op. cit.* pp. 89–90. Lord Hailey, who was in Curzon's time a junior undersecretary in the government of India, has told the author that Curzon had no manners at all, and carried his council not by the strength of his arguments but by the force of his character.

157 Curzon to Lansdowne 16 March 1902, Curzon Papers, vol. 161, part 2, no. 22.

158 To Curzon 28 April 1900, Curzon Papers, vol. 159, part 1, no. 30.

159 To Hamilton 5 April 1899, Hamilton Correspondence, D 510/1, fos. 241 ff.

160 O. Caroe, *The Pathans* (London, 1958), pp. 419–20.

161 To Morley 24 Dec. 1905, Morley Papers.

162 Curzon to Hamilton 8 April 1903, Hamilton Correspondence, D 510/13, fos. 283 ff.

163 Cf. 'Nothing in this wonderful land, which has fired the impulses and drained the strength of the best years of my life, has appealed to me more than the privilege of co-operation with the Chiefs of India—men sprung from ancient lineage, endowed with no ordinary powers and responsibilities, and possessing nobility of character as well as of birth. It seemed to me from the start that one of the proudest objects which the

representative of the Sovereign in India could set before himself would be
to draw these rulers to his side, to win their friendship, to learn their
opinions and needs, and to share with them the burden of rule.' Farewell
speech at Indore, 4 Nov. 1905, Raleigh, *op. cit.* pp. 236–7.

164 To Hamilton 16 Dec. 1901, Hamilton Correspondence, D 510/9,
fos. 309ff.

165 To Curzon 15 Nov. 1899 and 3 Jan. 1901, Hamilton Correspondence, C 126/1, fos. 400ff. and C 126/3, fos. 1ff.

166 To Hamilton 7 Dec. 1899 and 18 Sept. 1901, Hamilton Correspondence, D 510/3, fos. 303ff. and D 510/9, fos. 13ff.

167 Hamilton to Curzon 6 Nov. 1902, Hamilton Correspondence,
C 126/4, fos. 400ff.

168 Curzon to Hamilton 13 Nov. 1902, Hamilton Correspondence,
D 510/12, fos. 229ff.

169 To Hamilton 26 Oct. 1902, Hamilton Correspondence, D 510/12,
fos. 121ff.

170 Speech of 25 March 1903, Raleigh, *op. cit.* p. 308.

171 To Hamilton 19 March 1903, Hamilton Correspondence, D 510/13,
fos. 173ff.

172 To Hamilton 13 Jan. 1903, Hamilton Correspondence, D 510/13,
fos. 29ff.

173 Speech at Gwalior, 29 Nov. 1899, Raleigh, *op. cit.* p. 218.

174 Curzon to Barnes 16 June 1903, Curzon Papers, vol. 207, part 2,
no. 102.

175 See letter of the Resident to the Foreign Secretary 18 April 1902,
Foreign Department Proceeding Secret I, Nov. 1902, no. 24.

176 B. 1848; joined Indian civil service 1871; held various posts in
Bengal; resigned 1897; president of Indian national congress 1899;
minister at Baroda 1904–7 and chief minister 1909; d. 1909.

177 Curzon to Sir Arthur Havelock, Governor of Madras, 14 July 1900,
Curzon Papers, vol. 202, part 2, no. 11.

178 Curzon to Ampthill 5 Oct. 1903, Curzon Papers, vol. 208, no. 90.

179 To Curzon 8 Aug. 1900, Hamilton Correspondence, C 126/2, fos.
277ff.

180 Letter of E. K. Campbell, F.R.C.S. *The Times* 28 Aug. 1900;
Hamilton to Curzon 29 Aug. 1900, Hamilton Correspondence, C 126/2,
fos. 307ff.

181 Curzon to Hamilton 1 April 1901, Hamilton Correspondence,
D 510/7, fos. 249ff.

182 Gaekwar to First Assistant to the Resident in charge at Baroda
28 May 1902, Foreign Department Secret I, Nov. 1902, Proceeding 33,
enclosure 3.

183 Foreign Department Secret I, Nov. 1902, Proceedings 34–9.

184 Curzon to Hamilton 1 April 1901, 4 June 1902 and 12 March 1903,
Hamilton Correspondence, D 510/7, fos. 249ff.; D 510/11, fos. 229ff.;
and D 510/13, fos. 161ff.

185 Minute, 29 March 1905, Foreign Department Proceedings Secret
I, May 1905, nos. 25–48.

186 Curzon to Hamilton 25 Oct. 1899, Hamilton Correspondence, D 510/3, fos. 87ff.

187 Curzon to Hamilton 28 Dec. 1899, Hamilton Correspondence, D 510/3, fos. 405ff.

188 Curzon to Hamilton 4 Jan. 1900, Hamilton Correspondence, D 510/4, fos. 3ff.

189 Curzon to Hamilton 5 Nov. 1901, Hamilton Correspondence, D 510/9, fos. 97.

190 Resident at Hyderabad to Curzon 2 March 1902, Curzon Papers, vol. 205, part 1, no. 83.

191 *Ibid.* 21 March 1902, Curzon Papers, vol. 205, part 1, no. 124.

192 Viceroy's note of interview on 30 March 1902, Foreign Department Secret I, Dec. 1902, Proceedings 10–18. There are no papers regarding this transaction extant in the Hyderabad archives. The story was current in India that a report reached the Nizam that one of his ministers had censured his role in the Berars transaction. The Nizam had the minister tied to a bed and thrashed the air round him with a riding-whip. 'Now, minister, can you prevent me from beating you?' 'Please, Your Exalted Highness, no.' 'Ha. Now you know what is meant by voluntarily signing a perpetual lease at the request of Lord Curzon.' C. B. Fry, *Life worth Living* (London, 1939), p. 313.

193 Curzon to Dawkins 2 July 1902, Curzon Papers, vol. 182, part 2, no. 94.

194 Curzon to Hamilton 2 Aug. 1899, Hamilton Correspondence, D 510/2, fos. 221ff.

195 Speech 19 Oct. 1900, Raleigh, *op. cit.* pp. 381ff.

196 *Famines and Land Assessments in India* (London, 1900).

197 Hamilton to Curzon 1 Feb. and 18 April 1900, Hamilton Correspondence, C 126/2, fos. 37ff. and 131ff.

198 16 Jan. 1902.

199 Curzon to Hamilton 7 Aug. 1901, Hamilton Correspondence, D 510/8, fos. 287ff.

200 *Ibid.* 30 Oct. 1901, D 510/9, fos. 89ff.

201 Curzon to Brodrick 15 Nov. 1903, Curzon Papers, vol. 162, part 2, no. 87. Gandhi was during these years in South Africa and appreciated Curzon's efforts. He wrote of Curzon in May 1901 as 'the strong and sympathetic Viceroy', and this letter was forwarded by the government of India to the home government (*The Collected Works of Mahatma Gandhi*, vol. III, Delhi, 1960, p. 189). In 1902 Gandhi expressed a desire to wait in deputation on Curzon but the Viceroy thought that if he received Gandhi it might be resented as undue pressure. See Curzon to M. C. Turner 21 Jan. 1902, Curzon Papers, vol. 205, part 2, no. 13. So unfortunately Curzon and Gandhi never met. On 20 May 1905 Gandhi wrote an editorial in *Indian Opinion* appreciative of Curzon's 'watchful guardianship' (*Collected Works*, vol. IV, Delhi, 1960, pp. 439–40).

202 W. R. Lawrence, Private Secretary to Viceroy, to Sir Ernest Cassel 6 March 1902, Curzon Papers, vol. 182, part 2, no. 54.

203 Curzon to Hamilton 26 Nov. 1899, Hamilton Correspondence, D 510/3, fos. 251 ff.

204 *Ibid.* 20 Dec. 1900, D 510/6, fos. 433 ff.

205 *Ibid.* 23 April 1902, D 510/10, fos. 449 ff.

206 B. 1876; fellow of King's College Cambridge; director-general of archaeology in India 1902–31; d. 1958.

207 This architectural hybrid, largely completed by 1921, now serves as a museum of British Indian history.

208 MacDonnell to Curzon 18 May 1900, Curzon Papers, vol. 201, part 1, no. 213.

209 Curzon to MacDonnell 1 June 1900, Curzon Papers, vol. 201, part 2, no. 130.

210 Curzon to Ampthill 10 April 1901, Curzon Papers, vol. 203, part 2, no. 134.

211 Speech to the Educational Conference at Simla, 20 Sept. 1905, Raleigh, *op. cit.* p. 360.

212 Hamilton to Curzon 19 Sept. 1901, Hamilton Correspondence, C 126/3, fos. 396 ff.

213 Curzon to Hamilton 21 July 1902, and Hamilton to Curzon 13 Aug. 1902, Hamilton Correspondence, D 510/11, fos. 313 ff., and C 126/4, fos. 304 ff.; Curzon to Sir Henry Cotton 31 Aug. 1902, Curzon Papers, vol. 182, part 2, no. 124.

214 See the Resolution of the Government of India March 1904 and Curzon's speech of 20 Sept. 1905.

215 Hamilton to Curzon 10 Feb. and 8 June 1899, Hamilton Correspondence, C 126/1, fos. 26 ff. and 159 ff.

216 Curzon to Hamilton 2, 16 March and 14 June 1899, Hamilton Correspondence, D 510/1, fos. 117 ff. and 147 ff., and D 510/2, fos. 21 ff.; Curzon to Sandhurst 16 April, 2 July, 10 Aug. and 10 Dec. 1899, Curzon Papers, vol. 199, part 2, no. 112A and vol. 200, part 2, nos. 2, 17 and 111.

217 Hamilton to Curzon 10 Aug. 1899, Hamilton Correspondence, C 126/1, fos. 271 ff.

218 Curzon to Hamilton 30 Aug. 1899, Hamilton Correspondence, D 510/2, fos. 300 ff.

219 On 12 Sept. 1900 he wrote to Hamilton of the social reformer Malabari: 'Whether he is absolutely straight, I cannot undertake to say. It would be a difficult thing to assert of any Indian.' Hamilton Correspondence, D 510/5, fos. 381 ff.

220 'I hope I am making no false or arrogant claim when I say that the highest ideal of truth is to a large extent a Western conception.' Calcutta University Convocation Address, 11 Feb. 1905.

221 Curzon to Hamilton 23 Sept. 1903, Hamilton Correspondence, D 510/14, fos. 323 ff.

222 Curzon to Hamilton 14 June 1899, Hamilton Correspondence, D 510/2, fos. 21 ff.

223 Indeed on one occasion, when British soldiers wounded an Indian boy, they were menaced by the villagers nearby; the English district magistrate acquitted the soldiers, sentenced the villagers to long terms of imprisonment and had the wounded boy whipped.

224 Curzon to Hamilton 25 Oct. 1899, Hamilton Correspondence D 510/3, fos. 87ff.; Curzon to Chief Commissioner of British Burma 9 July, 10 Sept. and 17 Nov. 1899, Curzon Papers, vol. 200, part 2, nos. 9, 35 and 111.

225 A. C. Trevor to Curzon 24 March 1900, Curzon Papers, vol. 201, part 1, no. 128; Curzon to Hamilton 9 May 1900, Hamilton Correspondence, D 510/5, fos. 79ff.

226 Curzon to Hamilton 13 June 1900, Hamilton Correspondence, D 510/5, fos. 141ff.

227 Curzon to Northbrook 15 May 1901, Curzon Papers, vol. 181, part 2, no. 225.

228 See Dufferin to Cross 16 May 1887, Dufferin Papers, reel 518.

229 Curzon to Godley 18 June 1902, Curzon Papers, vol. 161, part 2, no. 46.

230 Curzon to Hamilton 29 May 1901, Hamilton Correspondence, D 510/8, fos. 83ff.

231 Hamilton to Curzon 27 Nov. 1902, Hamilton Correspondence, C 126/4, fos. 429ff.

232 Curzon to Hamilton 27 Nov. 1902, Hamilton Correspondence, D 510/12, fos. 307ff.

233 Curzon to Hamilton 8 Jan. 1903, Hamilton Correspondence, D 510/13, fos. 1ff.

234 *Ibid.*

235 Curzon to Hamilton 10 June 1903, Hamilton Correspondence, D 510/14, fos. 87ff.

236 *Ibid.* 17 June 1903, Hamilton Correspondence, D 510/14, fos. 115ff.

237 See article in *Hindustan Review* (Allahabad, June 1903).

238 Hamilton to Curzon 3 Jan. 1901, Hamilton Correspondence, C 126/3, fos. 1ff.

239 Curzon to Hamilton 4 June 1903, Hamilton Correspondence, D 510/14, fos. 65ff.

240 Curzon to Hamilton 13 Feb. 1902, Hamilton Correspondence, D 510/10, fos. 209ff.

241 Curzon to Hamilton 14 June 1899, Hamilton Correspondence, D 510/2, fos. 21ff.

242 See note by C. S. Bayley, General Superintendent of Operations for the Suppression of Thagi and Dakaiti, 18 June 1899, and report of Bombay Police 20 July 1899, Hamilton Correspondence, D 510/2, fos. 63ff., and D 510/3, fos. 33ff.

243 Curzon's memorandum of conversation with Gaekwar on 28 June 1899, Foreign Department Secret I, Dec. 1903, Proceeding 8.

244 Curzon to Hamilton 27 Sept. 1899, Hamilton Correspondence, D 510/3, fos. 27ff.

245 Dutt to Private Secretary to Viceroy 15 Sept. 1898, Curzon Papers, vol. 181, part 1, no. 51.

246 Hamilton to Curzon 5 Jan. 1900, Hamilton Correspondence, C 126/2, fos. 2ff.

247 Wedderburn to Curzon 9 March 1900, Curzon Papers, vol. 181, part 1, no. 98.

248 Curzon to Wedderburn 17 April 1900, Curzon Papers, vol. 181, part 2, no. 84.

249 Curzon to Hamilton 11 Jan. 1900, Hamilton Correspondence, D 510/4, fos. 57ff.

250 *Ibid.* 18 Nov. 1900, D 510/6, fos. 289ff.

251 Curzon to Wedderburn 31 Oct. 1900, Curzon Papers, vol. 181, part 2, no. 160; Curzon to Balfour 31 March 1901, Curzon Papers, vol. 181, part 2, no. 181.

252 Curzon to Hamilton 1 Feb. 1900, Hamilton Correspondence, D 510/4, fos. 85ff.

253 *Ibid.* 3 Jan. 1901, D 510/7, fos. 3ff.

254 *Ibid.* 23 April 1900, D 510/5, fos. 3ff. (Underlining in original.)

255 Hamilton to Curzon 22 Feb. and 17 May 1900, Hamilton Correspondence, C 126/2, fos. 55ff. and 169ff.

256 Hamilton to Curzon 22 Feb. and 13 Dec. 1900, Hamilton Correspondence, C 126/2, fos. 55ff. and 446ff.

257 Curzon to Hamilton 3 Jan. 1901, Hamilton Correspondence, D 510/7, fos. 3ff.

258 Hamilton to Curzon 24 Jan. 1901, Hamilton Correspondence, C 126/3, fos. 26ff.

259 Wacha to Private Secretary to Viceroy 7 March 1902, Curzon Papers, vol. 205, part 1, no. 96.

260 Wedderburn to Curzon 10 July 1902, Curzon Papers, vol. 182, part 1, no. 121; Curzon to Wedderburn 15 Aug. 1902, Curzon Papers, vol. 182, part 2, no. 116.

261 Curzon to Ampthill 15 June 1903, Ampthill Papers, vol. 17.

262 *Ibid.*

263 Hamilton Correspondence, D 510/11, fos. 59ff.

264 21 May 1902, Hamilton Correspondence, C 126/4, fos. 188ff.

265 For an interesting analysis of the causes which led to this problem of administration being taken up by the officials at this time and not earlier see J. M. Broomfield, *The Partition of Bengal*, Proceedings of the Indian History Congress 1960 (Calcutta, 1961), pp. 12ff. Mr Broomfield shows that with each year the administrative problem grew worse till it finally overcame official inertia, while the development of educated Indian opinion and growing interest in Britain in Indian affairs freed the Government of India from the influence of Calcutta interests.

266 Minute of 24 May 1902, Home Department Public A, Dec. 1903, Proceedings 149–60.

267 Acting Lieutenant-Governor of Bengal to Curzon 22 May 1903, Curzon Papers, vol. 207, part 1, no. 136.

268 Minute of 1 June 1903, Home Department Public A, Dec. 1903, Proceedings 149–60.

269 See Ampthill to Curzon 21 Dec. 1903, Curzon Papers, vol. 208, part 1, no. 198.

270 Letter from Secretary to Government of India to Chief Secretary to Government of Bengal no. 3678.

271 Letter from Officiating Chief Secretary to the Government of Bengal to the Home Secretary to the Government of India, no. 2556J dated 6 April 1904, paragraph 46, Home Department Public A, Proceedings Feb. 1905, nos. 155–67, p. 159.

272 Note 8 Feb. 1904, *ibid.*, p. 7. (Underlining in original.)

273 Note 6 Dec. 1904, *ibid.*, p. 47.

274 13 Dec. 1903.

275 Cited in P. C. Ghosh, *The Development of the Indian National Congress 1892–1909* (Calcutta, 1960), p. 106.

276 Curzon to Brodrick, 31 Dec. 1903, Curzon Papers, vol. 162, part 2, no. 96; Curzon to Ampthill 5 Jan. 1904, Ampthill Papers, vol. 17. Curzon had some justification for ignoring the Congress session of 1903, for even many Indian members of the party had been disappointed. See L. Samaldas to G. K. Gokhale 6 Jan. 1904, Gokhale Papers, National Archives of India; Ampthill to Curzon 9 Jan. 1904, Curzon Papers, vol. 209, part 1, no. 5.

277 Curzon to Brodrick 17 Feb. 1904, Curzon Papers, vol. 163, part 2, no. 9.

278 Note 3 March 1904, Home Department Public A, Proceedings Feb. 1905, nos. 155–67, p. 9.

279 Speech at Dacca 18 Feb. 1904, *Parl. Papers*, 1905, Cd. 2746, p. 222.

280 This and other resolutions passed by the Congress were forwarded to the Government of India by the President 'as the deliberately recorded views of this most influential and representative gathering of His Majesty's Indian subjects'. See Home Department Proceedings Jan. 1905, no. 280.

281 Curzon to Brodrick 5 April 1904, Curzon Papers, vol. 163, part 2, no. 18.

282 *Business and Politics under James I*, p. 131.

283 Cotton, *Indian and Home Memories* (London, 1911), p. 290; Private Secretary to Viceroy to Cotton 2 Jan. 1905, Curzon Papers, vol. 210, part 2, no. 27.

284 Curzon to Brodrick 29 Dec. 1904, Curzon Papers, vol. 164, part 2, no. 5.

285 See the correspondence with the governments of Bengal, Assam, Madras and the Central Provinces, Home Department Public A, Proceedings Feb. 1905, nos. 155–67, pp. 103–460.

286 Despatch 3 of 1905, *ibid.* pp. 461 ff.

287 Curzon to Brodrick 2 Feb. 1905, Curzon Papers, vol. 164, part 2, no. 15.

288 Despatch no. 75 (Public) 9 June 1905, Home Department Public A, Proceedings October 1905, nos. 163–98. The passage cited here was omitted in the papers presented to Parliament.

289 Note of 24 June 1905, Home Department Public A, Proceedings Sept. 1905, no. 302.

290 Letter to Curzon 6 June 1905, Curzon Papers, vol. 210, part 1, no. 231.

291 See his note of 14 July 1905, Home Department Public A, Proceedings Oct. 1905, nos. 163–98.

292 Resolution of the Government of India no. 2491 dated 19 July 1905.

293 See H. and U. Mukherjee, *India's Fight for Freedom or the Swadeshi Movement 1905–1906* (Calcutta, 1958), p. 33.

294 *Notes on Imperialism* (1908).

295 Telegram and letter of Leiutenant-Governor of Bengal to Curzon 12 July 1905, and letter 20 Aug. 1905, Curzon Papers, vol. 211, part 1, nos. 13, 13A and 55.

296 Note 26 Aug. 1905, Home Department Public A, Proceedings Sept. 1905, no. 302.

297 Despatch 35 dated 7 Sept. 1905, *ibid.*

298 Telegram from Secretary of State 7 Oct. 1905, Home Department Public A, Proceedings Sept. 1905, no. 302.

299 Telegram to Secretary of State 9 Oct. 1905, *ibid.*

300 Note of Curzon 3 Oct. 1905, Home Department Public Proceedings Oct. 1905, nos. 114–15, part B, confidential.

301 Telegram from Chief Secretary Bengal Government 7 Oct. 1905, *ibid.*; Lieutenant-Governor of Bengal to Curzon 8 Oct. 1905, Curzon Papers, vol. 211, part 1, no. 137.

302 Cited in K. Kripalani, *Tagore: A Life* (New Delhi, 1961), p. 104.

303 Curzon's notes of 13, 26 Aug. and 10 Oct. 1905, and his telegram to Secretary of State 9 Oct. 1905, Home Department Public A, Proceedings Sept. 1905, no. 302.

304 Cf. Aurobindo Ghose, at this time a revolutionary nationalist: 'whereas others regard the country as an inert object, and know it as the plains, the fields, the forests, the mountains and rivers, I look upon my country as the mother, I worship her and adore her as the mother. What would a son do when a demon sitting on the breast of his mother is drinking her blood? Would he sit down content to take his meals, and go on enjoying himself in the company of his wife and children or would he, rather, run to the rescue of his mother?' To his wife 30 Aug. 1905. A. B. Purani, *The Life of Sri Aurobindo* (Pondicherry 2nd edition, 1960), p. 101.

305 W. G. Archer, *India and Modern Art* (London, 1959), p. 37.

306 See Commissioner of Police, Calcutta, to the Chief Secretary to the Government of Bengal, 21 Sept. 1905, Home Department Public Proceedings Oct. 1905, nos. 114–15, part B, confidential.

307 See C. P. Ilbert, *The Government of India* (Oxford, 1922), p. 100.

308 Cf. the question put by Sir Donald Stewart, a former Commander-in-Chief, and the answer given by Sir David Barbour, a former Finance Member: 'But is it not a fact that the Military Member in Council is usually held to be a check on the Commander-in-Chief rather than a supporter?—That is the theory, and, no doubt, in some cases that is the practice. . . .' Evidence given on 12 Nov. 1895 before the Welby

Commission, *Report of the Indian Expenditure Commission*, Cd. 8258 (1896), vol. I, p. 74.

309 Lord Hankey, *The Supreme Command* (London, 1961), vol. I, p. 186.

310 6 Dec. 1905, *Journals and Letters* (London, 1934), vol. 2, p. 124.

311 Milner to Curzon 9 Nov. 1905, Curzon Papers, vol. 183, part 1, no. 196 a.

312 P. Magnus, *Kitchener* (London, 1958), p. 152.

313 Godley to Curzon 7 Feb. 1899, Curzon Papers, vol. 158, part 1, no. 4 c.

314 Hamilton to Curzon 14 July 1899, Hamilton Correspondence, C 126/1, fos. 225 ff.

315 Curzon to Hamilton 2 Aug. 1899, Hamilton Correspondence, D 510/2, fos. 221 ff.

316 *Ibid.* 27 Sept. 1899, Hamilton Correspondence, D 510/3, fos. 27 ff.

317 Godley to Curzon 22 June 1899 and Curzon to Godley 12 July 1899, Curzon Papers, part 1, no. 24 c and part 2, no. 29 c.

318 Curzon to Hamilton 15 Feb. 1900, Hamilton Correspondence, D 510/4, fos. 123 ff.

319 To Curzon 23 Feb. 1900, Hamilton Correspondence, C 126/2, fos. 59 ff.

320 Curzon to Hamilton 22 March 1900, Hamilton Correspondence, D 510/4, fos. 225 ff.

321 Hamilton to Curzon 9 March and Curzon to Hamilton 29 March 1900, Hamilton Correspondence, C 126/2, fos. 81 ff., and D 510/4, fos. 275 ff.

322 Curzon to Kitchener 21 Aug. 1900, Kitchener Papers; Sir Philip Magnus gives the date of this letter wrongly as 31 Aug., *op. cit.* p. 176.

323 To Lady Edward Cecil 27 Dec. 1900 and 20 May 1902, quoted in Edward Crankshaw, *The Forsaken Idea* (London, 1952), pp. 96 and 97.

324 Mosley, *op. cit.* p. 98; Curzon to Hamilton 23 April 1900, Hamilton Correspondence, D 510/5, fos. 3 ff.; Northbrook to Curzon 15 Nov. 1900, Curzon Papers, vol. 181, part 1, no. 206 A.

325 See Salisbury to Lansdowne 28 Sept. 1900, Newton, *Lansdowne*, p. 189.

326 Curzon to Hamilton 9 May and 13 Dec. 1900, Hamilton Correspondence, D 510/5, fos. 63 ff., and D 510/6, fos. 403 ff.

327 Magnus, *op. cit.* pp. 174–76; Hamilton to Curzon 18 Jan. 1901, and Curzon to Hamilton 7 Feb. 1901, Hamilton Correspondence, C 126/3, fos. 18 ff. and D 510/7, fos. 109 ff.

328 Curzon to Kitchener 31 March 1901, and Kitchener to Curzon 8 May 1901, Curzon Papers, vol. 181, part 2, no. 208 and part 1, no. 275 a.

329 Hamilton to Curzon 16 Oct. and 24 Dec. 1902, Hamilton Correspondence, C 126/4, fos. 373 ff. and 459 ff. Kitchener had been warned by General Sir Horace Smith-Dorrien, on the instructions of Sir Power

Palmer, of the difficulties of the Commander-in-Chief. Smith-Dorrien, *Memories of Forty-Eight Years' Service* (London, 1925), p. 314.

330 Hamilton to Curzon 24 Dec. 1902, Hamilton Correspondence, C 126/4, fos. 459 ff.

331 Dawkins to Curzon 25 July 1902, Curzon Papers, vol. 182, part 1, no. 131.

332 Curzon to Hamilton 29 March 1900, Hamilton Correspondence, D 510/4, fos. 275 ff.

333 Curzon to Hamilton 10 July 1901, Hamilton Correspondence, D 510/8, fos. 213 ff. Sir Edmond Elles b. 1848; entered Royal Artillery 1867; major-general 1900; military member of Viceroy's council 1901–5; d. 1934.

334 3 Dec. 1902, Hamilton Correspondence, D 510/12, fos. 355 ff.

335 *Ibid.*

336 Sir George Arthur, *Life of Lord Kitchener* (London, 1920), vol. 2, p. 205 footnote.

337 Curzon to Kitchener 13 Aug. 1902, Kitchener Papers.

338 In a letter to Lady Salisbury 25 Jan. 1903, Magnus, *op. cit.* p. 202; Dugdale, *Balfour*, vol. 1, pp. 404–5.

339 Curzon to Hamilton 19 Feb. 1903, Hamilton Correspondence, D 510/13, fos. 119 ff.

340 For an account of this dislike see Smith-Dorrien, *op. cit.* pp. 307–8.

341 See above, p. 277.

342 Kitchener to an unknown correspondent 6 May 1903, Kitchener Papers.

343 Hamilton to Curzon 24 April 1903, Hamilton Correspondence, C 126/5, fos. 133 ff.

344 Curzon to Kitchener 12 May 1903, Magnus, *op. cit.* p. 206; Curzon to Hamilton 7 May 1903 with enclosure Kitchener to Curzon 13 May 1903, Hamilton Correspondence, D 510/14, fos. 1 ff.

345 Curzon to Hamilton 14 May 1903, Hamilton Correspondence, D 510/14, fos. 19 ff.

346 Dawkins to Curzon 10 Nov. 1905, Curzon Papers, vol. 183, part 1, no. 196 b.

347 See Kitchener to Curzon 21 May, Curzon to Kitchener 24 May, Kitchener to Curzon 25 May and Curzon to Kitchener 25 May 1903, Hamilton Correspondence, D 510/14, fos 51 ff.; and Curzon to Hamilton 4 June 1903, *ibid.*, D 510/14, fos. 65 ff.

348 Curzon to Hamilton 17 June 1903, Hamilton Correspondence, D 510/14, fos. 115 ff.

349 *Ibid.* 9 July 1903, D 510/14, fos. 179 ff.

350 See Curzon's letters to Kitchener 26 April and 30 May 1904, Curzon Papers, vol. 209, part 2, nos. 123 and 136.

351 Hamilton had warned Kitchener again in 1903; letter of 5 June, Kitchener Papers.

352 Dugdale, *Balfour*, vol. 1, p. 405. Curzon may have secured more support from Salisbury who had never liked the presence of the Commander-in-Chief in the Council. 'I am not, therefore, very keen to inflate further a dignitary, who, to my mind, is more than full-blown already.' Salisbury to Lytton 23 Nov. 1877, Lytton Papers, vol. 516/2, no. 48. The retirement of Salisbury at this crucial stage was one more element in Curzon's run of ill-luck, but on the other hand Salisbury was reported as favouring Kitchener as Curzon's successor, Dawkins to Curzon, 25 July 1902, Curzon Papers, vol. 182, part 1, no. 131.

353 Brodrick to Ampthill 22 April 1904, Ampthill Papers, vol. 37, part 1, no. 3, fos. 3 ff.

354 See, for example, Kitchener to Roberts 27 April 1904, Kitchener Papers.

355 See Ampthill to Brodrick 22 June and 7 July 1904, Ampthill Papers, vol. 37, part 2, nos. 22 and 28, fos. 68 ff. and 94 ff.

356 9 June 1904, Kitchener Papers, Kitchener has here got his Latin phrases transposed.

357 Ampthill to Brodrick 9 June, Kitchener to Ampthill 10 June and Ampthill to Kitchener 11 June and 24 July 1904, Ampthill Papers, vol. 37, part 2, no. 16, fos. 51 ff.; and vol. 34, part 1, no. 84, fos. 85 ff. and part 2, nos. 65 and 138, fos. 55 ff. and 113 ff. Also Notes by Viceroy and Members of Council in Military Department Proceedings Oct. 1904, no. 1301.

358 Brodrick to Ampthill 17 June, and Curzon to Ampthill 23 June 1904, Ampthill Papers, vol. 37, part 1, nos. 19 and 22, fos. 34 ff. and 39 ff.

359 Curzon to Ampthill 4 Aug., Brodrick to Ampthill 5 Aug., and Godley to Ampthill 5 Aug. 1904, Ampthill Papers, vol. 37, part 1, nos. 37, 38 and 39, fos. 93 ff. Also Balfour to Curzon 3 Nov. 1904. Dugdale, *Balfour*, vol. 1, p. 407.

360 21 Sept. 1904, Kitchener Papers.

361 To Major Marker 15 Sept. 1904, Kitchener-Marker Papers, B.M. Add. MSS 52276.

362 Kitchener to Ampthill 23 and 24 Sept. 1904, Ampthill Papers, vol. 34, part 2, nos. 381 and 388, fos. 286 ff. and 292 ff.

363 28 Sept. 1904, Ampthill Papers, vol. 37, part 2, no. 62, fos. 228 ff.

364 Despatch no. 146 dated 13 Oct. 1904, Military Department Proceedings Oct. 1904, no. 1301.

365 Brodrick to Ampthill 6 Oct. and Godley to Ampthill 13 Oct. 1904, Ampthill Papers, vol. 37, part 2, nos. 61 and 63, fos. 138 ff. and 142 ff.; and Brodrick to Kitchener 13 Oct. 1904, Kitchener Papers.

366 Brodrick to Ampthill 15 Sept. and 13 Oct. 1904, Ampthill Papers, vol. 37, part 2, nos. 54 and 62, fos. 126 ff. and 140 ff.

367 Balfour to Lady Salisbury 4 Oct. 1904. Monger, *op. cit.* p. 171.

368 Quoted in Sir Charles Petrie, *The Powers behind the Prime Ministers* (London, 1958), p. 76.

369 3 Nov. 1904. Dugdale, *Balfour*, vol. 1, p. 407.

370 Brodrick to Ampthill 13 Oct. 1904 and Ampthill to Brodrick 2 Nov. 1904, Ampthill Papers, vol. 37, part 1, no. 62, fos. 140 ff. and part 2, no. 77, fos. 294 ff.; Kitchener to Brodrick 9 Nov. 1904, Kitchener Papers. Later Kitchener disliked the idea of any such commission for fear that

Curzon would gain influence with its members. Kitchener to Marker 12 Feb. 1905, Kitchener-Marker Papers, Add. MSS 52276.

371 Brodrick to Ampthill 11 Nov. 1904, Ampthill Papers, vol. 37, part 1, no. 74, fos. 172 ff.

372 Brodrick to Curzon 2 Dec. 1904, Curzon Papers, vol. 164, part 1, no. 1. Kitchener was believed to have got in touch with the Liberal leaders and to have shown an interest in the War Secretaryship in any Liberal administration. See Col. Repington to Maj. Marker 8 Nov. 1904, Kitchener-Marker Papers, Add. MSS 52278.

373 Kitchener to Brodrick 9 Nov. 1904 and to Roberts 27 Nov. 1904, Kitchener Papers.

374 Brodrick to Kitchener 9 Dec. 1904, Kitchener Papers,

375 Kitchener to Ampthill 19 Dec. 1904, Ampthill Papers, vol. 34, part 2, no. 625, fos. 446 ff.

376 Despatch of the Secretary of State 2 Dec. 1904, Correspondence regarding the Administration of the Army in India, *Parl. Papers*, 1905, Cd. 2572, no. 1.

377 Despatch to the Secretary of State no. 36 dated 23 March 1905, enclosure 1, Military Department Proceedings 1905.

378 *Ibid.* enclosure 2.

379 Despatch to the Secretary of State no. 36 dated 23 March 1905, enclosure 3, Military Department Proceedings 1905.

380 See notes of Sir Edward Law 23 April, Sir Denzil Ibbetson 24 April and Sir Arundel Arundel 25 April 1904, Military Department Proceedings Oct. 1904, no. 1301, notes pp. 9–10.

381 'Kitchener seems to treat the whole business as rather a bore and if the Viceroy asks him if he has any remarks to make throws himself back and says, "Oh, no".' Younghusband after attending a meeting of the Council Oct. 1903. Fleming, *op. cit.* pp. 89–90.

382 Kitchener to Marker 17 March 1905, Kitchener-Marker Papers, Add. MSS 52276.

383 Despatch 36 dated 23 March 1905, with Minute of Dissent by the Commander-in-Chief, Military Department Proceedings 1905.

384 To Roberts 26 Jan. 1905, Kitchener Papers.

385 Curzon to Balfour 26 Jan. and to Brodrick 16 March 1905, Curzon Papers, vol. 164, part 2, nos. 14 and 25.

386 Even on 6 Jan. 1905, while approving the transfer to the Commander-in-Chief of supply and transport services, the Secretary of State had remarked that he would have been prepared to consent to a further measure of control, both financial and administrative, being vested in the Commander-in-Chief. Military (Confidential) Despatch no. 4, Military Department Proceedings 1905.

387 Brodrick to Curzon 20 Jan. 1905, Curzon Papers, vol. 164, part 1, no. 15; Dawkins to Curzon 10 Nov. 1905, Curzon Papers, vol. 183, part 1, no. 196 b.

388 The Cabinet wanted Henry Fowler to serve on this committee. See Fowler to Sir Henry Campbell-Bannerman 22 April 1905, Campbell-Bannerman Papers, B.M. Add. MSS 41214, fo. 262.

389 Curzon to Brodrick 2 Feb., to Godley 2 Feb. and to Brodrick 9 Feb., 2 and 9 March 1905, Curzon Papers, vol. 164, part 2, nos. 15, 16, 17, 21 and 23.

390 Curzon to Brodrick 16 March and to Balfour 30 March 1905, Curzon Papers, vol. 164, part 2, nos. 25 and 29; Curzon to Ampthill 2 April 1905, Ampthill Papers, vol. 18.

391 Curzon's only supporter in the Cabinet was Lansdowne. See Esher 18 April 1905, *Journals and Letters* (London, 1934), vol. 2, p. 83.

392 Curzon to Ampthill 12 May 1905, Ampthill Papers, vol. 18.

393 Brodrick to Curzon 18 May 1905, Curzon Papers, vol. 164, part 1, no. 39.

394 Further Papers regarding the Administration of the Army in India 1905, *Parl. Papers*, Cd. 2718, no. 2.

395 Speech in the House of Lords, 1 Aug. 1905.

396 Military (Secret) Despatch from the Secretary of State no. 66 dated 31 May 1905, Military Department Proceedings 1905.

397 Military (Secret) Despatch from the Secretary of State no. 67 dated 31 May 1905, Military Department Proceedings 1905.

398 Letters of Lansdowne 26 May, Brodrick 26 May and Godley 26 and 30 May 1905, Curzon Papers, vol. 164, part 1, nos. 40, 41, 42 and 43; Roberts to Curzon 2 June 1905, Curzon Papers, vol. 183, part 1, no. 63.

399 Balfour to Curzon 9 June 1905, Curzon Papers, vol. 164, part 1, no. 46.

400 Brodrick to Curzon 2 June 1905, Curzon Papers, vol. 164, part 1, no. 44.

401 B. 1847; entered Indian civil service 1868; various posts in the Punjab; secretary to government of India 1896–8; chief commissioner of Central Provinces 1898–1902; member of Viceroy's council 1902–5; lieutenant-governor of the Punjab 1905–8; d. 1908.

402 B. 1854; joined Indian civil service 1877; served in home department 1886–1902; chief commissioner of Central Provinces 1902–4; member of Viceroy's council 1904–7; lieutenant-governor of United Provinces 1907–12; d. 1941.

403 B. 1848; joined Indian civil service 1865; various posts in Madras; member of Viceroy's council 1901–6; d. 1929.

404 Sir A. T. Arundel to Curzon 25 June 1905, Curzon Papers, vol. 210, part 1, no. 256.

405 Curzon to Balfour 27 July 1905, Curzon Papers, vol. 164, part 2, no. 50.

406 Curzon to Ampthill 23 July 1905, Ampthill Papers, vol. 19; Magnus, *op. cit.* pp. 219–21.

407 Kitchener to Marker 6 July 1905, Kitchener-Marker Papers, Add. MSS 52276.

408 Curzon to Ampthill 23 July 1905, Ampthill Papers, vol. 19.

409 Viceroy's telegram to Secretary of State 17 July 1905, *Parl. Papers*, 1905, Cd. 2718, no. 3.

410 In a conversation with W. S. Blunt 2 Oct. 1909. Blunt, *My Diaries*, part II (London, 1920), p. 287. Kitchener was never, of course, one of Churchill's heroes.

411 Telegrams from Secretary of State 1 and 4 Aug. 1905, *Parl. Papers*, 1905, Cd. 2718, nos. 4 and 6.

412 Curzon to Ampthill 12 Aug. 1905, Ampthill Papers, vol. 19.

413 Telegram to Secretary of State 5 Aug. 1905, *Parl. Papers*, 1905, Cd. 2718, no. 7.

414 See telegrams from Secretary of State 11 and 16 Aug. 1905, *Parl. Papers*, 1905, Cd. 2718, nos. 10, 12 and 13.

415 Curzon to Ampthill 12 Aug. 1905, Ampthill Papers, vol. 19.

416 *Ibid.*

417 See Curzon to Morley 24 Dec. 1905, Morley Papers.

418 Haldane to Curzon 22 June 1905, Curzon Papers, vol. 183, part 1, no. 74.

419 Sir Winston Churchill to Curzon 22 Aug. 1905, Curzon Papers, vol. 183, part 1, no. 134a.

420 Ripon to Campbell-Bannerman 3 Sept. 1905, Campbell-Bannerman Papers, Add. MSS 41225, fo. 41.

421 Curzon to Ampthill 23 July 1905, Ampthill Papers, vol. 19.

422 Curzon to Sir Winston Churchill 5 Oct., to Haldane 11 Oct. and to St Loe Strachey 10 Nov. 1905, Curzon Papers, vol. 183, part 2, nos. 120, 128 and 138.

423 19 July 1905. K. Young, *Arthur James Balfour* (London, 1963), p. 240.

424 To Morley 12 Dec. 1905, Morley Papers.

425 Brodrick, *Records and Reactions 1856–1939* (London, 1939), p. 208.

426 Ronaldshay, *The Life of Lord Curzon*, vol. 2 (London, 1928), pp. 372–412.

427 *The Times*, 20 Nov. 1930, cited in Fleming, *op. cit.* p. 289.

428 Curzon to Roberts 22 March 1905, Curzon Papers, vol. 183, part 2, no. 19; Curzon to Balfour 30 March 1905, Curzon Papers, vol. 164, part 2, no. 29; Curzon to Sir W. Churchill 5 Oct. and to Ripon 19 Oct. 1905, Curzon Papers, vol. 183, part 2, nos. 120 and 130.

429 Letter to Morley 31 Jan. 1906, Morley Papers.

430 Curzon to Hamilton 11 April 1900, Hamilton Correspondence, D 510/4, fos. 357ff.

431 Vansittart, *op. cit.* p. 254.

432 'One goes out amid the glare of magnesium. How shall I return?' Curzon to Elgin 17 Nov. 1898, Elgin Papers, Correspondence with persons abroad, vol. 5, part 1, no. 67. 'The conditions under which he [Curzon] enters his term of office are so exceptionally favourable that, knowing how the unexpected occurs in political life, I feel as if the auspices were almost too favourable.' Hamilton to Elgin 15 Dec. 1898, Hamilton Correspondence, C 125/3, fos. 517ff.

433 Crankshaw, *op. cit.* p. 112.

434 Cited in John Raymond, 'Cromer: The Proconsul', *History Today* (March, 1960), p. 181.

435 Dawkins to Curzon 17 May and 6 June 1900, Curzon Papers, vol. 181, part 1, nos. 133 and 137A.

436 To Hamilton 18 June 1901, Hamilton Correspondence, D 510/8, fos. 143 ff.

437 5 Jan. 1900, Hamilton Correspondence, C 126/2, fos. 2 ff.

438 Curzon to Hamilton 27 Dec. 1900, Hamilton Correspondence, D 510/6, fos. 441 ff.

439 Curzon to Balfour 20 Nov. 1902, Curzon Papers, vol. 161, part 2, no. 92.

440 Hamilton to Curzon 20 Nov. 1902, Hamilton Correspondence, C 126/4, fos. 415 ff.

441 Balfour to Curzon 12 Dec. 1902, Curzon Papers, vol. 161, part 1, no. 102. The letter has been quoted in part in Dugdale, *Balfour*, vol. 1, p. 396.

442 18 June 1903, *ibid.* p. 398.

443 To Ampthill 10 June 1904, Ampthill Papers, vol. 37, part 1, no. 17, fos. 29 ff.

444 Curzon to Godley 23 Sept. 1903, Curzon Papers, vol. 162, part 2, no. 69.

445 Curzon to Brodrick 2 Oct. 1903, Curzon Papers, vol. 162, part 2, no. 71.

446 Curzon to Ampthill 5 Oct. 1903, Curzon Papers, vol. 208, part 2, no. 90.

447 Brodrick to Curzon 15 Oct. and 29 Oct. 1903, and 19 Feb. and 3 March 1904, Curzon Papers, vol. 162, part 1, nos. 71 and 75, and vol. 163, part 1, nos. 11 and 13.

448 Curzon to Dawkins 9 March 1904, Curzon Papers, vol. 182, part 2, no. 231.

449 Godley to Curzon 27 Nov. 1903 and 1, 8 Jan. and 3 March 1904, Curzon Papers, vol. 162, part 1, no. 86 and vol. 163, part 1, nos. 1, 3 and 14.

450 Curzon to Ampthill 8 July 1904, Ampthill Papers, vol. 37, part 1, no. 30, fos. 65 ff.

451 To Ampthill 31 Oct. 1904, Ampthill Papers, vol. 37, part 1, no. 70, fos. 163 ff.

452 To Ampthill 23 July 1905, Ampthill Papers, vol. 19.

453 See Esher 20 June 1904, *Journals and Letters*, vol. 2, pp. 55–6.

454 Brodrick to Curzon 10 Feb. 1905, Curzon Papers, vol. 164, part 1, no. 20.

455 Curzon to Brodrick 2 March 1905, Curzon Papers, vol. 164, part 2, no. 21.

456 To Curzon 30 June 1905, Curzon Papers, vol. 164, part 1, no. 50.

457 To Hamilton 9 Sept. 1903, Hamilton Correspondence, D 510/14, fos. 307 ff.

458 Curzon to J. S. Sandars, private secretary to Balfour 5 July and to Balfour 19 July 1905, Curzon Papers, vol. 164, part 2, nos. 47 and 49.

459 Balfour to Curzon 23 Aug. 1905, Curzon Papers, vol. 164, part 1, no. 57.

460 Curzon to his successor Minto 5 Oct. 1905, Curzon Papers, vol. 183, part 2, no. 123.

461 To Hamilton 28 May 1902, Hamilton Correspondence, D 510/11, fos. 215 ff.

462 Sir Walter Lawrence, *The India We Served* (London, 1928), p. 236.

463 To Hamilton 31 Jan. 1901, Hamilton Correspondence, D 510/7, fos. 91 ff.

464 Curzon to Godley 23 Feb. 1899, Curzon Papers, vol. 158, part 1, no. 6 b.

465 *Ibid.* 9 Dec. 1901, Curzon Papers, vol. 160, part 2, no. 82.

466 Curzon to Lamington 27 Feb. 1904, Curzon Papers, vol. 209, part 2, no. 50.

467 Curzon to Brodrick 17 Feb. 1904, Curzon Papers, vol. 163, part 2, no. 9.

468 To Hamilton 16 Aug. 1899, Hamilton Correspondence, D 510/2, fos. 261 ff.

469 *Ibid.* 13 June 1900, Hamilton Correspondence, D 510/15, fos. 141 ff.

470 See obituary notice of Dag Hammarskjold in *The Guardian*, 19 Sept. 1961.

471 To Hamilton 17 June 1903, Hamilton Correspondence, D 510/14, fos. 115 ff.; to Brodrick 31 March 1904, Curzon Papers, vol. 163, part 2, no. 17.

472 Curzon to the Warden of Merton 2 May and to John Morley 17 June 1900, Curzon Papers, vol. 181, part 2, nos. 92 and 119.

473 Curzon to Brodrick 2 Oct. 1903, Curzon Papers, vol. 162, part 2, no. 71.

474 See, for instance, Curzon to Ampthill 17 Sept. 1900 and to Lamington 22 Oct. 1903, Curzon Papers, vol. 181, part 2, no. 146 and vol. 182, part 2, no. 214.

475 Curzon to Buckle 10 April 1902 and to Northbrook 21 July 1902, Curzon Papers, vol. 182, part 2, nos. 61 and 103.

476 Curzon to Godley 27 Jan. 1904, Curzon Papers, vol. 163, part 2, no. 4.

477 Curzon to Godley 17 Dec. 1903, Curzon Papers, vol. 162, part 2, no. 94.

478 *Ibid.* 9 April 1901, Curzon Papers, vol. 160, part 2, no. 27.

479 Curzon to Salisbury 21 June 1903, Curzon Papers, vol. 162, part 2, no. 43.

480 B. 1866; professor in Fergusson College Poona; member of Bombay legislative council 1900–2; member of Viceroy's legislative council 1902–15; founded Servants of India Society; president of Indian National Congress 1905; d. 1915.

481 Gokhale to Curzon 1 Jan. 1904, Curzon Papers, vol. 209, part 1, no. 1.

482 Curzon to Lamington 24 July 1905, Curzon Papers, vol. 211, part 2, no. 23.

483 Curzon to Godley 11 May 1905, Curzon Papers, vol. 164, part 2, no. 38.

484 Lamington to Curzon 20 March 1904, Curzon Papers, vol. 209, part 1, no. 104; Curzon to Lamington 16 April 1905, Curzon Papers, vol. 210, part 2, no. 107.

485 Curzon to Godley 29 Oct. and 13 Dec. 1900, Curzon Papers, vol. 159, part 2, nos. 69 and 76.

486 Curzon to Salisbury 21 June 1903, Curzon Papers, vol. 162, part 2, no. 43.

487 Wacha to Gokhale 4 Feb. 1904, Gokhale Papers. (Underlining in original.)

488 *Ibid.* 17 Feb. 1904 and 20 March 1905, Gokhale Papers.

489 Curzon to Sir M. M. Bhownaggree 7 Sept., to Dawkins, 14 Sept., to Valentine Chirol 14 Sept. and to Lord Selborne 5 Oct. 1905, Curzon Papers, vol. 183, part 2, nos. 103, 104, 105 and 121.

CONCLUSION, pp. 299–304

1   T. Martin, *Life of the Prince Consort*, vol. IV (1879), pp. 284ff.
2   Buckle, *Disraeli*, vol. V (1920), p. 435.
3   9 March 1876, *Hansard*, 3rd series, vol. CCXXVI, p. 1739.
4   23 July 1878, *Hansard*, 3rd series, vol. CCXLII, pp. 48ff.
5   'England's Mission', *The Nineteenth Century* (Sept. 1878), p. 580.

BIBLIOGRAPHY

This work is based almost entirely on manuscript sources, and an effort has been made to consult such official records and private paper collections as might prove of relevance.

MANUSCRIPT AUTHORITIES

INDIA OFFICE LIBRARY

Sir Charles Wood Papers (MSS Eur. F. 78)

India Office letter books 25 June 1859 to 1 Feb. 1866 (22 volumes).
India Office correspondence (boxes 2–7).

Papers of the 8th Earl of Elgin (MSS Eur. F. 83)

Section 1, part 1, Letters to Wood 17 Feb. 1862 to 4 Nov. 1863 (5 volumes).

Section 1, part 2. Vol. 11, Letters to Governor of Bombay; vol. 13, Letters to Lieutenant-Governor of Bengal; vol. 14, Letters to Lieutenant-Governor of North-West Provinces; vol. 15, Letters to Lieutenant-Governor of Punjab; vol. 16, letters to Members of Council; vol. 17, Miscellaneous; vol. 18, Letters from Governor of Bombay; vol. 19, Letters from Governor of Madras; vol. 20, Letters from Lieutenant-Governor of Bengal; vol. 21, Letters from Lieutenant-Governor of North-West Provinces; vol. 23, Letters from Members of Council; vol. 24, Miscellaneous.

Section 1, part 3. Vol. 29, Letters from Commander-in-Chief; vol. 30, Letters to the Queen.

Sir John Lawrence Papers (MSS Eur. F. 90)

Letters from Secretary of State, vols. 3–5, 1866–8. (The letters for the earlier years of the viceroyalty have been consulted in the Wood papers.)
Letters to Secretary of State, vols. 3–5, 1866–8.
Letters from Members of Council 1864–9 (3 vols.).
Letters to Members of Council 1864–9 (2 vols.).

Northbrook Papers (MSS Eur. C. 144)

Vol. 7, General Correspondence 1876–9; vol. 8, Letters to the Queen 1872–6; vol. 9, Correspondence with Argyll 1872–4; vol. 10, Telegrams to and from Secretary of State 1873–4; vols. 11 and 12, Correspondence with Salisbury 1874–6; vols. 13–19, Correspondence with persons in India 1872–80; vols. 20–3, Correspondence with persons in England 1872–6.

British Policy in India, 1858–1905

Lytton Papers (MSS Eur. E. 218)

Series 516, Correspondence with Secretary of State, 6 vols.; series 517, Letters from persons in England, 9 vols.; series 518, Letters despatched vols. 1–4 and 6; series 522, Letters to John Morley, vols. 15 and 16.

Dufferin Papers (microfilm copy)

Reel 516, Correspondence with the Queen and some letters of Secretary of State 1885–7; reels 517 and 518, Correspondence with Secretary of State 1884–8; reel 522, Correspondence regarding resignation 1888; reels 525–7, Correspondence with persons in England; reels 528–34, Correspondence with persons in India.

Lansdowne Papers (MSS Eur. D. 558)

Series VII, Correspondence with persons in India 1888–94, 10 vols.; series VIII, Correspondence with persons in England 1888–94, 5 vols.; series IX, Correspondence with Secretary of State 1888–94, 5 vols.; series XIII, Volume of Notes and Minutes 1889–94.

Papers of the 9th Earl of Elgin (MSS Eur. F. 84)

Volume of letters from Secretary of State 1894; Correspondence with persons in England and elsewhere 1894–8, 5 vols.; Correspondence with persons in India 1894–8, 10 vols.

Wolverhampton Papers (MSS Eur. C. 145 (Papers of Sir H. H. Fowler later Lord Wolverhampton))

Correspondence with Viceroy 1894–5, 3 vols.

Lord George Hamilton Correspondence

Letters to Elgin 1895–8, C 125, 3 vols.; Letters to Curzon 1899–1903, C 126, 5 vols.; D 508, Private telegrams 1895–9; Letters from Elgin 1895–9, D 509, 12 vols.; Letters from Curzon 1898–1903, D 510, 14 vols.

Curzon Papers (MSS Eur. F. 111)

Correspondence with Lord Salisbury, A. J. Balfour, St John Brodrick and Sir Arthur Godley, vols. 158–64; Correspondence with persons in England and abroad, vols. 181–3; Correspondence with persons in India, vols. 199–211.

Ampthill Papers (MSS Eur. E. 233)

Correspondence with John Morley 1906, vol. 13; Correspondence with Curzon 1901–5, vols. 15–19; Correspondence with Lord Kitchener, vol. 21; Correspondence with persons in India April to December 1904, vol. 34; Correspondence with India Office 1904, vol. 37; Correspondence with persons in England 1904, vol. 40.

Morley Papers (MSS Eur. D. 555)

These have not been listed.

Bibliography

PUBLIC RECORD OFFICE

Granville Papers (Series 30/29)

No. 21, Box of papers concerning India and Burma 1852–62. These include Granville's letters to Canning.

No. 51, Volume of correspondence with Argyll 1869–73.

Kitchener Papers

These are in three trunks and have not been listed.

BRITISH MUSEUM

Palmerston Papers

Add. MSS 48580, Correspondence with the Chairman of the East India Company, the President of the Board of Control and the Governor-General 1856–7; Add. MSS 48581, Correspondence with Lord John Russell 1859.

Gladstone Papers

Add. MSS 44099, Correspondence with Argyll 1861–4; Add. MSS 44101–4, Correspondence with Argyll 1869–80; Add. MSS 44112, Correspondence with John Bright 1853–71; Add. MSS 44145–6, Correspondence with Hartington 1879–83; Add. MSS 44228–9, Correspondence with Kimberley 1882–6 and 1889–96; Add. MSS 44151, Correspondence with Dufferin; Add. MSS 44156, Correspondence with Fawcett; Add. MSS 44266–7, Correspondence with Northbrook 1868–85; Add. MSS 44642–6, Memoranda of Cabinet meetings 1880–5; Add. MSS 44747, Memorandum on Indian legislation July 1858; Add. MSS 44769, Notes on Afghan affairs 1885.

Northcote Papers

These were consulted when they were still in the possession of the family. They are now in the British Museum.

Ripon Papers

These have now been renumbered; the old numbers are given in the notes. Letters received, 29 vols.; letters to Lady Ripon, 1 vol.; diary, 3 vols.; miscellaneous, 1 vol.; general correspondence, 15 vols.; correspondence with Secretary of State, 7 vols.; military operations and famine papers, 6 vols.; correspondence with the Queen, 1 vol.; official papers, 19 vols.

Cross Papers

Add. MSS 51275–7, General Correspondence 1886–90.

Campbell-Bannerman Papers

Add. MSS 41212, Correspondence with Col Bruce; Add. MSS 41214, Correspondence with Henry Fowler; Add. MSS 41221, Correspondence with Kimberley; Add. MSS 41224–5, Correspondence with Ripon; Add. MSS 41227, Correspondence with Lord Sandhurst, Governor of Bombay.

Kitchener-Marker Papers

Add. MSS 52276–8, Correspondence of Lord Kitchener with Major Marker.

CAMBRIDGE UNIVERSITY LIBRARY

Mayo Papers (Add. 7490)

Vols. 33–46, Letters despatched; vols. 47–50, Letters from Secretary of State; nos. 51–61, Bundles of correspondence.

CHRIST CHURCH LIBRARY, OXFORD

Salisbury Papers (I have consulted the microfilm copy in the National Archives of India)

Reels 807–10, Letters from persons in India 1866–73; reels 820–1, Letters from Members of the Council of India.

LINCOLN CASTLE

Welby Manuscripts. Lindsey Deposit, vol. 24/3/31.

HUGHENDEN MANOR

Disraeli Papers

These have not been listed.

Kimberley Papers (In the possession of the Earl of Kimberley who kindly granted me access)

D/2, Letters from Northbrook 1883–4; D/6, Letters from Hartington 1883–5; D/8, Letters from Cabinet Ministers 1882–5; D/18, Letters from Members of Council of India 1883–5; D/19, Cabinet minutes and correspondence regarding Afghan boundary 1882–5; D/21, 32c and 34, Miscellaneous; D/22a to d and D/28, Correspondence with Dufferin 1884–6; D/26a and b, Correspondence with Lord Reay; D/30, Correspondence with Cabinet Ministers 1886; D/37, Memoranda regarding Afghan boundary 1885; E/5, Letters from Godley 1892; E/6a and b, Correspondence with Gladstone 1893–4; E/7, Letters from Campbell-Bannerman 1892–3; E/8, Letters from Rosebery 1892–4; E/10, Correspondence regarding appointment of Sir Henry Norman as Viceroy 1893; E/14, Letters from Sir Owen Burne and Lord Elgin 1892–4; E/18a to e, Correspondence with Lansdowne and Elgin 1892–4; E/19, Telegrams 1892–4; E/36, Abstracts of letters from India 1892–4; E/13, 15, 17, 26 and 29, Miscellaneous.

Bibliography

Canning Papers (In the possession of the Earl of Harewood)
Volume of Correspondence with Secretary of State 1858–9; Volume of Letters from Her Majesty's Ministers 1856–62; Volume of Letters to Her Majesty's Ministers 1856–62; Volume of Correspondence with the Queen; Volume of Letters to Members of Council 1858–62; Volume of Minutes.

NATIONAL ARCHIVES OF INDIA

Tyabji Papers
The papers of Badruddin Tyabji have not been listed.

Gokhale Papers
The papers of Gopal Krishna Gokhale have not been listed.

Government of India Records
The Judicial, Political and Public Series of the Home Department, the Secret Series of the Foreign Department and the papers concerning tariffs in the Finance and Commerce and Industry Departments have been found particularly useful. The specific references have been given in the notes.

PRINTED AUTHORITIES

PARLIAMENTARY PAPERS

These again constitute a large number and are indispensable to the student of the period. Of those cited in the notes, particular mention may be made of those on Afghanistan and Central Asia 1878–9 C. 2190 and 1885 C. 4387; Local Self-Government 1883 nos. 93 I and 93 II; the Ilbert Bill 1883 C. 3512, C. 3545, C. 3650 and C. 3655 and 1884 liv and C. 3877 and 3952; the partition of Bengal 1905 C. 2746; and the Curzon-Kitchener controversy 1905 C. 2572 and C. 2718.

PUBLISHED WORKS

Mention is made here only of those works which merit more than a passing reference in a note but which are yet not the standard works of reference for all work on this period.

M. Maclagan, *Clemency Canning* (London, 1962).
Sir R. Temple, *Men and Events of My Time in India* (London, 1882).
T. Walrond, *Letters and Journals of James, Eighth Earl of Elgin* (London, 1872).
J. L. Morison, *The Eighth Earl of Elgin* (London, 1928).
Sir George Campbell, *Memories of My Indian Career* (London, 1893).
J. Beames, *Memoirs of a Bengal Civilian* (London, 1961).
Dharm Pal, *Administration of Sir John Lawrence in India* (Simla, 1952).
M. Cowling, 'Lytton, the Cabinet, and the Russians, August to November 1878', *English Historical Review*, vol. LXXVI (January 1961).

British Policy in India, 1858–1905

Lady Betty Balfour, *The History of Lord Lytton's Indian Administration, 1876–1880* (London, 1899).

W. W. Hunter, *The Indian Musalmans* (London, 1871).

G. R. G. Hambly, 'Unrest in Northern India during the Viceroyalty of Lord Mayo 1869–72: the Background to Lord Northbrook's Policy of Inactivity', *Journal of the Royal Central Asian Society* (January 1961).

R. P. Masani, *Dadabhai Naoroji* (London, 1939).

S. Gopal, *The Viceroyalty of Lord Ripon* (Oxford, 1953).

D. K. Ghose, *England and Afghanistan* (Calcutta, 1960).

M. Cumpston, 'Some early Indian Nationalists and their allies in the British Parliament, 1851–1906', *English Historical Review*, vol. LXXVI (April 1961).

I. P. Minayeff, *Travels in and Diaries of India and Burma* (Calcutta, no date).

C. C. Davies, *The Problem of the North-West Frontier* (Cambridge, 1932).

R. L. Greaves, *Persia and the Defence of India, 1884–1892* (London, 1959).

P. Fleming, *Bayonets to Lhasa* (London, 1961).

A. Lamb, *Britain and Chinese Central Asia* (London, 1961).

INDEX

Index

Index

Index

Index

Mayo, sixth Earl of, 74, 301, 304; evaluated, 64, 65, 120–3, 300; appointed Viceroy, 64; meets Shere Ali, 66–9; mediates in Afghanistan, 69–70; attitude to Russia, 70, 71; successful frontier policy, 70–2; famine policy, 91; financial policy, 91–6; public works policy, 92; local self-govt. policy, 93–4; army policy, 94; and Wahabism, 97–8; on British community in India, 97; and the Kukas, 99–101; murdered, 65, 101; against interfering in Upper Burma, 139–40

McMahon, Sir H., 244

Mecca, 95, 198

Meerut, 2, 11, 39

Mehta, Pherozeshah, president of Congress, 188; Curzon on, 297

Mekong river, 252

Mekran, 68

Merv, 73, 80, 81, 83, 133, 232; occupied by Russia, 135

Meshed, 73

Metcalfe, Sir C. T., 114

Midlothian campaign, 154

Miller, Sir A., rebuked by Lansdowne, 191

Milner, Viscount, 291; on Lansdowne, 180; compared with Curzon, 227; on Kitchener, 276 and 277

Mishmi pass, 89

Mitter, R. C., 192; on jury trials, 209

Mogul (emperor), 97

Mohammerah, 240; Sheikh of, 240

Mohurram, 201

Monroe doctrine, 141, 231, 234

Mookerjee, Raja Peary Mohun, on council reforms, 168

Morley, J., congratulates Lytton, 89; devoted to Lytton, 125; criticizes Curzon, 289

Moscow, 139

Moslems, 38, 41, 73, 81, 95, 99, 100, 101, 124, 165, 173, 175, 198, 201, 202, 303; uneasiness among, 95–8, 202; no conspiracy among, 102; distrusted by Salisbury, 104; encouraged by Dufferin, 158–60; participation in Congress, 159–60, 167; favour council reforms, 167–8; cow-killing

by, 193–4; dislike plague rules, 199; Curzon on, 159; Curzon appeals to, 271; *see also* Muhammadans and Mussalmans

Muhammadans, 46, 137, 183, 185; opposition to age of consent bill, 192; official bias in favour of, 194; *see also* Moslems and Mussalmans

Muhammadan Literary Society, 159

Muhammadan National Association, 159

Muir, Sir W., 95, 96, 103, 331 n. 221; replaced as finance member, 112

Multa Sittana, 96

Munro, Sir T., 12

Murdoch, Miss Iris, 298

Mussalmans, 72, 75, 95; *see also* Moslems and Muhammadans

Mymensingh, 269

Mysore, 9, 10, 154; Maharaja of, on the succession, 9–10, and the Congress, 170, 253

Nabha, Maharaja of, 100

Nana Sahib, 50

Naoroji, Dadabhai, 335 n. 283; in Baroda service, 105, 106, 108; member of Welby commission, 191; on recruitment of Indians to civil service, 191; evidence before Welby commission, 205

Nasratabad, 240

Natal, 258

National Gallery (London), 250

Natu brothers, detained without trial, 200, 201; Curzon secures release of, 260, 265

Nepal, 99, 195; govt. of, said to support Curzon's Tibetan policy, 237

Nil Darpan (Indigo Mirror), 28–9, 57

Ninth Lancers Regiment, 263–4

Nizam (of Hyderabad), Canning considers restoration of territory to, 8; Northbrook and Salisbury suspect, 104; and the Congress, 170; cedes Berar, 254–5, 384 n. 192

Norman, Sir H., 357 n. 3; declines viceroyalty, 180

North-eastern frontier, 52

North-west frontier, 96, 135, 139, 217, 277, 280; Curzon's policy, 249–50

Index

419

Index

Index